Social Psychology and Intergroup Relations

European Monographs in Social Psychology

Series Editor HENRI TAJFEL

EUROPEAN MONOGRAPHS IN SOCIAL PSYCHOLOGY 9
Series Editor HENRI TAJFEL

Social Psychology and Intergroup Relations

MICHAEL BILLIG
University of Birmingham, England

1976

Published in cooperation with the
EUROPEAN ASSOCIATION OF EXPERIMENTAL
SOCIAL PSYCHOLOGY
by
ACADEMIC PRESS London, New York and San Francisco

ACADEMIC PRESS INC. (LONDON) LTD.
24/28 Oval Road
London NW1

United States Edition published by
ACADEMIC PRESS INC.
111 Fifth Avenue
New York, New York 10003

301. 114
B 598s
1976

Library of Congress Catalog Card Number: 75 19617
ISBN 0 12 097950 0

PRINTED AND BOUND IN ENGLAND BY
HAZELL WATSON AND VINEY LTD
AYLESBURY, BUCKS

Preface

Initially this book was intended to fill a gap in contemporary social psychology. In the past fifteen or so years intergroup relations has become somewhat of a neglected topic. Early research work into intergroup relations has not by and large been followed up. Instead of investigating intergroup relations directly, social psychologists have tended to approach the subject obliquely, their perspectives deriving from interpersonal and individual psychology. It was hoped to outline and criticize this trend, as well as making a plea for the study of intergroup relations in its own right.

However, in attempting this it became apparent that broader and more political questions were involved. These relate to the underlying values and assumptions inherent in social psychology. There has been an influential line of thought which suggests, sometimes explicitly and sometimes implicitly, that interpersonal processes can serve as adequate models for large-scale social phenomena, including intergroup relations. By concentrating on small-scale processes social structures remain unexamined and thereby uncriticized. The resulting social psychology will by its nature be unquestioning; it will be based upon premises which preclude fundamental criticism of existing ideologies and states of affairs.

By considering the political dimension the present book attempts a wider perspective than is often the case in social psychological writing. However it is not the present intention to indulge merely in an exercise of political name-calling. A polemical attack which did not seek an understanding of the discipline would inevitably fall short of its target. Throughout the book there are both internal and external criticisms of a wide number of approaches to the study of intergroup relations. For instance, in the opening chapters there are detailed internal criticisms of models of intergroup processes derived from psychoanalytic theorizing. The explanation of social processes in terms of an unchanging "irrational" human nature is criticized, no matter whether these ideas come from thinkers on the political left such as Marcuse, or from Lorenz on the right. It is argued that Freudianism does not constitute an adequate basis for a social psychology of intergroup relations. Nor, it is suggested, do theories which concentrate on the prejudices of authoritarian or close-minded individuals.

There are detailed examinations of experimental approaches to the study of conflict. Laboratory investigations of aggression and gaming are considered at length and internal interpretations are offered. For instance it is suggested that a social-cognitive account of the frustration-aggression relationship is more appropriate than a motivational one. The issue of the relation between game theory and gaming experimentation is also considered. Naturally there are reviews of those experimental approaches which study intergroup phenomena directly. The classic work of Sherif is re-examined in the light of Tajfel's work on social categorisation and the creation of intergroup identity. In all these discussions the importance of cognitive variables in the experimental situation is emphasised.

At all times the intention is to go beyond specific internal criticisms in order to investigate their wider significance. In part this means considering the work of those social psychologists like Leonard Berkowitz, Morton Deutsch, Anatol Rapoport, etc. who look beyond the confines of the psychological laboratory to seek analogies between experimental behaviour and the behaviour of real-life social groups. For this reason an attempt has been made to complement social psychological findings with findings from other disciplines, notably sociology, anthropology and political science, when discussing such phenomena as social movements, dissident groups, international conflict, group identity and ethnocentrism. More than this, the intention is to examine the ideological implications of such attempts to extend the laboratory model. For instance it is argued that explanations of rebellious and revolutionary behaviour in terms of the frustration-aggression hypothesis often are based upon implicit premises favouring the *status quo*. Similar arguments are made in relation to gaming models of conflict. It is suggested that the conservative implications of both approaches are related to the tendency to reduce intergroup processes to interpersonal ones.

If a more critical and radical social psychology is sought it is not sufficient merely to lay greater emphasis on large-scale and intergroup processes. It is a constant theme of the present book that wider theoretical issues must be given greater prominence. As a preliminary step toward the development of a more critical framework it is proposed that certain concepts derived from the writings of Marx be incorporated into social psychological theory. The importance of such concepts as "ideology" and "false consciousness" is stressed. These concepts are employed in the discussion of traditional social psychological findings as well as in the more theoretical discussions. Just as the internal critique of experimental social psychology revealed the importance of cognitive variables, so too it is assumed that ideology and false consciousness have crucial cognitive dimensions. For example, in chapter nine there are discussions concerning the affinity between Marx's ideas of the practicality of language and recent notions about the social functions of group categorization.

Often attention is given to topics and issues which conventionally are not discussed by social psychologists. At times the internal and external critiques interweave; rigid separation of the two has not always been possible, nor has it been sought. It is to be hoped that those orthodox social psychologists who do not share the author's concern for the development of critical social theory will nevertheless be able to derive some value from the more technical discussions of the various research approaches. Similarly it is hoped that such discussions will not be seen as misplaced by those who have rejected orthodox social psychology on the assumption that it is incompatible with a radical social theory. Whilst an attitude of rejection is understandable in the light of the blinkered narrowness of much published social psychological writing, it is the present view that it is necessary to raise wider questions and extend the scope of social psychological discourse. Only then will it be possible to assess the contribution which existing formulations can make to a critical understanding of social forces.

MICHAEL BILLIG

September 1974

Acknowledgements

There is no doubt that this work would never have been started, let alone completed, without the encouragement and generosity of Henri Tajfel. I owe much to his guidance and assistance throughout my time as a graduate student at the Department of Psychology at Bristol University, and also subsequently. Henri Tajfel's influence is, I think, strongly reflected throughout this work, and I wish to pay tribute to the debt I owe him both personally and professionally.

This book has taken roughly two years to write. It arose from the Bristol project into intergroup relations supervised by Henri Tajfel and I am grateful for the one-year post-doctoral fellowship at Bristol which gave me uninterrupted time to read and write. The second year of writing has been at the Department of Psychology, University of Birmingham, where I have greatly benefited from the superb facilities of the University library.

I would like to thank the Institute of Psycho-analysis for allowing me to use their library. Similarly I would like to thank Jo Davies, Barbara Hudson, Annette Nuttall and Marjorie Sanger for typing the manuscript and also Kathy Crawford for suggesting certain changes and corrections. I am grateful to Nigel Flynn for his careful reading of the manuscript and for his helpful criticisms. Lastly I would like to thank my wife, Sheila, for her specific help with the references and preparation of the manuscript, and generally for much more besides.

Contents

1

Introduction

Social psychology has witnessed a considerable expansion in the past twenty years. In terms of sheer activity it is a thriving enterprise. The increase in academics committed to social psychological research, the numbers of students enrolling in their courses, the amount of published material all seem to testify to the vigour of the discipline. It has firmly established itself within the academic community and has all the outward symbols of intellectual success—professional associations, conferences, learned journals, etc. Nevertheless for all these symptoms of good health, there is an underlying disquiet.

This book is intended to be a commentary upon certain aspects of contemporary social psychology, as well as being an investigation into the social psychology of intergroup relations. The opportunity for one work to attempt these two tasks arises because the topic of intergroup relations has been largely ignored by social psychologists. The subject is dominated by the experimental method, as any glance at the leading journals would confirm. Moreover, the experimental methodology is creating a tradition which is almost exclusively devoted to the sophisticated analysis of person-to-person behaviour. For instance, the journals are filled with experiments examining the conditions under which a subject will like, help, obey, shock, insult, believe, etc. another. In this way the establishment of the discipline has been accompanied by a drift away from the investigation of large-scale social processes.

The limitations of the current trends have been noted by social psychologists themselves (e.g. Ring, 1967). Similarly the neglect of group processes at the expense of interpersonal processes has been regretted (Steiner, 1974): However, such dissenting voices are rare compared to the actual volume of work produced yearly by social

psychologists. It can be suspected that the pursuit of academic acceptance and respectability has divorced social psychology from the wider
questions which it is capable of asking. One of the central themes of
the present work is that a broader perspective is called for. The social
psychologist should not restrict himself to the collection of empirical
data; the wider theoretical issues must also be considered. In particular, questions relating to intergroup conflict and the possibilities for
attaining peace should not be pushed aside in favour of more circumscribed inquiries.

As a consequence the following pages will contain discussions of
topics often omitted in mainstream social psychological investigations.
If a critical re-evaluation by social psychologists is required, then it is
also necessary to consider alternative approaches to the social psychology of intergroup relations. For this reason there will be detailed
discussions of instinctual and psychoanalytic theories of large-scale
social processes. In the examinations of current social psychological
approaches there will be both internal and external critiques. It is
hoped that the social psychological findings can be assessed on their
own merits and that certain internal conclusions can be drawn. A more
wide-ranging external criticism will also be attempted, relating social
psychological investigation to wider social theory.

Since one of the main focuses of attention will be on wider theoretical issues, there will not be an emphasis upon the purely methodological issues, which seem to trouble so many contemporary social
psychologists. It can be argued that there is a somewhat unhealthy
obsession with methodology within the discipline. The critics and
advocates of experimental methods tend to draw attention away from
the wider society. Genuine advances in our understanding of the
relation of the individual to his society will not be gained merely by the
defence of, or the campaign against, a particular methodology. It
should not be thought that the vital issues concern whether or not
social psychology should be a purely experimental science. More
crucial questions concern the reasons for conducting experimentation
of any sort and the theoretical pictures which are constructed by the
social psychologist out of his data. For these reasons, when experimental studies are discussed in the following chapters, an eye will always
be kept on their potential implications for wider social theory. It will
be assumed that, if the experimental findings are to be ultimately
meaningful, then they must attempt to explain, or at least illustrate,

real-life processes. The mini-worlds of the experimental situation will be irrelevant, unless they can be related theoretically in some way or another to the real-world.

In making the connection between the laboratory and the real-world, one needs, at least, an implicit model of society. Such a model of society cannot itself be derived from laboratory experimentation, but must arise from a wider social analysis. In this sense, the macro-social sciences, e.g. sociology and anthropology, should not be thought to be ultimately reducible to problems of social psychology. Rather, it can be argued that, if social psychology is to make significant theoretical advances with respect to wider social issues, then it must be more closely allied than at present with theories of society. In any model of societal processes, the relations between large-scale social groups must be thought to be crucial. This is the case, no matter whether intergroup relations within a social structure are thought to be essentially harmonious, or based upon incompatible aims. Similarly, questions about intergroup relations become even more pressing if relations between societies are considered. It may well be the case that the neglect of social theory in social psychological research is connected with the neglect of intergroup relations. However, what does seem to be more obvious is that a systematic consideration of the topic of intergroup relations should lead more directly to matters of social theory, than does, for instance, the study of "dating behaviour", "helping behaviour" or interpersonal communication. In this way, a consideration of the intergroup, rather than the interpersonal, could bring about a closer relation between social psychological findings and basic social theory.

The exclusion of societal variables from the study of social psychology has encouraged the growth of a discipline which is basically conformist and politically conservative. If society is ignored, or if it is considered as a constant scenario within which social psychological dramas must be enacted, then there can be no possibility for the development of a socially critical science. Existing social structures will not be questioned and as a result criticised. It might be objected, however, that the neglect of societal variables in social psychology does not lead to a conservative social psychology, any more than a neglect of social criticism leads to a conservative biology or a conservative physiology. In other words, it might be argued that the social psychologist is studying phenomena which are important in their own right and which do not necessarily relate to the wider issues. Even if this argument were valid, it would not be strictly relevant. It would still admit the possibility of a critical approach. In this respect social values will be expressed by the questions which are not being raised just as much as by those questions which are. However, the basic argument is not itself strictly correct. Many social psychologists do consider their researches to be socially relevant and their mask of "scientific neutrality" can be observed to slip when they attempt to relate their findings to large-scale social issues. Instances of political bias, which underlie aspects of social psychological research, will be discussed, especially with respect to the frustration-aggression theory and the attempts to analyse intergroup conflicts by studying gaming situations. It will be suggested that these examples of political bias are by and large in favour of the existing *status quo*, and that the very attempt to conceal such bias behind the myth of complete neutrality is itself an instance of this ideology.

If experimental psychology has tended to neglect issues of social theory, and especially critical social theory, this is not the case of the social psychological tradition which is derived from psycho-analysis. By its very nature, psychoanalysis is a critical enquiry, but its criticisms are by and large directed at individual behaviour. Thus the outward forms of behaviour and thought are critically examined in order to reveal their "hidden and true" significance. It will be argued that too often psychoanalytic social psychology analyses problems of intergroup relations from the standpoint of the individual, and that any reduction of large-scale social processes to interpersonal or indi-vidualistic processes involves a distortion. What is more, such a reduc-tion inevitably precludes a critical social analysis. Nevertheless there have been attempts by psychoanalitically-minded writers to attempt a wider social analysis. Freud's own work contains not only theories of individual and group behaviour, but also accounts of the hypothe-sised social psychological dynamics underlying the development of civilisation. Similarly there have been of late a number of attempts to develop the social theories of Freud into explicitly critical theories of society and its present state of development. The most notable of such attempts is Marcuse's reconstruction of Freudian social theory; both Marcuse's and Freud's ideas will be discussed in some detail, at least in so far as they relate to topics concerned with intergroup re-lations. It will be argued that although these psychoanalytic models present the *prima facie* possibility of a critical social theory, they are nevertheless fraught with empirical and theoretical difficulties. Thus the present approach is in no way a flight into Freudianism from the rigours of a positivistic social science.

It will be suggested that one of the crucial issues involved in the study of intergroup relations is that of "ideology". This term will increasingly appear in the following discussions; it will be used in a somewhat loose sense to encompass not only the socially-derived beliefs of a particular group, but also the social functions of such beliefs. In this way, the concept of ideology will attempt to relate the subjectively-held beliefs to the objective social structure. The concept will be used in the sense given it by Marx, who specifically linked the ideological superstructure with the underlying infrastructure. Therefore the present discussion will stress the social context of variables associated with intergroup relations—as a consequence it will be emphasised that social identities, the social categorisation of groups into distinct social entities, the normative values of such groups, etc. are all themselves the social products of social situations. In particular the intergroup aspects of such situations will be noted, especially concerning objective inequalities of intergroup power.

By doing this, it is hoped to raise the possibility of a more critical social psychological analysis. In drawing attention to the ideological nature of group beliefs, it then becomes incumbent on the social analyst to seek the underlying significance and ideological function of such beliefs. Thus in the various discussions of social psychological approaches to the study of intergroup relations an effort has been made to draw out some of the ideological premises which underlie the various orientations. However, for major issues the task of seeking ideological significance must be more than an academic exercise and must inevitably relate to practical issues. Consequently, many crucial issues, relating to the study of contemporary intergroup relations, have been left untouched in this book, whose scope is essentially limited to an examination of social psychological descriptions of intergroup relations. As far as the ideological premises of the present work are concerned, it is hoped that at least some of the basic assumptions are made plainer than is usually the case in "scientifically-neutral" social psychology.

There will however be a certain fuzziness and lack of development of some of the basic assumptions of this work, mainly due to its explicitly limited aim. The flavour of the assumptions can be considered with respect to the remark made by the American sociologist Mills (1963), concerning Marx and modern social psychology. Mills wrote that Marx's assumptions about the nature of man were "in line with the most adequate assumptions of contemporary social psychology" (p. 40). Mills does not, however, detail the social psychology he had in mind. Nevertheless, much of the following survey of social psychological approaches to the study of intergroup conflict will aim to show some of the disparities between the contemporary approaches and Marx's theory. Thus the trend to reduce intergroup notions of interpersonal processes is at variance with the assumption that "activity and mind, both in their content and in their *mode of existence*, are social: *social* activity and *social* mind. The *human* essence of nature first exists only for *social* man . . . Thus *society* is the unity of being of man with nature" (Marx, *Philosophic and Economic Manuscripts of 1844*, 1973 edn., italics in original p. 137.) It is not only that many of the contemporary approaches neglect societal variables and intergroup divisions within societies, they also lack Marx's commitment to social change and the radical improvement of existing conditions.

2

Freud's Group Psychology

For those who are dissatisfied with the current state of an academic discipline it is a natural enough inclination to look back at the intellectual origins of their chosen field. This inclination may not merely be based upon a historical curiosity to find out how contemporary ideas have developed; it may also reflect a hope that the writings of past thinkers may contain hints for overcoming present intellectual impasses. This is especially so in a discipline like psychology; different schools of thought have produced widely different theoretical answers but the basic questions often remain fundamentally unchanged.

Given this, it is no surprise that a number of critics of contemporary social psychology are turning from the dominant experimental tradition to the psychoanalytic tradition initiated by Freud. The attractions of the psychoanalytic tradition are fairly clear. For instance, psychoanalytically inspired writers such as Fromm, Marcuse and Reich deal with important issues directly. They write with an air of seriousness and purpose which is all too often lacking in orthodox social psychology. Moreover, psychoanalysis offers the possibility that important facts lie hidden beneath the surface of everyday reality. Nevertheless claims to "hidden" truths must be investigated rigorously if one is to avoid the short fall from theory to mysticism.

For these reasons the theories of Freud and of some of his followers will be discussed in detail. This discussion will be critical and at times repetitive to the extent that similar theses often reoccur in different psychoanalytically influenced writers. It will be assumed that such a discussion is necessary and timely if only to argue the negative point that a Freudian foundation would be an inappropriate base for the development of a social psychology of intergroup relations.

The present discussion of Freud does not attempt any definitive

exegesis. It is well known that there are widely different interpretations of his views. For instance, the political substance of his ideas can
be seen as radical, liberal or conservative, (for such interpretations,
see Marcuse, 1969; Roazen, 1970 and Rieff, 1955, respectively). The
psychoanalytic movement is split into factions each claiming to uphold
the "true" spirit of Freud's thought. The present examination of
Freud will raise issues concerning the nature and level of any social
psychological explanation of large-scale social processes. This problem
can be illustrated by considering three possible levels of explanation
for a large-scale social event. Firstly, there is explanation at the level
of individual processes—this sort of explanation aims to derive the
ultimate causes of social events from constitutional processes common
to all human beings. Thus the individual explanation makes certain
assumptions about a pre-social "human nature" which is basic to all
individuals. Such an individualistic explanation of intergroup conflict
might be based on the assumption of an aggressive instinct to be found
in all men and which is the determinant of social aggression. A wider
level of explanation is offered by a social psychological exposition in
terms of interpersonal processes. At such a level, the causes of social
phenomena are sought in the face-to-face interaction between persons.
The individual *per se* is no longer the unit of explanation, but instead
the focus is on the relation between individuals. Such an explanation
of intergroup phenomena might be based on the derivation of outgroup prejudice from certain familial relations, i.e. that certain individuals are predisposed to negative outgroup attitudes because of their
early relations with their parents. In fact most psychoanalytic explanations of behaviour consist of interactions between individual and
interpersonal explanations—they assume that the basic constitution of
individuals together with certain common patterns of interpersonal
interaction combine to form the resulting behaviour patterns. The
final level of explanation is the social—at such a level, large-scale
processes are not reduced to smaller units, but are analysed in their
own terms. Cultural or societal variables are brought into prominence.
With respect to intergroup relations, such an explanation would seek
to offer descriptions in terms of properties of the groups themselves, or
of the wider social system in which the group interaction takes place.

Traces of all three levels of explanation, the individual, the interpersonal and the social, can be found in Freud's writings. At different times Freud seems to have placed varying amounts of empha-

sis on these respective levels. However, it should be recognised that he would not necessarily accept the distinctions outlined here. For instance, at the start of *Group Psychology and the Analysis of the Ego*, he claims that all psychoanalysis is in fact social psychology, and that there is no sharp distinction between individual and social psychology (Freud, 1921, Vol. 18, pp. 69–71; all references to Freud will be to the *Standard Edition of the Collected Works*, but will also contain the date of the original publication). There are also terminological difficulties; for example, Freud tends to distinguish individual and social psychology by subject matter rather than by their method of analysis and theoretical aims. He refers to the study of group leaders as being individual psychology, but the study of their followers as being a problem of social psychology (Freud, 1921, Vol. 18, p. 123). Notwithstanding these qualifications, it is nevertheless possible to differentiate these levels of explanation in Freud's social writings and also to note some of their inter-connections.

Before proceeding to discuss some of the details of Freud's social theories, a word is in order about his aims in extending psychoanalytic theory from the clinical setting to cover the widest possible questions of society and its origins. He believed that he had discovered the basic determinants of all human behaviour in psychoanalytic theory: he had uncovered the essential nature of man, and this essential nature must affect not only man's interpersonal relations, but also his wider social relations. Moreover it must relate to the creation and operation of society itself. As a result, Freud hoped that psychoanalysis could provide answers to questions about individual, interpersonal and social processes. He was attempting nothing less than an integration of these three possible levels of studying man's behaviour. As a consequence he saw the social level of analysis as applied psychology, rather than a discipline in its own right:

> . . . sociology . . . , dealing as it does with the behaviour of people in society, cannot be anything but applied psychology. Strictly speaking there are only two sciences: psychology, pure and applied, and natural sciences. (Freud, 1933, Vol. 22, p. 177.)

Nor was this attitude a product merely of his later "metapsychological" works which were concerned with developing wider theoretical statements from his basic psychoanalytic theories. The importance he placed upon psychoanalytic theory for any wider social analysis, is clearly outlined in *Totem and Taboo* (1913). Freud writes that, in any synthesis of our knowledge of religion, morality and society, psychoanalysis "could not play any other than a central part" (Vol. 13, p. 157). And of course Freud's own social writings contain the outlines for such a synthesis.

The success of Freud's own synthesis of social and individual psychology will be discussed below, especially with respect to his own theory of intergroup relations. Problems concerning the validity of his individual psychology will only be touched upon tangentially. The main burden of argument will not be directed to defending or attacking psychoanalysis as a study of personality. Rather the emphasis will be upon examining whether such a theory, derived as it is from the study of individual or interpersonal processes, can be said to lay the basis for a wider social theory. This question will be posed with respect to Freud's particular theories of society, and the implications involved in such theories. The problems, raised by Freud's approach and by his attempted synthesis, are not confined to his own formulations. These same issues will re-occur in later chapters, especially when the work of post-Freudian personality theorists is discussed. Nevertheless many of the problems faced by these writers are the same as those that confronted Freud. A clarification of these problems as they affect Freud's work should therefore pave the way for later discussions. In considering Freud's own theoretical formulations, the subject matter will be divided into three sections—his theory of ingroup ties, his theory of society as a whole, and his specific theory of intergroup relations. Although the last named should be the prime focus of the present discussion it will be suggested that it cannot be properly understood without reference to other aspects of Freud's social theories. Certainly the problems involved in the different levels of explanation cannot be appreciated without the wider focus, even if any answers will eventually be applied to the narrower topic of intergroup relations. Just as Freud's own theories ranged across the whole spectrum of human activities, so the present examination of his views on intergroup relations will take into account interconnections with other topics.

Ingroup ties

In describing Freud's account of group processes, the discussion will follow the arguments in *Group Psychology and the Analysis of the*

Ego. It is in this work that Freud most clearly states his ideas on the psychology of groups: the main emphasis being upon the psychological foundations of ingroups, rather than upon intergroup relations itself. However, this emphasis upon the ingroup has direct theoretical consequences for his notions of intergroup processes. As will be argued later, the primacy which Freud placed on ingroup processes is reflected by the theoretical primacy of the ingroup with respect to intergroup conflict. Thus it would not be inappropriate to follow Freud's own arguments and to start by discussing the ingroup and its psychological properties. Only after discussing this, will it be possible to consider in detail his specific ideas on intergroup processes.

Freud starts his consideration of the psychology of groups by quoting extensively from Gustave Le Bon's book *The Crowd* (1897). Freud's own formulations of group processes are not the direct outcome of detailed examination of group behaviour. He freely admits his own lack of empirical investigations into the topic, and begins his discussion by taking over Le Bon's "brilliantly executed picture of the group mind" (Freud, 1921, Vol. 18, p. 81). Le Bon's work is primarily a diatribe against mass movements, especially those that threatened the established order of the day. For Le Bon the crowd was something to be feared; he based his views on the actions of the Parisian mass movements of the 1870s, and proclaimed that "the advent to power of the masses marks one of the last stages of Western civilisation" (Le Bon, 1897, p. xviii). Throughout the book his conservative views are in evidence. For him, the crowd stood for mediocrity and barbarity; as such their growing power was ensuring the decay of all civilised standards. Such themes, as will become evident, are also to be found in certain of Freud's writings. However, it is not so much the political content of Le Bon's theses that most attracted Freud—rather it was the similarities between Le Bon's descriptions of the mental states of crowd members with some of the formulations of psychoanalytic theory.

The essential parallel between Le Bon's account and Freud's psychoanalytic theory was that Le Bon emphasised how, under the influence of crowds, individuals reveal their basic instinctual nature. Unconscious urges, which are normally held in check, come to the fore under mass conditions. The thin veneer of civilised behaviour is stripped off and individuals are shown in their true barbarous and primitive colours. This *prima facie* accords with the psychoanalytic picture of man, and Le Bon accepts the psychoanalytic premise that there is an irrational side to man's nature which lurks beneath his more rational behaviour. In stating that this irrationality comes to the surface in the case of mass behaviour, Le Bon provides a clue for Freud's quest of a synthesis between individual psychoanalytic theory and wider social theory.

Essentially Le Bon postulated that there is a "mental unity" in crowds, that is, the psychological state of the members of a crowd is homogeneous. He goes on to offer explanations for this. Firstly he states that the sheer numerical power of a crowd enables its members to consider themselves omnipotent and capable of achieving what is impossible for isolated individuals. As a result they loose all feelings of individual responsibility and the unconscious instinctual urges emerge. It is interesting to note that a modern version of this notion has been expressed in social psychological writings (for instance, Festinger, Pepitone and Newcomb, 1952; Cannavale, Scarr and Pepitone, 1970; Zimbardo, 1969). It is also interesting to speculate whether this new version is motivated by the same lack of sympathy for mass movements as Le Bon's original was. Certainly, Zimbardo's article (1969) [1] strongly suggests that this is the case. Le Bon goes on to describe two other features that characterise a crowd. He states that crowd behaviour resembles a contagion—every act or mood is rapidly spread throughout the crowd. The third characteristic of a crowd is that members are suggestible, and by virtue of their excited emotional states are likely to be swayed easily. Freud, in fact, made the point that these last two characteristics of the crowd, suggestibility and contagion, are part and parcel of the same basic phenomena. Notwithstanding, Freud accepted in essentials the general picture of the crowd outlined by Le Bon which can be illustrated by the following quotation:

> We see, then, that the disappearance of the conscious personality, the predominance of the unconscious personality, the turning by means of suggestion and contagion of feelings and ideas in an identical direction,

1. The tone of Zimbardo's analysis is apocalyptic. He contrasts rationality and order with impulse and chaos. He states that modern society is witnessing a return to a Dionysic age of irrationality and loss of personal control. He instances sexual permissiveness, mob violence, drug-taking, protest demonstrations, high murder-rates etc. as evidence for the decay of reasoned order. In this way Zimbardo argues that loss of control or deindividuation is leading to an increase of aggression and inhumanity. Although writing in the late 1960s, Zimbardo does not discuss how the ordered and disciplined part of American society could have come to be associated with the aggression and inhumanity in Vietnam.

the tendency to immediately transform the suggested ideas into acts; these we see, are the principal characteristics of the individual forming part of a crowd. . . . Moreover, by the mere fact that he forms part of an organised crowd, a man descends several rungs in the ladder of civilisation. Isolated, he may be a cultivated individual; in a crowd, he is a barbarian—that is, a creature acting by instinct. (Le Bon, 1897, p. 12.)

All in all, Freud endorses the general conclusions of Le Bon. Some of the specific differences between these two writers will emerge in the discussion of Freud's development of Le Bon's basic concepts. For the present one can note the similarity of outlook between the two in their disparagement of mass action—although, in passing it can be mentioned that Freud did not adopt all the lurid descriptions of Le Bon. For instance, he writes that Le Bon correctly compares the mentality of the crowd to the mentality of primitive people and children (Freud, 1921, Vol. 18, p. 77), but Freud omits the full nature of the comparison that Le Bon makes which is to "beings belonging to inferior forms of evolution . . . women, savages, and children, for instance" (Le Bon, 1897, p. 16).

Enough should have been said of Le Bon's characterisation of mass action to have shown the somewhat archaic flavour of his descriptions. His political prejudices are obvious and he gives full reign to antidemocratic sentiments. Certainly, there have been more sympathetic accounts of mass action in France in the nineteenth century. For instance, Rudé's two books, *The Crowd in History* (1964) and *Paris and London in the 18th Century* (1974), paint an altogether different picture—one that emphasises the reasonableness and political nature of the mass movements in question. Later in the present work, arguments will be advanced against attempts to view mass revolutionary action in terms of psychological emotionality or blind anger; it will be stressed that the so-called mob or crowd is normally engaging in a particular form of intergroup conflict, and that the ideological nature of such actions must not be ignored. However, the present problem can be said to revolve around the following simple question: if Le Bon's crowd descriptions are inadequate, is Freud's theory of group processes necessarily invalidated, because it is built upon a fallacious foundation?

The answer to this question can be given in the negative for two simple reasons. Firstly, Freud did not content himself merely with describing the behaviour of the volatile mass in his group psychology;

as will be seen, he developed his ideas to cover a much wider type of group. Secondly, the assumption of universality in Le Bon's descriptions need not be shared by Freud. It would still be legitimate for Freud to construct a psychoanalytic theory of group behaviour upon the rare exceptions of hysterical mass action without assuming that such hysteria is a general property of groups. This is a quite legitimate strategy in constructing psychoanalytic theories. For instance, in his individual psychology Freud examined the breakdowns of normal behaviour in order to discover the structure of the normal mind. He gave special importance to neuroses, slips of the tongue, dreams, etc. in his investigation of mental structures. Thus the parapraxes of normal life provided him with the clues for describing the familiar. In the same way, it could be argued that the complete breakdown of social organisations might provide the important clues for understanding the psychological determinants of the established group. Therefore it could be admitted that Le Bon was inaccurate in his description of particular crowds but that nevertheless the clues to understanding groups might be contained in the actions of hysterical mobs. However, it will be suggested that in making this move, the resulting psychoanalytic theory of group behaviour lays itself open to a number of criticisms.

Freud's development from the ideas of Le Bon takes the form of depicting the psychological connection between the phenomena described by Le Bon. As Freud points out, Le Bon's account is essentially descriptive rather than explanatory. When he refers to contagion and suggestion he does not state the psychological basis of these phenomena. Similarly, when Le Bon draws an analogy between the crowd and a hypnotised individual, he does not, according to Freud, attempt to portray the psychological aspects of hypnosis. He alludes to the surfacing of instinctual urges during crowd formation, but he has no general idea how these instinctual urges affect more normal mental functioning. In other words, Le Bon has no general psychology with which to illuminate his vivid descriptions of crowd bestiality. In Freud's opinion psychoanalytic theory could fill this gap, and by doing so illustrate the workings of more normal groups. This would constitute a first step towards the integration of individual and group psychologies necessary for his projected synthesis of the human sciences around psychoanalysis.

In developing his group psychology from Le Bon's descriptions,

Freud begins by concentrating on the analogy, mentioned above, between the crowd member and the hypnotised patient. If this analogy is correct, Freud argues, then it would show the importance of one factor that Le Bon tended to neglect—the role of the group leader. The hypnotised patient is not pliable and open to any suggestion, he is specifically under the influence of one man, his hypnotist. Similarly, he argues that the crowd's suggestibility relates specifically to its malleability in the hands of a dominant leader. Also, according to Freud, it is possible to characterise the leader-crowd relationship not as analogous to the patient-hypnotist relationship, but as one instance of the same basic phenomenon. But in order to do this, it is necessary to describe the psychological relationship between the leader and his followers. Le Bon, he claims, merely talked about the "prestige" of a great leader and the influence he achieves through this prestige. For Freud, such a concept is essentially unpsychological and in no way describes the full force of the tie between the leader and his followers —certainly it does not explain it in any way.

Freud specifically links the formation of groups with his concept of the Oedipus complex. His aim is to describe the psychological attraction of the leader in terms of the psychological processes that arise in the development of the psyche of the young child. As such, he is attempting an explanation of large-scale processes in terms of interpersonal processes. The Oedipus complex arises out of the interaction between the infant and his parents, and so by implication it is possible to analyse group behaviour in terms of such relationships. This implication is explicitly recognised at the start of *Group Psychology* when Freud states his intention of attempting to trace the beginnings of the social instinct in the narrow circle of the family (1921, Vol. 18, p. 70). The nature of this interpersonal explanation will become clearer as Freud's attempted integration of his Oedipal theory with his group theory is discussed. For the present, one can point to the key connection, which Freud makes, between the importance of the child's father in the Oedipus complex, and the leader of a social group. All that need be said at the moment is that in order for Freud to attain his interpersonal explanation in terms of the Oedipus complex, it is necessary for him to establish the importance of the group leader in group phenomena. The reasons for this, and the proposed psychological relationship between the Oedipal father and the group leader should become apparent in the following discussion.

In pursuing this aim of theoretical integration, Freud proposes a fundamental distinction between groups with a leader and groups without a leader. Although he does not attempt what he terms "a morphology" of groups, he does consider briefly other ways of distinguishing different sorts of groups. For instance, he notes that there are long lasting groups and fleeting groups; there are natural ones and artificial ones, primitive and highly organised groups, etc. (Freud, 1921, Vol. 18, p. 93). However, these distinctions are, in his opinion, psychologically trivial. Even the differences between the complex stable group and the transient group are not of great psychological importance: in the case of the former there are external forces that can be applied to keep the group members in check, whilst in the latter there are no such external forces. For Freud the actual *psychological* significance of these differences is minimal—they may have a certain sociological significance, but knowledge of sociological variables must of course be integrated with psychological knowledge, if the grand synthesis, that Freud was attempting, is to be possible. Thus Freud is not concerned with any organisational or structural differences between groups, but with their essential psychological nature. Of course, whether such psychological variables can be established with respect to large-scale groups as distinct from the more mundane sociological variables, is a crucial question. It is to be hoped that a clarification of Freud's attempt to provide an answer will throw light on the problem as it exists today.

The crucial distinction between groups with leaders and those without is not made by Freud at the end of a detailed examination of both sorts of group. In fact the distinction is made in order to concentrate exclusively on the group with a leader. The leaderless group is considered an aberration and of little psychological significance. Thus it is the group with a leader which, according to Freud, will reveal the basic psychological ties that underlie social behaviour. To this end, he makes a brief analysis of two real, stable groups. In contrast to most modern social psychologists, Freud does not choose for his examples small and simple forms of groups. Instead he grasps the nettle firmly, and proposes a brief analysis of the psychological ties which bind together the Catholic Church and the army as groups. His aim is to isolate what is common to these two forms of group formation, not so much in their organisational structure but in the psychological relationships of their members. Not only this, he also attempts to point out parallels between these two institutions and the unorganised crowds described by Le Bon. Whereas for Le Bon such organised groups as the church and the army present the antithesis of the dangerous mob, for Freud they are all part of the same psychological phenomena.

The first similarity which Freud notes between the Catholic Church and the army is that both groups have leaders, who exert more than just physical force over their followers. There is also an emotional tie that binds the followers to their leaders. In both the church and the army, he points out:

> ... the same illusion holds good of there being a head—in the Catholic Church Christ, in an army its Commander-in-Chief—who loves all the individuals in the group with an equal love. Everything depends on this illusion; if it were dropped, then both Church and army would dissolve, so far as the external forces permitted them to. (Freud, 1921, Vol. 18, p. 94.)

Not only are there emotional ties that bind the follower to his leader, but there are also ties that bind the group members to each other. All the believers in the church consider themselves to be equal members of the kingdom of God. Similarly all the soldiers in the army are comrades amongst themselves. Thus each group member is "bound in two directions by an intense emotional tie" (p. 95) to his leader and to his fellow group members. This two-way tie is also, of course, characteristic of the Le Bon type mob; in such a crowd the individual members were said to follow their leader blindly, and also to be easily affected by each other's mental state. In this respect the psychological ties, as outlined by Freud, are the same for the hysterical mob as they are for highly disciplined and organised groups, such as the Catholic Church and the army. When the secondary social characteristics are removed from such instances, they can be seen to be instances of more primary group formation, or so Freud argues.

It is one thing to identify the structure of the primary group's psychological bonds, but it is another matter to characterise those bonds. So far, all Freud has done in effect is to postulate that there are two sorts of emotional tie in a group. Both these sorts of ties obviously cannot be doubted to exist—it is almost a truism that in most groups with a leader there is some sort of psychological relationship between the leader and his followers, and also between the followers themselves. However, in admitting this, no suppositions are made about the nature of such ties and it does not need a psychoanalytic enquiry merely to identify them. In going further than mere identification it becomes possible to introduce psychological assumptions, and thereby to characterise such emotional bonds. In Freud's case, such emotional ties are described in terms directly taken from his individual psychoanalytic theory. At this point, therefore, in his study of groups, one can assert that he moves beyond a general social analysis into a specific psychoanalytic explanation.

Freud's explanation of the ties in a primary psychological group is derived from his theories of sexuality. In a nutshell, he characterises such ties as being sexual, with Eros being the guiding principle behind social formations. Stated baldly, this would seem to be as absurd as it is fallacious: it is simply not the case that armies are founded on explicit sexual relations between the soldiers; in fact in most modern armies such sexual relationships are expressly forbidden. Sexual attachments between a Catholic priest and members of his flock are likewise prohibited. However, Freud's contention would be that such bans on sexuality are indicative of the general truth of his proposition. This is because his use of the term "sexual", or "erotic" does not imply that there exist actual behavioural sex relations. It is characteristic of Freud's psychology that he seeks the origins of impulses, rather than just concentrating on the final behavioural manifestations of such impulses. Thus, he identifies numerous relationships as being outcomes of the sexual impulse, although there is no overt sexuality in the relationship. In this, he draws an analogy with the many uses of the word "love", which, he states, exemplifies the way he uses the term "sexual":

> The nucleus of what we mean by love naturally consists (and this is what is commonly called love, and of what the poets sing of) in sexual love with sexual union as its aim. But we do not separate from this— what in any case has a share in the name "love"—on the one hand, self-love, and on the other, love for parents and children, friendship and love for humanity in general, and also devotion to concrete objects and to abstract ideas. (Freud, 1921, Vol. 18, p. 90.)

The issue is more than a semantic one: Freud in fact states that the semantic usage correctly mirrors the underlying psychology. Freud had come to the conclusion from his individual psychoanalytic researches that those forms of love which were overtly non-sexual, were in point of fact covertly sexual, i.e. they were secondary manifestations of the sexual impulse. In the course of things, libidinal energy rarely achieves its goal of sexual union; however, when unsatisfied by its primary goal, such libidinal desires do not merely evaporate. It is one of the most basic tenets of Freud's psychoanalytic theory that such instinctual desires continue to affect the psyche of the individual. This unfulfilled energy emanates from the unconscious id and exerts pressure on the conscious and pre-conscious structures of the mind. In turn, the ego, the seat of the conscious and pre-conscious mental activity, may repress this instinctual energy and direct it along other channels. It is Freud's contention that the tie binding a leader to his followers is such a re-directed instinctual urge. It is more than a mere metaphor to state that the group members love their leaders, and that they believe they are loved in return—this form of "love" is a genuine form of love, which is derived from sexual love, the exemplification of all forms of love.

In chapter seven of *Group Psychology and the Analysis of the Ego*, Freud outlines the psychological process by which the libidinal energy is transformed into the social bonds of groups. In doing so, he introduces the important psychoanalytic concept of the superego—hitherto Freud had considered the human mind as being composed of two structures, the ego and the id. Much of his psychoanalytic theory had been based upon the conflicts which he hypothesised to exist between the ego and the id, the rational and the irrational. However, it was in this work that he first formulated the tri-partite schema of the mind, which he was to retain in all his subsequent writings. The introduction of this concept, of vital importance for psychoanalytic theory, explains the latter half of the book's title, and testifies to the fact that his individual psychoanalytic psychology was developing as he formulated his social theories. Thus Freud's social psychology cannot be seen as a straightforward application of his individual psychology to a wider set of problems: his projected synthesis was to be the result of a parallel development rather than a crude arrogation of theory and methodology.

The basic libidinal tie in the group is based on the feelings of the members for their leader. The group member loves the leader, who becomes the object-choice of his libidinal desires. However, the member cannot possess the leader sexually, and thus the libido is thwarted from achieving its goal with its object-choice. This frustrating situation is solved by the ego possessing the leader symbolically. It possesses the leader by "becoming" the leader, who is then set up inside the ego. This process Freud refers to as primary identification, by which the leader is introjected inside the ego. In doing this, the ego is irrevocably split. On the one hand there is the former part that still remains unchanged. On the other, there is the newer part, which is the introjected leader. This new part is the ego-ideal, or superego. It represents, and in a real sense is, the ideal figure which the individual loves but cannot possess physically. Thus the libidinal problem is solved, but there is a price to pay. The individual carries his ideal-standard— he cannot escape from the superego, which exacts strict codes of behaviour and thought from him. It requires a further instinctual renunciation over and above that which the ego requires. Not only this, the demands of the ego conflict with the demands of the superego, and so the individual's mind becomes a three-way battle-ground, between the conflicting structures of the id, ego and superego.

The tie between the group and its leader is therefore based on the introjection of the leader into the egos of his followers. This primary process of identification does not itself explain the ties between the group members themselves. This form of identification is a consequence of the primary form, according to Freud, and is not of itself a sexual identification. The group member does not introject his fellow group members as loved objects, but identifies with them because of the recognition of a common quality—this common quality being a similar superego. There is, in Freud's formulation, no need for the group members to be jealous of one another, and to compete for the favours of the loved leader. The followers are not rivals for the leader since, in a sense, they are that leader themselves—they all possess inside their psyche this same loved-object. Because of this psychic similarity, based on the primary identification, they develop the psychological ties that characterise the *esprit de corps* of an ingroup. This secondary identification is not such a deep-seated process as the primary identification, and it is mediated by the ego. By hypothesising these two forms of identification, Freud is then able to define the basic psychological structure of a social group. A group, therefore, can be said to consist of ". . . a number of individuals who have put one and the same object in the place of their ego ideal and have consequently identified themselves with one another in their ego." (Freud, 1921, Vol. 18, p. 116.)

By offering such a definition, Freud has by no means satisfactorily explained the psychological nature of social groups for his wider project of synthesising individual and social theories. In his own words, he admitted that "we cannot for long enjoy the illusion that we have solved the riddle of the group with this formula" (p. 117). So far, Freud had argued that the identification of the group member with his leader is the same sort of phenomenon as the identification of the patient with his hypnotist. Whereas Le Bon had drawn a parallel between the crowd and the hypnotised subject, Freud actually states that the group leader does in fact hypnotise his followers, at least in terms of the psychological mechanisms involved. However, as Freud correctly points out, equating the introjection of the ego ideal with hypnotism offers in itself no real explanation of the phenomena, but rather a categorisation. Freud has outlined the possible structures which can produce within-group emotional ties. He has not shown why these ties should be produced in the first place, and in particular, why the individual should come to love his leader. For this reason the problem of ingroup ties is traced back to more basic questions concerning the origin and nature of the instinctual libido itself.

Freud directly links the development of the superego to the Oedipus complex. He sketched this connection in *Group Psychology and the Analysis of the Ego*, and described in greater detail the relationship between the Oedipus complex and the splitting of the ego in his later work *The Ego and the Id* (1923, Vol. 19). There is no need to present a full account of Freud's formulation of the Oedipus complex; a brief outline should suffice in order to demonstrate its central significance both for his individual psychoanalytic theory, and also for the development of his social theory. The essential elements of Freud's account of the Oedipus complex are simple enough. The young child sexually desires the parent of the opposite sex—that is, the young boy develops an erotic attachment to his mother, and the young girl similarly desires her father. However, these desires remain unfulfilled and the same sex parent is seen as the major rival for the desired object. The young boy will see his father as the obstacle to his own libidinous fulfilment, and the young girl will view her mother in the same way. Consequently the same-sex parent comes to be hated and resented; although, at the same time, it is still loved as a parent. The full-blown Oedipus complex, which according to Freud affects every child, can be characterised as the sexual desire for the opposite sex parent, and the desire to kill the same sex parent, in order to remove the main rival.

It is not, however, the Oedipus complex itself that is of prime importance for the development of group ties, but the way that the child resolves this complex. The resolution of the complex paves the way for later adult identifications with group leaders. In the *Ego and the Id*, Freud detailed the resolution of the Oedipus complex mainly with respect to the young boy's love for his mother and hate for his father. The corresponding complex for girls, the Electra complex, and its resolution were to Freud "precisely analogous" to the Oedipus complex: this view was somewhat modified in a later essay, (*Some Psychical Consequences of the Anatomical Distinction Between the Sexes*, 1925, Vol. 19) in which differences between the two sorts of complexes were discussed. However, for the present, the concentration will be on the young boy's Oedipus complex, mainly because Freud himself concentrated upon this and because it is the Oedipus, and not the Electra, complex which constitutes the core of his social theory. The resolution of the Oedipus complex can crudely be summarised by stating that the young boy erects the obstacle to his desires within himself, i.e. he introjects his father into his own ego. The conflict between the love and hate, which he feels towards his father, is not completely annulled by this introjection; rather it is altered so as to become a permanent conflict within the individual, one that will last for the rest of his life. The battle is now fought between the ego and the ego-ideal; in the first instance it produces feelings of guilt for the previous desire to kill the father. This constitutes the origin of conscience which will now punish the individual for any future forbidden desires. In terms of the boy's relations with his parents, the original dilemma of the Oedipus complex has been resolved—by becoming the father, the boy is no longer the jealous rival for the mother, because in a sense he possesses the mother. The net result is that, with a non-neurotic resolution of the complex, the boy will strongly identify with his father and will copy his example. Similarly the girl will identify with her mother, following a resolution of the Electra complex. Thus the resolution of these complexes ensures that the young child will learn the correct socially-prescribed sex-role.

Freud interprets all later introjections in terms of the original introjection of the opposite sex parent by the young child. The superego becomes not only the individual's conscience, but is also an expression of the child's emotions towards its parents. All later introjections can be traced back to the original childish introjection, and the first and most crucial splitting of the ego. Therefore the fully developed adult superego is the heir to the Oedipus complex, as the love for the father finds other substitutes:

> As a substitute for a longing for the father, it (the ego ideal) contains the germ from which all religions have evolved . . . As a child grows up, the role of father is carried on by teachers and others in authority; their injunctions and prohibitions remain powerful in the ego ideal and continue, in the form of conscience, to exercise the moral censorship. (Freud, 1923, Vol. 19, p. 37.)

In other words, the resolution of the Oedipus complex is never completely satisfactory. It leaves the young boy with an increased love for his father, which causes him to search, throughout his life, for other father-figures. In this way the introjection of group leaders by adult group members can be interpreted in terms of the dynamics of the Oedipus complex. What is more, the problem of why such introjections should take place in the first place has been solved by Freud. If the Oedipus complex is a universal phenomenon in the development of children, as Freud thought it was, then it becomes easy to explain why individuals in later life are so ready to accept ego-ideals and to enslave their own egos. They are paying the price for their own infantile desires—they are condemned to seek father-substitutes and to torment themselves with strict standards of conduct.

The basic outline of Freud's description of the nature of ingroup ties can be summarised. The primary identification with the ingroup leader is psychologically derived from the infantile trauma of the Oedipus complex which affects every young child. The non-neurotic resolution of the complex leaves the individual searching for father-substitutes in later life. As such Freud's explanations of the primary group tie, which binds the group members to their leader, and of the secondary tie, which binds the members to each other, are in outward respects interpersonal explanations. The complex phenomena of social groups are reduced to descriptions of the child's relationships with his parents. The group leader becomes the father in the Oedipal triangle; and the Oedipal triangle is explained in terms of the interpersonal relations between the participants. However, this relationship is affected by the genetic constitution of individuals. Thus the Oedipal triangle would not arise if young children did not have libidinal desires and also aggressive instincts. In this sense the explanation is not purely an interpersonal one, but depends on an interaction between interpersonal factors and individual constitutional factors. What is clear is that there is a reduction of complex social phenomena, which might form the basis of a "mass" psychology, to an individual or interpersonal psychology, in which the family becomes the proto-type of the social group.

Having outlined Freud's characterisation of the psychological struc-ture of the ingroup, it is now necessary to make a few comments con-cerning Freud's approach. What is most striking about Freud's formulation is the importance he attaches to group leaders in his description of social groups. This importance is almost asserted *a priori* without any separate empirical investigation. The distinction is made between groups with leaders and those without leaders, but only the former are given any serious consideration. One can ap-preciate the theoretical reasons for this, given: (a) Freud's aim of a synthesis between his individual psychoanalytic theory and social psy-chological theory; and (b) the importance of the Oedipus complex in his individual psychology. If his individual researches suggest that most non-neurotic individuals desire to submit to a higher authority, or father-figure, then the existence of non-authoritarian groups clearly constitutes a problem for his formulation. In a sense it looks as if his social psychological theory is being made to complement his individual theory in a somewhat arbitrary fashion.

The problem of leaderless groups becomes an important one for the Freudian outline of group structure. Such groups would be an obvious embarrassment for his projected synthesis. Although anthropological knowledge was comparatively undeveloped when Freud was formu-lating his views, it is however possible now to cite examples of com-munities that are run on non-authoritarian lines, without an obvious leader. For instance, the volume edited by Middleton and Tait (1958, *Tribes without Leaders*) contains a series of essays describing African societies which have no central authority. Such groups are not easily accommodated in Freud's theoretical formulation.[2] There is a hint in Freud's writings concerning his reaction to the difficulty of leaderless groups. In *Civilization and its Discontents* (1930, Vol. 21) he mentions

2. Similarly, the Freudian account faces difficulty in explaining those forms of government which are based on the dual authority of two equal leaders. Instances of such diarchies are the twin chieftains of the Iroquois, the two consuls of the Roman republic, and the two kings of ancient Sparta. The psychoanalytic basis of such states must, according to a crude application of Freud's arguments, be the introjection of two father-figures.

social groups that do not accord their leader due significance. Such a group is, in Freud's view, an unhealthy aberration. He refers to the "psychological poverty" of such groups (p. 113) and although this notion of psychological poverty is not developed and only America is offered as an example of such an impoverished group, the implication is clear: any group that does not fit into the authoritarian pattern is only an exception to the general rule insofar as it is an unhealthy variant. The suspicion is that *a priori* value judgements have replaced detailed social analysis. In view of Freud's failure to state why leaderless groups are psychologically impoverished, the conclusion must be that his group psychology has not adequately considered the exceptions to the hypothesised general rule.

Another difficulty with Freud's description of group leadership can be briefly mentioned. This relates to the fact that his account is based primarily on the Oedipus, rather than the Electra, complex. His theory is over-concerned with male identification of male leaders. Freud's anti-feminist views, as reflected in his psychoanalytic theory, have been commented upon (for instance, Millett, 1970; Brown, 1973). However, the present issue is not so much one of male sexism, as such, but Freud's neglect of explaining how sex differences could affect his social theory. For instance, if the Electra complex is precisely analogous to the Oedipus complex, then one would expect that women would identify only with female group leaders. But one does not find separate political, national or religious groups, some of which are run by men for men, and others by women for women. It would seem that throughout history many of the important political and religious leaders have gathered support equally from men and women. Similarly Freud's conception of the group leader is essentially a masculine one; he seems to be assuming a patriarchal society. In fact, he seems only to have considered matriarchal societies as specific reactions to male societies at particular and distant times in the development of civilisation (e.g. *Moses and Monotheism*, 1939, Vol. 23, pp. 82–3, 113–114). One might surmise what his views would be concerning the "psychological impoverishment" of matriarchal societies.

Two different sorts of difficulty, then, have been mentioned with respect to Freud's theory of ingroup ties—the first relates to his lack of specific social analysis and his *a priori* assumption derived from his psychoanalytic theory. The second relates to the way in which lacunae in his individual theory are reflected in his social theory. Social variables relating to the roles of men and women in social groups are not dealt with, neither are intercultural differences or the possibility of a woman filling the role of the "substitute father". Both these two sorts of difficulty arise from Freud's aim at explaining complex social events in terms of interpersonal processes. The secondary characteristics of groups are downgraded in theoretical importance; thus the purely structural or cultural variables relating to social formations have to be explained in relation to primary characteristics, namely the instinctual strivings of infants.

Social theory

So far the elements in Freud's social theory that explain group processes in interpersonal terms have been mentioned. However, the projected synthesis between individual and social psychology was not to be effected merely by such a reductionist approach, in Freud's view. The explanation of the group leader's power in terms of the infantile Oedipus complex only goes part of the way to forming a psychoanalytic social psychology of group processes. This form of explanation can be called an ontogenetic explanation, in that the complex social process is explained in terms of the ontogeny of the individual—in this case the leader's power is explained in respect of a developmental stage, hypothesised to be a universal characteristic of mankind. To achieve the synthesis, more than an ontogenetic theory is required; a corresponding phylogenetic theory is also necessary, such that the development of society as a whole can also be explained. Consequently Freud attempted to construct a psychoanalytic phylogenetic theory to complement his ontogenetic account; and this was to form the basis of the synthesis of individual and social psychology.

Before proceeding to a discussion of Freud's phylogenetic social theory, one can illustrate why he thought it necessary to develop his account of group processes beyond the interpersonal account. Freud's account of the development of the adult superego does not provide in itself an integrated picture of society. His account of the effects of the Oedipus complex can be interpreted as providing a psychological mechanism by which such cultural values are passed down from one generation to another. As such, the superego "represents tradition and the ideals of the past" (Freud, 1933, Vol. 22, p. 178). But this does not provide an explanation of the content of these ideals. If Freud had left his theory at this stage of development, he would still be allowing for the possibility of a non-psychoanalytic social theory. He would have formulated the psychological mechanism, which motivates individuals to accept cultural standards and develop social consciences— but he would not have explained the social origins of such standards and of conscience itself. He would merely have described the psychological form of the superego. The substantive content would not necessarily be describable in terms of psychoanalytic theory. Certain social theorists have interpreted Freud in this way, and have used his theory to provide the outlines for a psychological account of cultural transmission (for instance, Parsons, 1954, 1958; and the ego psychologists whose work will be discussed in chapter four). In doing this, such writers are primarily inserting a psychological variable into a theory of society which itself is not based upon psychological theory.

For Freud himself this was insufficient: he wished to explain the dynamics of society itself in terms of his psychoanalytic model of cultural transmission. This meant the development of a phylogenetic theory to parallel the ontogenetic theory and in particular to give due importance to the Oedipus complex. In this section, this phylogenetic theory will be discussed. This will be done not only because it contains the nub of Freud's social theory, but also because it embraces an implicit model of revolutionary conflict. His account of the psychological basis of society also enabled him to assess revolutionary attempts to change social forms. This assessment concerns both the psychological significance of revolutionary action and also its chances of achieving revolutionary objectives. As such, Freud's account of revolutionary group conflict will provide a useful prelude to his discussion of intergroup relations in general.

Basically Freud's phylogenetic theory endeavours to chart the development of the cultural superego in an analogous way to his account of the development of the individual's superego. Consequently Freud hypothesises that similar processes operate at both individual and group levels, and also that the history of the individual is essentially a retelling of his species's history. Just as the individual's mind preserves all its past experiences, so the cultural superego retains elements remembered from the dawn of civilisation. The cultural parallel also contains an account of the Oedipus complex as a significant social event in the history of man's development, in the same way that the Oedipus complex constitutes a crucial stage in the life history of each individual. These then are some of the basic features of the phylogenetic theory by which Freud hoped to synthesise individual and social theory.

Freud described his phylogenetic theory in a number of separate publications, notably *Group Psychology and the Analysis of the Ego* (1921, Vol. 18); *Totem and Taboo* (1913, Vol. 13); *Civilization and its Discontents* (1930, Vol. 21); *Moses and Monotheism* (1939, Vol. 23). The details of the theory are complex and relate to a number of matters outside the present scope of interest, especially those discussions concerning the genesis of religions. However, it is hoped to present briefly what appear to be the main elements, at least as far as they affect the present discussion. Basically the phylogenetic theory centres around an Oedipal-type event in the history of man; this historical event bridges the period in which men lived by brute force and instincts, and the period which saw the first beginnings of a developing moral consciousness. Freud maintained that prehistoric man lived in small hordes. The horde differs from the herd, in that it is a social group with a specific social structure: it consists of one all-powerful leader who dominates all others in the group by force. This primal father, or group leader, tyrannised the other males in the group, and monopolised all the women. The other males had no sexual or civil rights. The primal horde, therefore, can be characterised as a society which was ruled by the physical authority of one man, who acted according to the dictates of his own will. The primal father was like the young child, who seeks instinctual pleasure; his id was only curtailed by the demands of reality, and he possessed no internal restraints.

In passing beyond the pleasure-seeking stage, the child suffers the Oedipal trauma, which results in the development of an internal authority. The primal horde undergoes a similar traumatic development. Unlike the Oedipus complex, whose drama is enacted in phantasy, the drama of the primal horde was, in Freud's view, an actual historical event. Or rather, it constituted a series of events, since the original drama was to be re-enacted and repeated on numerous occasions. What was necessary for the state of affairs in the primal horde to change, was for the leader's sons to unite. Only by a combination of the primal brothers could the despotic rule of the father be broken.

If one of the brothers were more powerful than the others, he would establish himself as the new primal father, and the pattern of horde existence would be continued. But this pattern could be broken if there were deadlock and none of the brothers were sufficiently strong enough to become the new primal father. In such a case they would be forced to come to an agreement amongst themselves. Such an agreement forms the basis of civilised society, and is the historical foundation of the "social contract" that political theorists have talked of. Freud describes it thus:

> A realisation of the dangers and uselessness of these struggles, a recollection of the act of liberation which they had accomplished together, and the emotional ties with one another which had arisen during the period of their expulsion, led at last to an agreement among them, a sort of social contract. (Freud, 1939, Vol. 23, p. 82.)

But this physical liberation from the power of the primal father is not accompanied by a psychological liberation. Since the old man had been their father, the brothers loved him as well as hating and fearing him. These feelings of love prevent them from enjoying their triumph, and give rise to feelings of remorse in each of the brothers, which help to unite them more closely. This union is celebrated in a commemorative meal, in which the slaying of the father is re-enacted by the slaying and eating of an animal. This, claims Freud, is the origin of totemic phenomena, in which tribes worship certain animals and hold taboos about the eating of such animals. Freud also traces the incest taboo to this remorse of the brothers—because of their guilt they are unable to take over the women of the horde and to compensate for their erstwhile sexual denials. Eventually the conflicting emotions of triumph and remorse within each brother are resolved by the introjection of the dead father. In this way the original primal father becomes the first ego-ideal. However, the original character of the father becomes altered in the minds of the brothers—he becomes a benevolent god. Nevertheless, the previous hatred the brothers felt for their father does not disappear. Instead it is directed inwards, and is used by the ego-ideal to oppress the ego. Thus the story of the primal killing is essentially one of irony—the hated father returns after his death to dominate the brothers, this time with even more ferocity than previously. The revolt of the brothers against their father is a failure; they do not achieve the liberation they had desired. All that they have achieved is the exchange of an external authority for an internal authority. No real psychological liberation has been attained by the heroic act, which lays the foundations for the development of civilisation. The renunciation of instinct, then, is the psychological basis of civilisation, and according to Freud this is as true of modern societies as of ancient ones. He postulates that "civilisation is largely responsible for our misery" (1930, Vol. 21, p. 86), and that social consciousness consists of a curtailment of individual instinctual desires. This pessimistic conclusion he traces back to the inevitable Oedipal stage that mankind as a whole had to pass through. In formulating this notion, Freud then can claim to have united the phylogenetic and ontogenetic theories around the Oedipus complex:

> . . . the beginnings of religion, morals, society and art converge in the Oedipus complex. This is in complete agreement with the psychoanalytic finding that the same complex constitutes the nucleus of all neuroses, so far as our present knowledge goes. It seems to me a most surprising discovery that the problems of social psychology, too, should prove soluble on the basis of one single concrete point—man's relation to his father. (Freud, 1913, Vol. 18, 156–57.)

Clearly the phylogenetic theory can be criticised on a number of grounds. From its original publication, the primal horde theory has been attacked by anthropologists for lack of firm evidence which could be used to support its many assumptions (for instance, Kroeber's 1920 classic review of *Totem and Taboo*). More recently Lévi-Strauss, (1969) has criticised Freud's explanation of the totemic phenomena, on the grounds that he completely misunderstood the phenomena that the primal legend was intended to explain. Sahlins, (1960) has discussed the implausibility of the existence of the primal horde; he argued that such a community, with all its interpersonal relations based on power, would be unable to survive. Many other such criticisms coming from anthropologists could be cited. For the present, criticism will be confined to the part of the primal legend which directly affects Freud's account of revolution. It is hoped that in this way a key weakness in the phylogenetic theory will be made clear. It is also the present aim to show that attempts to explain intergroup conflicts in general, and revolutionary conflicts in particular, by referring to a psychoanalytic phylogenetic theory are bound to raise a number of difficulties.

It was mentioned above that one of the assumptions of the phylogenetic theory was that important previous experiences should be remembered and preserved in the psyche of the species—this paralleled the assumption from individual psychoanalysis that the mind preserves "all the earliest stages alongside of the final form" (Freud, 1930, Vol. 21, p. 71). It is only by making this assumption that subsequent revolutions can be explained in terms of the original revolution of the primal brothers. Freud, of course, wished to make such explanations. For instance, in *Moses and Monotheism* he formulates the hypotheses that the children of Israel killed Moses, and he interprets this revolt against a non-primal leader in terms of the original killing. He offers a similar explanation for the crucifixion of Jesus. These acts can only be seen as psychological repetitions of the original act, if there is some way of connecting them to the primal killing; otherwise alternative forms of explanation need to be sought.

The connection proposed by Freud was that the memory of the primal killing is somehow preserved in the psyche of the species in the same way that the individual remembers his wish to kill his own father. Later, when a similar situation arises, these memories surface. Thus when the group members hate and wish to overthrow their leader, there is a "return of the repressed memory" of the primal killing. In this way the primal scene has been re-enacted on many occasions throughout history, (Freud, 1939, Vol. 23, pp. 132–137). For example, any explanation of the crucifixion that does not refer back to the original primal killing misses, according to Freud, the crucial significance of the act. The primal killing can be said to affect later dethronements of group leaders, and attempted revolutions by the latter-day heirs of the primal brothers. Thus the primal killing serves as a model of later revolutionary action, in Freud's account. The important implication of this notion is that the failure of the original rebellion of the brothers is the prototype for all future action, which in turn must result in failure.

The problem then for Freud's phylogenetic theory is how such memories are transmitted from one generation to another. Clearly this is a key issue for Freud's projected synthesis of individual and group psychology, since he needs some way of demonstrating how the most important event in the history of the species can affect the individual members of the species. To solve this problem he posits an "archaic heritage" which contains the memories of the primal legend; this assumption is of crucial theoretical importance and allowed Freud to claim to have "bridged the gulf between individual and

group psychology", (Freud, 1939, Vol. 23, p. 100). The importance of
this archaic heritage for Freud's syntheses becomes apparent when one
considers the mechanism by which these memories could possibly be
transmitted across generations. The memories obviously are not conscious memories which are deliberately taught as part of the folklore
of all civilisations. If they were, there would have been no need for
psychoanalytic investigation to have "discovered" the primal legend:
it would have been common knowledge to all humans. A second possibility is that the archaic heritage is transmitted subconsciously through
the conscious culture—however this assumes that all cultures, whatever their forms, transmit this knowledge in a way that is not consciously perceived. The implication of this is that all persons must
have the subconscious mechanisms for interpreting this universal form
of symbolism. The problem is then to discover what these mechanisms
are and how they are to achieve such an immense task of interpreting
and coding the same messages hidden in the many forms of human
culture. It is no wonder that Freud rejected this possibility to account
for the transmission of the archaic heritage; but in rejecting it he was
forced to accept the third possibility, that such memories are genetically transmitted. It is this acceptance which leads to the collapse of his
bridge between individual and group psychology.

Freud was well aware of the radical character of the assumption that
the archaic heritage was genetically transmitted. He assumed that the
heritage contained "memory-traces of earlier generations", (1939, Vol.
23, p. 99) and also "particular psychical contents, such as symbolism",
(1937, Vol. 23, p. 240). Thus each individual in the species carries within him a subconscious and inherited memory of the original killing,
and presumably of its aftermath. Freud realised that this assumption
ran contrary to modern biological thinking, in which the inheritance
of acquired characteristics is seen as an impossibility. However, such
was the importance that he attached to the archaic heritage that he was
fully prepared to fly in the face of modern scientific theory. This is
revealed in the following passage from *Moses and Monotheism*:

> My position, no doubt, is made more difficult by the present attitude of
> biological science, which refuses to hear of the inheritance of acquired
> characters by succeeding generations. I must, however, in all modesty
> confess that nevertheless I cannot do without this factor in biological
> evolution . . . Granted that at the time we have no stronger evidence
> for the presence of memory-traces in the archaic heritage than the resi-
> dual phenomena of the work of analysis which call for a phylogenetic

derivation, yet this evidence seems to us strong enough to postulate that such is the fact. If it is not so, we shall not advance a step further along the path we entered on, either in analysis or in group psychology. The audacity cannot be avoided. (Freud, 1939, Vol. 23, p. 100.)

It is hard to resist the conclusion that the synthesis between the two sorts of levels of explanation has not advanced a step further along the path that Freud suggested—indeed that it ever could advance further so long as it rests upon the assumption of the genetic transference of the archaic heritage, which Freud himself recognised as being one of its main planks. Although Freud was prepared to set aside his normal scientific attitude in order to preserve his theory, it is hard to see how such can be justified today. His bridge between individual and group psychology has not only been unsupported by subsequent anthropological evidence, but it also still contradicts biological theory. In the light of the untenability of the archaic heritage, an overall negative judgement must be made on Freud's synthesis of ontogenetic and phylogenetic psychoanalytic theories.

Because the phylogenetic theory has been found to be unsatisfactory there is no need to refute in any great detail Freud's views on revolutionary action. As has been mentioned, the primal killing was intended to be the model of future revolutionary action. Similarly the primal legend points to the failure of all revolutionary action which only attempts a political or economic transformation of society. The brothers only overthrew the elementary political organisation of their community, but did not manage to achieve psychological emancipation. Freud's comments on the Russian revolution can be seen in relation to this. He criticises the Bolsheviks for not attempting to revolutionise human nature, but only changing the economic basis of society. Without "a transformation of human nature" (*New Introductory Lectures*, 1933, Vol. 22, p. 180.) there will be no genuine emancipation from the burdens that civilisation places on man (cf. also Freud, 1933a, Vol. 22; 1930, Vol. 21, p. 113). Thus, the economic reorganisation of society promulgated by the communists cannot lead to an abolishment of the aggressive instincts of mankind. Whatever the particular economic and political arrangement of society, man is still condemned to his instinctual nature and history.

But if man's social forms need not be explained in terms of Freud's specific theories of individual and social nature, then it is no longer necessary to seek understanding of all social events in the archaic heritage. In the case of revolutionary action it is no longer necessary to accept the premise that political and economic revolutions need necessarily result in as much or more enslavement for men. In other words, revolutionary acts can be interpreted in their own terms and not in terms of hypothesised psychological principles underlying the course of human history. This would seem to be a far more reasonable course than criticising the efficacy of revolutionary action *per se* with some sort of Olympian detachment.

Intergroup theory

Contained in Freud's analysis of ingroup ties is a theory of intergroup relations. It is not so developed as his account of ingroup structure, and is more properly a sketch of a theory rather than a theory itself. However, it does contain a number of features which have influenced later theorists, and also it does raise a number of issues in its own right. In separating Freud's model of revolutionary conflict from his theory of intergroup relations, it is not implied that revolutions are necessarily different forms of conflict than other intergroup conflicts. In fact it is one of the intentions of this work to dispute such a claim. For Freud revolutionary conflicts have separate psychological origins from conflicts between national or religious groups. It was shown that his model of revolutionary conflict was derived from his phylogenetic theory. His intergroup theory, on the other hand, is not dependent on the myth of the primal killing, and can be discussed separately from it. If much of Freud's social psychology has been neglected by later social scientists, the separation of revolutionary from other sorts of group conflicts has been followed by later social psychologists. It will be suggested later that it is a dominant trend in present day social psychological research to seek different social psychological determinants for revolutionary conflicts than for national conflicts. If this separation is being followed here, it is only because separate theories have been propounded by Freud, and because he associated different psychological processes with the different types of group conflict.

To begin with, one can note Freud's early views on the subject of national war before *Group Psychology and the Analysis of the Ego*. During the First World War he wrote to a friend that the psychoanalytic picture of human nature was being verified by current events, (1914, Vol. 14). In an article written at about the same time he men-

tions how the war unleashed the aggressive instincts which are normally repressed in civilised society, (1915, Vol. 14). But he did not feel
able at that time to specify how and why the aggressive instincts could
be responsible for such a widespread cataclysm. He felt that there was
a close connection between the aggressive instincts and nationalist
fervour, but he could not stipulate the psychological nature of this
connection. Certainly he thought that the more "objective" explanations offered for such national conflicts were unsatisfactory—for
instance he considered that a conflict of national interests could not by
itself explain the bestiality of the war. In fact he felt sure of the
primacy of the aggressive instincts, and that rational reasons for conflicts were mere *post hoc* justifications of those instincts. Nations, he
wrote:

> . . . put forward their interests in order to be able to give reasons for
> satisfying their passions. It is, to be sure, a mystery why the collective
> should in fact despise, hate and detest one another—every nation against
> every other—and even in times of peace. I cannot tell why that is so.
> (Freud, 1915, p. 288.)

In this work Freud is both offering and also delineating the limitations of an individualistic interpretation of national conflict. An
explanation based on the genetic constitution of mankind is one such
individualistic interpretation—and in effect Freud is only asserting
that all individuals have aggressive instincts. The most obvious in-
adequacy of such an explanation is that it can offer no account of why
sometimes nations are at war and why sometimes they are not. Presumably the genetic endowment of their national subjects is constant
whether there is war or peace. All that such a universal instinctive
explanation can predict is that there will always be wars, or at least
manifestations of aggression, but it cannot say anything about particular wars. The limitations of such an explanation were freely admitted
by Freud—in fact he hardly considers it as an explanation. Notwithstanding this, it can be noted in passing that subsequent writers have
offered "explanations" of wars based on some sort of general aggressive
instinct—instances of such individualistic approaches will be discussed
in the following chapter.

If, in 1915, Freud was unable to offer an explanation for national
conflicts and ethnocentric pride, six years later he was to formulate
the outlines of a theory of intergroup behaviour in *Group Psychology
and the Analysis of the Ego*. As has been mentioned, the main empha-

sis of this work is upon the libidinal structure of the ingroup. It should come therefore as no surprise that Freud's analysis of intergroup relations should be directly derived from his account of the psychology of the ingroup. Intergroup conflict is in his view a product of events within the ingroup. In relating the topic of intergroup relations specifically to the structure of the ingroup, Freud makes use of the important psychoanalytic concept of "ambivalence". In his individual psychology, Freud attached great significance to ambivalent feelings, which are a mixture of love and hostility. Early in his psychoanalytic investigations he acknowledged that the aggressive instincts would invariably accompany the sexual instincts. In *Three Essays on the Theory of Sexuality*, (1905, Vol. 7) he describes how libidinal feelings towards a cathected object will produce sadistic impulses, which were an integral part of object–cathexis. This basic idea was to be referred to as "instinctual fusion" in *The Ego and the Id*, (1923, Vol. 19); in this work Freud postulated that in the course of human development the instincts of love and hate become fused together, such that a manifestation of the one instinct will always contain a component of the other. In *Group Psychology* he summarises the interaction of ambivalent feelings:

> The evidence of psychoanalysis shows that almost every emotional relation between two people which lasts for some time—marriage, friendship, the relations between parents and children—leaves a sediment of feeling of aversion and hostility, which only escapes perception as a result of repression. (Freud, 1921, Vol. 18, p. 101.)

Thus psychoanalytic theory predicts that when there exist strong feelings of love, there are also correspondingly strong feelings of hate. In the case of ingroups, Freud had characterised the relation between the group leader and his followers as being one of love. One can predict from these two assertions that group members will hold feelings of antipathy against their loved leader. These feelings have to be repressed. It will be recalled that the primal brothers loved, as well as hated their father. The libidinal structure of the ingroup would collapse if the ambivalent feelings of hate were allowed to be freely expressed. Such feelings have to be redirected along other channels, since instinctual energy does not evaporate if it fails to achieve its true goal. According to Freud, the redirection of hostile feelings must be towards objects outside the ingroup. In this way, outgroup hostility is a natural concomitant of the formation of an ingroup: "it is always possible to bind together a considerable number of people in love so long as there are other people left over to receive the manifestations of their aggressiveness" (Freud, 1930, Vol. 21, p. 114). Outgroup hostility is a secondary phenomenon, which is psychologically speaking dependent on the formation of primary ingroup ties. Moreover, it is a necessary condition of harmony within an ingroup. This Freud seems to have considerd to be a general law of social psychology. He asserts that this formulation even holds true for religious groups, which profess a love for all mankind. However, according to Freud, this love only goes as far as those in their own religious group—the love shown to their own god is in direct proportion to the hate shown towards outsiders:

> ... even during the kingdom of Christ those people who do not belong to the community of believers, who do not love him, and whom he does not love, stand outside this (libidinal) tie. Therefore a religion, even if it calls itself the religion of love, must be hard and unloving to those who do not belong to it. Fundamentally indeed every religion is in this same way a religion of love for all those it embraces; while cruelty and intolerance towards those who do not belong to it are natural to every religion. (Freud, 1921, Vol. 18, p. 98.)

Freud has thus provided a psychological mechanism to explain the problem which puzzled him in 1915: the intense libidinal feelings enabling ingroup formation bring with them aggressive pressures which need to be directed outside the ingroup. The notion that the stability of the ingroup harmony necessarily implies outgroup conflict, is one that has been modified by later social psychologists—for instance a variant of this basic notion will be discussed in the later chapter on frustration-aggression theories. It can also be mentioned that Freud's approach in deriving outgroup relations from ingroup structure is in contrast to that of later experimental social psychologists who have seen ingroup cohesiveness to be the effect, not the cause, of outgroup hostility, (cf. for instance Sherif *et al.*, 1961; Thibaut, 1950; Pepitone and Kleiner, 1957). Freud as a consequence, can be said to have presented a theoretical hypothesis which at the least would seem to be worthy of further empirical verification.

However, the present purpose is not empirical verification, but to draw out some of the theoretical implications of Freud's position. Although Freud did not present his views on intergroup relations in any great detail, he does mention one form of the basic phenomenon that ingroup-ties lead to outgroup-hostility. This is the "narcissism of minor differences" which governs relations between groups that are physically close to one another or who have many close connections. The relations between these groups will be characterised by ambivalent feelings. They will become jealous rivals, although this rivalry can serve the function of strengthening the positive ties—thus the narcissism of minor differences can be a "convenient and relatively harmless satisfaction of the inclination to aggression" (Freud, 1930, Vol. 21, p. 114) as is the case between the English and the Scottish. The implication of this notion is that close similarities between different groups lead to a softening of antipathetic outgroup feelings, and that there are also libidinal feelings in this sort of intergroup relationship. In discussing the narcissism of minor differences in *Group Psychology*, Freud spells out this implication quite clearly. He states that "we are no longer astonished that greater differences should lead to an almost insuperable repugnance", (1921, Vol. 18, p. 101). However, it is a measure of Freud's lack of detail in his views of intergroup relations that he should assert the very opposite proposition in *Moses and Monotheism*. There he states that "the intolerance of groups is often, strangely enough, exhibited more strongly against small differences than against fundamental ones", (1939, Vol. 23, p. 91). It can also be noted in passing that in *Group Psychology* Freud cites anti-Semitism as resulting from major differences, whereas in the later work, anti-Semitism is seen as a product of minor differences.

Although Freud's intergroup theory is clearly undeveloped, its format nevertheless is plain. Complex social phenomena like nationalism, religious hatred and large-scale wars, are to be explained in terms of interpersonal processes. The crucial concept is that of ambivalence, and intergroup rivalries are explained in terms of the displacement of ambivalent ingroup feelings. The obvious example of such ambivalent feelings are the love-hate sentiments which each individual group member feels for his leader. It is interesting to note that there is a convergence here between Freud's theory of revolution and his intergroup theory—the basic feeling that ensured the implementation and the eventual failure of the primal killing was the ambivalence that the brothers felt for their father. Even the concept of "narcissism of minor differences" is taken directly from Freud's non-social theories—he first mentions the concept in 1918 (Vol. 11, p. 199), to explain interpersonal relations between very close and similar individuals. Once again his intergroup theory can be seen as an attempt to translate concepts from the interpersonal level of explanation to the social. The success or failure of this translation can be considered in relation to some of the problems that arise from the theory.

The first problem relates to the concept of ambivalence itself. In the clinical setting its meaning is clear, and it seems quite reasonable to expect that strong emotional ties are comprised of a number of mixed feelings. Similarly it is quite reasonable to expect that life in any social group involves restrictions and irritations to the individual, and also that such irritations cannot be expressed openly if the group is to survive as a social unit. But the question is whether social restrictions can be equated with strong personal emotions in the way that Freud suggests, and whether both sets of phenomena can be explained with reference to basic instincts. This problem can be illustrated by comparing outgroup hostility with interpersonal hostility. The expression of hostility by an individual against another individual whom he knows well may be interpreted as an expression of, or a reaction against, more positive feelings—it seems quite legitimate to search for hidden motives and repressed feelings in such a case, in the absence of obvious conscious motives. In the case of intergroup hostility the matter does not seem to be completely analogous.

Freud's contention that the instincts of love and hate nearly always are mixed together, leads to a curious conclusion with respect to intergroup relations, which Freud himself does not seem to have considered. Certainly Freud thought that instinctual fusion was the norm: "the two kinds of instinct seldom—perhaps never—appear in isolation from each other, but are alloyed with each other in varying and very different proportions and so become unrecognisable in our judgement." (Freud, 1930, Vol. 21, p. 119.)

However, if one accepts that any instinctual act is the product of both love and hate, then one must perforce find evidence of love in even the most brutal outrage. To be consistent, outgroup hostility should not be seen as merely a displacement of hostility from the ingroup but also should reflect certain ambivalent feelings towards the outgroup. By concentrating on ingroup processes Freud has largely neglected to account for the selection of outgroups as targets for displaced aggression, (except of course for his contradictory statements on the importance of similarities and differences). One might expect that any act of outgroup hostility should reflect the love and hate felt towards the ingroup, and also the love and hate felt towards the outgroup. The conclusion from this must be that in any large-scale intergroup conflict individuals must in some sense love their enemy as well as hate him. This conclusion as stated must be untenable with respect to large-scale intergroup conflicts. Roheim, whose work will be discussed in the following chapter, was forced to this conclusion in his psychoanalytic theory of intergroup relations. The ramifications of making such a step will be discussed there. For the present it can be noted that the conclusion would seem to be unacceptable with respect to organised intergroup conflicts. It would surely be absurd to state that the Nazi persecution of the Jews, the dropping of the atomic bomb on Hiroshima or the trench battles of the First World War were all in some sense expressions of love for the enemy. It was Freud who emphasised that the word "love" correctly reflected the underlying psychological reality—it would now be wrong to use the word in a way that conflicted with social reality.

That there might not be an isomorphism between individual and social processes can be illustrated further by considering a paradox in Freud's intergroup theory. This paradox resides in Freud's assertion that the superego tended to use up surplus aggression by tormenting the ego. In this way aggressiveness is directed inwardly—the aggression:

> is taken over by a portion of the ego, which sets itself over against the rest of the ego as a super-ego, and which now, in the form of "conscience", is ready to put into action against the ego the same harsh aggressiveness that the ego would have liked to satisfy upon other extraneous individuals. (Freud, 1930, Vol. 21, p. 123.)

This mechanism of coping with instinctual aggression is different from the one that Freud described as determining intergroup relations —in that account, the aggression is not directed inwards to one's own ego, but is directed outwards onto outgroup members. If these two accounts are combined then the following paradox emerges: those with the strongest superegos will be the least likely to project their aggressiveness onto outsiders. In other words, those members of an ingroup who have most strongly identified with that group will not be those who will show the greatest amount of hostility to non-group members, for all their surplus aggression will be used against themselves. Aggression towards outgroup members will, then, probably be produced by those with weaker ingroup identifications and who cannot cope with their own aggressive impulses internally. That Freud meant such a conclusion is doubtful, and it would conflict with his views about the hostility of religious believers towards non-believers. In *Group Psychology*, he argued that there is a positive relationship between the strength of religious belief and the existence of religious intolerance:

> If today that tolerance no longer shows itself so violent and cruel as in former centuries, we can scarcely conclude that there has been a softening in human manners. The cause is rather to be found in the undeniable weakening of religious feelings and the libidinal ties which depend on them. (Freud, 1921, Vol. 18, pp. 98–9.)

One can characterise this paradox as arising from the conflict between interpersonal (or even individualistic) explanations and social explanations. In this case the description of the individual psychological process does not seem to be consistent with that of the wider social phenomena. If for a moment one continues with the paradox, the need for a social, *qua* social explanation can become apparent. In his essay, *The Future of an Illusion*, Freud points to the possibility that ethnocentrism might be especially strong amongst the suppressed classes of a society, "since the right to despise the people outside it compensates them for the wrongs they suffer within their own unit" (1927, Vol. 21, p. 13). Freud also mentions on the preceding page that "an internalisation of the cultural prohibitions among the suppressed people is not to be expected" (1927, Vol. 21, p. 12). One might attempt to resolve the paradox between internal and external aggression on a class basis, i.e. that it is those without the strong superegos and the material wealth in a society that are the most nationalistic. This is an empirical hypothesis; it brings, however, into the analysis, the important variable of "class" which is essentially a sociological rather than a psychological variable. This would also involve a social analysis of the relations between the ruling and the suppressed classes. If it is true, as Freud asserts, that the masses are "lazy and unintelligent" (1927, Vol. 21, p. 7) then one would want to know how they come by their negative outgroup stereotypes. Also, one would wish to know for any intergroup conflict why the leaders of the society have declared war or made peace. If the masses are incapable of making such decisions, and if their instinctual aggression is kept constant, then one must analyse the group leaders to uncover the secrets of particular intergroup conflicts. It would be wrong to assume *a priori* that all political decisions reflect the psyche of particular social rulers and ruling classes. One must take into account overt political, economic and social factors, especially since it seems that the hostilities of the masses are directed outwards so as not to threaten the *status quo* within the society, (e.g. 1927, Vol. 21, p. 13). It seems necessary therefore to account for such power relations within a society, and also to investigate the ways in which a ruling group might contain non-ruling groups.

Consequently Freud's psychological account of intergroup relations would seem to neglect variables which are specifically social. He himself considered that his theories dealt quite adequately with such variables. However, if his social theory is rejected, then non-psychological variables present a dilemma for any psychoanalytic investigation of large-scale social phenomena. On the one hand the psychoanalytic theorist might attempt to reduce such variables to basic psychological mechanisms—examples of this form of reductionism will be given in the following chapter. In taking this step the psychoanalyst would be committed to explaining economics and politics in terms of instinctual processes. Alternatively, the theorist might eschew reductionism and hope to integrate psychological and non-psychological variables in a non-reductionist manner. Examples of such attempted integrations will also be discussed in subsequent chapters. However, the purpose of such integrations is not the grand synthesis which motivated Freud's metapsychology; rather the aim is a more limited correlation between different sorts of variables.

Before concluding this discussion of Freud's social psychology, a few strands of his theory of groups can be emphasised. His concentration upon the ingroup as the determinant of intergroup relations does provide the potential for a critique of various views of ingroup–outgroup behaviour. For instance this notion would seem well fitted to describe such phenomena as imperialism and imperialistic ideologies. Similarly the emphasis on the division between leaders and followers would suggest that fundamental power divisions within a society might be related to external intergroup relations. Moreover, the emphasis on probing beneath the surface of all phenomena, instead of accepting surface explanations for actions, carries the implication that in an intergroup context the official reasons given for particular intergroup conflicts should not necessarily be accepted at face value. A

deeper significance can be attached. It is, however, the present contention that Freud has not established that this deeper significance is
necessarily a psychological one. Before seeking instinctual explanations for intergroup phenomena, it might be possible to relate them
to the social contexts of the groups and also to the social structure
within groups.

3

Post-Freudian Group Psychology: Reductionism

It was argued in the last chapter that Freud's group psychology represented an attempt to synthesise three levels of explanation: the individualistic, the interpersonal and the social. Criticisms were made of his plan for such a synthesis, built around the theories of psychoanalysis. If Freud's own synthesis can be deemed a failure, nevertheless numerous elements of his theory have been adopted by later theorists in order to give a more circumscribed picture of human society. In this chapter and the following one the ideas of several writers, who have taken up certain of Freud's notions, will be discussed. The influence of Freud on later generations of social scientists and psychologists has been enormous and the present discussion is in no way intended to be a documentation or history of this influence. Rather the focus will be on the ideas themselves and their usefulness for understanding intergroup relations. Inevitably the choice of authors to be discussed will be somewhat arbitrary and some important thinkers will be omitted. However, the intention is not to present intellectual biographies, but to assess the value of the ideas themselves and to draw out any implications for a social psychological description of intergroup relations. In this sense, the discussion will elaborate on a number of the themes introduced in the last chapter. In particular, the background can be explained in terms of the basic instincts postulated by individualistic psychoanalysis. In turn this will involve a discussion of reductionism and the special forms of reductionist explanations offered by psychoanalytic theorists for social phenomena. Thus the issues to be considered involve the relations of an aggressive instinct, intrapsychic processes, personality types etc. to intergroup relations. The answers to such issues given by post-Freudian theorists reflect a number of different intellectual and political standpoints, and it is hoped to separate some of the main divergences of these theorists.

The systematic reductionism of Roheim

To begin with, systematic psychoanalytic reductionism will be discussed. Essentially this form of reductionism involves two stages in its approach to social phenomena. Firstly all social phenomena are considered in terms of individual psychological processes, i.e. social variables are reduced to individual variables. The second stage is that individual processes are interpreted in terms of hidden unconscious processes; in other words individual psychology is explained by the workings of the id. Thus all social forms are explained by psychoanalytic reductionism with respect to unconscious and instinctual forces. In this way the id constitutes the ultimate explanatory variable. In the previous chapter, Freud's explanation of group formation and intergroup relations was shown to depend on the instinctual erotic and aggressive feelings shared by all individuals. This is essentially a reductionist explanation of group phenomena in that pre-social, unconscious instincts are the ultimate determinants of social phenomena. Freud, of course, went further and developed his explicitly social or phylogenetic explanation based on the primal horde myth, which he intended to parallel his individualistic explanation. The systematic psychoanalytic reductionist, on the other hand, dispenses with this development—the phylogenetic explanation is abandoned in favour of the individualistic or ontogenetic explanation.

The reductionism to be discussed in this section will be that found in the theories of Geza Roheim. Other well-known reductionists will be considered in the following section—such writers will include Menninger, Storr and Lorenz. However, none of these latter are professional social-scientists. Roheim, himself, was a trained anthropologist who spent many years engaged in anthropological field-work. His writings represent a detailed and determined attempt to produce a psychoanalytic social science. As such, a number of key issues relating to such a reductionist enterprise are highlighted in his work.

Before proceeding to discuss Roheim's social theories, a brief preliminary word about the psychoanalytic doctrines of Melanie Klein is in order. This is because Roheim was directly influenced by the substantive content of Klein's views and also because they shared the same methodological presupposition of reductionism. Klein's psychoanalysis represented a determined attempt to trace the origins of all adult behaviour in infantile strivings. The forces of the id represented the ultimate determinants of her psychology. Conscious and overt phenomena are merely the surface manifestations of the unconscious. Thus the superego, which contains the prescriptions and traditions of a culture, needs to be explained in terms of infantile dramas. Its surface form is "superficial" and "if we wish to reach the real superego, to reduce its powers of operations and to influence it, our only means of doing it is analysis" (Klein, 1948, p. 171). This entails discussing the origin of the superego with respect to the child's earliest relations to its mother. In Kleinian psychoanalysis this relation is compounded of both love and hate. The mother's nipple offers security, but its withdrawal brings about "anxiety of a persecutory nature" (Klein, 1959, p. 4). Thus the infant develops a split picture of its mother: there is the Bad Mother, the origin of all its frustrations, and the Good Mother, the origin of its nourishment and comfort.

In Klein's view these infantile impulses towards the good and bad mothers constitute the ultimate realities of human behaviour. Explanations of human phenomena, which do not cite the infantile id as the ultimate causal determinant, must necessarily be incomplete and superficial. Therefore, her psychoanalytic methodology must inevitably entail reductionism. When applied to social phenomena, there must be the two-stage reduction—firstly of the social to the individual, and secondly of the individual to the instinctual. Melaine Klein makes this quite clear when she refers to social groups:

> A group—whether small or large—consists of individuals in relationship to one another; and therefore the understanding of personality is the foundation for the understanding of social life. An exploration of the individual's development takes the psychoanalyst back, by gradual stages to infancy. (Klein, 1959, p. 3.)

Although her own psychoanalytic theories placed great emphasis upon the importance of instinctual aggression, nevertheless, Klein did not undertake any systematic investigations into the ways in which the impulses of the id might affect social forms. In particular, she does not make the direct connection between the death instinct and intergroup conflicts. In fact she appears more interested in the effects of war upon individual aggression than in individual aggression as a determinant of warfare, (see, for instance, Klein, 1948, pp. 341–3, and Klein, 1961, for discussions of the effects of war on the mental states of her patients).

Klein's interest in intergroup conflict, therefore, is primarily as an independent variable, whose psychological effects rather than causes need investigation. However, had warfare been treated as a dependent variable, then it can be assumed, in the light of the preceding comments, that a rigidly reductionist methodology would have been adopted. Klein herself did not undertake an analysis of complex social phenomena; but Geza Roheim can be seen as applying Kleinian presuppositions to the social sciences. At least this is the case with respect to his later writings. In his earlier works his theories were more orthodoxly Freudian in that he sought a phylogenetic explanation of social forms. Much of his early field-work consists of attempts to substantiate empirically the myth of the primal crime. Thus Roheim (1925) claimed to have formed indirect substantiation for the existence of the primal horde from his detailed study of Australian aboriginal tribes. Similarly in his book *Animism, Magic and the Divine King* (1930), Roheim attempts to explain many of the features of kingship, to be found in primitive societies, in terms of the brother's crime against the primal father.

If there was an implicit social reductionism in Klein's thinking, then Roheim makes it explicit. He accepts the two steps of psychoanalytic reductionism and he openly states that "psycho-analytic thinking is *reductionist*" (Roheim, 1950, p. 450, italics in original); he consequently devoted much effort to reducing complex social institutions to what he considered to be their psychological origins in the infantile situation. In this, he followed many of the leads offered by Melanie Klein. Thus, where Klein had been able to give a psychoanalytic account of symbol-formation, based on infantile instinctual strivings, Roheim saw that this process could be extended: he realised that all social objects, and even society itself, could be illuminated by similar explanations:

> if Melanie Klein regards symbolism as a necessary consequence of the infant's aggressive trends and the mechanism mobilised against these trends and also as the basic elements in the subject's relation to the outside world and in sublimation, this implies an explanation of culture in terms of the infantile situation. (Roheim, 1941.)

This is the basis for what Roheim called his "ontogenetic theory" of culture. His psychoanalytic social science resembles traditional individual psychoanalysis, in that both seek the determinants of developed phenomena in the infantile situation. Unlike Freud, Roheim in his later works does not pursue the analogy between cultural and individual development, to the extent of relating cultural forms to the infancy of civilisation. Rather he derives specific cultural forms from infancy itself. His thesis is that the longings and strivings of the infant are constant throughout time, and these longings contain the seeds from which societies are developed. By implication also, these longings contain the seeds of conflicts between societies. However, before considering Roheim's account of intergroup relations, a brief description of his general social theory will be given.

Because of his anthropological training, Roheim was not trying to claim that there were no cultural influences in the mother-child relationship; in fact much of his first-hand anthropological work was concerned with cross-cultural comparisons of child-rearing practices. Nevertheless he believed that the age-old chicken-egg problem, whether society determines its child-rearing practices or vice versa, was a pseudo-problem. The chicken-egg sequence could be broken if attention were paid to what was biologically constant about human infancy and not subject to cultural variations. In his view, the universal fact of human's prolonged infancy was "the key that will unlock many doors" (Roheim, 1941).

Roheim laid great stress on the fact that the human infant undergoes a longer period of helplessness than the young of any other species. The tie between the mother and its young is biologically given and not dependent on particular cultural forms. The dependence of the new-born child on its mother is the closest possible human relationship, and Roheim characterises it as a "dual-unity"—the state of dual-unity is "the basic psychological fact which makes society possible" (Roheim, 1945, p. 25). In this state the infant is completely secure —the dual-unity constitutes its Garden of Eden, as it were. However, the infant is soon banished from its paradise. The nipple is withdrawn, frustrations and consequent anxiety ensue. Roheim borrows heavily from Kleinian theory in his description of the development of the images of the Good and Bad Mother. What is important about the dual-unity situation, from the point of view of future behaviour, is that it is never forgotten. The infant, and later the adult, retains the image of its brief experience of total security, and much of its later behaviour is designed to recapture and recreate this initial dual-unity.

However, the paradise lost is never regained. The continual search is inevitably unsuccessful. Nevertheless this search determines much of human behaviour, and especially human social behaviour. According to Roheim, cultural developments are merely "attempts to deal with infantile anxieties" (Roheim, 1934, p. 416), and culture itself is no more than "the parent-child situation extended over many generations by the aid of language" (Roheim, 1950, p. 420). Roheim traces civilisation to the human urge to prolong infancy and to return to the blissful dual-unity state. The history of civilisation is not, on this account, the story of man's progressive maturity, as some of Freud's more optimistic works implied. On the contrary, according to Roheim, civilisation is an attempt by man to prolong his infancy, not to reach an independent maturity. Cultural development, then, implies more infantilism, "which means that the savage is more infantile than the ape and civilised man more infantile than the savage" (Roheim, 1934, p. 411).

Therefore Roheim's ontogenetic theory, based on Kleinian psychoanalytic theories, is an attempt to explain social psychological phenomena in terms of the individual's infantile situation with his mother. The two-step reductionism implies that society is composed of individuals striving to find an answer to their own particular versions of a universal human problem. Roheim expresses it thus:

> It seems that we only grow up in order to remain children. Human society is like a group of authors who are not really very keenly interested in what the other has to say. Yet they attend each other's lectures in the hope of an audience when it is their turn to have their say. (Roheim, 1943, p. 31.)

Roheim applies his reductionist arguments to account for various cultural forms. These are explained in terms of the general features of man's infantile situation. It is a tenet of Roheim's reductionism that economic life is determined by emotional life, not vice versa, and of course emotional life is determined by the infantile situation. He examines various forms of economic life to be found in primitive societies, and gives a psychoanalytic explanation of them. He derives gardening from anger and reaction to infantile deprivation; agriculture he sees as a genital response to the castration fears involved in the Oedipus complex; cattle-farming a reduplication of the Oedipal complex, with Father Bull and Mother Cow acting in symbolic roles, (see *The Origin and Function of Culture*, 1943, for a summary of Roheim's views on the psychological bases of economic activities).

Roheim argues that all such economic activities originated from play activities or from fantasies which expressed instinctual strivings. Because of their function and adaptive value these forms of fantasy expression were continued rather than discarded. For Roheim, economic activities "which are originally due to id causes acquire a secondary Ego function in the course of human history" (1943, p. 71). Even less basic cultural phenomena than food production can be explained in this same way. For instance, Roheim derives the use of money from certain anal feelings, and not from any functional or societal value which a monetary system can afford:

> The desire for . . . anal symbols comes first, the practical application afterwards. *That is, originally people do not desire money because they can buy things with it, but you can buy things for money because people desire it.* (Roheim, 1934, p. 402, italics in original.)

Roheim's is a systematic and explicit psychoanalytic reductionism. He stresses the commonalities of human beings and assumes what he calls the "psychic unity of mankind". If id processes are to be seen as basic causal determinants of social phenomena, then relativistic explanations are out of the question. The timeless id exists for itself, and is not subject to geographical or sociological variation. "The unconscious is the same for every culture" (Roheim, 1950, p. 444).

Roheim's difficulties in dealing with cultural differences become particularly noticeable when one considers his account of intergroup relations. In his monograph entitled *War, Crime and the Covenant* (1945), Roheim discusses the topic of intergroup relations. He bases his discussion of this topic on his anthropological studies of the aboriginal tribes of Australia. Roheim's anthropology was itself essentially psychoanalytic: he pioneered anthropological techniques for dream analysis (e.g. Roheim, 1949) and adapted Melanie Klein's technique of play analysis to use in the field (Roheim 1941a; 1943a). The exact details of his anthropological findings will not be presented here; the discussion will mainly concern his general theoretical conclusions and their relation to the social psychology of intergroup relations.

Roheim (1945) explains the effect of dual-unity on the formation of social relations. The libidinous forces, which seek to return the individual to dual-unity, direct him to form relations with others. The other members of a particular society are introjected and become surrogate parents. Cultural objects, too, have a psychodynamic significance, relating to infancy. They are also introjected because they "unite one human being to the other, (and) are cunning devices adopted by man, the infant, against being left alone" (Roheim, 1943, p. 84). Thus, it is Eros which binds men together in social relations. In this respect Roheim's account resembles Freud's; but, whereas Freud's main concern is to trace the libido involved in social relations back to the Oedipal situation, Roheim characteristically sees their origin in the mother-child dual-unity.

Like Freud, Roheim also maintained that the aggressive instincts, as well as the libidinal ones, contribute to social phenomena. The existence of elaborate rules to combat criminality and complex mourning ceremonies suggested to Roheim that these are means of containing aggression within a social group (see Part 3 of *War, Crime and the Covenant*). The ceremonies and rituals he encountered in Australia only made sense to him if seen as methods of sublimating aggression away from destroying the social bonds. Just as important as these methods for combating aggression within an ingroup are those which deflect hostility onto an outgroup—in this way personal frustrations and aggressions are projected onto people outside the ingroup. Like Freud, Roheim considered this projection of aggression onto outgroups as a necessary fact of group life. Ingroup cohesion would be impossible without it:

> Every unity achieved means the projection of hostility into the environment, a nation cannot be really a nation without having enemies. In war an attempt is made to reaffirm a threatened unity by projecting hostility beyond the frontiers. (Roheim, 1945, p. 38.)

Roheim, however, goes further than Freud in detailing the psychological mechanisms underlying the projection of ingroup hostility onto an outgroup. Typically, Roheim traces the phenomenon back to the relationship of the infant with its mother, whereas Freud's account described the ingroup leader as a father-figure. Roheim follows Klein by arguing that aggression felt by the infant against its mother is followed by extreme feelings of anxiety and guilt. These feelings are only assuaged by the introjection of the mother. However, this is not a satisfactory resolution of anxiety—the cost of introjection is the splitting of the ego into two conflicting factions. This in turn produces increased aggression, followed by increased guilt and greater re-identification. This process is according to Roheim "an endless cycle" (1945, p. 37). The father is inserted into this scheme at the Oedipal stage, with the result that "the mother becomes more the goal of sexual desire and the father the object of identification and aggression" (ibid.).

The love for the mother, thus, gives rise to the desire for unity within the ingroup. Eros has to seek substitutes for the mother, and it finds these in binding social ties: "in its eternal search the family, the tribe and the nation are formed" (Roheim, 1943, p. 99). The death instincts, on the other hand, take a different path; they become associated with the father, and aggression is directed away from the libidinal ties. This gives rise to the need for enemies and the projection of aggression onto such enemies. As a consequence, in Roheim's theory of intergroup relations, the outgroup enemy becomes the father-figure. This is in complete contrast to Freud's account where the ingroup leader is the father-figure, or substitute for the paternal imago.

Roheim's evidence for this original theory of intergroup relations comes from his detailed analyses of the aboriginal blood-feuds. He gives psychoanalytic interpretations to the many bizarre customs and rituals associated with the blood-feud. For instance, he notes that the blood-avengers *par excellence* are the sons-in-law of the dead man, rather than his natural sons. This is interpreted in terms of the repressed hostility deriving from their struggle to obtain their wives. Similarly he notes the use of decapitated enemy heads in initiation rites and the fact that slayers often adopt the names of their victims, and also mourn for them. Roheim's theories of the blood-feud are not mere speculations without any anthropological or psychoanalytic evidence to support them. He is not an armchair anthropologist, who has also dabbled in a bit of psychoanalysis. This should be borne in mind when considering his quite remarkable conclusion that the enemy represents the father-figure:

> The guilt felt in connection with the dead is derived from the Oedipus situation and the victim of the blood feud with whom they subsequently identify themselves represents the father. (1945, p. 55) . . . *Whatever is killed becomes the father* . . . The father was the enemy, the enemy becomes the father. The difference between the cult of one's own dead and the cult of the enemy killed in a raid is not as great as one might think. (1945, p. 57, italics in original.)

In this way Roheim is able to solve a problem that was noted in Freud's theory of intergroup relations—namely, that feelings towards outgroup enemies should be an ambivalent mixture of love and hate. Roheim goes on to assert that the identification of the enemy with the father is itself part of the endless cycle of aggression-guilt-identification. As such, this form of identification is caused by, and itself in turn causes, further aggression; intergroup hostility becomes an ever-present and ever-increasing phenomenon. It is, according to Roheim, like most other human social products, only a partial and unsuccessful solution to a universal psychological problem.

There are two points to notice about Roheim's description of intergroup relations. In the first place, it assumes the dichotomy between ingroup and outgroup. He maintains that the ingroup is formed by the introjection of the mother-image, and that the outgroup, psychologically, is the projection of the father-image. This, in itself, is insufficient to account for the existence of stable real-life groups; it implies that all the members of a particular ingroup will introject each other as mother-substitutes, and not introject other people in the same way. Also it implies that the ingroup members will project their aggressions onto the same outgroup. This uniformity of ingroup introjection and projection is itself in need of explanation. The question is why there should be relatively stable patterns of uniform introjection and projection, if their determinants are individual and instinctual.

To solve this difficulty Freud used the phylogenetic account of the primal horde; but Roheim on the other hand is committed to an ontogenetic description. Also, because of his psychoanalytic reductionism, he is precluded from explaining the uniformity of ingroup and outgroup perceptions in terms of the transmission of normative cultural values—these would themselves have to be derived from the infantile situation. In other words his individualistic account implies that each individual recreates his own society out of his own infancy. However Roheim is at a loss to explain how the same infancy can regularly lead to the recreation of different societies by different groups of people. In fact, the existence of cultural differences can be said to create an especially difficult problem for Roheim, since his psychoanalytic explanation rests on the essential "psychic unity of mankind." His explanatory variables for cultural phenomena are the instincts common to all men and as such would seem to be ill-suited to explaining the formation of culturally distinct groups. In the words of one sympathetic critic ". . . one is left with the feeling that Roheim simply had no ultimate answer to the question how cultural differences arose" (Robinson, 1972, p. 87).

The second point to notice about Roheim's theory of intergroup conflict is that it is primarily based on the blood-feud. Although he discusses it under the general heading of "war", the blood-feud does seem *prima facie* a very special form of intergroup conflict. In most intergroup situations the actors can be said to act and function as group members, not as individuals. However, in the case of the blood-feud, particular individuals are killed and avenged. The whole ritual is conducted at a personal level and it is easy to see that personal unconscious motivations could be operating (although it is just as easy to suppose that they need not be as uniform and ritualised as Roheim paints them to be). On the other hand, it is not easy to imagine that the same unconscious motivation could play the same part in modern large-scale depersonalised warfare. It is fanciful to think that the modern fighter-pilot bombing ground targets imagines even unconsciously those, whom he cannot even see, to be father-substitutes.

Roheim does not apply his findings from blood-feuds directly to complex and developed group conflicts. However his assumption that Eros is responsible for increasingly larger social units (Roheim 1943, p. 99) can find its parallel in the assumption that Thanatos is responsible for ever larger group conflicts. This would make the modern full-scale war psychologically similar to the blood-feud. Roheim does not deny or admit this in his discussion on war, but in his conclusion he makes the following comment:

> These considerations throw some light on the role of super-ego conflict as one of the factors that lead to war. We all remember the tremendous role the problem of German war guilt played in Nazi propaganda, the furious denial and the paranoia or projection that followed. (Roheim, 1945, p. 68.)

Such an allusion is tantalising; the role of unconscious motivating factors is suggested but not spelled out. It should be noted that Roheim's allusion is a guarded one—he refers to "one of the factors that lead to war", without saying whether the other factors are also psychological derivations from infancy. The suggestion however does seem to imply that factors other than the psychoanalytic have to be taken into account, when dealing with complex social phenomena.

The feeling that systematic psychoanalytic reductionism may be insufficient to account for complex social phenomena is reinforced by Roheim's comments on modern society. There are clear indications that he did not advocate the blind use of psychoanalysis to explain every facet of modern Western culture. For instance, he criticised Margaret Mead's *And Keep Your Powder Dry* and Geoffrey Gorer's *The American People* on the grounds that they were based on "use and misuse of psychoanalysis in a simplified way" (Roheim, 1950, p. 366). Examples of further psychoanalytic oversimplifications will be given in the following section. For the moment, it might be asked whether such oversimplification is a product of particular psychoanalytic approaches or whether it is a necessary consequence of applying psychoanalytic reductionism to problems of modern society.

That the latter may be the case is hinted at by Roheim himself. For instance, he explicitly makes a distinction between the modern nation and the primitive tribe and he warns against equating the two (Roheim, 1950, p. 390). In particular, he states that class divisions need to be taken into account in the case of the modern state. Such class divisions need economic explanations. Previously in *The Origin and Function of Culture* (1943), Roheim had attempted to explain economics in terms of unconscious psychological motivations. However, with regard to modern classes, he seems to be advocating that economic variables should be considered in their own right and not be reduced to psychological variables. Thus, when dealing with modern societies, he calls for "a new kind of interpretation which combines the economic with the psychological" (Roheim, 1950, p. 376). This new sort of interpretation, of course, denies the reductionist presupposition that the ultimate reality underlying all manifestations of human behaviour is to be sought in the unconscious workings of the id.

In the case of modern intergroup conflicts, Roheim seems to be admitting that purely psychological explanations must be insufficient. However, if one accepts that unchanging individual instincts by themselves cannot account for the manifold differences in cultural development, then the position becomes more serious for the reductionist. Roheim admits that the differences in cultural customs of modern states are not instinctually determined. He writes that they "are not dependent on the infantile situation but on events in history", (1950, p. 455). There is, of course, no *a priori* reason why this argument should not be extended to cover the history of primitive tribes; and also there would seem to be no *a priori* reason for denying the existence of economic factors in determining conflicts between primitive societies. Roheim, in fact, establishes no firm reasons for stipulating different forms of explanation of modern complex social phenomena than of more primitive phenomena.

The conclusion would seem to be that even Roheim admitted that modern social phenomena are not amenable to a completely reductionist explanation. Such phenomena, of course, include conflicts between complex social groups. In taking this step Roheim would seem to have arrived at a paradox: namely, that psychoanalytic theories, developed from the examination of some of the most articulate members of modern society, are most fitted to describing primitive societies. This paradox will not be probed further except to suggest that Roheim may well have been oversimplifying the primitive. It is however apparent that his explanation of primitive warfare cannot cope adequately with modern organised conflict. To divorce economics from class conflicts is as absurd as stating that the combatants in a modern war are really fighting their own fathers. Roheim seems to have been aware of these absurdities. However, not all psychoanalytic reductionists have saved themselves from gross oversimplification.

Dogmatic reductionism

In contrast to Roheim, other psychoanalytic theorists have been oblivious to the difficulties inherent in reductionism and have thrown themselves headlong into the task of deriving complex social phenomena from asocial instincts. In doing so they often dispense with any social analysis; instead they dogmatically assert connections between psychoanalytic concepts and overt social forms. Moreover, they often import political assumptions in order to amplify their rudimentary psychological explanations.

Examples of dogmatic reductionism can be found in the works of Money-Kyrle (1950, 1951 and 1961), Glover (1946) and Menninger 1942). These writers all emphasise the unconscious and infantile origins of group phenomena. For instance, Money-Kyrle (1950) writes that the individual seeks to rediscover his childish fantasies throughout his life and that he imposes them on "all the varieties of group formation he will enter, and help to mould", (p. 315). Glover states that it is the psychoanalyst's task to lay bare "in the situation of con-flict between two countries *all* the threads of infantile conflict", (1946, p. 26, italics in original). The ways in which they relate the psychology of the child to intergroup phenomena differ considerably. Money-Kyrle states that ingroup attitudes are the product of identification with the Good Mother and outgroup attitudes are derived from the image of the Bad Mother. Glover specifically links intergroup conflict with infantile sadism. For Menninger outgroup prejudice arises out of infantile feelings of rejection, (1942, pp. 224 ff).

In none of these cases are the connections between infantile instincts and social phenomena spelt out in any detail. Rather they are dog-matically asserted. For instance Money-Kyrle offers no detailed argu-ments to back up his description of intergroup attitudes in terms of the Good and Bad Mother; in particular he does not discuss the alternative psychoanalytic accounts of Freud and Roheim. Similarly Glover writes that the normal inhibitions against instinctual aggres-sion are by no means secure. In times of intergroup conflict an indi-vidual's "inhibiting mechanism will give way under the strain of social sanction, and the full sweep of his aggression will once more turn out-wards", (1946, p. 24). However, Glover does not describe what the relevant social sanctions are and how precisely they might interact with the individual's instinctual structure. Menninger (1959) argues that men sublimate their aggressive fantasies against their mothers by en-gaging in communal masculine pursuits. This sublimation, according to Menninger, is inevitably unsuccessful; the destructive impulses sooner or later "must foment a war with someone", (p. 622). The cer-tainty of warfare following the hatred of the maternal imago being sublimated into all-male activities is asserted *a priori* without reference to specific instances.

Where there is more specificity there is often unsatisfactory over-simplification. For instance Menninger (1942) advocates the free ex-pression of emotionality as a way of reducing aggression. He claims that it is significant that "among the Jews, where there is such a notice-able tendency to express aggressions in argument and verbal contact, there are few divorces and so little physical violence" (1942, p. 274). The mere association of certain social and cultural phenomena with psycho-analytic concepts by itself cannot constitute an adequate explanation. Money-Kyrle is likewise prone to generalisations. He states that "Eng-land entered the Second World War still largely in that state of de-

pression which had prevented her from stopping it before it started",
(1961, p. 149). The meaning of such a statement is unclear. Money-
Kyrle could be interpreted as psychoanalysing a whole society—in
which case he is committing the "group mind fallacy" and applying
psychological concepts to mythical abstractions. If he is describing the
mental states of individual Englishmen then one would require some
further social analysis; in particular one would wish to know who
exactly was depressed and how the feelings of passive dependency
could be dramatically changed into patriotic aggression.

The absence of social analysis is sometimes accompanied by political
assumptions in the works of dogmatic reductionists. Money-Kyrle
(1951, p. 103) writes that class conflict is based on feelings of guilt and
repressed aggression. In stating this he is asserting that class conflict is
essentially irrational; it arises from instinctual psychic dramas, rather
than from realistic social inequality. Consequently those who rebel
against an existing social structure are seen to be rebelling against the
image of the bad parent instead of attempting to improve their social
position. This orientation reduces the intergroup to the intrapsychic;
it also implies that the prevention of intergroup conflict depends upon
changes within the individual rather than changes within the social
structure. Glover (1946) puts this succinctly in the maxim: "take care
of your own aggression and the aggression of nations will take care of
itself" (pp. 31–2). By reducing intergroup aggression to individual
aggression, the reductionist is theoretically forestalling explicit social
criticism. Even so implicit values can be readily detected.

Money-Kyrle's views are in obvious disagreement with those who see
class conflict as being the concomitant of particular social orders. If
class conflict arises out of some sort of clinical pathology, then
Money-Kyrle can characterise certain group relations as "clinically
normal" (1951, p. 105). These occur when the group members have
rational and adult world-views. An instance of an unhealthy world-
view, according to Money-Kyrle, is communism which is based on
Marx's "envy of his parents pictured as greedily keeping their inex-
haustible goodness to themselves" (1961, p. 166). In this way communism is explained away as a bad identification, just as class conflict is
dismissed as guilt. Money-Kyrle's description of healthy world-views
is an outline of a liberal humanism, which understands the psychological basis of opposing viewpoints. As a consequence Money-Kyrle is
able to defend a particular ideological stance, and to criticise others,

by his casual linking of psychoanalytic terminology with complex social issues.

The dogmatic reductionism of Money-Kyrle, Glover and Menninger has been mentioned. It should not be thought that this mode of thinking is confined to psychoanalysts of their generation. The errors of dogmatic reductionism may have been long recognised by some members of the psychoanalytic movement (Alexander, 1937); nevertheless it would be wrong to suppose that dogmatic reductionism is dead and buried. Mitscherlich (1971) notes the lack of psychoanalytic studies of large-scale mass aggression, which employ findings from the social sciences and which are not derived solely from individualistic accounts. He repeats Otto Fenichel's criticisms of Glover, made in 1935, that the latter's exclusively psychoanalytic approach does injustice to complex social phenomena. Mitscherlich says of Fenichel's criticisms that they are just as timely today as they were over thirty years ago.

Two modern examples of dogmatic reductionism will be briefly mentioned. In his book, *Human Aggression* (1968), Anthony Storr reveals a basic orientation similar to Glover and Menninger; he also attempts to explain social phenomena in terms of human instincts. Nevertheless there is an important difference between Storr's account and those of Glover and Menninger. Whereas the latter two writers tend to stress the harmful effects of the aggressive instinct, Storr emphasises its positive side. He sees aggression as a basic human instinct which "is an inherited constant, of which we cannot rid ourselves, and which is absolutly necessary for survival" (Storr, 1968, p. 109). According to Storr, it is the aggressive instinct which ensures that children achieve emotional independence, and which is also at the root of all creative endeavours. He specifically distinguishes between the positive and negative sides of aggression. Aggression can be, according to Storr, an "active striving" or a "destructive hostility" (1972, p. 20). He sees the psychiatrist's job as releasing the positive sides of the aggressive drive and curtailing its negative effects. To attempt to eliminate aggression altogether is in Storr's opinion undesirable.

Storr stresses the immutability of the aggressive instinct, and his comments upon social phenomena, and in particular on intergroup relations, arise directly from his belief that there is a basic aggressive instinct. He argues that this instinct in man is endogenous, and needs periodic discharge. He suggests that outlets for aggression will be sought if "aggressive tension" is allowed to accumulate. He writes that "it is probable that when no outside stimulus for aggression exists, men actually seek such stimuli out in much the same way as they do when sexually deprived" (1968, p. 18). However, Storr offers no direct evidence to support such assertions. This is especially critical since he uses the term "aggression" in a wide sense to cover a multitude of human activities from actual violence to Beethoven's composition of his ninth symphony (Storr, 1968, p. 88). The evidence which is offered in support of an aggressive instinct is indirect. Storr quotes several experiments on animal behaviour; for instance, he mentions that rats reared in isolation will attack strange rats, and that cichlid fish seem to need a hostile neighbour in order to survive. However, such animal experiments cannot be said to demonstrate that man has an inborn aggressive instinct, which seeks periodic release. The fact that the cichlid fish will attack its mate in the absence of an aggressive neighbour is no evidence that similar behaviour must be found amongst humans. Similarly the fact that many other species do not behave in the same way as the cichlid fish does not of itself entail any necessary facts about human social behaviour. There would seem to be no *a priori* reason why human behaviour should parallel the behaviour of the cichlid fish or of the laboratory rat. In fact there are good reasons for believing that human social behaviour is unique in the animal kingdom in a number of significant respects. Certainly Storr recognises that it is not possible to describe human aggression "in the same kind of terms which ethologists use of animal behaviour" (1968, p. 26). Nevertheless, he concentrates upon the animal studies in order to substantiate his notion of an aggressive instinct.

Having postulated the existence of a human aggressive instinct, Storr then proceeds to make certain inferences about the instinctual basis of complex human behaviour. For instance, he asserts that men are instinctively more aggressive than women, and that this biological difference underlies differences in sex roles. Since aggression has its positive effects as well as negative ones, male aggressiveness endows men with superior powers of mind and physique: "It is highly probable that the undoubted superiority of the male sex in intellectual and creative achievement is related to their greater endowment of aggression" (1968, p. 62). The woman is by her nature passive, whilst the man is active. According to Storr, there are biological reasons for such differences. He writes that "in the relation between the sexes, the spermatozoon swims actively, whilst the ovum passively awaits its penetration. The anatomy of the sexual organs itself attests the differentiation of the sexual role" (1968, p. 62). Storr does not pursue this analogy between sex role and anatomy in any greater detail. Had he done so, he might have been forced to admit that the woman biologically creates something out of the sperm and ovum—this would, of course, conflict with the belief that women are biologically endowed with inferior powers of creation.

Just as Storr ascribes sex differences to immutable biological constitution, so too does he seek a reductionist account of conflicts between social groups. He asserts that intergroup aggression is natural and that "the need for weapons is rooted in man's biological weakness and vulnerability" (1968, p. 113). As a consequence he denies that intergroup conflicts can ever be eliminated—a man's biological aggression would always seek such an outlet. However, he does advocate the substitution of ritual intergroup struggles for actual warfare. He argues that sporting tournaments and scientific competition, such as the "space-race", could provide an acceptable substitute for warfare, and in this way the aggressive instinct could be sublimated along socially productive lines (Storr, 1964). He does not present any detailed argument to support such a contention, but merely derives it from his biological premises. He does not discuss the necessary social context, in which any substitute intergroup conflict must be enacted—in particular he does not discuss the role of those powerful agencies which would establish the substitute warfare, and which no doubt would have vested interests in seeing that all less powerful groups sublimated their aggression along the prescribed channels. Moreover, Storr does not consider the opposing psychological thesis that such intergroup competition might enhance existing intergroup conflicts. Certainly there is some evidence that under certain circumstances sporting competition can increase aggression (e.g. Heinila, 1966; Goldstein and Arms, 1971; and in particular, Sherif and Sherif, 1953; Sherif et al. 1961).

Storr also derives certain ideological statements from his biological premises. He offers a biological justification for the British parliamentary system. He states that in parliamentary democracies the problem of the disposal of aggression is "solved" by allowing an opposition to the government (1968, p. 27); he goes on to suggest that "the House of Commons might stand as an exemplar of how men should deal with their aggressive drives" (p. 121). One might wonder how many times British parliamentarians have acted out their aggressions in an exemplary fashion by dispatching gun-boats around the world. Similarly, Storr justifies a "mixed-economy" on biological grounds. He states that both individual competition and group cooperation are necessary for the existence of animal and human societies—from this he draws the conclusion that a mixture of capitalism and communism provides the correct social form for human instincts (Storr, 1972, p. 24). Again he provides no systematic analysis, and he leaps directly from assumptions of human instinctual constitution to statements about the desirability of particular complex social forms. It is by such leaps that he hopes to deal with questions like the stability of liberal democracies, the inferiority of women, the role of sport in intergroup relations, etc. He does not seem to notice that these questions raise wider social issues than the hypothesis of a diffuse and ill-defined aggressive instinct.

The final example of dogmatic reductionism is not in fact taken from a psychoanalyst but from an ethologist. Konrad Lorenz, in his book *On Aggression* (1967) draws implications from his studies of animal behaviour for human social behaviour. Like Freud he sees the sciences of man as possessing an essential unity, but unlike Freud he does not place psychoanalysis at the centre of that unity. Rather he gives pride of place to biology. He writes that "expert teaching of biology is the one and only foundation on which really sound opinions about mankind and its relation to the universe can be built" (1967, p. 288). The justification for including Lorenz under the heading of psychoanalytic reductionism is his belief that the findings of psychoanalysis have complemented ethological findings and together they enable a diagnosis of the human condition. Even if the existence of an aggressive instinct is given a biological explanation it is assumed in the case of humans to be mediated by processes described by psychoanalytic theory. For instance Lorenz writes that "psychoanalysis has shown very convincingly that many patterns of altogether laudable behaviour derive their impulses from the 'sublimation' of aggressive or sexual drives" (1967, p. 270). Although Lorenz tends to concentrate upon the biological significance of basic instincts, he nevertheless assumes the psychoanalytic model as an intervening variable between the biological origin and the final output of complex human social behaviour.

Lorenz's animal studies convinced him of the reality of the aggressive drive, and that such a drive has important biological functions. Just as he attempts to explain the evolutionary significance of animal instincts, so he likewise extends the evolutionary argument to account for man's aggressive drive. In this way he has added a third stage to the two-stage arguments of psychoanalytic reductionism. Thus, there is still the reduction of social aggression to individual instinctual aggression—then there is the explanation of individual and instinctual aggression in terms of its significance for the species. As such, Lorenz's arguments progress beyond the reduction of the social to the individual; nevertheless they do contain this element and like Money-Kyrle, Glover and Storr, Lorenz dispenses with any specifically social scientific analysis.

Like the psychoanalytic writers just mentioned, Lorenz seeks underlying and irrational reasons for intergroup conflicts. He calls mass social behaviour "abjectly stupid" and states that "the ever-recurrent phenomena of history do not have reasonable causes" (1967, p. 228). Intergroup conflicts are therefore the product of "unreasoning and unreasonable human nature", which causes nations "to compete, though no economic necessity compels them to do so" (p. 228). This irrationality in man's behaviour can only be explained, therefore, by considering his evolutionary inheritance, and in particular his capacity for instinctive aggression. It should be noted that Lorenz gives no detailed arguments to back up his contentions about the irrationality of intergroup conflict, nor does he offer reasons for rejecting alternative views of human social conflict. Rather he takes a detached Olympian view of mankind, or to use a favourite example of his, the view of the unbiased investigator from Mars. From a great distance he notes the continual existence of human warfare and from this fact alone he deduces that there must necessarily be something in man's genetic make-up that preconditions him to organised group conflict. This "something" is of course his innate aggressive drive.

Originally, according to Lorenz, intra-specific warfare had great evolutionary advantages for mankind. It enabled the balanced distribution of human communities. Moreover, because instinctual aggression could be directed against a neighbouring community, it was possible to control its expression within the group. In stating this Lorenz is adding an evolutionary and biological gloss to Freud's theory of intergroup relations, which stipulates that ingroup cohesion is only possible with the direction of aggressive instincts onto an outgroup.

Also Lorenz links the aggressive drive to sexuality and states that intra-specific aggression can aid the sexual selection of partners to good evolutionary advantage. Without going into the details of Lorenz's arguments, one can summarise his position by stating that modern man is a captive of his evolutionary heritage and that modern social be-haviour needs to be explained in terms of man's hidden biological nature. This behaviour includes a "specialised form of communal aggression" (p. 259) in which the individual is willing, nay, enthu-siastic to commit any act in the name of duty. There is a special posture that the individual adopts when he is "militantly enthusiastic" in which "the facial muscles mime the 'hero face', familiar from the films" (p. 260). What is important, according to Lorenz, is how this behaviour has outlived its usefulness. Originally it ensured the defence of the community; but now to be militantly enthusiastic has become a drive in itself, which needs to be satisfied:

> Humanity is not enthusiastically combative because it is split into poli-tical parties, but it is divided into opposing camps because this is the adequate stimulus situation to arouse militant enthusiasm in a satisfying manner. (Lorenz, 1967, p. 262.)

This form of explanation resembles Roheim's explanation of money —just as Roheim asserted that money exists because people desire to spend it, so Lorenz asserts that group divisions exist because people desire intergroup conflict. The underlying psychological motive is seen as determining the social form and not vice versa.

The implication from this sort of evolutionary analysis is that there is not much profit to be gained from analysing particular intergroup conflicts. The Olympian detachment implies that all warfare is of the same order and derived from the same set of irrational instincts. The occurrence of any particular outbreak of war will no longer occasion any surprise on the part of the visitor from Mars. Consequently, it might be thought that the postulation of unchanging instincts as underwriting human behaviour would lead to a position which denies the importance of social change. If the instincts are considered im-mutable, then changes in social forms will leave the "basic" deter-minants of human conduct untouched. As a result, the reductionist might be thought to decry the usefulness of making social changes, and in turn to defend existing social arrangements. Certainly Storr and Money-Kyrle lend weight to this interpretation of reductionism by their commendations of British parliamentary democracy. However, the matter is not quite so simple, as a closer discussion of Lorenz's social views will reveal.

Although Lorenz and Storr hold similar positions about the nature of the aggressive instinct, their social views differ substantially. Storr's liberalism has already been mentioned; Lorenz explicitly criticises liberalism and is no defender of present social trends. Some of his most stringent criticisms of modern life are contained in his recent book *Civilized Man's Eight Deadly Sins* (1974). He argues that modern man has become divorced from his instinctual structure. In particular he attacks life in the Western world, especially the competition and "supply-and-demand escalation" of capitalism (p. 21). However, he does not relate such criticisms to an analysis of the Western social system and contrast this system with other forms of social existence, in order to isolate the important social variables responsible for the present malaise. To do this would be to abandon the attempt to reduce social questions to matters of basic instinct.

Lorenz is especially scathing of democratic and liberal principles. He attacks what he calls the "pseudo-democratic doctrine", which includes a belief in the equality of men and the importance of social conditioning upon behaviour. He claims that the pseudo-democratic doctrine "undoubtedly bears a considerable part of the blame for the moral and cultural collapse that threatens the Western world" (1974, p. 66). His anti-democratic bias leads him to distrust the popular viewpoint. He writes:

> Public opinion is inert: it reacts to new influences only after a protracted hush; moreover it loves gross simplifications, mostly exaggerations of the facts. Therefore the opposition, criticising a general opinion, is nearly always in the right. (Lorenz, 1974, p. 37.)

Lorenz does not develop these notions into a coherent social analysis. It is as if he considers that his criticisms of democratic doctrine follow from his biological presuppositions just as naturally as Storr considered that the defence of democracy followed from the same presuppositions.

Although Lorenz is critical of modern trends and adheres to the belief that human nature is immutable, he is nevertheless not entirely pessimistic about the future of mankind. In the final chapter of *On Aggression* he makes certain suggestions for reducing intergroup conflict. Like Storr he advocates the use of sporting tournaments as a harmless substitute for actual warfare. In common with Menninger and Glover, he also advocates the spread of scientific knowledge for reducing international tensions. Similarly he attaches an importance to psychoanalytic knowledge and he states that a deeper understanding of the processes of sublimation "will do much toward the relief of undischarged aggressive drives" (1967, p. 268). However, it is in the biological sciences that Lorenz puts his greatest faith. All in all, he believes that scientific knowledge can bring about an amelioration of the human condition, and can unite men, where now they are divided. It can do this because "more than any other product of human culture, scientific knowledge is the collective property of all mankind" (1967, p. 279).

There are a number of difficulties with Lorenz's faith in science. Since Lorenz, in common with other dogmatic reductionists, considers that the social organisation of man is unimportant compared to his innate character, he does not recommend any particular social changes, which might bring about the required respect for science. In the absence of any social analysis of the transmission of scientific ideas, his recommendations for an extension of the scientific spirit must appear to be optimistic hopes, rather than as practical guides for social improvement. More seriously, there are certain contradictions in Lorenz's position. Particularly, he does not view all scientific endeavour as being of equal value. In *Civilized Man's Eight Deadly Sins* he is especially critical of those behavioural sciences, which, in his view, promote pseudo-democratic values. The behaviourist belief in the plasticity of human nature is, according to Lorenz, a widespread and fallacious dogma. Psychological and social science has thus become a part of the erroneous public opinion, which Lorenz attacks. In this respect, he recognises that the dogmas of a particular age will create their own scientific justifications.

Given that Lorenz strongly criticises those sciences which contribute to the "pseudo-democratic doctrine", the suspicion must be that he only supports the scientific spirit so long as he agrees with the resulting theories. However, his support for the scientific spirit is in certain respects less than total. Throughout *Civilized Man's Eight Deadly Sins*, and to a lesser extent throughout *On Aggression*, Lorenz makes pronouncements on a variety of social issues, whilst ignoring what evidence there is from the social sciences. It is as if he feels safe to reject, or at least neglect, studies pointing to the importance of social differences in human behaviour—such studies might be thought to be part of pseudo-democratic science and therefore to be dangerously erroneous. Certainly Lorenz's commendation of the scientific spirit is not itself absolute, since he advocates a respect for older non-scientific traditions. He criticises the youth of today for showing scant respect for their elders, especially when they do this in the name of science:

> The erroneous belief that only the rationally comprehensible or the scientifically provable belongs to the fixed knowledge of mankind produces disastrous effects. It encourages "scientifically enlightened" youth to throw overboard the enormous fund of knowledge and wisdom contained in the traditions of every old civilisation and in the teaching of the great world religions. (Lorenz, 1974, p. 48.)

Consequently Lorenz seems to champion the scientific spirit only so far as it supports his own values.

The values which Lorenz upholds seem to be a mixture of authoritarian conservatism and romantic idealism, viz. his criticism of democracy and of the quality of modern life. One further aspect of his values can be mentioned, since it not only relates to intergroup relations but also it illustrates his lack of social analysis. In all his accounts of the evolutionary significance of intergroup warfare and of militant enthusiasm, he assumes that social groups are distinct bounded entities. He does not investigate the structure of the group as such, but accepts that social groups are autonomous creations. Modern anthropological thought has doubted this assumption; it has stressed the interrelatedness of different human social groupings and that group boundaries are not always easy to define, (e.g. Moerman, 1965; Cohen and Middleton, 1970; LeVine and Campbell, 1972). However, Lorenz goes further and adds a certain normative element to his account—he deprecates attempts to reduce the distinctiveness of national or cultural groups. He writes that it "usually proves highly dangerous to mix cultures" and that "to kill a culture, it is often sufficient to bring it into contact with another, particularly if the latter is higher" (1967, p. 253). Not only does Lorenz fail to deal with the considerable evidence which suggests that cultural contact is the normal state of affairs in intergroup relations, but he also seems to be introducing certain values relating to the purity and worth of various cultures. He does not develop his notions on "higher" and "lower" cultures and the need for each to preserve their own purity. In the absence of any detailed argument or empirical evidence, it is hard to escape the conclusion that Lorenz is adding a nationalist ideology to his conservative anti-democratic views. Certainly it is difficult to accept such social views as being merely the product of "neutral" biological science.

The aggressive instinct and social analysis

The one element common to all the psychoanalytic reductionists is their desire to seek the hidden determinants of human behaviour. They scorn the more obvious surface explanations in their attempts to uncover the deeper springs of human conduct. The overt reasons which men give for their actions are considered as rationalisations. On a social level, the overt ideological reasons for intergroup warfare are likewise considered as rationalisations, which conceal the true instinctual bases of social behaviour. The psychoanalytic reductionist would think it naive and simplistic to accept at their face value the political and economic justifications given for any intergroup conflict. Roheim specifically criticised non-psychoanalytic explanations on the grounds of superficiality; he wrote that "after Freud managed to dive to the bottom of the ocean, people now tell us that the ocean has a surface" (1950, p. 450).

Although the psychoanalysts might share this same basic premise, nevertheless the details of their theories contain substantial differences. The reductionists discussed in this chapter are not all of one accord in their descriptions of intergroup phenomena, but embrace a variety of positions. In particular, they differ amongst themselves in their descriptions of the aggressive instinct. It would be true to say that there is no one universally accepted theory of aggression within the tradition of psychoanalysis. Freud himself entertained at least three different theories of the aggressive drive. His theorising progressed from the notion that aggression was the result of the conflict between the ego and the id to the idea that the aggression was an ego, as well as id, instinct. In his last theoretical formulations, Freud developed the notion that the basic instincts were Eros and Thanatos, and that aggression was a manifestation of the death instinct, which was deflected from the self to the outside world. Roheim, Klein and Menninger all accepted this last theory of Freud and postulated that aggressive behaviour is a manifestation of the death instinct. Glover, Storr and Lorenz, on the other hand, deny the reality of the death instinct and urge for the existence of a distinct aggressive drive analogous to the sexual drive. Other psychoanalytically minded theorists have stressed the relation of the aggressive instinct to the structures of the ego—for instance the ego psychologists, to be discussed in the following chapter, have emphasised the "particularly close tie between the ego and aggression", (Hartmann, Kris and Loewenstein, 1949, p. 23). Other psychoanalysts, who will also be more fully considered in the next chapter, have denied that aggression is an instinct at all—for instance Horney and Sullivan deny that aggression is a function of Thanatos, ego or id instinctual structures. Consequently it can be seen that there are a number of opposing accounts of aggression; it will be suggested that this presents a serious problem for any attempt to explain social behaviour in terms of individual instinctual aggression. Without a firm theory of individual aggression, the task of illuminating large-scale social phenomena in terms of a hypothesised instinctual theory becomes well-nigh impossible.

Some of the theoretical positions just mentioned are not particularly modern, but it should not be imagined that psychoanalysts have of late mended their differences on the matter of the aggressive instincts. Subsequent psychoanalytic research has not led to a general convergence of opinion on the basic instinctual structure of man. The Twenty-Seventh Psychoanalytical Congress, held in Vienna in 1971, devoted a considerable portion of its time to the discussion of problems relating to the concept of aggression. The printed reports of the congress convey the impression that progress in theory and empirical research into aggression has not been as pronounced as psychoanalysts would have wished. The main divisions between the theoretical positions of the different psychoanalytic schools of thought still persist, and this is well illustrated by Lussier's (1972) report on the informal discussions on aggression at the congress.

Some of the positions of leading psychoanalysts of today can be briefly mentioned. For instance, Freud's concept of aggression as a manifestation of the death instinct still has its champions (Eissler, 1971). This view is rejected by those psychoanalysts who see a direct parallel between aggression and the libido, and argue that aggression, like sexuality, is a primary instinctual drive (Brenner, 1971). This position is rejected by others who dispute that aggression is a primary drive at all; for instance, according to Gillespie (1971), aggression is not "a fundamental irreducible element in the human constitution", rather it is "a *way* of doing things rather than an activity in its own right" (Gillespie, 1971, p. 159, italics in original).

It is not just that present day psychoanalysts are unsure of the theoretical status of the concept of aggression—they are also unsure of the way aggression works in the individual. Their disagreements are both empirical as well as metapsychological. Brenner, who argued at the Congress that there was a separate aggressive instinct, concluded his survey of the topic with the following words: "We cannot say whether aggression and sexuality are separate at birth and gradually mix or fuse in the course of development or whether the two differentiate gradually from a common matrix." (Brenner, 1971, p. 143.)

This would appear to be a fairly basic matter in the discussion of the instinctual status of aggression. If the empirical evidence is not forthcoming, then the debates cannot be resolved about whether or not there is an aggressive instinct, and if so whether it is a separate instinct or an offshoot of the libido. Anna Freud (1972) summed up the discussions at the Congress by stating that the theoretical disagreements revealed a lack of empirical studies by psychoanalysts into the topic of aggression. Too often, she argues, psychoanalysts have tended merely to assume that aggressive development parallels sexual development, without providing any evidence to support this assumption. All in all, according to her, the Congress revealed the differences of opinion that exist in psychoanalytic thinking concerning aggression, and "listeners were left with the impression that the problem of the source of aggression is unresolved so far" (A. Freud, 1972, p. 165).

Thus substantial divisions exist within the official psychoanalytic movement today concerning the status and nature of aggression. This is not to mention the differences between the official movement and breakaway groups. There is no need to outline the variety of theoretical positions that psychoanalysts, both within and without the official movement, have adopted. It is sufficient to note the psychoanalysts' own admissions that the problem of individual aggression has by no means been resolved. The divisions amongst the psychoanalysts therefore suggest that there is no one generally accepted theory of aggression that the social scientist could adopt for the purpose of explaining large-scale intergroup aggression. Given the differences of opinion that exist about individual instinctual aggression, it should not be surprising that there exist a multitude of psychoanalytic theories concerning the determinants of social aggression. There has been occasion to mention a number of these competing theories. Freud could see the outgroup enemy as a projection of hostility felt towards the ingroup leader, or father-figure. Roheim, however, viewed the outgroup enemy as the father-figure itself, whereas Money-Kyrle could characterise it as the Bad Mother. Lorenz and Storr could start from similar premises concerning the nature of the aggressive drive, but still derive very different social analyses. Similarly there have been a number of other psychoanalytic accounts of outgroup attitudes, which seek the roots of intergroup relations in a variety of unconscious phenomena. For instance, Sterba (1947) developed a theory of out-group prejudice based upon genitality and the jealousy of younger siblings. Zilboorg (1947) sees outgroup hostility as a projection of anxiety derived from a failure to find herd security. Kubie (1965) and Kovel (1970) view outgroup prejudice, and especially racial prejudice, as deriving from feelings of guilt about faeces. Lowenthal and Gutter-man (1972) argue that the outgroup represents a rejection of the self's infantile helplessness together with an ambivalent longing for that parasitic early stage of development. On the other hand, Erikson (1946) described outgroup prejudice in terms of images and fears of violation and castration.

All in all there would seem to be a plethora of psychoanalytic accounts of intergroup aggression. Faced with such a disarray in both individualistic and social accounts of instinctual aggression, the temp-tation must be to deny that there is an aggression instinct at all. This is especially compelling, given the dangers of concentrating upon interpersonal aspects of intergroup situations, and of postulating an unchanging human nature as a barrier to social change. In this respect, Gorer (1968) denies that "man has a killer instinct" and he specifically quotes the findings of anthropologists who have discovered "a few societies where men seem to find no pleasure in dominating over, hurt-ing or killing the members of other societies, where all they ask is to be left at peace and to be left in peace" (Gorer, 1968, p. 34). Instances of such societies are, according to Gorer, the Arapesh of New Guinea, studied by Margaret Mead, the Pygmies of the Ituri rain forests, studied by Colin Turnbull, and the Lepchas of the Sikkim, studied by Gorer himself. Gorer argues that the findings of psychoanalysts, who have depicted man as a naturally aggressive savage, need to be com-plemented by anthropological discoveries.

Gorer is certainly correct in advocating that the barbaric picture painted by certain instinct theorists needs to be balanced by accounts of man's more social achievements. However, just as psychoanalytic findings should not be applied simplistically to explain large-scale social phenomena, similarly there are dangers in basing conclusions about man's natural instincts, or lack of them, on the evidence of a few anthropological studies. Gorer (1968) quotes Mead's (1935) finding that the Arapesh were essentially peaceful and unwarlike. However, he does not mention the qualification of Fortune (1939) who suggested that the principal reason why the Arapesh conducted no wars was because they were explicitly prevented by their German colonialists. Prior to colonisation "warfare was good Arapesh custom" (Fortune, 1939, p. 27). From this it should not be concluded that Gorer is after all incorrect, and that man does have an aggressive instinct. Rather the moral should be that it is imperative to seek the social conditions under which warfare is more likely to occur. In the case of Mead's and Gorer's descriptions of the Arapesh, a simple and obvious social variable was neglected—in the search to uncover basic truths of human nature the fact of colonial subjugation was overlooked. In this way the "anti-instinct theorist" is capable of adopting the same narrow focus as the instinct theorist himself, and as a result wider social variables are ignored.

It is not the present position to assert confidently either that there is an aggressive instinct or that no such instinctual drive exists. This issue, as such, will be left in abeyance. It has been repeatedly argued throughout this survey of psychodynamic accounts of intergroup relations that individual and interpersonal theory should not replace social theory. As a consequence, it will be suggested that a distinction can be drawn between the individual and social aspects, at least as far as they relate to matters of intergroup relations and to social identity. It will not be assumed that problems of individual aggression hold the key to mass social aggression. Similarly it need not be thought that unconscious and social demands necessarily combine to form a unity, which might be called an "identity". There is no reason why the two elements, the personal and the social, cannot be distinguished in theory. Deeply felt loves and hates need not be reflected in socially acceptable attitudes—and as a result a distinction between the two levels of experience can be drawn. Such a distinction can be illustrated by quoting the novelist Christopher Isherwood. In his autobiographical novel, *Down There on a Visit,* Isherwood describes his life in Greece prior to the Second World War. He tells how a conversation with another Englishman brought back all the deep and hostile feelings he felt towards his homeland. He had forgotten that such feelings existed within himself:

> That's because I've been living outside England myself, and in the presence of public enemies, the Nazis, against whom you feel a different sort of hostility—public and proper and respectable.
>
> The other sort of hostility—which isn't respectable or proper, but which sometimes goes much deeper—you can perhaps only feel for your own class and kind. (Isherwood, 1968, p. 95.)

Later in the book, Isherwood again makes this point. This time he is back in England, after the outbreak of war. He passes by his old school and compares the hatred he feels for that institution with his hatred for the Nazis:

> If the Nazis got over here, I should be terrified of them, of course; but I could never, at the deepest level of my consciousness, take them quite seriously. Not as seriously as I took my first headmaster. (Isherwood, 1968, p. 144.)

These two quotations from Isherwood's novel illustrate the point that there need not be any simple correlation between individual personal feelings and the "public and proper and respectable" social feelings. In Isherwood's case the public hatreds are not isomorphic with the personal hatreds, and therefore cannot be explained merely in terms of his personal and unconscious feelings. Although, as Isherwood implies, the personal feeling may be the more intensely felt, the public feelings have a wider practical and social significance. What is suggested by the quotations is that the distinction between the personal and the socially normative is a valid one, and that attempts to equate the two oversimplify the phenomenology of the feelings. In the present argument this distinction is made because it has been argued that attempts to reduce social phenomena to matters of individual aggression oversimplify social analysis. The determined attempt by Roheim to reduce the social to the instinctual foundered upon accounting for cultural differences, and he himself admitted that complex modern social phenomena were not amenable to a straightforward instinctual explanation. Other reductionist explanations, expounded with less subtlety than Roheim's have been criticised for providing an inadequate account of large-scale social events and for neglecting specifically social variables.

4

Post-Freudian Group Psychology: Theories of Society and Personality

In the previous chapter the reductionist tradition of social psycho-analysis was discussed. This chapter will consider explicitly non-reductionist attempts to link post-Freudian thought to a social analysis. The reductionist attempts to explain social phenomena ultimately in terms of asocial and individualistic instinctual structures; the non-reductionist social psychoanalyst on the other hand offers explanations in terms of an interaction between individual and either interpersonal or genuinely social variables. It was mentioned in the previous chapter that the reductionists, despite their varying theoretical positions, shared a similar basic premise, concerning the importance of instincts. There is however no such broad unifying link between the non-reductionist social psychoanalysts. Their views embrace contrasting psychoanalytic and social standpoints, and their differing interpretations of psychodynamic processes mirror their different views of society. There are however two main themes, which will underlie the discussion of the nonreductionists' thought. These are the questions whether individual, and interpersonal, psychoanalytic theory can be united with a wider social analysis; and whether personality can be seen as an important determinant of intergroup relations. With respect to the first issue the theories of the radical Freudians and of the ego psychologists will be particularly considered, and the limitations of these approaches for the study of intergroup relations discussed. With respect to the second issue, the standpoint of the interpersonal theorists and the concept of authoritarianism will be examined. Having said this, it must be emphasised that these two broad issues cannot entirely be separated one from another, and in a sense both are variants of the broader problem concerning the relevance of psychoanalytic and personality theory for the analysis of large-scale social processes.

Radical Freudianism: Herbert Marcuse

Whereas the reductionists reviewed in the last chapter attempt to develop the individualistic elements of Freudian theory, the radical Freudians to be discussed in this section explicitly aim to enlarge upon Freud's social theory. The differences between the radical Freudians and the reductionists cut deeper than just their chosen levels of explanation. In the discussion of the reductionists, some of their social and political assumptions were mentioned; for instance, the right-wing nationalist implications of Lorenz's evolutionary analysis and the "middle-of-the-road" liberalism of Storr and Money-Kyrle, (for a clear exposition of some of the political implications of the British psychoanalytic movement, see Winnicott, 1950). In this section left-wing social analyses, based upon Freudian social theory, will be considered. In discussing the left wing of post-Freudian thought, the main emphasis will be on the writings of Herbert Marcuse. This will be done not only because in recent years Marcuse's work has achieved a considerable measure of popularity and/or notoriety, but also because his writings contain a detailed and systematic re-interpretation of Freud's social theory.

Reductionism, by its nature, is hard to present as a radical social critique, because it stresses the unchanging, and thereby unchangeable, instinctual nature of mankind. With respect to intergroup conflict, it lays emphasis upon the primitive and the savage forms of instinctive drives, and implies that man is constitutionally an aggressive war-mongerer. The remedy advocated by the dogmatic reductionists to combat this instinctive brutality is the patient education of the masses by an enlightened and scientifically trained elite—only in this way can the first steps be taken to gain mastery of the aggressive instincts that continually threaten harmonious social life. The dogmatic reductionist's philosophy does not allow for an explicitly political critique, in which certain socio-economic forms are seen as the determinants of social conflict, and which postulates that changes in these forms may produce substantial improvements in social relations. With the dogmatic reductionist, all has to be traced back to the savage nature of man, (with the exception, perhaps, of the underlying pre-suppositions of the reductionist himself, who seems to allow his own views to transcend the impulsive irrationality of the mass).

Radical Freudianism, on the other hand, does not accept the premise that human nature is essentially and immutably savage. In the works of Wilhelm Reich, Norman O. Brown and Herbert Marcuse, the present sorry state of humanity is contrasted with the utopian po-tentialities which are contained in human nature. These potentialities are unfulfilled under existing social conditions; and therefore the possibilities contained in man's nature provide the basis for a radical critique of the present societal organisation. These theorists look for-ward to the overthrow of the present repressive system and the start of a new era, in which man's true and hitherto stunted psychology can be revealed. In this way the analysis of the individual is closely allied to the analysis of the society which moulds the individual. Unlike the dogmatic reductionist, the radical Freudian does not accept the present balance of instinctual forces as being a necessary constant throughout the history of mankind. With respect to the topic of intergroup rela-tions, the radical Freudian denies that the aggressive instincts must seek a social outlet in some form of actual, or substitute, warfare. On the contrary, the radical Freudian argues that the present social struc-ture and its attendant social psychology can be transcended. With revo-lutionary social changes, the seemingly endless pattern of international warfare, interpersonal cruelty and exploitation can be destroyed; and the present nature of intergroup conflict can be transcended to the benefit of mankind.

One of the features of the radical Freudianism of Marcuse and Brown is its vigorous anti-empiricism; although it is fair to say that Reich's work, especially his earlier theorising, is very different in this respect. Neither Marcuse nor Brown are practising psychoanalysts, and both are explicitly critical of the scientific methodology in itself. Brown, (1968) refers to the basis of science as being anal sadism, and calls for a new "nonmorbid" scientific spirit (p. 210). Similarly Mar-cuse, especially in *One-Dimensional Man* (1968), adopts an attitude of anti-scientism. He equates scientific progress with the spread of a "technological reality", which suppresses critical thought. The result-ing science, according to Marcuse, is by its nature conservative and re-pressive. It only demonstrates what *is* the case, and not what *can* be the case. As such it denies the unfulfilled possibilities of human nature.

The realm of possibility can only be discovered by intuitive reason, and not by empirical observation. Marcuse's anti-empiricism, and its ideological presuppositions, need to be born in mind when considering his re-interpretations of Freudian social theory.

Marcuse can be seen as attempting to provide a psychological basis to Marxist analysis and social theory. Marx, especially in his early writings, had argued that the capitalist system of economic production had blunted human potentialities and had alienated the worker from his true self. Marx's writings on alienation, and the necessity of a proletarian revolution for its transcendence, are most fully expounded in the *Economic and Philosophic Manuscripts of 1844*—yet it would be true to say that his descriptions of alienation do not rest upon any systematically formulated psychological theory. Marcuse's intentions, then, basically are two-fold: first to relate Marxist theory to the situation of the mid-twentieth century; and secondly to supply explicitly psychological concepts to detail Marx's concept of alienation and thereby state the psychological preconditions for its transcendence. He claims to have found the psychological basis for Marxist social thought in Freud's later metapsychological writings.

It is at first glance curious that an avowed anti-empiricist, such as Marcuse, should attempt to demonstrate the theoretical harmony of two such champions of the scientific spirit as Marx and Freud. For Marx, socialism was a utopian pipe-dream if it could not be "scientific socialism"; Freud, as was argued in chapter two, saw psychoanalysis as occupying a central position in the human sciences. It will be suggested that there is a definite tension in Marcuse's writings between his own anti-scientism and his borrowed "scientific" notions. For the present, one can note that he specifically and deliberately concentrates on Freud's "most speculative and 'metaphysical' concepts not subject to any clinical verification" (1969, p. 172). It is from such concepts, largely ignored by the empirically-minded followers of Freud, that Marcuse derives his radical social psychology.

Like Freud before him, Marcuse claims that there is an essential unity between individual psychoanalytic theory and the wider speculations that can be derived from it. He asserts that "Freud's individual psychology is in its very essence social psychology" (1969, p. 31), thereby echoing Freud's own claims in the opening pages of *Group Psychology and the Analysis of the Ego*, (1921, vol. 18). Marcuse also accepts Freud's view that the psychology of the individual closely mirrors the psychology of the species, and consequently he is committed to a theory that parallels ontogenetic development with phylogenetic development. Whereas Freud considered the phylogenetic development had been halted with the creation of the socially repressive superego, Marcuse, like Marx, envisages a future development which will herald genuine freedom.

The exact details of Marcuse's Freudianism need not be discussed here. However, it will be necessary to outline some of the basic arguments contained in *Eros and Civilisation* (1969), the book in which the Freudian critique is most extensively developed, and also those of *One-Dimensional Man* (1969) in which Marcuse applies the critique to contemporary Western society. It is only through considering the general directions of Marcuse's ideas that some of the difficulties and presuppositions involved in his account of revolution and group conflict can be brought to light. No overall assessment of Marcuse will be attempted; rather, the intention is to examine the extent to which his non-empirical brand of Freudianism can constitute an adequate basis for the social psychological study of intergroup relations. This will, of necessity, entail a rather arbitrary selection from the many themes and ideas to be found in the works of Marcuse, and also a considerable simplification of much of his sophisticated argumentation.

The basic concepts in Marcuse's Freudianism are the two instincts, which Freud considered as underlying the activity of all organisms: Eros and Thanatos—the Life instinct and the Death instinct. From the former is derived sexuality and from the latter comes aggression. In *Beyond the Pleasure Principle*, Freud used these concepts to denote more than the sexual or aggressive instincts to be found in the id. He argued that these desires are merely forms of the two basic instincts, life and death, which are present in all living matter. Marcuse adopts these notions of Eros and Thanatos, and he was following Freud in giving them a wider interpretation than could be derived from the clinical setting. It is Marcuse's aim to give an account of the development of human society in terms of these two basic instincts. This is the core of what he calls "the dialectic of civilisation".

First, Marcuse aims to bring out the hidden sociological presuppositions in Freud's theory of the instinctual basis of civilisation. Freud had written that civilisation was based upon the suppression and sublimation of instinctual forces, and he traced this denial of the instincts back to the myth of the primal horde. Marcuse specifically denies that the Freudian account is an ahistorical description of unchanging psychological structures. He states that the Freudian description of civilisation rests upon one important assumption: the existence of scarcity. The primal myth assumes the existence of economic scarcity —the primal father would never have been able to impose his will upon the rest of the horde, had this not been an effective way of combatting economic necessity. Similarly the instinctual renunciation, which has enabled the progressive development of civilisation, can be seen as occuring against a background of scarcity. In this way, Marcuse argues that Freud's account of the phylogenetic development of mankind rests on the nonpsychological assumption that economic conditions of scarcity exist; and thus Freud's account is at one and the same time both psychological and sociological.

In order to elucidate this hidden sociological dimension, Marcuse introduces two further concepts: "surplus-repression" and "the performance principle". Surplus-repression is clearly intended to be the psychological equivalent of Marx's concept of surplus-value and denotes the unnecessary repression that society demands of its members. According to Freudian theory, every society requires a certain minimal amount of instinctual repression, in order for there to be communal living. However, Marcuse argues that the development of civilisation has seen the development of unnecessary instinctual restrictions on the individual. The performance principle is the current ideology or version of the reality principle which ensures the continuing accretion of surplus-repression. Basically the performance principle is the ideology of self-denial and of the work ethic; the performance principle discourages immediate instinctual gratification and seeks to justify the sublimation of the basic human instincts. It is important to note that Marcuse links the concept of surplus-repression to that of domination. Surplus-repression which Marcuse defines as "the restrictions necessitated by social domination" (1969, p. 42), has not arisen haphazardly in the course of the history of civilisation. By domination, he is referring to intergroup or interindividual inequalities of power: "domination is exercised by a particular group or individual in order to sustain and enhance itself in a privileged position" (1969, p. 43). In the primal horde the interests of domination clearly refer to the individual domination by the father over his sons and womenfolk. However with the growth of civilisation, domination has shifted from the powerful individual to the powerful group. It can be seen that one of Marcuse's key concepts, that of surplus-repression, refers at one and the same time to individual instinctual repression and also to its cause, which in the case of developed societies is unequal intergroup power distribution.

With the failure of the first revolution by the primal brothers against their tyrannical father, there is a continuing and ever-increasing sublimation of Eros and of the aggression instincts. The sublimation of Eros contributes to the growth and strengthening of ingroup ties. Aggression is sublimated against those who do not belong to the ingroup. This psychological process of sublimation has, according to Marcuse, reached its zenith in the modern industrial state. He coins the phrase "the welfare state is the warfare state" to describe the contemporary situation. The material welfare of the individual members of the modern state is by and large looked after; but this ingroup security is only possible if there can be an outgroup Enemy, on which aggressive impulses can be vented. Thus, according to Marcuse, the communist state needs its capitalist enemy, and the capitalist state needs the communist as an enemy. As a consequence, the welfare state is in a perpetual readiness for warfare, (cf. chapter two of *One-Dimensional Man*, for a detailed discussion of this issue). Such continual outgroup hostility is, in Marcuse's opinion, incomprehensible, if the instinctual structure of modern society is neglected. It is the product of "accumulated aggressiveness" which must "be turned against those who did not belong to the whole" (1969, p. 81). This instinctual balance between Eros and aggression require a complete social mobilisation:

> The difference between war and peace, between civilian and military populations, between truth and propaganda, is blotted out. There is regression to historical stages that have been passed long ago, and this regression reactivates the sado-masochistic phase on a new and international scale. But the impulses of this phase are reactivated in a new, "civilised" manner: practically without sublimation, they become socially "useful" activities in concentration and labour camps, colonial and civil wars, in punitive expeditions, and so on. (Marcuse, 1969, p. 81.)

In this passage can be seen the two integral features of Marcuse's method of explaining social phenomena. In the first place complex social and political actualities are explained in terms of the underlying instinctual dialectic of civilisation. Secondly, it should be noted that this explanation is essentially an historical one; instinctual impulses are "reactivated" and the present stage of development is seen as a novel combination of older features. Marcuse is not just referring to an ontogenetic reactivation—his account is also phylogenetic. Just as Marx had interpreted the capitalist economy in terms of its historical development, so too does Marcuse interpret present-day patterns of dominance in terms of their historical and instinctual development. He takes seriously the Freudian notions of the "archaic heritage" and the "return of the repressed", especially in a social context. The important happenings in the history of the dialectic of civilisation return to affect later events; these can only be understood in terms of their historic precedents. The most important of all events in the history of man was, of course, the rebellion of the primal brothers against their father and the unsuccessful outcome of this rebellion. Marcuse uses the myth to explain later events, such as the persecution of non-conformists (1969, pp. 63–5) and the lack of success of all later revolutionary exploits (1969, pp. 74–5). He states that the persecution of non-conformists throughout history needs an instinctual explanation—the "sadistic extermination of the weak suggests that unconscious instinctual forces broke through all rationality and rationalisation" (1969, p. 64). In this way wars waged against heretics in the name of the Christian church must be understood as an overreaction against the return of "the spectre of liberation". This spectre, which continues to haunt mankind, is the image of unrepressed freedom—it is the image shared by the primal brothers as they attempted their revolution, and at later times it returns in the persona of rebels and nonconformists to trouble the powers that be. These powers overreact in order to prevent the actual return of the repressed, and in so doing they deny their own possibilities for freedom. Certain wars, and here Marcuse mentions the campaigns against the Cathari, Albigensians and Anabaptists, are in fact battles against the repressed image of true liberation which returns to haunt societies built upon unnecessary surplus-repression.

In a similar vein, Marcuse interprets the course of subsequent revolutionary acts in terms of the primal myth. He argues that there must be a psychological explanation for the ease with which revolutionary demands for an end to all domination are defeated. Such an explanation is offered by considering the guilt of the primal brothers in the crime they committed against their father. This guilt reappears in later revolutionary struggles and explains why, in every revolutionary conflict, no advantage is taken of the "historical moment when the struggle against domination might have been victorious" (1969, p. 75). This is because the revolutionary forces themselves feel guilt at the possible destruction of the basis of surplus-repression. In revolutions there is accordingly an "element of *self-defeat*" (1969, p. 75, italics in original); and the "successful" revolutions end by instituting new and more repressive orders of domination. The archaic feelings of guilt return to prevent the abolition of surplus repression and of the pernicious performance principle which supports it.

Therefore Marcuse interprets revolutionary conflict, as well as certain other forms of intergroup conflict, in terms of his instinctual dialectic of civilisation. So far only the barest outlines of his views have been presented. Both his account of the persecution of nonconformists and his explanation of the psychological basis of revolutionary failure will be discussed below. For the present, this sketch of Marcuse's dialectic of civilisation can be continued. His dialectic leads him to a savage criticism of the quality of modern industrial life—this criticism is most forcefully expressed in *One-Dimensional Man*, but also permeates *Eros and Civilisation* and *An Essay on Liberation* (1972). However, he argues that the instinctual repression, which is demanded by the modern industrial state, contains an inherent contradiction. Because of this contradiction, Marcuse allows that the possibility of freedom can be raised and the modern industrial state contains the seeds of its own destruction as well as the means by which man can find his true nature. In this sense Marcuse's dialectic is forward looking, and offers the very real possibility of rational political activity against the forces that perpetuate the system of domination, (see, for instance, the "Political preface" to *Eros and Civilisation* written over ten years after the main text).

The contradiction of the modern industrial state is a simple one. Just as the demands for instinctual repression are increasing to an unprecedented and intolerable level, so has civilisation succeeded in abolishing the preconditions and necessity for instinctual repression. The original act of repression was a function of scarcity or necessity—economic survival dictated that each individual could not pursue his own asocial instinctual inclinations. Now for the first time in history, economic scarcity is no longer the objective situation in which society must develop. Technological progress, argues Marcuse, has conquered scarcity and permits the possibility of abundance. This means that the trend of ever-increasing surplus-repression can be reversed. Man no longer has to renounce his natural instincts and devote himself to a life-time of toil. Surplus-repression and the performance principle serve only the interests of domination—the true instinctual interests of mankind lie in a liberation from psychological and social repression. In this way technology can be said to provide the precondition for a new revolutionary life-principle, based upon the celebration, rather than the repression, of Eros. As a consequence Marcuse looks forward to a new society, in which Eros will be supreme. The human body will be resexualised, and Thanatos will serve the interests of Eros. Man will cease to be alienated from his instinctual structure, and the forces of the id will be free to seek their natural goals. Eros will be un-trammelled and Thanatos will not be deflected into aggression against man or nature. Instead Thanatos will serve its true function of ensuring that the organism returns to its former inorganic state, at its appointed time of death.

In short, Marcuse envisages a future social order, in which the present social psychological relations within and between groups will be transcended. The present state of the dialectic of civilisation is by no means permanent: the self-defeating revolutions, the persecutions of non-conforming groups, the increasing aggressivity of the welfare state are not immutable facts. If the underlying instinctual and sociological factors are altered, then the interests of domination can be broken once and for all. Man can then transcend his present state of alienation, and the liberation of sexuality is the key to this transcendence. In stressing the significance of repressed sexuality for the maintenance of repressive social orders, Marcuse is in agreement with many of the arguments of Reich, although he bases his views more on the wider social theories of Freud than does Reich—in particular Marcuse gives a wider interpretation than Reich to the concept of sexuality. In this, his theories contain many similarities with those of Brown. Like Marcuse, Brown, recognises the importance of scarcity in the Freudian primal myth of the foundations of civilisation, and similarly he draws conclusions from this about subsequent repression. Brown, too, believes that technology may enable a radical instinctual reconstruction, which will free man from the tyranny of repression. In contrast to Marcuse, Brown (1968) anticipates an instinctual refusion between Eros and Thanatos, rather than the triumph of Eros over Thanatos. Further comparisons between these two thinkers will not be pursued here (see, for instance, Robinson's, 1972, comparison between Marcuse and Brown); since Marcuse's work embodies the more systematic political and social critique, the emphasis will still be placed upon his theories.

It must be stated that Marcuse's dialectic of civilisation contains a number of attractive features. Quite apart from its merits as a powerful piece of Freudian scholarship, it also offers the possibility of a nonreductionist social psychology based upon Freud's psychoanalytic theories. More than this, the importance placed on the distinction between necessary and surplus repression enables Marcuse to engage in a radical critique of social forms. The insistence on certain "objective" nonpsychological concepts means that psychological states of mind can be evaluated by some outside criterion. As a result in Marcuse's hands, as in Marx's hands, the concept of alienation is essentially a critical concept, which relates psychology to social structure; it does not merely describe, in a relativistic manner, the states of mind of those "suffering from the disease of alienation". However, having admitted this, it is nevertheless necessary to look at Marcuse's Freudianism more closely, in order to reveal some of its less satisfactory features.

First, it is necessary to examine Marcuse's use of the concepts of Eros and Thanatos. These quite clearly constitute the major theoretical building-blocks with which he constructs his dialectic of civilisation. They are also his main explanatory tools for examining patterns of intergroup relations. As a consequence one would wish to enquire exactly what these concepts refer to. At times they appear to represent certain metaphysical principles derived from abstract philosophy, and at other times they seem to refer to specific psychological drives. The history of Eros and Thanatos appear also to contain the history of the human race—significant historical changes are marked by significant changes in the relations between these two instincts. Yet on the other hand, Eros and Thanatos underwrite the ontogenetic development of each individual and seem to do so in the ways described by classic psychoanalytic theory. As a consequence the same questions must be raised about Marcuse's analysis, that were raised about Freud's social theory, concerning the relationship between ontogenetic theory and phylogenetic theory. These questions relate to the extent to which individual and large-scale processes can be assumed to be similar—ultimately these questions refer to the relationship between individual and social psychology.

With respect to intergroup relations, this problem refers primarily to the correlation between individual aggressiveness and large-scale social aggression. If the same concept is used to explain both phenomena, then their relationship must be demonstrated—it should not be assumed *a priori*. In the case of Marcuse's use of the concepts of Eros and Thanatos, the suspicion is that he ranges from the abstract and metaphysical to the particular and scientific; because of this wide range it becomes correspondingly difficult to ascertain exactly what he means by Eros and Thanatos. Even if the same criticism can be raised against Freud's use of the terms in his later metapsychological writings, this still does not absolve Marcuse from the necessity of elucidating his own use of the terms. This is especially so since he often departs substantially from the psychology of Freud, as will be argued below.

Two brief examples can be given to illustrate Marcuse's vague usage of the terms "Eros" and "Thanatos". He seems to accept Freud's hydraulic model of instinctual energy, and its premise that there is a fixed quantum of energy which seeks release. Applying this hydraulic model to the conflict between Eros and Thanatos, one is left with the simple equation, that the more energy, which is pressed into the service of Eros, the less there will be at the disposal of Thanatos, and vice versa. Society, therefore, forbids the free-play of the sexual instincts, which are sublimated to forming cohesive ingroup ties; but this repressed Eros can also be pressed into the service of Thanatos and produce outgroup aggression. However, having assumed the fixed-quantity energy model, Marcuse is faced by an awkward paradox. In the modern world there is an unparallelled amount of aggression—this is demonstrated by the savage wars that man wages against man, and also in man's unprecedented destruction of nature. The amount of instinctual aggression released by the modern state would seem to be inordinately high; however this would seem to conflict, theoretically at least, with the increasing sexual permissiveness which is evident particularly in the Western world. According to the fixed-energy model one should not expect to find an increase in aggressive behaviour at the same time as an increase in sexual behaviour. The instinctual energy that Eros requires for sexual expression should be competing with the energy that Thanatos uses for producing acts of aggression. Marcuse, however, does not take this as a disconfirming case of his dialectic of civilisation, and the way he accounts for this apparent contradiction throws light on his use of the concepts of Eros and Thanatos.

In *One-Dimensional Man* (1968, pp. 73f), Marcuse deals with this problem by introducing the notion of "controlled desublimation". He states that controlled desublimation presents an exception to the Freudian fixed-quantum model of energy. The sexuality allowed by the modern state is, according to Marcuse, not a free-sexuality, but is narrowly localised. It is essentially genital sex, and as such is the antithesis of the free sexuality, which sexualises the whole body. This localised sexuality does not allow a proper release of sexual energy but is "tantamount to an actual compression of erotic energy and this desublimation would be compatible with the growth of unsublimated as well as sublimated forms of aggressiveness" (Marcuse, 1968, p. 73). In other words, the "controlled genital sexuality", which is characteristic of present-day industrial society, in no way affects the accumulation of aggressive instincts within the modern world. Marcuse offers no detailed proof that modern sexuality is essentially genital, nor does he offer any justification for the exception which genital sexuality presents to the fixed-quantum model. He merely asserts that localised sexuality has no effect upon the aggressive instincts, and psychoanalytic evidence is regarded as unnecessary. By introducing a new concept such as "controlled desublimation", defined in terms of localised sexuality, the apparent contradictions in Marcuse's theory are resolved.

In this way Marcuse is able to "preserve" his analysis of the instinctual basis of modern civilisation. However, the move is too neat and without further explication it must remain superficial. In effect he is saying that civilisation is built upon a balance between the forces of Eros and the forces of Thanatos, but that the amount of sexual behaviour demonstrated in the modern industrialised society is irrelevant to this balance. The instinctual basis would remain the same, whether there was strict Puritanism or rampant genital licentiousness. It would seem hard to demonstrate the substance of this basis if it can produce such widely differing outward manifestations; the suspicion is that the concepts of Eros and Thanatos must become less meaningful, if their manifestations have little demonstrable substantiality. Real theoretical and empirical difficulties cannot be resolved merely by the introduction of a new abstract category which is given no factual basis (for a more detailed discussion of Marcuse's treatment of "localised sexuality", see Sedgwick, 1966).

A second example can be given of Marcuse's unrigorous use of the concepts of Eros and Thanatos. He argues that in the liberated society of the future, Eros will be freed through the auspices of technology. However, Marcuse does not mean by the liberation of Eros that everyone will spend all their time and energy engaging in sexual intercourse. His criticisms of genital sex have already been mentioned, and the free play of Eros will, in his opinion, lead to the resexualisation of the whole body. Since economic abundance, produced by technology, is a precondition for any such liberation, it follows that technological work would still be necessary in the state of freedom in order to maintain the necessary abundance. There would seem to be, as a consequence, a contradiction between the necessity of work and the demands of an unrestricted Eros. However, as before, Marcuse resolves the contradiction by introducing into his analysis a new concept—in this case, that of "non-repressive sublimation". He argues that Eros will freely sublimate itself into the necessary work. He bases this belief on the assumption that the life instinct has in itself a natural and spontaneous tendency for self-sublimation; he cites in support of this a remark by Freud that erotic desires subside as they become attainable. From this, Marcuse derives the principle that Eros does not really strive for sexual union, but seeks to sexualise all things. These would include, of course, work conditions—freed from the tyranny of the Performance Principle, Eros would "create an instinctual basis for the transformation of work into play" (Marcuse, 1969, p. 152).

Again the suspicion is that Marcuse has resolved a potential contradiction in an elegant, but unsubstantial, manner. The concept of "non-repressive sublimation" is essentially a theoretical concept, which rests upon an important assumption about the nature of the sexual instinct. Marcuse does not document this assumption, except by quoting the remark of Freud's, which itself is open to a number of different interpretations. Independently of the fact that he does not provide any empirical justifications for this assumption, his theoretical analysis can still be considered incomplete. If Eros has a tendency to self-sublimation, then it might be thought that Thanatos likewise had such a tendency. If Thanatos were to be self-sublimating, then the future state of liberation would be characterised not only by sublimated sexuality but also by the sublimation of the death instincts— such a sublimation would lead to the acts of aggression that are typical of the non-liberated society. As a result, Marcuse must assume that Eros, and only Eros, has this property of self-sublimation.

It is all very well making these distinctions and assumptions in theory but the force of the argument is lost if they cannot relate to the every-day world. If all is to be explained at the drop of a new category, then one must wonder what is the nature of such an "explanation". It would seem that Marcuse's anti-empiricism is enabling him to fight paper battles, and introduce what seem at first sight to be psychological assumptions, without using psychological evidence to support his case. Certainly the tactic of introducing a new theoretical concept in order to resolve potential contradictions is out of spirit with his two intellectual forbears, Freud and Marx. Freud's theories had a firm basis in psychoanalytic practice and experimentation, and within his own methodology he was by and large rigorous. Similarly Marx's scientific socialism was based upon detailed socio-historical study, rather than on broad unsupportable generalisation. He especially criticised the theoretical and non-empirical approaches of the Young Hegelians, who were prone to an abstract analysis of man and his history. Thus in *The Holy Family*, Marx criticises those who are capable of "inventing *new categories*, and . . . of re-transforming *man* into a category and indeed into the principle of a whole series of categories" (Marx, 1963 ed., p. 78, italics in original). In the absence of any detailed discussions of the differences between repressive and non-repressive sublimation, between desublimation and controlled desublimation, it would seem that Marcuse is an example of one who transforms mankind by the invention of a new category.

Marcuse might counter these criticisms by arguing that a concept like "unrepressed sublimation" refers to future psychological developments, and so cannot be adequately described by the psychology of the present repressive society. It is, however, possible to make more detailed criticisms of the way in which Marcuse uses Freudian concepts to describe present and past states of affairs. Here the main emphasis will be on those aspects of his writings that relate most directly to the social psychology of intergroup relations. There has already been occasion to mention and quote passages from *Eros and Civilisation*, in which Marcuse discusses the aggressiveness of modern society in terms of a regression to a sado-masochistic stage. Again he offers no direct evidence to support such an assertion. There are no detailed psychoanalytic case histories to reveal how the present social structure releases in individuals sado-masochistic urges, and whether this release occurs along socially predetermined lines. The details of the dialectic are left to the imagination: one is given the broad general statement that the aggressive instincts *must* lie at the root of human social aggressiveness, otherwise wars could not possibly occur on such a large-scale. For instance, Marcuse comments:

> Beneath the manifold rational and rationalised motives for war against national and group enemies, for the destructive conquest of time, space and man, the deadly partner of Eros becomes manifest in the persistent approval and participation of the victims. (Marcuse, 1969, p. 51.)

Similar sorts of assertion can be found in the works of the dogmatic reductionists—namely, that the pattern of history seems to suggest that there must be underlying irrational instincts guiding human behaviour. Freud, too, felt that the enormities of the First World War confirmed the existence of an aggressive instinct; but Freud realised that this was only an intuitive feeling which was in need of considerable theoretical refinement and detailed empirical validation. Similarly, Marcuse's broad assertion would need to be backed up by a detailed study of the psychology of both the perpetrators and the victims of mass social aggression. It is not enough to explain the occurrence of warfare by postulating an aggressive instinct, and then to claim that the occurrence of warfare itself is proof enough for the existence of an aggressive instinct.

In the light of these comments, Marcuse's account of two particular forms of intergroup conflict can be considered—these two forms are the persecution of non-conformists and the self-defeat of revolutions, which have already been mentioned. Both forms of conflict are produced by the spectre of liberation. Characteristically, Marcuse offers no evidence to link religious or other persecutions with the return of the repressed image of liberation. More than this, he changes the formula, without specific exemplification, when dealing with the modern technological society. Today he argues the "Great Refusal" is impossible, because non-conformism is "absorbed into the prevailing state of affairs" (Marcuse, 1968, p. 63). The rebel is forced to become part of the prevailing repressive social order. Under such circumstances the spectre of liberation is transformed into a constantly appearing "national enemy"—for the communist this enemy is the capitalist, and likewise the capitalist views the communist as his enemy. There is an underlying psychological significance to this, for, writes Marcuse, "the Enemy is not identical with actual communism or actual capitalism—he is in both cases, the real spectre of liberation" (1968, p. 55).

It would appear that "the spectre of liberation" can underwrite any "irrational" manifestation of aggressiveness. Whereas formerly it explained persecution of heretics, today it explains conflicts between communism and capitalism; or more accurately it might be said to have explained the cold-war situation of ten years ago. Since Marcuse wrote *One Dimensional Man* East-West relations have improved considerably and might no longer be thought to conceal the spectre of liberation. It might be argued that the spectre has now shifted onto the guerrilla and terrorist movements, whose actions constitute a more publicised threat to existing governments. But in stating this the concept of "the spectre of liberation" becomes equivalent with any outgroup which threatens the *status quo*. Thus the spectre adopts many guises on its frequent returns. It would seem, as a consequence, far too simplistic to state that all negative feelings toward outgroups, (except those held by a few unspecified revolutionary groups), are manifestations of a desire to keep the spectre of liberation repressed. This would appear to be an *a priori* formula, rather than an attempt to understand different forms of social conflict in all their complexity.

Unsuccessful revolutionary activity is the second form of intergroup conflict which Marcuse explains in terms of his social psychoanalytic dialectic. Marcuse argues that all revolutions have been unsuccessful until the present day because none has accomplished the abolition of domination and alienation; at best they have only achieved the limited success of replacing one system of domination by another. It will be remembered that Marcuse believes that in every revolution there is an historic moment, in which domination *per se* could be abolished, but that guilt feelings prevent the revolutionary group from taking advantage of this moment. Once again these notions are presented *ex cathedra*, without any supporting facts. One would particularly like to know whether in fact it is the case that every revolution possesses such an historic moment, and more particularly when precisely this moment occurs. For instance, one would wish to know whether the participants of the revolutionary group are aware of this historic moment, and whether it generally occurs during the heat of the revolutionary struggles, or after the defeat of the counter-revolutionary forces or at the start of the task of reconstruction. One might also ask how long this historic moment lasts, etc.

Marcuse does not offer answers to these questions. In the passage where he discusses the "self-defeat" of revolutions, he is probably making an oblique reference to the Russian revolution—but he declines details and does not mention when this moment could have occurred. It surely could not have been before the Bolsheviks had taken command of the country; similarly it seems unlikely that it could be identified in the first moment of Bolshevik rule, given that the first Bolshevik government was an *ad hoc* affair, still fighting to maintain its control (Rigby, 1973). Nor does it seem possible during the War of Intervention and the campaigns against the counter-revolutionary White armies. Marcuse's own analysis of the development of communist rule in the USSR, *Soviet Marxism* (1971), does not discuss when this historic moment may have occurred. It would seem, therefore, that the notion of an historic moment in all revolutionary struggle, which could see the end of all domination, is a fanciful or metaphorical one—it does not seem to relate to the heat and practicalities of actual historical revolutionary struggles. Most importantly, it does not seem to take into account the very real dangers of counter-revolutionary attack, which must face any new "system of domination". In this respect, one would particularly wish to know how this historic moment relates not only to the actions of the revolutionary group, but also how it relates to those of the counter-revolutionary groups; especially since a revolutionary situation is essentially an intergroup situation, involving at least two sides. A social psychological analysis of such situations should be alive to its intergroup nature and not concentrate exclusively on one side or the other.

Marcuse states that the hypothesis of revolutionary guilt "elucidates" the failure of revolutionary movements to abolish domination (1969, p. 75). However, he does not say exactly what he means by the term "elucidate". It would seem to be less strong than the word "explain", which would imply that the psychological variable of guilt is the independent cause of such failure. Perhaps Marcuse is suggesting that guilt is merely a contributing factor, albeit an important one. However, there is a vagueness about his formulation—he does not specify the nature of this guilt, except to suggest that it stems from an "'identification' of those who revolt with the power against which they revolt" (1969, p. 75). The generality of this guilt would seem to suggest that it is more than an individual reaction which occurs coincidentally in the psyche of every revolutionary. Rather it would appear to be some sort of generic response, in which the repressed returns only to be repressed again. If it is such a response, and Marcuse's allusions to the primal legend support this interpretation, then there are certain important theoretical implications arising out of this conception.

A generic response would imply that the primal guilt feelings return at later stages; as such it is a notion culled from Freud's phylogenetic social psychology. Similarly, when a concept such as "the return of the repressed" is given an historical interpretation, a phylogenetic account is being assumed. In the same way, when Marcuse talks of the present age reactivating past stages of sado-masochistic aggression, he seems to be saying more than that individuals regress to their own childhood stages of development. He would appear to be saying something about the past history of mankind, and assuming that past events can return to haunt the psyche of modern man. Not only does the individual's childhood affect his later behaviour, but also the childhood of civilisation determines the present state of social behaviour. As was discussed in chapter two, Freud made the connection between ontogenetic and phylogenetic development by introducing the controversial concept of the "archaic heritage". This heritage contains the memories of the species and is transmitted genetically, and as a result forms part of each individual's psychological make-up. It is through this archaic heritage that the psychological past can repeat itself, and the primal legend can continue to exert its influence on modern man.

Marcuse follows Freud in recognising the importance of the concept of the archaic heritage for uniting individual and social psychology within a psychoanalytic framework. He states that the archaic heritage binds individual psychology to the historic context; he argues that it "reveals the power of the universal in and over the individuals" and ensures that "the mature ego of the civilised personality still preserves the archaic heritage of man" (1969, p. 56). Thus in Marcuse's account the notion of the archaic heritage plays a crucial role in binding together individual psychology and the psychology of the species. In this way the dialectic of civilisation depends upon a notion which will connect the phylogenetic with the ontogenetic. Without such a notion there is no way of emphasising the *psychological* dependence of modern man upon the history of instinctual renunciation. The elucidation of modern man's predicament with respect to the dialectical history of human instincts is the basis of Marcuse's arguments—their force is substantially reduced if present psychological alienation cannot be related to social psychological history of alienation.

In the discussion of Freud's social theory, some of the difficulties associated with the notion of an archaic heritage were mentioned. It was stated that Freud himself was aware of these difficulties, especially as the concept contradicts biological theory. Marcuse, likewise, is alive to the difficulties inherent in the concept. However, he seems more concerned with the lack of anthropological evidence to support the myth of the primal legend which forms the backbone of the archaic heritage. He notes that the hypothesis of the archaic heritage "is not corroborated by any anthropological evidence" (1969, p. 57); but significantly he does not mention that the hypothesis actually flies in the face of biological evidence. One might wonder whether this is an accidental oversight on the part of Marcuse; or whether, on the other hand, it is a deliberate omission. A deliberate omission would be perfectly comprehensible in the light of his anti-scientism. If science is a repressive tool, then it might be argued that revolutionary ideas should not be answerable to scientific (and therefore repressive) validation. One might speculate whether Marcuse might adopt the stance of Freud, who stated that if biological evidence contradicted the notion of primal inheritance, then so much the worse for biological science. In the case of Freud this attitude was criticised as being an aberration from his usual rigorously empirical approach. In the case of Marcuse, the criticism must be more basic. If Marcuse warns against the tyranny of the scientific spirit, then it is just as possible to warn against the tyranny of anti-scientific dogma which creates and rejects its own facts on the basis of pure speculation. Marcuse, especially in *One Dimensional Man*, draws attention to the totalitarian implications of blind empiricism—however, it is possible to see even more clearly totalitarian implications in an approach which allows the theorist to describe and categorise the world with complete disregard for factual matters.

If Marcuse is willing to accept that the primal legend has no anthropological corroboration, nevertheless he does not consider that this nullifies its theoretical significance. He claims that above all the primal legend has value as a symbol:

We use Freud's anthropological speculation only in this sense: for its symbolic value. The archaic events that the hypothesis stipulates may forever be beyond the realm of anthropological verification; the alleged consequences of these events are historical facts, and their interpretation in the light of Freud's hypothesis lends them a neglected significance which points to the historical future. (Marcuse, 1969, pp. 57–8.)

This interpretation is in itself a departure from Freud who viewed the primal legend as historical fact. Marcuse's admission that the primal legend is essentially symbolic is revealing and it throws into doubt the exact status of his social psychology. If the primal legend is a symbol, then presumably it can be argued that his entire use of the Freudian phylogenetic theory is also symbolic. In this case one need not worry about biological difficulties regarding the concept of the archaic heritage, since it denotes a metaphorical rather than a scientific truth. Following this line of reasoning, the union between individual and social psychology must likewise be essentially symbolic, and what is more, the whole dialectic of civilisation, which Marcuse constructs from psychoanalytic premises, then becomes a symbol. If this is so, then Marcuse's disdain for supporting his generalisations and theoretical distinctions with factual evidence becomes entirely reasonable, as does his somewhat loose use of Freudian terminology. His psychoanalytic interpretations of history and of present society are thus essentially metaphorical. The spectre of liberation which returns and has to be repressed anew during intergroup conflicts is an allegory to elucidate our present plight. Its truth, then, does not depend on a present state of mind reflecting a past actuality—which could be proved or disproved by a combination of psychoanalytic and anthropological enquiry. Rather its function is to emphasise present atrocities and hold up the image of a better future. But one might nurture the doubt that, if Marcuse's vision of the past is symbolic, then so might his vision of the future be likewise a symbol of the imagination. If a utopian society is to be constructed, and the present system of domination is to be defeated, then these will surely be accomplished on a basis which is more substantial than a metaphor.

This is not the place to probe more deeply into the political implications of Marcuse's Freudianism and its place with respect to Marxist thought. It has been the present intention to pursue a much more limited enquiry into the limitations of his anti-scientific methodology, particularly as it relates to his accounts of the social psychology of intergroup relations. The main argument has been that Marcuse's use of psychoanalytic terms, in the description of his dialectic of civilisation, has been somewhat arbitrary, and does not arise from any empirical investigation of social phenomena. The result is that potential contradictions and theoretical difficulties are resolved in a way that throws doubt on the usefulness of Marcuse's theoretical framework for understanding concrete social phenomena. If the resulting dialectic is intended to be primarily metaphorical, then he is using the central concepts of Eros and Thanatos in a particular, and even eccentric, way. The Freudianism on which Marcuse bases his dialectic, is thus open to theoretical modification and reinterpretation without any form of empirical justification. In this sense the Freudian categories of repression, instinct, sublimation, etc., find themselves in a half-way house between psychoanalytic concepts, amenable to investigation by psychoanalytic enquiry, and symbolic categories, arising from *a priori* theory. As a result, sublimation can be split into "controlled sublimation" and "non-repressive sublimation", without great theoretical difficulty or empirical justification, and psychoanalytic concepts can be invoked in order to elucidate, without detailed argument, complex social phenomena.

If Marcuse's phylogenetic account is to be treated primarily as some sort of symbolism, then one can ask what, in his system, has more than a symbolic value. The dialectic of civilisation, based upon the underlying opposition of Eros and Thanatos, is hard to accept at face value. Stripped of its symbolism, Marcuse's basic thesis might be restated as being an account of the development and continuation of unnecessary social coercion in the course of social evolution. It will be remembered that Marcuse defined "surplus-repression" in terms of the interests of domination. In the course of his dialectic of civilisation, this aspect of surplus-repression becomes comparatively neglected. The ideological efforts of dominating groups and individuals to preserve and augment their positions of power become of secondary importance, as Marcuse seeks universal underlying psychoanalytic principles. The empirical investigation of the interests of domination should be possible, without sacrificing the ideal that domination *per se* can be defeated. In fact it might be argued that an empirical investigation is a necessary condition for producing the tools with which to defeat present interests of domination. Belief in the future transcendence of alienation, therefore, does not entail that present alienation should be metaphorically described and explained. Similarly the transcendence of the present form of intergroup relations does not imply that its present determin-

ants need to be considered in symbolic terms. Such an approach is
especially limiting if transcendence is to occur as the result of some
form of revolutionary (and therefore intergroup) conflict, whose actuality will be far less elegant than a theoretical symbolism. Marcuse
complains that the logic of scientific enquiry limits the potential universe of discourse; this charge can, however, be reversed, and it can
quite feasibly be argued that his own brand of radical anti-scientism
can have its own limitations and restrictions.

Interpersonal theories

In the psychoanalytic theories of intergroup relations considered so
far, the role of the aggressive instincts has been of paramount importance. In Freud's own account, and in both Roheim's and those of the
dogmatic reductionists, organised conflict and warfare were explained
in terms of instinctual aggression. Similarly Marcuse's dialectic of
civilisation is built upon the twin instinctual forces of Eros and Thanatos, and intergroup conflict is seen as the consequence of the repression
of these instincts. The theorists to be considered in this section, however, reject the instinctual basis of Freud's later metapsychology. As
a consequence, they neither attempt to reduce intergroup conflict to
individual instinctual forces, as do the psychoanalytic reductionists;
nor on the other hand do they attempt to construct a social theory out
of the concepts of Freudian instinctual theory. Their psychoanalytic
explanations which are advanced for intergroup phenomena are
pitched neither at the individualistic nor the social, level. Instead they
fall in the intermediate level of interpersonal processes.

Two aspects of the interpersonal theories to be discussed relate to
the study of intergroup relations. On the one hand there is a tendency
for the theorists to deny the relevance of their work to the phenomena
of large-scale groups. On the other hand there is the opposite tendency
to interpret intergroups relations in terms of interpersonal approaches.
At first sight this latter tendency would seem to be a variant of psychoanalytic reductionism, in which the determining variables for large-
scale social phenomena are sought in interpersonal psychology. Thus
macro-social phenomena are reduced to micro-social phenomena. But
this picture is only partially accurate; it fails to cover the whole story.
It will be argued that the reductionism present in the interpersonal
theories is not strictly analogous to the dogmatic psychoanalytic re-

ductionism, which has already been discussed. It constitutes a narrowing of focus, rather than a reductionist approach pure and simple. It will be suggested that to a certain extent the theorists themselves are aware of this narrowing of focus, and hence their reluctance to speculate about large-scale intergroup relations. Nevertheless, there are, over and above the scientific innovations of this narrow perspective, certain ideological presuppositions contained in their formulations.

The two interpersonal psychoanalysts whose work will be considered first are Karen Horney and Harry Stack Sullivan. Both criticise orthodox Freudianism for neglecting cultural factors and both aim to rectify what they consider to be the non-social nature of Freudian instinctual theory. In the first place they reject Freud's insistence on the primacy of basic instincts. For instance, Horney denies the universality of the Oedipus complex (e.g. Horney, 1937, pp. 285 ff.), and rejects the Freudian notion of the death instinct. Of direct relevance here is her assertion that large scale intergroup conflicts should not be seen as the products of instinctual aggression. What is more, she rejects the instinctual argument because she perceives it to be "positively harmful in its implications" (Horney, 1939, p. 132). She states that acceptance of the Death Instinct commits one to a pessimistic view of mankind, in which wars are fatalistically tolerated as being inevitable byproducts of an unchanging human nature. She argues that such ideas lead to a political passivity which must "paralyse any effort to search in the specific culture conditions for reasons which make for destructiveness" (1939, p. 132).

Like Horney, Sullivan rejects the instinctual theories of Freud. He aims to seek the determinants of behaviour in interpersonal relations rather than in basic instinctual structures. He writes that "everything that can be found in the human mind has been put there by interpersonal relations" and he claims that "this statement is intended to be the antithesis of any doctrine of human instincts" (Sullivan, 1950, p. 302). At face value Sullivan's interpersonal theory does seem to be more of a social theory than a theory of individual psychoanalysis. However, it should be remembered that Freud never studied the individual *in vacuo*—he always claimed that the individual's relations with his parents constituted the subject matter of psychoanalysis (e.g. chapter one of *Group Psychology*). Even that most rigid reductionist, Roheim, based his whole ontogenetic theory on the infant's relations with its mother. The concepts of object-choice and object-relations ensure that the individual is not socially isolated in traditional Freudian theorising. Thus the fact that Sullivan's psychiatry concentrates on interpersonal relations does not, of itself, separate it from classical psychoanalysis.

Like the orthodox Freudian, Sullivan does posit certain innate strivings in the individual. However, unlike the Freudian he does not characterise these strivings as being libidinal. Instead he considers that the major determinant of the infant's behaviour is the desire to avoid anxiety. This resembles some of Melanie Klein's ideas, and Sullivan states that the capacity to form interpersonal relationships in adult life is directly affected by infantile anxiety; in particular it is affected by the infant's personification of the threatening Bad Mother. In the same way the child is motivated to learn language to ward off anxiety. Anxiety is seen as the force which underlies interpersonal relations, and can all too often cripple them.

Sullivan's interpersonal theory, therefore, is based upon the vicissitudes of face-to-face interaction in the individual's development. It is the relationship of the individual to his immediate fellows which forms the basis of his studies, as indeed it does in Horney's theorising. The wider relationship of the individual to his society is correspondingly neglected. To use Sullivan's own terminology, the psychiatrist is concerned with the conceptual "you" and the conceptual "me", and the vagaries of social interaction between the two. Mass social phenomena, which are neither "you" or "me", fall outside his scope. When Horney denies that the Death instinct can explain human warfare, she does not offer any other psychological explanation. Instead, she is content to leave the study of warfare to anthropologists. A similar distinction between the province of the psychoanalyst and the social scientist is made by Sullivan. In discussing the limitation of his own form of social psychology, he explicity distinguishes between the study of interpersonal relations and the "study of persons and groups" (Sullivan, 1938–9, p. 73). The former is the province of the psychiatrist, and the latter is the province of the sociologist. The scope of the two studies is, according to Sullivan, quite clearly defined into two distinct areas:

to the psychiatrist "society" is practically a matter of two-groups and three-groups, real or illusory or a blend, and of larger, less durable integrations of two-groups and three-groups having members in common. If the sociologist, in studying the movements that concern him, looks to the individuals concerned and not to the processes integrating him with some of them, his data are incomprehensible. (Sullivan, 1936–7, p. 26.)

This, therefore, is one of the tendencies of interpersonal psychoanalysis: a clear distinction is made between the range of interpersonal theory and the range of social theory. According to this view, there would seem to be little or no overlap between these respective intellectual disciplines. The fragmentation of the ontogenetic from the phylogenetic would appear to be absolute in the revision of classical psychoanalysis offered by Sullivan and Horney: the notion of a psychoanalytically based social science is rejected, at least officially.

If this were the sole tendency in the writings of interpersonal theorists, there would be little point in discussing them in the present context. Sullivan's firm distinction between small interpersonal groups and large-scale social movements would seem to suggest that he has nothing to add to the study of intergroup relations: any such contribution is liable to come from the sociologist rather than from the interpersonal psychologists. Nevertheless, there is an opposing tendency—and this is for the interpersonal psychotherapist to offer suggestions for reducing international tensions. There is evidence that the interpersonal psychotherapist does consider that his findings may have certain practical, if not theoretical value, for real-life intergroup situations. As a result it becomes necessary to examine the nature of this contribution and to offer an assessment of it.

It should come as no surprise that Sullivan's analysis of international affairs should be devoid of any explicit social theory, and narrowly focus upon certain interpersonal aspects of intergroup affairs. In his essay entitled *Tensions Interpersonal and International* (1950), Sullivan discusses problems associated with war and peace. However, in doing so he concentrates almost entirely on the interpersonal aspects of the topic: his discussion focuses on problems of face-to-face interaction between people of different nationalities, on face-to-face interaction between political leaders, and so on. In other words his emphasis is on direct communications and their breakdowns. The nearest Sullivan gets to discussing explicitly large scale social processes is when he writes about "personifications" or stereotypes. The problem of personifications is likewise dealt with on an interpersonal level. He discusses intergroup stereotypes in the same way as interpersonal perception. Personifications of groups, like interpersonal perceptions, can be "parataxic", i.e. based on anxiety-fraught mental states and therefore unlikely to be conducive to healthy adjustment. The answer to the problem of parataxic personifications, or negatively-charged outgroup stereotypes, is according to Sullivan, through the reinforcement of the individual's self-esteem. Such a recommendation can hardly be considered a major and original contribution to the social psychology of intergroup relations.

However, the present interest is not upon the quality of Sullivan's analysis but upon the implications of his general approach. His methodology inevitably reduces complex social events to interpersonal phenomena. There is a narrowing of focus, in which only interpersonal data are considered; at best, the wider issues, such as group stereotypes, are only considered with regard to their interpersonal aspects. It may be argued that this is a reasonable undertaking, given Sullivan's own admitted theoretical limitations. However, it will be suggested that there is a hidden ideological element in such analyses which, if not recognised as such, can lead to fallacious assumptions about international affairs. In discussing this point, the argument here will concentrate upon the intergroup analyses of two psychotherapists: Hoedemaker (1968), who draws analogies from psychotherapy to international relations, and Muench (1960), who discusses labour-management conflicts in terms of psychotherapeutic processes.

Hoedemaker (1968) argues that in any interpersonal situation "the more realistic partner has the sole responsibility of evaluating the realities of the overall situation and of determining the framework of the relationship" (p. 73). Starting from this premise he discusses three incidents of American-communist confrontation, which occurred during the cold war. Hoedemaker has the same diagnosis for each of these situations: the Americans have the more realistic appraisal of the "overall situation" and the communists are being unreasonably distrusting and aggressive. Having accepted the dictum that the interpersonal psychotherapist should concentrate on those phenomena which he understands best, Hoedemaker professes to make his diagnosis solely on the interpersonal behaviour of the international delegates within the negotiating hall. The wider political and social questions fall outside the province of the interpersonal psychotherapist. In the three examples cited by Hoedemaker, he claims that the communists' fears and distrust of the Americans belied their desire to continue talks—this desire to keep in contact is evidence that they subconsciously were demanding help from the Americans. By entering into a discussion of international relations Hoedemaker must inevitably raise political issues in one form or another. His psychological criterion for diplomatic reasonableness would seem to be naïve in the extreme; but this naïvety, combined with a refusal to consider political matters as such, creates in itself a highly political picture. By refusing to consider the wider context, he neglects the possibility that communist fears of the Americans might well have been justified. Each incident is considered on its own—consequently when discussing the Cuban missile crisis, Hoedemaker does not mention the American aggression of the Bay of Pigs invasion. The net result of his narrow interpersonal focus is that the Americans have reasonable aims and intentions and thus have "sole responsibility" for imposing a sense of reality on the unrealistic communists. Inevitably such a judgement must rest upon assumptions about the "realities" of international politics.

Muench (1960) discusses an industrial conflict in terms of interpersonal psychotherapy. The company concerned had a series of labour disputes after they had tried to "inculcate greater discipline and dedication" (pp. 165–6) in their employees, and had changed the piece-rate system of payment. Like Hoedemaker, Muench analyses the intergroup conflict only in terms of interpersonal dynamics and excludes all wider social issues. His three recommendations to the company all reveal his limited focus; he advocates that there should be more effective communication, a diminishment of distrust and a renewed emphasis on human relations. It should be noted that Muench's recommendations say nothing about the original decisions of the management which set in train the disputes. These are accepted as outside his scope of reference, not surprisingly since he was appointed by the management and not the union. In this way, Muench's interpersonal analysis avoids making any fundamental criticism of the management and also fails to provide any deeper analysis of the social issues involved in the disputes.

Both Hoedemaker and Muench reveal some of the pitfalls facing an interpersonal psychotherapist, who attempts to move outside his consulting room in order to diagnose larger social ills in an intergroup situation. Inevitably he will be forced to make certain assumptions concerning the nature of the conflict—assumptions, which strictly speaking fall outside the realm of psychotherapeutic diagnosis. Hoedemaker assumed to a considerable degree the irrationality of the communists and Muench on the other hand does not question the rationality of the company management. The narrowing of focus to the interpersonal from the intergroup inevitably means that the wider social issues are not considered in their own right, and also that certain presuppositions are made. These issues will be examined in somewhat greater detail, when interpersonal approaches in experimental social psychology are discussed. For the present it is sufficient to note the limitations of applying the interpersonal therapeutic model to the intergroup situation. In this respect one should commend the reluctance of Sullivan and Horney to carry their particular methodologies beyond their restricted scope; for the analyses of the interpersonal psychotherapist should not be considered an adequate substitute for a social analysis of intergroup relations.

The psychotherapist is trained to differentiate between the sick and the healthy, between realistic and unrealistic pictures of the world. However, in translating this training from his clinic to real-life political confrontations, he must inevitably make certain political judgements as he differentiates unreasonable political statements from reasonable ones, and distinguishes the "sick" and the "healthy" participants of a diplomatic dialogue. It seems that this approach lends itself readily to the *ad hominem* argument: in Hoedemaker's case the communists' actions are not analysed in a wider context, but the communists' "psychological health" is impugned. The tactic is to undermine your opponent rather than to defeat his argument—in this instance the undermining is done by imputing an unbalanced or unreasonable psychological state. This surely cannot be held to be a reasonable basis for a serious scientific analysis.

Ego psychology and prejudice

In a very real sense the arguments so far have had an essentially negative character. Reductionism, whether to instinctual or interpersonal processes, has been criticised for not providing a satisfactory basis for social scientific enquiry. Similarly, it has been suggested that there are fundamental flaws in the Freudian phylogenetic account of social forces. There would seem to be an intellectual opposition between psychoanalytic and social scientific theory: whereas psychoanalytic thinking, by its methodology, seeks underlying individual or interindividual causal determinants of social processes, social theory aims at a macro-analysis of large-scale phenomena. Nevertheless, there is an approach, which explicitly aims at reconciling these levels of analysis: this is the approach of the "ego psychologists", who have developed certain lines of thought arising from Freud's later work, notably *Inhibitions, Symptoms and Anxiety* (1926, Vol. 20), in which Freud emphasises the importance of ego processes as opposed to id processes (e.g. Hendrick, 1942; Hartmann, 1958).

An alliance between ego psychology and the social sciences was the explicit aim of such ego psychologists as Heinz Hartmann, as well as such sympathetic social scientists as Talcott Parsons. Parsons (1952) argued that Freud's tri-partite scheme of the human mind—the id, ego and superego—was too rigid. Freud had considered that an individual is bound to his culture through his superego. Cultural values and normative prescriptions operate in the individual through the psychological mechanism by which ego-ideals are introjected into the ego to form the super-ego. Parsons argued that this is an unsatisfactory account of the individual's acculturation, because of its narrow focus on the super-ego. He maintained that object-cathexis and ego-functions are also affected by cultural processes. For instance, Parsons postulates cultural effects affecting mother-child communication before the formation of the superego; he argues that the child learns to communicate its emotions to its mother, and that this process does not occur in a cultural limbo where all actions are spontaneously created by the id.

Similarly, according to Parsons, the child has to learn the frames of reference required by his culture. This involves learning his own social identity and his relation to others in the immediate family and in the society at large. He has to learn the prescribed affective meanings of these roles and identities (Parsons 1954); the child's emotional perception of his parents is to a certain extent determined by his culture, rather than solely by the free play of the instinctual forces. Even the solution to the Oedipus complex is not biologically given, but the child has to choose "standardised solutions provided by his society" (Howe, 1955, p. 71).

The upshot of Parsons's criticisms of traditional Freudianism is to emphasise the influence of cultural processes upon the ego. Culture affects the child before the formation of the superego and so therefore cannot be confined to that structure. In this respect Parsons is correct; subsequent social psychological research has shown the influence of culture on perceptual processes, which are held to be ego functions according to psychoanalytic terminology, (examples of such research are Liberman *et al.* 1957, reporting experiments on auditory perception, and Segall, Campbell and Herskovits, 1963, on visual illusions). Parsons's emphasis on the cultural influences upon ego functions is also shared by Hartmann. According to him these functions are not spontaneous developments, but are adaptations to the environment; different cultures require children to impose different adaptations and systems of defence on their instinctual structures (e.g. Hartmann, 1951, and also Erikson, 1945 and 1946).

Ego psychology recognises the ego as a dynamic structure in its own right; the ego as it were has become an equal partner to the id. Unlike the id, it can be culturally biassed and determined. The upgrading of the ego and the recognition of its cultural dependency mean that the psychoanalyst need not feel obliged to seek causal explanations for complex social events in the forces of the id. Problems concerning the creation of social identity and the adoption of social roles need not be reduced to the level of the instincts. Whereas the infantile id processes were the root of all significant later behaviour for Melanie Klien, the ego psychologists stress the importance of the relationship between the autonomous ego and the environment. Therefore, with respect to intergroup relations, social variables can be recognised as such by the ego psychologist. As a result large-scale social phenomena can be studied in their own right, and not be considered a by-product of psychoanalytic processes. Parsons (1952) claimed that ego psychology enabled a synthesis between the sociology of Durkheim and the psychology of Freud. The sociological descriptions of normative value complement the psychological descriptions of their internalisation; according to Parsons, this convergence of Durkheimian and Freudian thought marks "one of the truly fundamental landmarks of the development of modern social science" (1952, p. 322).

The possibility for such an integration rests primarily upon the assumption that reductionism is false. Hartmann (1964) makes this clear in an essay entitled *The application of psychoanalytic concepts to social science.* He specifically repudiates the psychoanalytic reduction of social events to unconscious forces. He states that to understand "specific social structures in specific historical situations our approach cannot only be through an understanding of the unconscious contents and mechanisms" (pp. 95–6). Similarly, one of Hartmann's collaborators makes the following assumption when discussing the problem of anti-Semitism.

> The fate of human beings depends only occasionally and only to a small extent upon their unconscious, much more on other human beings who act under the influence of various complicated social and psychological factors. (Loewenstein, 1947, pp. 352–3.)

Hartmann and Parsons attempt to integrate ego psychology not with the social sciences *per se*, but with a particular view of society. This is the functionalist view, which emphasised the structural unity of society. This unity is presupposed to exist *a priori* to the individual and, therefore, determines individual development. As a result the stress is upon the way the individual learns and internalises the norms of the social system and upon "the social functions which the system requires of him" (Hartmann, 1964, p. 29). The individual is assumed to be moulded by his society—his genetically determined and instinctually-based constitution has a considerable plasticity. Hartmann writes of individuals being "driven into different developmental channels according to whether they belong to a society of one social structure or another" (1964, p. 25). Parsons, likewise, stresses the importance of individual learning and re-interprets the Freudian concepts of "object-relations", "identification", "internalisation" and even the Oedipus Complex in terms of role learning. According to Parsons, the various stages of development, described by Freud, are all aimed to bring about the incorporation of the individual into his given social structure. He states that "Freud's theory of object-relations is essentially an analysis of the relations of the individual to the *structure of the society* in which he lives," (Parsons, 1958, p. 38, italics in original).

The general picture derived from the combination of ego psychology and functionalist sociology is clear. Society is an independent entity to which the individual has to adapt his instinctual structure. He has to learn his place within the social structure and to accept what Kardiner (1946) calls "the basic personality" of his culture. Included in the social values which the individual internalises are ingroup and outgroup attitudes. Such attitudes are to be accepted as social constants, and in functionalist sociology are to be examined with respect to their integrative function for the social structure. As far as the integration of psychology and sociology is concerned, the end product is one that stresses "man the conformer". It concentrates almost exclusively on the problems of cultural influence, to the neglect of social change and the dynamic properties of social conflict. It plays down the role of intergroup divisions within a society and the social changes which could be produced by such divisions. Since ingroup–outgroup attitudes are seen as static social products, changes in intergroup relations are correspondingly neglected.

The functionalist synthesis can be summarised by saying that it examines the effect of social structure on individuals, but neglects to examine the way that the social structure itself is produced. There is, in Hartmann's or Parsons's accounts, only a one-way input from society to the individual which describes the individual being driven along certain pre-ordained grooves. There is no mention of social structure being moulded in turn by the actions of men. Throughout the present work it will be assumed that the relationship between man and his society is essentially a two-way process: man produces his society and likewise society produces its own men. The two halves of this relationship are in mutual dependency and influence—they are dialectically united. A detailed theoretical description of this essential dialectic can be found in Berger and Luckman (1967, especially Part II).

It has been suggested that when the relationship between the individual and his society is a one-way input from society to the individual, then the result is the alienation of individuals who have no possibility for original or creative expression. Since this is the relationship described by ego psychology, there have been critics, who have accused ego psychologists of being apologists for an alienated society. For instance, Fromm (1971) has attacked ego psychology on the ground that it is conservative and conformist. He argues that Hartmann defines mental health in terms of adaptation to society, and does not in turn consider the health of the society (pp. 32–40). Social pathology is not what is at question here, but the limitation of social enquiry by the refusal to ask questions about society, through accepting it as an established independent variable. An example of this, as well as a good example of ego psychology's incipient conservatism, is a study by Anne Parsons (1961) of slum-dwellers in Naples. She found that certain of the symptoms for classically described schizophrenia were an "adaptive reaction" by the slum-dwellers to their social environment. Because the social system (in this case the slum) is considered as given, it is something which has to be adapted to. It surely is a distortion of reality, as well as being socially irresponsible, to accept a slum as a given reality, and to describe the psychological harm it does to its occupants as an adaptation. It should not be forgotten that the slum has been constructed by men, is maintained by them, and can be torn down by them.

Another example of the conservatism of ego psychology is provided by a study more closely-related to the topic of intergroup relations. Bird (1957) in a psychoanalytic study discusses the role of sibling rivalry in the development of prejudice against outgroups. His basic thesis is that outgroup prejudice is a defence mechanism of the ego to maintain ego-integrity. Since the integrity of the ego is highly-prized by ego psychologists as a sign of mental health, Bird is forced to accept the conclusion that prejudice "is not without a positive measure of value for the individual and in a broad way for society as a whole" (p. 512). Realising that this seems to be a defence for the very worst forms of racial atrocity, Bird hastens to assure the reader that: "The Nazi atrocities perpetrated against the Jews could in no way involve the active participation of a normal ego and therefore cannot be compared to prejudice" (Bird, 1957, p. 511).

This is obviously absurd; it implies that prejudiced beliefs can only be healthy if they do not lead to prejudiced behaviour. Rather the criterion for a healthy psyche should be re-examined. No society can possibly be healthy, if the majority of its members harbour irrational and vicious outgroup prejudices, no matter how well-integrated their egos. The society might appear to be functioning smoothly and efficiently—however, if the ingroup and its despised outgroup are considered together as a unit, then it is more difficult to maintain that the situation is an altogether healthy one.

Two main elements of ego psychology have been highlighted in the preceding discussion. In the first place there is the basic non-reductionist orientation, which provides the possibility for a genuine social analysis. In the second place there is the limited functionalist model of society. However there is no reason to presuppose that these two elements must necessarily be conjoined, and that a non-reductionist psychoanalytic social theory must inevitably present a one-sided view of the relation between man and his society. It is perfectly plausible to envisage a synthesis between some form of ego psychology and a social theory, which acknowledges the dialectical basis of society. Therefore, questions still remain about any possible relationships between internal psychological processes and patterns of intergroup relations.

The idea that outgroup perceptions are projections of individual psychological processes has been a constant theme in psychoanalytic writings on the topic of intergroup relations. Freud's and Roheim's respective theories of ingroup-outgroup relations rest upon the concept of projection. If outgroup perceptions are held to be the result of psychoanalytic projection, then they must in some sense be irrational; their particular content is not the result of a rational appraisal of the outgroup's characteristics, but is the consequence of internal disturbances. The outgroup stereotypes, which are the result of irrational projections, can be said to be prejudiced. For the psychoanalytically-minded social scientist, then, the major problem becomes the extent to which ingroup-outgroup relations can be described in terms of prejudices.

There is no better way of discussing the topic of the relation of psychological projection to large-scale intergroup phenomena, than by considering the investigation of Adorno *et al.* (1950), into the causes of anti-Semitism. Racial discrimination against minority groups would seem to be the paradigm case of irrational and projected prejudice; the mammoth enquiry conducted by Adorno *et al.* into prejudice amongst white Americans will serve to raise most of the important issues regarding personality characteristics and intergroup prejudice. The study itself combined a variety of techniques, derived from both psychoanalytic and behavioural traditions in psychology. The end-product was a detailed picture which was said to characterise the typical anti-Semite. Adorno *et al.* claimed there was a definite syndrome of emotional and cognitive elements that together formed "the authoritarian personality". The typical authoritarian in their sample was someone who had a strict, disciplined upbringing, and has suppressed all feelings of resentment and aggression he might have felt towards his parents. Instead the authoritarian tends to idealise his parents, but at the same time he still retains a subconscious hostility towards them. His attitudes toward authority in general parallel his attitudes towards his parents. Outwardly the authoritarian is respectful, and even deferential, towards authority-figures—the inward anger is tightly repressed and is displaced onto those he considers to be his inferiors. Thus the authoritarian has an excessive concern for rank and status. He likes social position to be clearly defined, and in general he is intolerant of ambiguity and is unable to handle his ambivalent feelings. Just as he cannot handle his aggressive feelings, so too does the authoritarian find it difficult to develop a balanced outlook on sexual matters. He is obsessed by sex, but in a puritanical and hypo-critical manner. He generally finds personal intimacy difficult and prefers to follow the "correct" social roles rather than express his own emotional feelings. The general picture of the authoritarian painted by Adorno *et al.* is of a weakling, who copes with his own inadequacies by excessive reverence to the powers that be and by venting his aggres-siveness upon his social inferiors and upon "inferior" outgroups—particularly on Jews and Negroes.

Like most other major studies in psychology *The Authoritarian Personality* has been subjected to a great deal of methodological criticism (see, for instance, Kirscht and Dillehay (1967) Wilson and Nias (1973) for reviews); also alternative descriptions of the prejudiced personality have been offered (e.g. Eysenck, 1956; Rokeach, 1960; G. D. Wilson, 1973). However what is of prime interest here is not so much the detailed characteristics of the prejudiced individuals, nor the precise methodology of Adorno *et al.*, but the social significance of the attempt to account for outgroup stereotypes in terms of a theory of personality. The important issue is whether the existence of such a personality constellation would mean shifting the focus of social psy-chological analysis of intergroup relations onto problems of personality development. For this reason too, the concern will not be on the hundreds of studies which have assumed the existence of the person-ality constellation and employed the scale of measurement devised by Adorno *et al.*, the California F scale. Such studies have by and large merely employed the instrument of measurement and have not been concerned with the wider theoretical issues raised by the original study.

Certainly in *The Authoritarian Personality* social factors are not ignored. It was found that high prejudice on the authoritarian F scale was correlated with low socio-economic status, and Adorno in chapter sixteen specifically makes the point that lower- and middle-class anti-Semitism may well be psychologically different phenomena. Later studies have confirmed this linking of anti-Semitic prejudice with socio-economic variables (e.g. Frenkel-Brunswik, 1954; and from a different theoretical standpoint, Bettelheim and Janowitz, 1950 and 1964). Likewise Christie (1954) demonstrated a negative correlation between educational attainment and authoritarianism. All of which suggests strongly that there is a strong class bias in the development of authoritarianism (cf. Lipset, 1960, especially chapter four). This in itself implies that any definitive description of the aetiology of out-group prejudice would have to take into account the interaction between personality and social factors, especially with regard to the possibilities of the personality constellation changing as there are corresponding changes in underlying social forces.

Certainly it is the view of at least two of the collaborators of *The Authoritarian Personality* that the interrelation between social and psychological factors needs to be considered as an integral part of out-group prejudice. Adorno (1951) specifically discounts the view that a psychological account of the roots of Fascism in any way vitiates the need for political or social analysis. He denies that the psychological variables can in themselves be held to be the prime determinants for the historical facts of Fascism's popularity during the 1920s and 1930s.

> Psychological dispositions do not actually cause Fascism; rather Fascism defines a psychological area which can be successfully exploited by the forces which promote it for entirely nonpsychological reasons of self-interest. (Adorno, 1951, p. 298.)

Adorno's concept of "nonpsychological reasons of self-interest" resembles in essentials Marcuse's notion of "the interests of domination" and both concepts point the way to a nonpsychological analysis of socio-historic forces. In particular, they allow a critical analysis of economic and political trends. In a similar vein another of the original collaborators to *The Authoritarian Personality*, Nevitt Sanford, has written of the limitations of personality studies of prejudice. He writes that "nothing we know of personality in relation to racism contradicts the principle that overt manifestations of prejudice depend on socio-economic conditions" (Sanford, 1973, p. 73). It is interesting to note in this context that the psychoanalytic originators of the concept of "authoritarianism" (Reich, 1946 and Fromm, 1941), both emphasised the dialectical interplay between psychological and social factors. Both these writers specifically linked the psychological phenomenon of authoritarianism in Nazi Germany with the economic and political situation, and they particularly concentrated upon the social position of the lower middle class in their analyses.

The general point is that any personality syndrome, such as that of authoritarianism, does not develop in a cultural limbo. Central to the authoritarian's make-up is a whole series of beliefs about the nature of the world. These beliefs do not merely embrace attitudes towards "inferior" outgroups, but also contain views on sexual morality, attitudes toward authority, political beliefs, and precepts for handling interpersonal relationships. In short, there is according to Adorno *et al.* (1950) an authoritarian *Weltanschauung*. Such an ideological system of beliefs, although shot through with contradictions and inconsistencies, could not have been fortuitously created by each authoritarian solely as a result of his relations with his parents. Cultural and social influences must have inevitably shaped the ideologies of the post-war American authoritarian. The mass-media, schooling, beliefs of parents etc. must have all gone some way to producing the final belief-system.

The Authoritarian Personality can be said to show the psychological processes which mediate certain cultural beliefs. In particular it hypothesises an isomorphism between those beliefs and their underlying psychological dynamics. The racial prejudice of the bigot is seen in itself as a form of projection—the Jews and Negroes are blamed for ills that they could not possibly have caused, and therefore ideological scapegoating can be seen as a form of cultural projection. What Adorno *et al.* argue is that this cultural scapegoating is mediated by a form of psychological scapegoating, in which the aggression that the authoritarian feels towards his father is projected onto outgroups. It is this assumption (that the psychological processes mirror the form of the ideological beliefs about outgroups) which brands the authoritarian as being irrational. The ideology, based as it is upon psychodynamic projection, is seen as a means by which the individual can avoid facing up to reality. He is thus protected by an irrational cocoon of beliefs which save him from his own potentially destructive aggressive impulses.

In this way the concept of "authoritarianism" can itself be seen as an ideological one. It is a variant of the *ad hominem* argument. In this case the authoritarian is criticised because his beliefs are seen as the product of irrational psychodynamic processes. By implication the beliefs themselves are criticised as being irrational. The critical values, which are implicit in *The Authoritarian Personality*, have frequently been discussed by psychologists (e.g. Titus and Hollander, 1957; Brown, 1965). Recently, debates about the psychological significance of the concept of authoritarianism have been revived. The particular issue, around which the recent debate has revolved, concerns the psychological health of the right-wing authoritarian. Eckhardt and Newcombe (1969 and 1972) repeat the *ad hominem* argument, which seeks to undermine the psychology of the authoritarian, whilst other researchers give him a clean bill of psychological health (Elms, 1970; Ray, 1972a and 1972b). Ray has conducted studies which show no positive correlation between authoritarianism and neuroticism; from these he concludes that the notion of authoritarianism as proposed by Adorno *et al.* "would now seem to be irretrievably fallacious" (Ray, 1972a, p. 329). It should however be mentioned in passing that Adorno *et al.* predicted a negative relation between authoritarianism and neuroticism—in their study it was the non-authoritarian who had "an internalised, and rather strict, superego of the sort that often leads to neurotic symptoms" (1950, p. 410).

The present argument has stressed the connection between the concept of authoritarianism and ideological influences, both upon the psychological investigator as well as upon the authoritarian personality. There have however been attempts to eliminate such ideological influences from the study of prejudice, in order to reveal the basic psychological processes which determine the personality of the prejudiced individual. In such studies an attempt is made to investigate the psychology of prejudice *per se* apart from any particular historical manifestation of prejudice. Foremost amongst such attempts is that of Rokeach (1960). In his book *The Open and Closed Mind* he attempts to look beyond the social context of prejudice to reveal the basic, and unchanging, psychological dynamics. To this end he distinguishes between the content of particular prejudiced beliefs and their structure. Rokeach aims to eliminate ideological influences by concentrating exclusively upon the structure of beliefs; he writes that "if we focus on ideological structure rather than content, our own ideological biases become more irrelevant" (1960, p. 6). In this way Rokeach claims that his own presuppositions do not affect his investigation of the psychology of prejudice.

By examining the structure of beliefs, Rokeach aims to uncover the underlying dogmatic style of thought, which he claims is the hallmark of prejudice. He does not accept that prejudiced thinking is confined to the right-wing and entertains the possibility that there can be left-wing authoritarianism. He states that "if our interest is in the study of authoritarianism, we should proceed from right authoritarianism not to a re-focus on left authoritarianism but to the general properties held in common by all forms of authoritarianism" (p. 14). As such Rokeach explicitly calls his investigation ahistorical, in that he is not concerned with the content of actual prejudiced beliefs, but with underlying personality variables.

Rokeach distinguishes between the open (nondogmatic) mind and the closed (dogmatic) mind. This distinction is made not on the basis of beliefs which the dogmatic and nondogmatic individual might hold; it is specifically made on the way in which their beliefs are espoused. The closed mind is not receptive to new ideas and refers all new information to pre-set standards of reference. The open mind on the other hand is more willing to countenance new ideas and to evaluate them independently. In this way the distinction between the open and the closed mind is made deliberately upon the style of cognitive functioning and not upon the content of cognitive beliefs. The dogmatic person places an irrational over-reliance on authority (pp. 62–3) and seeks refuge from his own personal anxieties in a fixed system of thought. According to Rokeach the nondogmatic person has a much lower level of personal anxiety and can evaluate beliefs more rationally by considering them upon their own merits rather than automatically referring them to an outside standard.

The crucial question for Rokeach's theory is whether he has succeeded in distinguishing between prejudiced and non-prejudiced thinking without referring to the content of beliefs. It will be suggested here that both his concept of dogmatism and the scales he uses to measure dogmatism contain ideological bias and are not based solely upon the structure, as opposed to the content, of beliefs. Firstly, two of Rokeach's distinguishing criteria can be noted. He argues that the dogmatist has a comparatively rigid and systematised belief system, compared to the open-minded person. Also the dogmatist has "an overconcern with the remote future or remote past", whereas the open-minded person has "both feet in the here and now" (pp. 63–4). However, it has been claimed that both these two criteria can be features of different forms of ideological systems, rather than different forms of personality. Later in the present work, Karl Mannheim's concept of ideology will be discussed in some detail. At the moment one might note that in *Ideology and Utopia* Mannheim discusses the ways in which ideologies differ in their degrees of systematisation and in their conception of time. He suggests that groups which represent the *status quo* rarely have highly systematised ideologies. Also he argues that groups which are trying to effect radical social changes have different time perspectives from groups who are attempting to maintain existing conditions. If Mannheim's descriptions of ideological thought are accepted, then it is possible that Rokeach's concept of dogmatism could refer to the nature of different ideologies, and not merely to individual psychological processes. Moreover there is also the possibility that ideologies of social change may be defined by Rokeach as being dogmatic, and the ideologies of social stability as being open-minded.

The biases within Rokeach's analysis can be illustrated by considering in detail the two scales of measurement he designed to measure prejudiced thinking. These are the Dogmatism Scale and the Opinionation Scale. If these scales are to fit his stated theoretical purpose then they should properly probe only the structure of attitudes, rather than their specific content. However the Dogmatism scale contains such politically-loaded items as "The United States and Russia have just about nothing in common", and "Communism and Catholicism have nothing in common". One might wonder why it is necessarily dogmatic to stress the differences between a religion and a materialist political philosophy. Other items are intended to tap the "coexistence of contradictions within belief systems", which allegedly characterises dogmatic thinking. For instance, it is dogmatic, and contradictory, to believe that "while the use of force is wrong by and large, it is sometimes the only possible way to advance a noble ideal". However, such a view need not be interpreted as being the expression of a contradiction, rather that sometimes moral principles conflict. In such circumstances one has to choose between principles. The fact that one principle rather than the other is chosen would not itself seem to be the product of dogmatism, rather it would have to be the product of a more general outlook on the world. Similarly, Rokeach implies that it is contradictory, and dogmatic, to believe that the principle of freedom of speech might sometimes have to be waived. Here he seems to be equating open-mindedness with the classic liberal position that freedom of speech is the most important moral principle. This equation is made irrespective of the way in which the liberal argues his case.

An *a priori* linking of a "moderate" or liberal political stance with open-mindedness can be seen clearly in the Opinionation Scale. This scale is composed of two sets of items. Half the items express left-wing "opinionated views" whilst the other half expresses right-wing "opinionated views". Rokeach does not include in the Scale views from the centre of the political spectrum. It is as if he discounts the notion of there being centrist opinionated views. In the absence of any attempt to identify directly opinionated views in the centre, the suspicion must be that Rokeach is abandoning his attempt not to assess belief-systems by their content, and is to a certain extent pre-supposing that right-wing and left-wing ideologies are more dogmatic and less open-minded than liberalism.

One of Rokeach's major contentions is that there is a dogmatism of the left-wing as well as a dogmatism of the right-wing. This conclusion is based primarily on his study of thirteen British communists, who scored higher on the Dogmatism Scale than did Conservatives, Liberals, Attleeites or Bevanites (although it should be mentioned that these differences do not actually reach significance level). In the first place Rokeach's data does not support his basic theory—far from the "dogmatic" communists having high levels of personal anxiety, they in fact had the lowest level of the five groups of British subjects studied. Nor were they uniformly more dogmatic than the non-communists; on a number of items the communists were revealed to be significantly less dogmatic than the other groups of subjects. More-over it is possible to discern certain effects of ideological content if the items on which there was the greatest difference between communist and noncommunist responses are considered.

The five items, on which there was the greatest difference were: "To one who really takes the trouble to understand the world he lives in, it's an easy matter to predict future events"; "Most people are failures and it is the system which is responsible for this"; "Of all the different philosophies which exist in this world there is probably only one which is correct"; "Even though I have a lot of faith in the intelligence and wisdom of the common man I must sometimes say that the masses behave stupidly at times"; "It is only natural for a person to be rather fearful of the future". None of these five items would seem *prima facie* to be tapping basic personality variables, as opposed to more general views about the world. In fact the result that the communists agreed with the first three items and disagreed with the last two could be predicted solely on the basis of Marxist ideology, quite apart from any knowledge about the personal characteristics of individual communists. Since these are the items which revealed the greatest differences between communists and non-communists, again it must be suspected that Rokeach is, to a certain extent, linking left-wing views with his concept of dogmatism by definition, rather than by a value-free empirical investigation.

Rokeach's concept of dogmatism has been discussed in some detail because it represents an attempt to separate "basic" personality variables from social and ideological variables. However, it has been argued that Rokeach is unsuccessful in this endeavour; his concepts and research into dogmatism have ignored the content of ideological beliefs in order to look solely at their psychological structure. Given that there are certain ideological biases in Rokeach's own formulations, his criticism of the bias in *The Authoritarian Personality* is somewhat vitiated. Rokeach's analysis contains its own form of the *ad hominem* argument—the dogmatist is considered to have the cognitive style he has, in order to ward off personal anxieties. In this respect Rokeach can be said to be paralleling the *ad hominem* descriptions of the extreme right-wing as offered by Adorno *et al.* The important question, which still remains to be answered, is how much significance should be attached to these psychological accounts of the dynamics of ideological belief. Before attempting to tackle this issue, one point can be noted; that the psychological *ad hominem* argument need not be confined to the description of fascists and communists. It can be applied to any shade of political opinion. In this way it should be perfectly feasible to construct a psychoanalytic account to "explain" the moderation of the centrist, and to postulate what it is about his personality which prevents him from taking a more "positive" political stance. The fact that the psychological *ad hominem* argument is not generally applied to the centre of conventional political debate says more about the biases within psychological science, than about the necessary scope of such forms of argument.

Bearing this in mind, it is now possible to examine the proposition that the psychodynamic projection of interpersonal aggression must mediate an ideological projection of hostility onto outgroups. Nothing which has been said so far suggests that the connection between the two forms of projection is a necessary one. There is no contradiction in assuming that an ideology of prejudice against Jews and Negroes cannot be taught in the context of a closely united family; nor is there any contradiction in asserting that negative outgroup stereotypes could be socially transmitted in exactly the same way as other more innocuous folk-beliefs or ways of interpreting social reality. In this respect, one can note the arguments of Brown (1965). He argues that the weakest connections in *The Authoritarian Personality* are those that link the cluster of authoritarian attitudes with the postulated psychodynamic mechanisms. What is more, Brown suggests that the personality syndrome need not be explained by projective mechanisms of defence. Instead, he offers the guide-lines for a potential explanation based upon socio-economic status and acculturation into the norms and ethics of lower-class white American society. Thus he concludes his analysis by stating that "low IQ, education, and SES can account for the syndrome without recourse to personality dynamics" (p. 526). What is at stake is not whether Brown's explanatory schema is the best possible interpretation of the facts—rather it is that a social explanation, not based upon psychodynamic assumptions, is possible.

It is possible to go further than this, and argue for the necessity, rather than for the possibility, of a social analysis. So far it has been argued that the authoritarian syndrome must be linked to social conditions, and that this was recognised by the proponents of the concept of "authoritarianism". By implication this suggests that the authoritarian personality cannot offer a timeless and ahistorical theory of outgroup prejudice. Similarly Rokeach's (1960) attempt to provide an ahistorical account has been criticised. It has also been suggested that psychodynamic projection need not be considered a necessary condition for the existence of ideological outgroup prejudice. Now it will be suggested that the isolation of a particular personality syndrome cannot be a sufficient condition for explaining intergroup prejudice; to consider that it is sufficient is to ignore some of the more crucial aspects that relate to the wider intergroup context and to the aetiology of prejudice in particular.

To illustrate this, the studies by Dicks (1950, 1966 and 1972) can be considered. These studies investigated the personality structure of German Nazis, and Dicks's samples include both prisoners-of-war and convicted war criminals. Among the committed Nazis, Dicks found a pattern of intellectual and emotional responses similar to those found by Adorno *et al.* in their high authoritarian subjects. Dicks, however, stresses that it would be an over-simplification to attribute the phenomenon of Nazism purely and simply to a particular personality constellation—Nazism cannot be explained by saying that its rise in the 1930s was due to the existence of large numbers of people who were unable to resolve their intra-psychic conflicts without projecting hostility onto convenient scapegoats. Similarly, the decline of Nazism as a social movement cannot be attributed to the resolution of these intra-psychic conflicts. Dicks (1972), writes that the determinants of Nazism must be sought in "the two-way interaction between the inner world of individuals and their culture patterns, and of the way this dynamism creates not only social institutions but also the climate in which they are worked" (p. 264).

The complex interrelations which combine to produce any historical manifestation of outgroup prejudice do not involve just one particular personality type. Also involved must be a variety of social factors which combine to form a social unity out of disparate psychological characters. To illustrate this, one can assert that the rise of Nazism did not just affect those Germans who had highly authoritarian personalities; non-authoritarians, who were not even members of the Nazi party, also fought for the Third Reich and failed to register any protests against the persecution of the Jews. Dicks (1966) refers to the fact that the average "decent" individual can find himself caught up in the fight for authoritarian ideals which he himself does not necessarily share. This, according to Dicks, is one of the most tragic aspects of warfare (1966, pp. 109–110). Similarly, when considering the rise of Nazism, one should not forget Adorno's concept of "the nonpsychological reasons of self-interest" (1951, p. 298). For instance, the role of German industrialists in promoting the career of Hitler should not be forgotten, nor should the help given him by a number of the political figures of the time. To equate the phenomenon of Nazism with the psychology of the right-wing bigot oversimplifies both the historical and the social psychological aspects of the situation.

This oversimplification can have certain dangerous consequences. In particular it can lead to an underestimation of the social significance of racist and prejudiced ideologies. The study by Adorno *et al.* 1950, locates the roots of anti-Semitism, together with racial bigotry in general, in one type of irrational personality structure. There is, as a consequence, the implication that prejudice might possibly be eradicated, if authoritarians could be in some way "cured" of their irrational predilections. This implication, however, conflicts with the view that there are sound historical reasons for the development of prejudiced ideologies in particular places at particular times; similarly it conflicts with the view that outgroup prejudice is more than the product of individuals' psychological disturbances, since it is linked to fundamental social forces.

The dangers involved in an overemphasis upon the extreme bigot can be illustrated by referring to the current racial siuation in Britain. Recent studies on racial attitudes in general have emphasised the complexity of attitudes which can fall under the broad heading of "prejudiced" (e.g. Noel, 1971; Dummett, 1973; Hiro, 1973; Sanford, 1973). Dummett (1973) has described the variety of views, which can be seen to rest on racist assumptions. These range from the out-and-out fascist hatred of Blacks to the overtly liberal, but essentially racist, ideology of "kindness to inferiors", based upon a "cotton-wool condescension" (p. 86). Dummett argues that it would be completely mistaken to concentrate exclusively upon the fascistic type of racism, since that would severely underestimate the true extent and viciousness of racism as a social reality. For instance, the report by Rose (1969) into the state of race relations in Britain reported that only about ten per cent of the British were highly prejudiced against Black persons. If one assumes that these ten percent resemble the classic authoritarian bigot and that authoritarianism is isomorphic with racial prejudice, one is left with the optimistic conclusion that ninety per cent of the British are not colour-prejudiced.

However, this optimistic conclusion does not square with the realities of racial discrimination in Britain. For instance, the Political and Economic Planning Committee (1967) found that discrimination was widely practised in employment and housing. Rex and Moore (1967) have argued that racial prejudice is, in fact, the dominant attitude amongst the white community, and is not confined to the minority of disturbed individuals. Similarly Lawrence (1974), has shown the hidden extent of racism in an English city. The danger of equating racism with extreme bigotry is that racist presuppositions of presumably well-adapted persons are neglected. More than this, it ignores those legal and political acts which transcribe the racist presuppositions into actual discrimination. Allen (1973) has pointed out that a society can develop racist institutions without its members possessing strongly bigoted motivations. Foot (1965) has shown how race became an issue in British politics for purely political ends. It has also been argued that British politicians have institutionalised racism by placing on the statute book successive immigration acts, based upon implicit racist premises (Allen, 1973; Dummett, 1973; Hiro, 1973), and that the mass-media continually transmit subtly racist assumptions (Hartmann and Husband, 1974). Thus it would appear that racist ideology is being fostered in Britain for "nonpsychological reasons of self-interest". Instead of attempting to describe all racist premises as attempts to project individual hostilities, it would seem altogether more responsible to seek the social sources of such premises.

In the same way the authoritarian personality should not be taken as explaining Nazism and anti-Semitism. At most it can only state why a number of persons seem predisposed to aggressive hatreds. It cannot explain the direction of these hatreds purely in psychodynamic terms. The historian analysing Nazism has to explain why it was the Jews that became the scapegoats of the Germans, and why they should have been chosen as scapegoats at that particular moment. The psychoanalytic descriptions of projective mechanisms cannot answer such questions. In order to seek answers to these questions the ideological and social significance of anti-Semitism would need to be examined. This discussion would seek to analyse the historical roots of anti-Semitism in order to explain its recrudescence in the 1930s (e.g. Cohn, 1967). One might enquire about the prevalence of anti-Semitic premises before the rise of Hitler, and whether the "regular German" shared such premises. The pathway to Fascism should not be thought to lie merely in psychological dispositions—there are more obvious factors that ease the way of a Hitler. The exact role of purely psychodynamic factors with respect to the genesis of social movements needs, quite obviously, painstaking analysis; however, the search for significant variables should not conceal those more obvious features of a society which propagate irrational outgroup hatreds. The psychoanalytic enquiry in no way obviates the need for social analysis, and more importantly, for social action. People may not be able to undo their own childhoods, but they are able to change collectively the nature of their society. This fact should not be forgotten in the face of the conformist assumptions of ego psychology and in the light of the tendency to focus upon the individualistic aspects of intergroup bigotry. The need, therefore, is for an avowedly social analysis of social phenomena.

5

Frustration–Aggression and Rebellion

The frustration-aggression hypothesis

One of the principle aims of laboratory experimentation in social psychology is to provide tangible evidence for particular hypotheses. A single experiment by itself will seldom, if ever, prove or disprove a general theory of social behaviour. The champions of the experimental method do not seek instant revelation; they adopt a more gradual approach to understanding social life and hope that knowledge will be accumulated piecemeal through continuing series of empirical investigations. It is their belief that this patient approach will yield more reliable results in the long term.

If Freudianism is seen as too diffuse and grandiose a theory to be the basis for a social psychology of intergroup relations, this does not mean that all Freudian insights have to be discarded. Particular ideas and hypotheses can be isolated and subjected to rigorous testing. Within the history of psychology there have been numerous instances of researchers adopting this method. Initial insights derived from the psychoanalytic tradition are translated into the language and procedures of the behavioural tradition. The influential book *Frustration and Aggression* by Dollard *et al.* (1939) is a classic case in point.

Dollard *et al.* (1939) aimed to combine Freudian hypotheses linking frustration to aggression with concepts derived from learning theory. By so doing they hoped to provide a conceptual whole which could then be tested empirically primarily, but not exclusively, by the methodology of experimental psychology. This reformulation of psychoanalytic ideas has provided the impetus for a continuing interest in the two variables of frustration and aggression and has given rise to countless experimental studies into the social psychology of aggressive behaviour.

Most frustration-aggression experiments have been concerned with interpersonal rather than intergroup aggression. In fact it is true to say that little of the vast amount of research directly studies aggression in a group context. Nevertheless throughout the history of frustration-aggression research intergroup relations has been a constant underlying preoccupation. Hypotheses and theories are often intended to refer to group, as well as individual, aggression. This is certainly true of the original work of Dollard et al. (1939). The second part of their book is devoted to a discussion of the social applications of their theory. Not only do they derive a general theory of intergroup relations but they also use their frustration-aggression conceptual framework to illustrate issues such as race prejudice and the psychological foundations of outgroup attitudes. Even before the publication of this work Dollard (1937) had incorporated the basic notions of the frustration-aggression hypothesis in his study of the social psychology of race and class relations in the American southern states. In a similar spirit, two of the other collaborators of Frustration and Aggression produced a correlational study of economic indices and social unrest which was intended to be an indirect social psychological test of the basic hypothesis (Hovland and Sears, 1940). Another of the original authors conducted an experiment which directly linked the scapegoating of outgroups to the frustration-aggression theoretical framework (Miller and Bugelski 1948).

This linking of frustration-aggression theory to problems of intergroup phenomena is not confined merely to the early formulations of the hypothesis. Leonard Berkowitz, who did much to revitalise frustration-aggression research in the 1960s, has continued this tradition. In his book, Aggression: a Social Psychological Analysis, Berkowitz (1962) makes it plain that he considers his experimental laboratory programme to be directly relevant to problems of group prejudice and stereotypes. He devotes two full chapters of his book to the topic of intergroup relations which he discusses in relation to the experimental evidence. He has since then continued connecting the findings from small-scale frustration-aggression experiments with large-scale intergroup phenomena; in particular he has explicitly related his experimental research to the Black urban ghetto riots which took place in the United States in the 1960s (Berkowitz, 1971b and 1972). In these articles, the laboratory frustration-aggression experiments are used in an attempt to explain certain phenomena concerned with civil disturbances.

This linking of psychological research with large-scale group phenomena has not been confined to the writings of psychologists investigating the frustration-aggression relationship. There has been of late a growing interest in the theory from outside the discipline of psychology; a number of political scientists have attempted to offer explanations for revolutionary conflict and civil turmoil in terms of the basic tenets of frustration-aggression theory, (for instance, Lupsha 1971; Horowitz 1973; Feierabend and Feierabend 1966; Feierabend, Feierabend and Nesvold 1973). One of the most systematic translations of frustration-aggression theory into political science has been undertaken by Gurr (1970). In a detailed analysis of revolutions and rebellions, Gurr has stated how important he conceives the frustration-aggression hypothesis to be. He calls the relation between frustration and aggression "the basic motivational link" necessary for understanding the occurrence of collective civil violence. He goes on to illustrate the importance of this link, when he likens the frustration-aggression hypothesis to the law of gravity. Gurr asserts that it is even less feasible to construct a theory of social violence without taking into account the frustration-aggression relationship, than it is to construct a theory of flight without reference to the law of gravity (Gurr 1970, pp. 36–7). There is therefore a growing body of political scientists who consider the work of the frustration-aggression theorists to be crucial to an understanding of mass social phenomena.

Despite these examples of group studies arising from the frustration-aggression hypothesis, it will nevertheless be inevitable that, in any detailed discussion of the hypothesis and the psychological evidence for it, the focus will shift from intergroup relations. All too few experimentalists have followed the example of Miller and Bugelski (1948). Therefore in the following discussion, the topic of intergroup relations will be temporarily pushed into the background, while the mainstream frustration-aggression work is analysed. The justification for making this detour has already been outlined—it is the acknowledged relevance by the research workers themselves of their theories for large scale social events. The discussion will roughly take the following form: first the various theoretical positions will be outlined, starting from the original hypothesis of Dollard *et al.* and ending with some of the more recent theoretical statements. Then the empirical evidence supporting these positions will be outlined. Only then will the topic of intergroup relations be returned to. By then it is hoped a number of points can be made about the relevance of this line of research to the social psychology of intergroup relations. Also a number of speculations concerning the relation between social discontent and social violence will be made in the light of the frustration-aggression evidence.

To start with, the theoretical statements of Dollard *et al.* must be considered. Their book *Frustration and Aggression* begins with a bold assertion on the first page that the variables of frustration and aggression are necessary and sufficient conditions for each other:

> This study takes as its point of departure the assumption that *aggression is always a consequence of frustration.* More specifically the proposition is that the occurrence of aggressive behaviour always presupposes the existence of frustration and, contrariwise, that the existence of frustration always leads to some form of aggression. (Dollard, *et al.*, 1939, p. 1, italics in original.)

From this basic theoretical position the authors elucidate the psychological nature underlying the necessary and sufficient connections between frustration and aggression. One of the more important elements of their theory is the postulation of an intervening variable between a frustrating stimulus and an aggressive response. Specifically, this intervening variable was an "instigator" to action. A frustrating stimulus, defined in terms of the blocking or prevention of a goal response, does not produce aggressive responses directly: it produces in the subject an instigation to aggress, which in the normal course of events gives rise to actual aggression. Dollard *et al.* acknowledge that this basic notion is not an original one—they explicitly recognise their debt to Freud, and especially to his *Mourning and Melancholia* (1917, Vol. 14). In that work Freud argued that the blocking of pleasure-seeking, or erotic impulses, causes frustration, with aggression being "the primordial reaction" to frustration. It can be noted however that this is not the only reaction to frustration suggested by Freud. In *Civilization and its Discontents* (p. 138, 1930, Vol. 20) he remarks that frustration gives rise to feelings of guilt. The important assumption of *Frustration and Aggression* is not so much that the two variables are indissolubly linked. The actual relationship between the two variables is, according to the authors, hypothetical and in need of empirical validation. Dollard *et al.* made an assumption which gives the hypothesis great theoretical interest, and which allows a number of predictions to be made about the displacement and projection of prejudices onto outgroups. This assumption is one that is taken from the writings of Freud: it is that the energy which motivates human behaviour does not dissipate of its own accord if it cannot attain its original goal. In its application to the relationship between frustration and aggression, the assumption works in the following way. Frustration provokes an instigation to aggress—if, however, the frustrator cannot be attacked, the instigation to aggress does not evaporate but ensures that some other form of aggression will take place. Notably, aggression will be displaced onto some other target. The instigation to aggress can only be diminished by aggression itself. That is to say, after an act of aggression there will be a cathartic reaction, and further aggression will be less likely, except of course if there is a further frustration. In chapter three of *Frustration and Aggression*, Dollard *et al.* outline some of the reasons why aggression might not be directly expressed against the frustrator, and so has to be displaced onto some other target; for instance, they suggest, the frustrating agent may be too powerful, or there may be strong internal sanctions which forbid the subject from expressing his anger directly. An example of the former case would be the man who is insulted by his boss and who dare not answer back for fear of losing his job. An example of the latter case would be the child who is frustrated by his mother but cannot, even to himself, recognise any hostility towards his loved mother. In both these cases, Dollard *et al.* predict that the frustrated individual will be inhibited from expressing direct aggression and so will "take it out" on something or someone else.

Two major predictions are thus incorporated into the frustration-aggression model: (1) aggression, which cannot be expressed directly against the frustrating agent, does not dissipate, but is displaced onto some other target; and (2) the expression of aggression is cathartic—it diminishes the probability of further aggression without a fresh instigation. These two assumptions provide the cement which binds together the variables of frustration and aggression in the tight necessary and sufficient relationship of the theory. The authors were well aware of the fact that there are very many different forms of frustrations and aggressions, dependent on a multitude of social factors. Nevertheless it was their contention that behind all these different

forms there was a psychological unity. The importance of the assumptions of catharsis and displacement for establishing this psychological
unity amongst diverse manifestations of aggressive behaviour was not
lost on Dollard *et al.*:

> The phenomena of catharsis and displacement seem to point to a func-
> tional unity in the variety of reactions to which the label of aggression
> has been attached in this presentation. To the extent that the type of
> functional unity which has been illustrated occurs generally and to the
> extent that it is strong enough to make the relationship between two
> so-called aggressive responses closer than that between one such response
> and many other totally different types of response, the suggested usage
> of the word aggression seems justified. On the other hand, to the extent
> that the hypothesised functional unity is found, upon closer examina-
> tion, to break down, the present use of the term "aggression" will have
> to be modified or abandoned. (Dollard *et al.*, 1939, pp. 52–3.)

Much of the subsequent research has tended to neglect the functional unity of aggression and not to follow up the suggestion by Dollard *et al.* of the theoretical importance of displacement and catharsis.
Not that these topics have escaped empirical investigation; but they
have not received the systematic study accorded to the determination
of the gross relationship between frustration and aggression. In this
respect much of the history of frustration-aggression research can be
seen as a withdrawal from the categorical assertions of the first page of
Frustration and Aggression and an emphasising of other variables
affecting the hypothesised relationship between frustration and aggression. Even in the original formulation the tight necessary and sufficient
relationship between the two variables is modified, or at least qualified.
Dollard *et al.* make a distinction between overt aggression and non-
overt aggression. They state that not every frustrating experience
leads to overt aggression. If there is an inhibition against committing
an actual aggressive act some sort of covert aggression might be the
result. This covert aggression can take the form of aggressive fantasies
or day-dreams. Miller (1941) makes it quite clear that the authors of
Frustration and Aggression never intended to take the extreme position that every frustrating experience necessarily produces an overt
violent aggressive act. The behaviourist reinterpretation of Freud was
not taken to those lengths. Rather, according to Miller, it was the
intention to postulate that frustration inevitably produces an instigation to aggress—whether this instigation gives rise to overt aggression
depends on a number of social factors, including internal inhibitions

and external circumstances. Of course this emphasis on the instigation to aggress, rather than on overt aggression, makes the empirical problem of verifying the hypothesis all the harder. The intervening variable, the instigation, and not the actual response, is the direct result of frustration; as such it is difficult to identify and measure, since any act of frustration failing to evoke an overt aggressive response could still have provoked an instigation to aggress, which has been displaced or sublimated along harmless channels.

Notwithstanding this, a great deal of subsequent empirical research has concentrated on determining the likelihood of overt aggression following frustration. For instance, an important modification to frustration-aggression theory was suggested by social learning theorists, such as Bandura and Walters (1963). The nub of their criticism is that not all aggressive behaviour is a response to frustrating experiences— on the contrary, much of it is a learnt response which has been positively reinforced through socialisation processes. They argue that frustration is not a necessary condition for aggression. Aggressive behaviour can be taught like any other form of socially learnt behaviour, and can be performed in order to achieve future rewards. Thus, according to Bandura and Walters, aggression can have an instrumental value in daily life.

Several empirical findings can be cited in favour of the proposition that aggression, if reinforced, can occur in the absence of a prior frustration. McCord, McCord and Howard (1961), in a longitudinal nature study of children and their parents, stressed the role of parents teaching their children inner controls to deal with aggressive responses. They concluded that children substantially modelled themselves on their parents and that aggression in childhood is not an innate response; rather it is a specific response to environmental conditions mediated through early family experience. Bandura et al. (1963) showed that, in the absence of frustration, children will imitate an aggressive and rewarded model, but not imitate a similarly aggressive but punished model. Lovaas (1961) and Walters et al. (1962) likewise found that children exposed to an aggressive model and not punished will show an increase in aggressive responses. This effect has also been demonstrated by Kuhn et al. (1967) who found that an aggressive model, and not a frustrating experience, determined children's aggressivity. In this experiment the children were promised some sweets, but only half of them were given sweets at the appointed time, the others were told that they would have to wait for their sweets. This form of frustrating experience did not produce the increase in the children's aggressive behaviour which exposure to an aggressive model did. Drabman and Thomas (1974 and 1974a) argue that exposure to film violence increases children's tolerance of everyday aggression.

The findings that aggression can be a learnt response are not confined to studies involving young children. Hartmann (1969) has shown that adolescents can show an increase in aggression after watching an aggressive film. Berkowitz and Geen (1966) and Wilkins *et al.* (1974) found the same effect with nonfrustrated adult subjects. Zillman (1971) and Doob and Kirshenbaum (1973) showed that watching aggressive films could raise the arousal level of nonfrustrated subjects. Berkowitz (1970) also found an increase in aggressive reactions among nonfrustrated women students who had listened to a tape-recording of aggressive humour. Although it cannot be conclusively shown that the increase in aggression in these situations is a learning or an imitative process, there have been other studies where aggressive responses have been explicitly taught in the laboratory situation in the absence of any frustrations. For instance, in experiments by Loew (1967) and Geen and Pigg (1970) subjects were conditioned to act aggressively in response to certain stimuli. Reinforcement for shocking a confederate in these experiments increased the likelihood of subjects later in the procedure administering electric shocks.

The importance of such studies for the frustration-aggression hypothesis is that they demonstrate the implausibility of postulating that frustration is a necessary condition for the occurrence of aggression. If aggressive behaviour has an instrumental and utilitarian value under certain circumstances (Buss, 1961 and 1966) then there is every reason to suppose that (a) aggressive behaviour will be employed purposefully to achieve particular goals, and (b) will be taught to children as part of the general socialisation process in which they learn how to attain certain socially prescribed goals. Aggression was defined by the Yale psychologists as "an act whose goal response is injury to an organism (or organism-surrogate)" (Dollard *et al.*, 1939, p. 11), and there is no *a priori* reason why such an act should inevitably follow from a frustration. This point will be made again later in this chapter when the social implications of the frustration-aggression hypothesis are discussed. The general argument will be that, when large-scale aggression is considered, social variables, including the socially sanctioned use of violence, are of more importance than individually endured frustrations.

For the moment however, the general survey of frustration-aggression theories can be continued. Although the original theory was attacked by the social learning theorists, frustration-aggression research received nevertheless a pronounced impetus from Berkowitz's reformulations of the original theory, (see Berkowitz, 1962 and 1965). In this reformulation, Berkowitz takes note of some of the difficulties involved in asserting that frustration is a necessary condition for the occurrence of aggression. Instead of postulating a one-to-one relationship between frustration and aggression, Berkowitz acknowledges the role of external mediating factors. In the modified version of the theory, frustration (or the interference with an expected goal attainment) is still held to create an aroused or angered state. Whether or not this state produces aggression depends on the existence of appropriate situational (external) ones. Without such cues aggression will not ensue. Implied in this reformulation is a modification of the Freudian assumption; according to Berkowitz the aroused state, which corresponds to the instigation to aggress in the original formulation, must coincide with certain external properties for there to be any aggression. Presumably in the prolonged absence of these external conditions, the arousal or anger subsides, and is not automatically displaced or sublimated.

The many experiments, which Berkowitz and his colleagues have conducted to demonstrate the importance of situational cues for the frustration aggression relationship, will be discussed below. At the moment the implications of this revised theory can be briefly mentioned. The idea that aggression as a response to frustration is the product of an interaction between the organism's internal state and the external environment means the abandonment of any simple theory of scapegoating. Outgroup stereotypes and attitudes cannot solely be considered in terms of the psychology of the ingroup. The energy model pure and simple, which was implicit in Freud's theory of intergroup relations, cannot be applied—it is insufficient in Berkowitz's view to postulate that tensions bubble up within a person and/ or group and then are displaced as a matter of course onto some outgroup or other person. The particular features of this outgroup, or other person, need to be taken into account in order to explain (a) why a particular outgroup, rather than any other, is selected as an object for displaced hostility and (b) what are the circumstances under which scapegoating will and will not take place. Berkowitz (1962) in his discussion of these problems stipulates that any theory of scapegoating must take into account features and characteristics of the outgroup. In particular he stresses the visibility, the strangeness and prior estimation of any potential target group.

More recently Berkowitz has somewhat revised his description of the role of external conditions in determining the relationship between frustration and aggression (Berkowitz 1969). In this newer formulation Berkowitz has returned some way to the original ideas of Dollard *et al.* and he accords the role of internal emotional states more importance than he had done hitherto. He argues that the emotional state of the organism can be strong enough to produce an aggressive response even in the absence of the relevant situational cues; in other words, the occurrence of aggressive behaviour following frustration is not necessarily dependent upon certain hypothesised stimulus qualities in the environment. In this regard, the experiment conducted by Geen and O'Neal (1969) showed that it was possible to produce an increase in aggressive behaviour by increasing the emotional arousal of the subject through exposing him to white noise. Thus it was not frustrations as such that produced the increase in aggression, but emotional arousal. In stressing the importance of internal emotional arousal, Berkowitz (1969) is returning to a more motivational approach.

It is unclear, however, how this modification of Berkowitz's theoretical standpoint affects his views on outgroup scapegoating and the displacement of hostility. It would seem that situations in which Berkowitz considers situational cues to be comparatively unimportant are those where the emotional arousal is at an extremely high pitch. It might therefore be thought implausible to attribute such peaks of arousal to large-scale intergroup situations. To do so would be to revert to some of the crudities of Le Bon-type psychology; some criticisms of this sort of approach have already been offered in the discussion of Freud's group psychology, and in the course of the present chapter further arguments will be advanced against the idea of considering social movements as being due to the actions of highly emotional and irrational individuals. But until now Berkowitz has not related this particular theoretical modification to his wider views on social disturbances. In fact in his most recent theoretical statement

Berkowitz (1974) has returned to his earlier positions (1962 and 1965a). He does not develop the motivational ideas suggested by Berkowitz (1969); instead he concentrates upon situational cues as determinants of "impulsive" aggression. He emphasises the ways in which neutral stimuli can become associated with aggression and thereby act as facilitators for further aggression from angered subjects. Consequently Berkowitz (1974) is essentially developing in greater detail, and citing more experimental evidence for the basic theoretical notions he has previously advanced. In these the motivational variables are given less importance than the situational cues as determinants of impulsive aggression.

It is clear that Berkowitz's approach is essentially a non-cognitive one. Whether the emphasis is upon the internal motivational state of the individual, or upon the stimulus connections in the environment, it is not the individual's cognitive appraisal of the situation which forms Berkowitz's main object of study. Part of the argument of the present chapter will be that cognitive variables are crucial to the understanding of the frustration-aggression relationship; this is especially the case if wider social ramifications are to be drawn from the research into frustration and aggression. For the present it is sufficient to note the theoretical opposition between a predominantly motivational approach, based upon individual arousal, and a more cognitive-social approach, which emphasises the importance of socially-mediated cognitive meanings. It should be pointed out in passing that the Geen and O'Neal (1969) study has not shown unequivocally that emotional arousal *per se* can lead to a greater probability of aggression. The arousal produced by white noise would seem to be *prima facie* most unpleasant, and analogous in this respect to the negative feelings (or frustrations) produced by direct attack or insult. Certainly the subjects might well be ill-disposed towards the experimenters for subjecting them to such unpleasantness. Thus emotional arousal may not have been adequately separated from situationally-produced frustrations in this experimental design. In this respect, studies investigating the effects of a more pleasant form of arousal (sexual) upon aggressive behaviour have produced conflicting results: no clear trend has emerged as to whether sexual arousal inhibits or enhances aggressive responses (cf, for instance, Zillman, 1971; Meyer, 1972a; La Torre, 1973; Baron and Bell, 1973; Baron, 1974). It cannot therefore be said that there is clear and unambiguous evidence that internal arousal, whatever its nature, is correlated with aggressive behaviour. It is only by examining the experimental studies themselves that a clearer picture can emerge of the role of motivational states, learnt associations and social-cognitive variables in the frustration-aggression relationship.

Experiments on frustration and aggression

The first type of experimental findings to be discussed are those investigating the phenomenon of aggression against frustrator. The frustration-aggression hypothesis predicted that aggression would be directed against a frustrator so long as there were no inhibitions against such aggression. One of the simplest forms of frustration is a direct attack by someone else; one can say that an attack constitutes an interference with whatever "ongoing goal-seeking activity" the subject happens to be engaged in. There have been, therefore, a number of experiments conducted by frustration-aggression researchers investigating aggressive responses to direct attack. Primarily these experiments have tended to show that subjects will generally aggress against their attackers—although there have been notable exceptions to this.

Berkowitz (1966) showed that subjects, who had received electric shocks, will then in turn shock their aggressor, and Berkowitz and Le Page (1967) found that they would do this in proportion to the number of shocks they had received. For instance, subjects who had received one shock aggressed less than subjects who had received seven shocks. Gentry (1970), found that insulted subjects will aggress against their insultor, and Hanratty *et al.* (1972) found a similar response with young children. Many more studies could be cited which show that subjects will react aggressively to attack or insult (for instance Taylor and Epstein, 1967; Shuntich and Taylor, 1972; O'Leary and Dengerink, 1973). However, it scarcely seems to be a particularly interesting finding that retaliation can be demonstrated experimentally. Of more interest are those situations which had failed to find such an effect. The general emphasis in psychological research to find positive results should not hide the importance of negative results (Smart, 1964)—especially where a rather obvious effect is concerned.

Epstein and Taylor (1967) and Greenwell and Dengerink (1973) have shown that it is not the actual attack that is crucial for eliciting an aggressive response. Rather it is the subject's perception of the other's intention to attack. Support for this notion comes from an interesting experiment by Schuck and Pisor (1974). They found no difference in aggressive responses between subjects who were actually shocked by a confederate and subjects who were placed in exactly the same experimental condition, except that the shock apparatus was not wired up. These subjects were told that they were acting as control subjects and so would not in fact receive the shocks administered by the confederate. Schuck and Pisor interpret their negative results in terms of the "demand characteristics" of the experiment; a simpler explanation would be that the subjects in both conditions were responding to the deliberate intention of the confederate to administer shocks rather than to the shocks themselves. Thus it would appear that it is not the frustration as such that is the prime determinant of aggression in such situations, but the perceived intention to frustrate. This evidence suggests than an accidental attack may in itself be frustrating to the subject, but will not produce an aggressive reaction, whereas the intention to attack is more likely to elicit an aggressive response. Negative results were also found by Taylor and Epstein (1967), when they discovered that males were unlikely to counter-aggress against female attackers. Even more to the point are Lange's (1971) findings— not only do these show no evidence for aggressive retaliation at all, they even suggest that a direct attack can diminish aggression. Lange's study contains a number of findings which contradict results from other frustration-aggression studies. It will therefore be discussed in some detail later in this section.

Theoretically, some of the more interesting findings from the frustration-aggression research concern questions relating to the displacement of aggression, catharsis, facilitating cues, and the effects of differing sorts of frustrations. From the point of view of intergroup relations, the question of displacement is one of the more important issues arising from this line of research—the mechanism of displacement provides the psychological basis for theories of outgroup scapegoating and irrational outgroup prejudice. Therefore the experimental research relating to the displacement of aggression will be discussed in some detail. An attempt will be made to discuss displacement as a variable on its own; however, a considerable number of experiments have suggested that certain complicated interactions between variables determine the subsequent amount of aggression, (e.g. Berkowitz and Geen, 1966 and 1967; Berkowitz and Le Page, 1967; Geen and Berkowitz, 1967; Meyer, 1972a). Because of this empirical interaction, there will inevitably be some overlap in the following discussion, although an effort will be made to present the issues separately.

In order to simplify matters a distinction will be made between frustrators and non-frustrators as targets of aggression—the former will be referred to as "proper" targets, and the latter as "improper" targets. Such a distinction is valid in the context of experimental investigations, since proper and improper targets can be operationally defined. The distinction may be less clear-cut when considering natural groups; in such cases adherence to particular political and economic theories of social causation may determine how the distinction is made. One of the crucial differences between competing political ideologies is which group or class of persons they see as the natural enemies of the desired political order—these natural enemies will then be seen as proper targets for aggression, and any other type of enemy as a counterproductive diversion, or improper target. However, in the context of the experimental situations, the distinction can be drawn with the minimum of controversy. One can also differentiate between two different sorts of improper targets for aggression. This difference is not based on any characteristic of the targets themselves, but on the psychological processes by which they are selected as targets in the first place. A distinction can be made between the improper target who is the victim of displaced aggression and the target who is the victim of generalised aggression. These two psychological processes are not always sufficiently distinguished, but it is hoped to show that this distinction is important from a theoretical point of view.

This distinction between generalised and displaced aggression is clearly drawn in the work of Dollard *et al*. They predicted that an aggressive response can be generalised to targets sufficiently similar to the frustrator. This prediction was derived from stimulus response learning theory—according to this theory stimuli sufficiently similar to a particular stimulus which elicits a conditioned response will tend to elicit a similar response. In other words, aggression can be generalised to someone similar to the original frustrator, and the more similar he is to the proper target the more aggression will be shown towards him. An example might be a man who believes he is being frustrated by a particular group of persons, say policemen, generalising his aggression to traffic-wardens and then to all forms of uniformed authority. The theory predicts that he should show maximum aggression to policemen, and aggression towards other uniformed authority figures in direct proportion to their similarity with policemen (i.e. more to traffic wardens than to bus conductors).

This rather trivial example of hostility generalisation will serve to illustrate the difference between this process and displacement. The displacement of aggression only occurs if there is some inhibition against attacking the proper target or frustrator. If the man frustrated by the police feels unable, for one reason or another, to aggress against the police, then he may "take it out" on a traffic warden. In this case his aggression toward the traffic warden will be as great as his aggression towards the police would have been had there been no inhibition. This therefore constitutes the major difference between displaced and generalised aggression—in the former case the improper target receives the full force of the aggression caused by violence. In the case of generalised aggression the improper target receives less aggression than the proper target.

Some of the implications from the difference between generalised and displaced aggression have been drawn by Miller (1948) and Berkowitz (1962). One of these implications is that with displaced hostility, but not with generalised hostility, the strongest aggression is not directed against targets similar to the proper frustrator. The inhibiting mechanisms against attacking the proper target will be generalised to targets sufficiently similar to the proper target. These inhibiting mechanisms become progressively weaker with increasing dissimilarity to the original frustrator. Thus the inhibiting mechanism acts as a psychological counterpart to the generalisation of aggression. An example can be provided by considering the case of the classic "authoritarian": his aggression towards his father is inhibited, but this aggression does not find expression in figures similar to the subconsciously hated father. In fact, the authoritarian treats authority in general with the same exaggerated obsequiousness that he shows towards his father. The authoritarian's hostility is directed towards targets sufficiently dissimilar from his strong father image, i.e. onto defenceless minority groups.

This example shows that the two processes of displacement and generalisation can be interrelated (see Berkowitz, 1962). In the case of displacement, the selection of the target can be described as dependent on processes of stimulus generalisation. However, this should not conceal the fact that hostility displacement initially depends on an inhibition against attacking the proper target. Berkowitz's theory is that the displacement of hostility results in the selection of a target moderately dissimilar from the proper target through the process of generalisation. The possible interrelation of the two processes of displacement and generalisation should be born in mind when considering the empirical evidence for the existence of displaced aggression. The findings from a few studies which have failed to produce experimental scapegoating should not be taken as having disproved the frustration-aggression hypothesis. Nor should the existence of confirmatory evidence be taken as proving the hypothesis.

One of the first experiments investigating scapegoating was also one of the few experiments which have attempted to investigate the dis placement of aggression onto social groups (Miller and Bugelski, 1948). This experiment was conducted in a boys' summer camp; the boys had been promised a night out in town, but they had to do a number of boring tasks beforehand. It was arranged that these tasks would take longer than they should; midway through doing them the boys were told that their visit to the town would unfortunately have to be cancelled. It was found that after being told this the boys tended to rate Mexicans and Japanese more unfavourably on rating-scales than they had done previously. In other words, the frustration the boys had suffered by not being allowed into town seems to have provoked stronger negative outgroup attitudes. This semi-naturalistic experimental situation seems to have created an instance of scapegoating and hostility displacement.

Nevertheless a word of caution should be sounded in interpreting the results of the experiment: the increase in negative outgroup attitudes could have been predominantly produced either by displacement or by generalisation. If the former were the psychological process at work, then the boys might have felt themselves unable to express hostility towards the camp authorities, who they accepted as legitimate but frustrating authorities. In this case they might have displaced their inhibited aggression onto other groups, including the Mexicans and Japanese. Alternatively, the boys might have been seething with anger against the camp authorities, and this anger might have been generalised to all adults, including hypothetical Mexicans and Japanese. Of course, it is quite possible that the results may have been the product of both processes. Unfortunately Miller and Bugelski offer no way of discovering the relative strengths of both processes.

Given that the direction of aggression onto improper targets is not theoretically a simple psychological process, it is not surprising that a number of contradictory results have been found in experiments investigating scapegoating. For instance, Stagner and Congdon (1955) failed to find any aggression towards improper targets; Lindzey (1950) and Weatherley (1961) found the effect only with high authoritarian subjects. On the other hand, Cowen *et al.* (1959) were able to show frustration increasing negative outgroup attitudes as had been the case in the Miller and Bugelski (1948) study. In more recent years, the phenomenon of scapegoating has been extensively investigated by Berkowitz and his associates. In Berkowitz's research, interpersonal scapegoating has been the focus of attention rather than the scapegoating of innocent minority groups. However, as was explained earlier, Berkowitz clearly sees his research to be relevant to a social psychology of group relations.

Two early experiments by Berkowitz and Holmes (1959 and 1960) found significant evidence for aggression against improper targets. In these experiments subjects worked together with a partner, who was in fact a confederate of the experimenter. As a preliminary experimental manipulation, subjects were induced either to like or dislike their "partner". The subjects were then insulted by the experimenter. In the 1959 study the subjects were found to rate the partner more unfavourably after the experimenter's insult, and in the 1960 study they administered more electric shocks to the partner after insult. Berkowitz and Holmes interpreted this increased hostility as generalised hostility—in this they were almost certainly correct, since the subjects also expressed hostility towards the genuine frustrator, the experimenter. Thus there did not seem to be the inhibition necessary for the phenomenon of displacement to take place. Berkowitz and Green (1962) conducted a modification of this basic design; there was also a neutral, as well as a liked and disliked partner. They found that hostility was generalised to the neutral partner as well as to the disliked one.

There have been other experiments which have provided evidence for aggression against an improper target following frustration. Turner and Berkowitz (1972) found subjects to be more hostile to the experimenter after being insulted by a "partner"; similar results were found by Geen and Berkowitz (1967) where subjects were punished for acts of the experimenters. Hanratty *et al.* (1972) found that frustrated children attacked a non-frustrator as much as they attacked their frustrator. This last finding was in accord with the possibility of hostility displacement, rather than generalisation, since the amount of hostility was not diminished by attacking an improper target rather than a proper one. However, the experimental situation was not specifically designed to separate hostility displacement from generalisation, and so firm conclusions cannot be drawn on this issue. Holmes (1972) has also shown that subjects will aggress against a non-frustrator. In this experiment the subjects were "kept waiting" by a "partner" who, depending on experimental condition, either showed up eventually or was replaced by an innocent bystander. The subjects were then allowed to shock the partner; the results showed that the subjects who had been kept waiting shocked the partner more than subjects who had not been kept waiting. Also, there was no difference between the amounts of shocks given to the "innocent bystander" as against the "late partner". This result does suggest that the aggression could have been caused by displacement rather than generalisation: the subjects in the "innocent bystander" condition were unable to aggress against the real frustrator, because he never showed up. Thus there was an enforced inhibition in the situation preventing aggression against the proper target.

An experiment by Fenigstein and Buss (1974) seems to support Holmes's findings on the displacement of aggression. This study represents an attempt to distinguish empirically between displaced and generalised aggression. The subjects were insulted by an experimental stooge; they then had the opportunity of administering shocks to one of two other "subjects" in what was ostensibly a learning task. The subjects had to choose which of the two confederates to shock. One of the subjects was a friend of the original frustrator and the other was unconnected with the frustrator. It was arranged that in one of the experimental conditions the subjects had to choose between giving low shocks to the "friend" or high shocks to the unconnected party. In another experimental condition the "friend" could receive the high shocks and the unconnected subject the low shocks. By comparing the amounts of shock given in these two conditions Fenigstein and Buss aimed to test whether the subjects would generalise part of their anger to the friend, or displace it all on the innocent target. They claim that their results show that the subjects chose to displace a greater amount of aggression in preference to generalising a smaller amount. They state that "the target of displaced aggression was determined mainly by the opportunity to aggress more intensely" (pp. 311–312). Their results show a difference in the number of shocks given to the friend depending on experimental condition. The subjects shocked him less when they could only give him a few shocks. Although these results do suggest that motivational factors can be important in such experimental situations, nevertheless they are insufficient to support their general conclusion that displacement of affect is the main determinant of aggression. The crucial condition for examining this proposition would seem to be the one in which the subjects are faced with the dilemma whether to give low shocks to the "friend" or high shocks to the unassociated stooge. If affect were the main determinant one might expect that they would overwhelmingly choose to give the high shock. Fenigstein and Buss present no separate analysis of this data, but the data does not suggest any significant preference for the high shocks.

Another way of distinguishing between generalised and displaced hostility is in terms of catharsis. According to the frustration-aggression theory, generalised hostility should have a lower cathartic value than displaced hostility, since psychologically speaking it has not replaced aggression against the proper target. Although the notion of catharsis is a central one to the frustration-aggression hypothesis (see, for instance, the quotation above from Dollard et al., pp. 52–3), there has been surprisingly little of the frustration-aggression research devoted to it recently. As far as can be told, there have been only two studies which compared the cathartic value of aggression against proper and improper targets. The first was an experiment conducted by Hokanson et al. (1963) which used the physiological measure of blood pressure as an indication of emotional arousal, (this had previously been found to be a good indicator of the cathartic value of aggression; see Hokanson and Burgess (1962) and Hokanson and Shelter (1962)). Hokanson et al. (1963) measured the emotional arousal of subjects, who had been insulted by the experimenter, following aggression against (a) the experimenter, (b) the experimenter's assistant, and (c) a fellow subject. Catharsis, following aggression, was strongest for those who could aggress against their frustrator (the experimenter) and weakest after they aggressed against a fellow subject. These results then give credence to the notion that, in this situation, aggression against the improper targets was not true displaced aggression. However, an experiment by Konecni and Doob (1972) produced different results. The measure of catharsis in this study was a behavioural one—the amount of further aggression likely to be shown after administering a fixed amount of electric shocks to another. Subjects were annoyed by a "confederate", and had to shock either that confederate or another subject, depending on condition, a fixed number of times. Following this, the subjects had the opportunity to shock the annoying confederate as much as they wished. The intermediate fixed amount of shocks had been found to diminish the likelihood of further aggression (see Doob and Wood 1972), and in this study the intermediate aggression had as much cathartic effect when it was directed against the improper target as against the proper target. This result is, of course, consonant with the idea that the aggression against the improper target was displaced aggression. These two studies (Hokanson *et al.* 1963 and Konecni and Doob, 1972) reveal by their contradictory results, that much is still to be discovered between generalised and displaced aggression and the cathartic effects of both. Because of the theoretical importance of the notions of displacement and catharsis, it is unfortunate that these two topics, and their interrelations have been comparatively ignored, and not subjected to systematic investigation, (for a review of studies into catharsis, and their relation to frustration-aggression research generally, see Hokanson, 1970. For recent studies showing no behavioural evidence of catharsis, see Goldstein *et al.* 1975, and Manning and Taylor, 1975).

So far studies which have demonstrated aggression against an improper target have been discussed. To counteract these experiments, there are other studies which have failed to demonstrate any "improper" aggression. For instance, in the study by Kuhn *et al.* (1967), young children did not show aggression against a non-frustrator. Berkowitz (1965) reported an experimental condition with no improper aggression: in this condition there were two experimenters— one who angered the subjects and one who did not. There was no "carry over" of aggression directed towards the hostile aggressor onto the neutral experimenter. In a study by Berkowitz and Knurek (1969) it was found that subjects rated their fellow subjects more *favourably* after being insulted by the experimenter. The authors refer to a "judgemental contrast-effect", by which subjects favourably contrasted their fellow subjects with the experimenter. In this case, therefore, there was the reverse of any hostility displacement or generalisation.

Finally, there is the curious set of experimental results reported by Lange (1971). These results dispel any lingering hope of finding a simple relation between frustration and aggression. Lange failed to find that frustration in general increased aggressiveness—in fact, his results point to the opposite conclusion: namely, that frustration can diminish aggression. This was the conclusion from two experiments conducted on schoolboys, aged about 13 years. In the first experiment the subjects had to take part with an adult who was ostensibly a fellow subject. In the "frustration conditions" this confederate abused the young subjects by saying that "it was a waste of money to use such young, and therefore stupid, subjects for an investigation like this". There was a neutral condition in which the confederate said nothing. Afterwards, all subjects had the opportunity to deliver noxious stimuli to the confederate. The results showed that the insulted subjects delivered significantly *less* noxious stimuli than the non-insulted subjects. In a second experiment with young boys, reported by Lange (1971) some of the insulted subjects had the opportunity to administer noxious stimuli to a neutral confederate. It was found that subjects aggressed against the improper target *more* than they did against the proper target. Not only this, all the insulted subjects aggressed less than the non-insulted ones in the control condition. These results suggest that frustration, far from creating an instigation to aggress, created in this situation an inhibition to aggress. Furthermore, it seems that this inhibition was generalised to improper targets. These results contradict practically every theoretical position concerning the frustration-aggression hypothesis.

This brief review of some of the studies investigating aggression against improper targets has revealed no basic uniform trend. It cannot be said that aggression is or is not consistently directed against non-frustrators. Berkowitz's theory is that this must depend on certain features of the target. However, it has been argued that progress on this score is unlikely unless systematic attempts are made to distinguish between hostility displacement and generalisation. This is especially important since, according to frustration-aggression theory, the two processes work in different directions according to the nature of the "improper" target and its similarity to the proper target. If this complicates what was originally quite a simple hypothesis, then a point will now be made that should complicate it still further. It is not just the similarity between the proper and improper target that is crucial, but the social relations between the three main actors in the situation, the frustrated subject, the proper and the improper targets. If displacement is to take place then there has to be some sort of inhibition against attacking the proper target. The form and nature of this inhibition has been generally neglected in frustration-aggression research; it is the present argument that this inhibition not only prevents aggression against the proper target, but can also influence the choice of improper target. Furthermore the inhibition can only be understood in terms of the social relations and normative influences which bind together the social relations between the frustrator and the frustrated. It is not enough just to look at the overall consequences of the inhibitions—its causes need examination, as well as its meaning for the inhibited subject.

The importance of social relations can be illustrated by considering Lange's (1971) findings. In contrast to the series of experiments conducted by Berkowitz and his associates, Lange found that frustration decreased aggression. It is therefore important to know in what way Berkowitz's experiments differed from Lange's. The most obvious difference is that Berkowitz's experiments were conducted on American subjects whereas Lange's participants were Dutch. There seems to be no *a priori* reason why this should make a difference; but if it did, it would of course dispel the idea that the relationship between frustration and aggression was a basic psychological relationship which existed independently of values and systems of cognitive beliefs. A more interesting difference between the two sets of experiments than that of nationality, relates to the age of the subjects. In Berkowitz's experiments, students were used as subjects, while in Lange's study schoolboys were used. These schoolboys were insulted by an adult, and they possibly accepted the authority of the adult who said that they were "too young" to take part in the experiment. The authority would in this case be considered as a legitimate or powerful one, and thus not one to be attacked. If this were the case then one would expect an inhibition of aggression, and also that this inhibition would be generalised to all other adult "authority" figures in the experimental situation.

Such a *post hoc* explanation would explain Lange's results. It would also explain why he obtained slightly different results in the two experiments in which he did not use schoolboys as subjects. When he used older subjects, who would be less likely to kotow to adult authority, no inhibition of aggression was found. The importance of this *post hoc* explanation from a theoretical point of view is that it stresses the social relation between the frustrator and frustrated. The reason for any inhibition is based on the social context and perceptions of the participants. From this one can hypothesise that the target for displaced hostility will be affected by this social relationship between frustrator and victim. For instance, it might be predicted that if Lange had provided even younger boys as improper targets, instead of adults, his schoolboys might then have shown displaced aggression. For the social relationship of the subjects to the adult might have found its mirror-image reverse in the relationship of subjects to younger boys, several years their junior. A parallel then would have been created with the authoritarian person who inhibits all aggression towards those he sees as superior to himself, and directs his hostility against inferiors. On this account Berkowitz's notion that there must be some dissimilarity between proper and improper target for displacement to occur would be correct, but only as far as it goes. This dissimilarity would need to be specific and to be related to the reasons for the original inhibition. One can state that any such inhibition does not occur in a social vacuum—it may be dependent on specific social norms, upon defined social relationships, or an individual's ability or inability to relate to others, etc. All of these possible reasons relate to various sorts of social relationship which link the frustrator and his victim.

The above explanation of Lange's findings is of course without direct empirical validation. There are some indications from other frustration-aggression studies which tend to give it credence. Pastore (1952) and Rothaus and Worchel (1960) showed that people are more tolerant of justified frustrations; although such an effect was not found in one of the conditions of the Thompson and Kolstoe study (1974). In an experiment by Burnstein and Worchel (1962) subjects in a discussion group with a "deaf" confederate, who because of his infirmity kept interrupting the proceedings, tended to show greater hostility towards the experimenter than towards the deaf confederate. This was in contrast to control subjects, whose discussion was continually interrupted by a confederate without any infirmity. In this case one can say that certain norms relating to the treatment of handicapped persons influenced the expression of aggression—also one might wonder whether any displacement would occur if the experimenter were similarly deaf. A study by Cohen (1955) points directly to the relevance of the frustrator's status in determining aggressive reactions. His results suggested that the aggressive response could be affected by an interaction between the status of the frustrator and the arbitrariness of the frustrator. Ellis *et al.* (1971) found that status could affect aggression, when they found that there was less aggression against an armed policeman as a target than against a student. This result was in contradiction to the Berkowitz and Le Page (1967) conclusion that weapons *per se* increased the aggressiveness of angered subjects, (see also Buss *et al.* 1972, for a further failure to show weapons as facilitator to aggressiveness). An effect for status was also reported by Doob and Gross (1968) who found in an observational study that more horn-honking was directed at low-status cars than at high-status cars. However, this finding was not replicated by Chase and Mills (1973). Although no clear pattern is discernable in these results, there is nevertheless an indication that social status does under certain circumstances interact with the hypothesised "normal" frustration-aggression relationship. This is, of course, entirely reasonable if the concept of "inhibition" is held to be a crucial one for frustration-aggression theory; thus the basis of inhibition might, under many conditions, be sought in the social relations between the frustrator and the frustrated.

The importance of social relations within the experimental situation can be further illustrated by the Berkowitz and Knurek (1969) study. These experimenters found that a negative evaluation of the experimenter could be increased by interaction between the subjects, in this way the "unpleasantness" of the experimenter could be contrasted with the "pleasantness" of the fellow subjects. Thus the interacting subjects may well have been constituting some sort of rudimentary ingroup, whose cohesiveness is strengthened in the face of an external aggressor, (cf. Pepitone and Kleiner, 1957). If this was the case, then it might help to explain why, in the Geen and Berkowitz (1967) study, hostility toward the experimenter was also generalised to other subjects; in this case there was no inter-subject interaction, and thus no possibility of building incipient ingroup ties. This would also suggest that the phenomenon of generalisation is affected by social relations. It is, of course, quite legitimate to attempt to describe such relations in terms of stimulus similarity and dissimilarity, (e.g. Berkowitz 1962); however, it does seem to be more reasonable to recognise and evaluate the complexities of such relationships before endeavouring to translate them into the rather arid language of stimulus-

response theory; this is so especially since such translations often involve misconceptions (see Harré and Secord, 1972), and since the
social variables in the frustration-aggression relationship have not yet
been fully identified.

The original formulation of the frustration-aggression hypothesis
was couched in the language of stimulus-response learning theory. Just
as the subsequent history of the frustration-aggression research can be
seen as a continued qualification of the bold early statements of Dollard *et al.*, so can it also be seen in terms of a drift away from the simple
stimulus-response schema. Cognitive elements, which have no place in
a strict behaviourist language, have consistently crept into the frustration-aggression framework; even Berkowitz, who has attempted to
retain a great deal of the original stimulus-response orientation in his
theories, has been forced to introduce substantial cognitive elements
into his descriptions. For instance, his definition of "frustration"
differs from that of Dollard *et al.* in that he recognises the difficulty of
defining the term purely and simply in relation to goal responses.
Instead, Berkowitz offers a definition of "frustration" based on "expected" goal attainments, thus introducing a cognitive element where
none existed previously (Berkowitz 1962; see also Berkowitz, 1969, for
a discussion on the necessity of agreeing upon a definition of frustration in order to clarify contradictory experimental results).

This shift away from behaviourist concepts is not due just to the
particular orientations of the researchers themselves; the experimental
results have demonstrated the importance of cognitive variables
which mediate between frustration and aggression. Studies which
show that crucial variables include the *intention* to frustrate, the
arbitrariness of frustration etc. have already been mentioned. It has
also been argued that the perceived social relations between the frustrator and frustrated are crucial to the understanding of the phenomenon of displacement. The perceptions and intentions of the actors
involved are of critical importance. A model which only posits a
stimulus, a response and an intervening aroused state, is too simplistic.
Essentially the frustration-aggression experimental paradigm is an
interpersonal situation which can be affected by the full gamut of
variables pertaining to social interaction.

The importance of cognitive variables does not just relate to
frustration-aggression research—it applies to research upon human
aggression generally. Two studies illustrate the cognitive element in

aggressive arousal (Berkowitz, Lepinsk and Angulo, 1969, and Geen and Pigg, 1973). Both these studies found that subjects who had been told that they were aggressively aroused according to certain electronic measurements, aggressed more than subjects who were not so informed. Geen and Pigg (1973) also told some subjects that they had been sexually aroused, and these subjects showed a preference for seeking sexual stimuli, as opposed to the subjects who believed that they were aggressively aroused.

The state of arousal, which according to frustration-aggression theory exists between the two main variables, is itself subject to cognitive control. It is not physiological arousal *per se* that is important, but the perception and/or interpretation of any such "arousal"; this statement is consistent with Schachter's (1964) theory of the cognitive control of emotion. Similarly the evidence from studies investigating the importance of cues facilitating aggressive responses suggests that the important variable is not so much the presence or absence of such cues; it is the way the cues are interpreted by the subjects (Berkowitz and Alioto, 1973; Geen and Rakosky, 1973; Geen, Stonner and Kelley, 1974; Leyens and Picus 1973). The theoretical importance of such cognitive variables will become clearer, when the role of mass frustration is assessed with respect to large-scale social disorder.

Before this is done, another aspect of the cognitive control of aggression must be mentioned. Many of the recent experiments testing the frustration-aggression hypothesis have involved subjects engaging in actual acts of aggression, normally the administration of electric shocks to an experimental "partner". This happens in many of the experiments conducted by Berkowitz and his co-workers. In these studies different sorts of frustration, modelling stimuli, victims, etc., have been used in order to discover whether they noticeably increase the subjects' level of aggression. The assumption behind these experiments is that subjects will aggress anyway in the absence of these variables. This assumption is quite reasonable since it is regularly verified by the results of experimental control conditions; in such conditions, the variables which theoretically are supposed to elicit aggressive responses, are absent; yet control subjects will still administer a certain level of shocks. Buss (1963) makes the point that the aggression shown by frustrated subjects represents only a minimal increase when compared to the baseline aggression shown by non-frustrated subjects. Thus one can say that normal non-frustrated subjects are willing to commit acts of aggression in the experimental situation when required to do so by the experimenters. Similarly there have been several experiments which have demonstrated increases in aggression, if the aggressive response has instrumental value for the subjects (e.g. Buss, 1966; Lange and Van de Nes, 1973; Thompson and Kolstoe, 1974). The experimental subjects seem to be quite willing to use aggression as a means to obtain an end without being angry in any way. These experiments have revealed instrumentality to be a more potent determinant of aggression than frustrations. In this sense the "rational" use of aggression seems to be more predominant than its "irrational" use.

When considering experimental aggression which is not the product of frustration, the studies by Milgram (1963, 1965 and 1974) should be noted. Milgram used an experimental situation very similar to the paradigms used in countless frustration-aggression experiments— similar, that is, except for one crucial aspect. As in many other studies, Milgram's subjects were required to "teach" another "subject" by administering electric shocks for every error made by the learner. Where Milgram's situation is unique, is that these shocks were not ostensibly of a low voltage. His experiments were designed to investigate what were the highest levels of shock subjects would be prepared to administer. He found that a large number of subjects were willing to administer a 450-volt "danger-level" shock, when told to do so by the experimenters. Thus, not only was very extreme aggression shown by the subjects in the absence of frustration, but also these studies displayed dramatically the importance of social influence (from experimenter to subject) as a determinant of aggressive responses. These studies have shown how the variable of social influence has produced, experimentally at least, far greater amounts of aggression than experimental manipulations of frustration.[1]

The Milgram experiments were extremely stressful for the majority of the subjects. He reports that most of the subjects entertained grave doubts about obeying the experimenter, and also that they resolved their moral dilemmas by disclaiming personal responsibility for their actions (Milgram 1974). Instead they placed responsibility onto the

1. A recent replication of the Milgram experimental paradigm by Kilham and Mann (1974) has shown the importance of social communication in this situation. They found that subjects were prepared to order others to administer higher levels of shock than subjects who actually had to administer the shocks.

experimenter, who in fact explicitly accepted it (see for instance Mixon's (1972) detailed discussions of the Milgram experiments). It is not inconceivable that even in the less extreme "normal" frustration-aggression paradigm, subjects may have certain qualms about administering the electric shocks, and that any such qualms are resolved by attributing responsibility to the experimenter (see for instance discussions by Holmes 1972; Katz *et al.* 1973; Manning and Taylor, 1974, on the difficulty of studying guilt reactions in such situations). The possible effects of such social influence can be considered with respect to the one experimental study that has claimed to show the greatest support for a non-cognitive account of hostility-displacement. (Fenigstein and Buss, 1974). In this experiment as in most frustration-aggression experiments, the angered subject is explicitly offered by the experimenter a channel for displaying aggression.

In view of the possible demand-characteristics of the situation, (Page and Scheidt, 1971; Schuck and Pisor, 1974) it is possible that the subject interprets the experimenter's actions as suggesting—"go ahead, get it out of your system, I'm taking responsibility". If this is the case, then it would not be true to say that such an experimental situation had eliminated cognitive variables in order to investigate the "pure and uncontaminated" effects of motivational states. What seems to have been done instead is that a particular social situation is provided in which the subject feels free from normative sanction. Consequently he indulges in certain impulses, which otherwise might have been more restrained. The social context of the experimental situation might be one of the most crucial variables affecting the choices facing the subjects in the Fenigstein and Buss (1974) study. It could be that changes in this social context, whilst keeping the amount of frustration endured constant, could well lead to a reduction of aggression. In this respect, Scheier, Fenigstein and Buss (1974) and Carver (1974) found that the presence or absence of a mirror could affect the level of aggression shown by subjects; they hypothesise that the subjects become more self-aware when there is a mirror. Borden and Taylor (1973) found that subjects' aggressive behaviour could be increased or diminished by pressure from an audience. They conclude that "the typically observed relationship between attack and retaliation can be drastically modified by manipulations of the immediate social surroundings" (p. 360).

The general point is that the subject's hypothesised internal motivational state does not occur in a social vacuum, and that the social context as well as the subject's beliefs and interpretations all combine in determining his course of action. This suggests that it would be advisable to investigate the effects of responsibility (and other social influence variables), in the frustration-aggression situation with a view to discovering whether the social context affects the occurrence or non-occurrence of aggressive responses, as in fact it seems likely to. In conclusion, therefore, it can be said that the present discussion has pointed to the importance of social variables in understanding the frustration-aggression relationship as it affects individual behaviour in laboratory situations. It can be hypothesised that such social variables will become increasingly more important when group aggression, rather than individual aggression, is considered.

Frustration-aggression theory and social discontent

The basic two questions which will be considered in this section are: firstly, the extent to which frustration-aggression theory can be applied to a large-scale social phenomena; and secondly, what theoretical implications are involved in the translation of the theory from the individual to the social. In offering a partial answer to the first question, the present strategy will be to follow the arguments of those who have attempted to use frustration-aggression theory to explain social phenomena, in particular to explain riot behaviour and revolutions. As close an analogy as possible will be drawn between social and individual aggression, and at all stages parallels will be made between the experimental findings and the social phenomena. This will not be attempted because it is the present view that the laboratory findings and the frustration-aggression theory constitute a sound basis for understanding intergroup aggression. On the contrary it is hoped to show by this method of argument the limitations of this approach and to reveal important social variables neglected by the frustration-aggression theorists. It is also hoped to demonstrate some of the underlying normative presupposition involved in the straightforward applications of frustration-aggression theory to intergroup relations.

Any theory of group aggression must be incomplete if it does not deal with the social and cognitive factors which have been found to affect individual aggression. Frustration *per se* can explain all too little by not taking into account the cognitive meaning of that frustration for those who suffer it. Not to take account of the cognitive and social variables in a theory of group aggression would be to state that wars and revolutions are due to a coincidence of individual states of emotional arousal. Such an implication is contained in the intergroup theories of Dollard *et al.* (1939). These writers derive a theory of racial prejudice from the concept of displacement. However, the deficiencies of this approach can be illustrated by their account of the rise of Nazism in Germany. In *Frustration and Aggression* they refer to the frustrations and resentments that "almost every German experienced and resented . . . personally" (p. 153) after the treaty of Versailles. This frustration provoked an aggressive response which could not be directed against the powerful Allied victors; fifteen or so years later these hostile feelings were increased by the frustrations arising out of economic deprivations. The net result was the displacement of this hostility onto the Jews, who were "ideal victims for the aggression of the German people" (p. 155). This explanation is altogether too neat. Although social factors are touched upon, with the power of the allies and the relationship between the Jews and the German people, the prime cause of Nazism is still based on the individual hydraulic model of motivation. It is too fanciful to imagine that the Germans were kept in a state of increasing emotional arousal for fifteen years, and at the end of this time simultaneously millions happened to rid themselves of their tensions in an identical manner. What one surely wishes to know more about is the social causation of Nazism—not only about the relations between the perceived characteristics of the Jews and German discontent, but also how the Nazis were able to mobilise this discontent to form a powerful ideological movement. In other words, the purely psychological explanations of Nazism in terms of displacement are meaningless without taking into account their social context.

Dollard *et al.* not only put forward a theory of German anti-Semitism based on the concept of displacement, they also offered a general theory of intergroup relations. This theory is similar in most important respects to that of Freud. In *Frustration and Aggression* they argue that life in an organised society, by necessity, involves frustrations. Societies could not exist if they did not impose restrictions on their members. One of the most important processes of socialisation is when the child is taught to restrict his own inclinations and to accept interference from others. All in all, Dollard *et al.* argue that frustrations are an integral part of communal life. However, in order to preserve the social fabric there must be strict sanctions against the expression of aggression within the community. Social order would collapse if individuals met every frustrating experience with an aggressive response. For this reason, groups develop social pressures which ensure that this aggression is displaced, and in particular is displaced onto individuals outside the ingroup:

> Displacement of aggression to race groups or movie villains within a society is apparently not sufficient to produce a complete catharsis. The chronic burden of intra-group frustration is too great to make this possible. Instead out-groupers are, as it were, blamed for the frustrations which are actually incident to group life; and a host of aggressive responses are displaced to them. (Dollard *et al.*, 1939, p. 89.)

This theory of intergroup relations basically only differs from Freud's in that Dollard *et al.* do not specifically relate intragroup frustrations to the function of the leader; nor do they adhere to Freud's notion of the "narcissism of small differences". They state that the best target for displaced aggression should be as dissimilar to the ingroup as possible. No actual proof for this is given, and this general theory of intergroup relations only takes up a few pages in *Frustration and Aggression*. Thus many of the criticisms which were made previously of Freud's theory can be applied equally well to that of Dollard *et al.* Likewise too, there is the potential importance of the idea that ingroup structure can affect outgroup attitudes. Simply to posit that displacement is responsible does not resolve the problem; there is still the need to explain how such displacement is contained in within-group norms and how it operates in the social context. If a concept such as displacement, culled as it is from descriptions of individual psychological processes, is to be useful to an understanding of the social psychology of groups, then it must be properly integrated in a social analysis.

The criticisms of the theories of prejudice and intergroup relations proposed by Dollard *et al.* should not be taken as all-embracing; they do not imply that the concept of frustration is irrelevant to the study of intergroup behaviour. It is not that frustration is a negligible factor in mass social violence, but that a crude application of the concept is unsatisfactory to account for large-scale phenomena. Revolutions and wars do not occur because a large number of people coincidentally have similarly aroused emotional states—and because these people happen by chance to discharge their emotionality in similar directions.

The uniformity found in mass behaviour cannot be explained purely and simply in terms of a basic motivational relationship between frustration and aggression. Having said that, it would be absurd to go to the other extreme and to deny that frustrations, using the term in its loosest possible sense, have no part to play in intergroup dramas; quite clearly, social discontent is a potent factor in determining group conflicts. What therefore is needed is not some blanket confirmation or disconfirmation of the frustration-aggression hypothesis as it relates to intergroup phenomena; rather there is a need to relate frustration-aggression findings and concepts to the analysis of social discontent.

The most obvious way to do this is to equate the aroused emotional state, which frustration-aggression theory claims precedes acts of aggression, with the emotionality of crowd behaviour. Berkowitz (1972) does this in his analysis of black urban rioting in the United States during the 1960s. According to his arguments, the frustrations suffered by the blacks, together with the requisite situational cues, cause pent-up hostility to erupt. The implication of this argument, which is admitted by Berkowitz, is that the eruption of hostility in such circumstances is basically irrational. Thus Berkowitz refers to the Goranson and King (1971) findings that the timing of the riots was correlated with unusually hot weather, and he suggests that "unusual heat can be an irritant, fraying tempers" (Berkowitz, 1972, p. 81). This is not supported however by the experimental results of Baron (1972) who found that heat inhibited the aggressive response to frustration. Nevertheless it can be seen that the basic premise of Berkowitz's model is non-cognitive—human behaviour is accordingly guided by the accumulation and dispersal of emotional energy and irritations, rather than by the shared hopes and fears of men.

It will be argued here that the equation between the emotional "instigation to aggress" of frustration-aggression theory and the emotionality of riot behaviour is too simple. The equation neglects an important point about the structure of frustration-aggression theory— in the theory the "instigation to aggress" was posited as an intervening variable between cause (frustration) and effect (aggression). However, the emotional arousal of a rioting crowd should not be seen as such an intervening variable between cause and effect. On the contrary it should be seen as part of the effect, and as a necessary concomitant of the "aggression". It is possible to argue that the riot does not occur because its participants are emotionally aroused, but that they become emotionally aroused because they are rioting. This accords well with Fogelson's (1970) account of the feelings of jubilation experienced by the rioters. This jubilation sprang from the fact that they had taken over the streets and were offering a determined challenge to the existing order. The feelings of jubilation are incomprehensible if they are seen purely and simply as a precondition for action.

If emotional arousal is not to be seen as the crucial intervening variable between social frustration and social violence, then one might well ask what *can* act as the salient link between the two variables. The experimental laboratory studies provide a clue to this. It was argued that the findings suggest that the interpretation of arousal can be more important than the state of physiological arousal itself (e.g. Berkowitz *et al.* 1969; Geen and Pigg, 1973). Translated into social terms, this suggestion means that the interpretation of social discontent or deprivation is more important than the actual feelings of suffering; more important, that is, for the production of social violence as a response to social deprivation. In other words the crucial intervening variable which links the cause (social deprivation) with the effect (a riot or revolution) is the social interpretation of the deprivation. In particular, this fits in with one of the most common dicta about revolutions—that they occur not at the times of the greatest oppression, but when the lot of the underprivileged is improving. The "revolution of rising expectations" is a well-documented phenomenon (Davies, 1962) but its relation to frustration-aggression theory still needs to be outlined.

What is meant by "the social interpretation of social discontent" needs some amplification in order to explain its relevance as an intervening variable. It has been suggested that experimental aggression is dependent on social and cognitive variables. Similarly, revolutionary movements do not occur in a social vacuum where the crucial determinant would be a certain level of physiological arousal. They occur because the participants believe that certain social, economic or political ends are being denied them, and furthermore that they should rightfully possess such ends. The participants' belief systems and theories of social causation are of prime importance. In brief, the ideology of a revolutionary movement acts as its instigation to aggress. The importance of ideology in mass movements, rather than their diffuse emotionality, can be shown by reference to a few examples. Rudé (1964) in his detailed analyses of crowd behaviour in the

eighteenth and nineteenth centuries dispels the notion that the discontented crowd strikes out blindly and is driven to mass action by
irrational emotionality. He emphasises the role of ideology and ideological slogans which unify the crowd and give it definite social aims.
Its actions are directed by and large to these aims and do not lead to
diffuse acts of random and wanton violence. Instead, the aggression is
determined by the ideology. Also, cross-cultural comparisons have
shown the influence of cultural and political traditions on mass protest behaviour. If crowd behaviour were merely the product of asocial
states of emotional arousal, then one would not expect the development of different traditions and rituals of protest (Mann, 1972).
Studies of the comparative history of violent protest point to a similar
conclusion (e.g. Tilly, 1969).

A large number of studies which have been conducted in the aftermath of the black ghetto riots in America point to similar conclusions.
These riots cannot be properly understood if they are seen as mere
emotional outbursts, not dependent on the political beliefs of the
participants. Although the editor of the black radical magazine who
declared at the time that "every brother on a rooftop can quote Fanon"
was accused of exaggeration, there can be little doubt that the riots
were motivated by an ideology of discontent. For instance Marx (1967),
Tomlinson (1970) and Paige (1971) found that the rioters were more
politically aware and sophisticated than blacks who did not riot, (see
Caplan, 1970 for a review). The riots took place in areas of greater
political awareness (Abudu et al. 1972), and the rioters believed that
their actions would have beneficial political consequences (Hahn,
1969). Moreover, the disturbances resembled the historical movements analysed by Rudé (1964) in that the riots took definite forms:
the rioters concentrated upon actions which were related to specific
grievances. Geschwender (1973) has described the tactics underlying
black violence and Fogelson (1970) has outlined the social meaning
behind the acts of looting and burning which were common to all the
ghetto riots. The rioters did not attack and pillage without reason—
the looters believed that the merchandise they took was theirs by
right, as a repayment for years of economic exploitation. Similarly the
arson was selective—in the main it was confined to shops which had
charged excessive prices and white-owned businesses (see Fogelson,
1970). Thus the slogan "Burn, baby, burn!" was not a hysterical cry
for indiscriminate and unthinking arson; it was a crystallisation of an

ideology of discontent, every bit as much as the rallying cry of the Parisian crowds during the French revolution "Vive le Tiers Etat!" (Rudé, 1964).

A mass movement depends on some sort of social ideology to articulate and crystallise its discontent. If this ideology is revolutionary then it will provide the instigation to aggress, and similarly, without this ideology there will be no concerted mass action which challenges the existing order. Although the ideology is here seen as a precondition for the social movement, this is not to say that there will not be an interplay between the ideology and the events it produces. In fact almost certainly there will be such an interplay. In the course of the revolution or struggle the ideology will become more refined and clarified (see for instance Rule and Tilly's (1972) account of the emergence of "ideological groups" in the course of the 1830 French Revolution). Not only this, the ideology will itself produce and be the product of practical action. Even comparatively spontaneous group action cannot be understood without a back-drop of certain beliefs shared by the participants. Without an articulation of these beliefs mass action cannot be maintained, despite the individual feelings of frustration. An illustration of this is provided by Beynon's (1973) description of an unofficial wild-cat strike at a car factory. The strike occurred without prior organisation during one dinner-break. This action was outside the normal run of organised trades union activity, and has all the hallmarks of being an angry gesture rather than being a coherent social action:

> The symbolism of women, militancy, grades, humanity, dole, equality, and much more besides, were jumbled together with an antagonism and a defiant *no—fuck off*. They'd had enough and they didn't want to know any more. They wanted to do *something*. (Benyon, 1973, p. 170.)

This unofficial strike fits into the paradigm of the angry reaction to the frustrating situation. But just to say that is to miss out two factors central to the event. Firstly, even this spontaneous and defiant gesture needed some mutual agreement among the men that things generally had come to a bad pass. The action could not have taken place without this agreement, tacit at least, about the unfairness of the company and the ineffectiveness of their trades union leaders to deal with this unfairness. Moreover, when the men walked out of the factory, they held immediately a mass meeting in order to formulate the aims and structure of their protest. The fact that the meeting failed in this aim meant that the unofficial strike soon collapsed and it was not translated from a gesture into determined social action. In the absence of a strong binding ideological force, the wildcat strike appears as a simultaneous and angry response to frustration. But nevertheless, even in this case, one of the crucial elements was the interpretation by the men of what had been happening in the factory to their trades union representatives. Thus one can see the importance of the beliefs of the participants for mass social action. Feelings of frustration may seem to trigger-off an aggressive response, but for this response to have any social strength, it must be backed up by an ideology of action. In saying this and in emphasising the ideological context of social action, there is simultaneously an implication that the final straw that triggers-off a disturbance has in itself less importance than the conditions which precede it. The last straw may evoke an aggressive response, in the manner predicted by frustration-aggression theory, but this should not lead to the neglect of the context in which the action takes place. There is consequently an agreement in the present argument with those sociologists who maintain that the precipitating factors leading to a hostile outburst should be distinguished from the underlying structural conditions (e.g. Smelser, 1963 and 1972; Lieberson and Silverman, 1965; Spilerman, 1971; Morgan and Clark, 1973).

So far it has been suggested that if a social movement of protest is to be strong and effective, it must ideologise and articulate its discontent. To the extent that the discontent is weakly articulated, as in the wildcat strike described by Benyon (1973), the social movement will be a weak force of social protest and change. The cognitive interpretation of the deprivations and frustrations suffered by ingroup members must provide the basis for a determined social action. Without the coherence provided by an ingroup ideology, frustrations will merely produce individual reactions; these will take diffuse forms and will not be vehicles of mass social change. Having stated this, it must be recognised that little has been said about the nature of the cognitive interpretation of frustrations—only the mere fact of its existence as necessary to social movements has been stated. The question can be asked whether such a cognitive interpretation takes any particular form and what are its consequences for a social psychological analysis. In order to throw light on these questions, one characterisation of social discontent will be considered. This is the descrip-

tion of dissidence in terms of "relative deprivation", which theoretically has been closely linked to the frustration-aggression framework.

The concept of "relative deprivation" revolves around "perceived
discontent" rather than objectively measured discontent. As such it has
been used to explain the phenomenon of the revolution of the rising
expectations (Davies, 1962; Gurr, 1970). If it is relative deprivation,
rather than objective deprivation, which is the spur to social discontent, then there is no mystery in the notion that the worst conditions of
deprivation do not usually produce the most revolutionary situations.
Gurr (1970) in his analysis of revolutions specifically combines frustration-aggression theory with the concept of relative deprivation; he
defies relative deprivation as the "actors' perception of discrepancy
between their value expectations and their value capabilities" (Gurr,
1970, p. 24). Relative deprivation increases when people receive less
than they expect to receive; an increase in relative deprivation, according to Gurr, correspondingly increases the likelihood of violence. Revolts will occur when expectations increase to a greater extent than
received benefits. The discrepancy between expectations and received
benefits is frustrating and predisposes the individual towards an
aggressive response. In this way the frustration-aggression hypothesis
is seen as providing the motivational link between relative deprivation
and social revolution. Given these assumptions, the revolution of rising
expectations becomes a predicted phenomenon, rather than a puzzle.

A major difficulty with the frustration-aggression approach to social
movements can be pointed out here. This is the tendency towards the
reduction of complex social events to individual reactions. It has been
argued that ideology is a central phenomenon in large-scale social
action, and in particular revolutionary activity. What is meant by
ideology is a pattern of beliefs about the social world and about the
possibilities for social action. These beliefs are essentially group beliefs
that emerge from, and shape the activities of, social groups. This conception of ideology will be developed in later chapters. For the present
it can be noted that this view does not reduce ideology to individualistic reactions and that it also stresses the practical nature of ideology.
With respect to revolutionary ideology, the present position is in
agreement with the view of Wolin (1973) that one cannot analytically
distinguish the ideological beliefs from their practical application.

Frustration-aggression theory can posit ideologies of discontent (or
of social change) as intervening variables between frustration and

aggression. But the essential unit of analysis is individual frustration and individual instigations to aggress; because of this, ideology is reduced to individualistic components. Gurr's (1970) definition of relative deprivation is in terms of the perceptions of individuals and does not specifically link such perceptions to social determinants. This is because the frustrating feeling of relative deprivation is assumed to be a basic unitary variable. Ideology is assumed to be the sum total of such individually produced perceptions; it is a by-product of more basic processes. This outlook is not confined to the work of Gurr, but is to be found in other applications of frustration-aggression theory to social phenomena. Thus, Feierabend, Feierabend and Nesvold (1973) refer to "systemic frustrations" which are "simultaneously experienced by members of social aggregates" (p. 404). This account resembles that of Gurr in that individually experienced frustrations are given theoretical primacy over ideology. It is for such reasons that Gurr and the Feierabends have been accused of neglecting ideology completely in their analysis of revolutions (for instance, Kochanek, 1973); it can be noted that in his latest model of civil strife Gurr has, however, abandoned psychological concepts such as "relative deprivation" and frustrations (Gurr and Duvall, 1973).

If there is a reductionist trend in the application of the frustration-aggression model to civil conflict, then its unsatisfactory nature can be shown by considering particular examples. Firstly, certain aspects of Berkowitz's (1972) explanation of the urban ghetto riots can be mentioned. The reduction of social ideology to individual reactions seems to imply, in Berkowitz's work at least, that particular beliefs can be considered on their own, without referring to their possible interrelations in a complex ideology of the social world. Berkowitz attempts to explain the riots by considering possible feelings of relative deprivation alone, out of all the possible beliefs that the participants might hold. He links relative deprivation to social comparison, and argues that people feel deprived in relation to others. If the rioters felt relatively deprived, and thus frustrated, then the problem is to identify those with whom they were comparing themselves. Berkowitz answers this by considering the responses to two items from a survey by Caplan and Paige (1968). This survey revealed that the rioters did not feel that the income difference between black and whites was increasing, but that they did feel that the difference between rich and poor blacks was increasing. Berkowitz concluded from this piece of evidence that the black rioters did not feel deprived in relation to whites but in relation to rich blacks. His analysis does not seek the causes of the riots in the structure of U.S. society or even directly in racist discrimination. Responsibility is not seen to rest with dominant white groups: firstly, extraneous factors, such as the weather, are blamed for upsetting the blacks, and secondly it is held that the blacks' most keenly felt grievances relate to members of their own community.

Such an explanation is far too simplistic, and leaves too many factors unaccounted for. It should be noted that Berkowitz has not established any dynamic connection between riot behaviour and the rioters beliefs about income differences, which would suggest in any way that the blacks were rioting *because* rich blacks were getting richer. There is no consideration of the ideological context of such a belief and its consequences for practical activity. Instead, the ideological outlook of the blacks is fragmented and isolated aspects are given prime attention. Even if the answers to Caplan and Paige's two questions were in some way directly relevant to riot action, then other possible explanations are possible to the one offered by Berkowitz. Instead of saying that the blacks were only frustrated by other blacks and not by whites, it might have been the case that the rioters believed that successful blacks were being "bought off" by the white society, and so the black community was losing its most powerful leaders—thus direct action from the grass-roots was what was required to continue the battle for economic and social equality. It is not being suggested that this was in fact the ideological motivation behind the ghetto riots, merely that Berkowitz's 1972 account is by no means the only one that can be offered.

The limitations of a purely psychological approach to the phenomena of social protest is further illustrated by a study conducted by Crawford and Naditch (1970). These authors also attempt to offer an explanation of riot behaviour in terms of relative deprivation and frustration-aggression theory. Essentially they posit two basic variables to describe the psychology of social change—high and low relative deprivation, and internal/external control. From this they aim to provide a typology of the four basic stages of movements for social change. These variables combine to form a 2×2 matrix, depicting four stages in a sequential model of social change. In the first stage potential dissidents have low feelings of relative deprivation and believe that they have little control over their destiny (external control). This stage gives way to high feelings of relative deprivation, but the belief of helplessness still persists. In this stage, according to Crawford and Naditch, there is instability and emotional mass action. The next stage is the development of internal control, which heralds the start of instrumental mass action and the belief that changes can be made. The fourth and final stage marks a happy ending to this troubled progression—internal control is maintained, whilst relative deprivation disappears and the erstwhile revolutionaries settle down to a life of "content activism".

Crawford and Naditch's matrix of social change is essentially a model of individual modes of action. They define internal and external control not in terms of a socially produced ideology of action or acquiescence, but with respect to Rotter's (1966) Scale of Internal-External Locus of Control. Their interpretation thus refers to individual styles of action rather than to ideological interpretation of political realities. One of the main weaknesses of their model is that they offer no evidence for the temporal sequence that they describe— it is merely postulated, rather than detailed. Nor do they say how individuals pass from one stage to another. In fact Crawford and Naditch admit that "the transition from an external to an internal perceived locus of reinforcement is difficult to explain theoretically, and it is probably even more difficult to bring about the change in an individual or group" (Crawford and Naditch, 1970, p. 216). Certainly such a change is difficult to explain given their individualistic premises. The problem of the uniformity of mass action faces any individualistic account, especially one that attempts to chart the development of determined revolutionary activity from the emotional feelings of frustrated individuals without taking into account social variables. The social context of a revolutionary ideology must be considered: its origins must be sought farther afield than the hypothesised emotional states of its adherents. Not to do so means misunderstanding the nature of civil strife and revolution. In particular, it devalues the ideological, and, as will be argued, ignores the intergroup context.

If it is assumed that civil strife is more than an expression of individual emotion, then it becomes necessary to identify the issues and grievances driving men to rebel. It must be remembered that in a rebellion there are two sides, the rebels and those whom they rebel against. The prior context of the rebellion, revolution or protest must be taken into account, and this relates to the relations between the two sides. In chapter five of *Why Men Rebel*, Gurr (1970) recognises that in any society there are a number of values, which are difficult to share. These values are the prerogative, by definition, of a ruling élite or class. Dissidence is created when a group excluded from these values begins to demand a greater share as of right. Thus Gurr and Duvall (1973) in a nonpsychological statistical analysis of civil conflict, have found that the prime source of political conflict was "strain"—by "strain" the authors mean inequalities and cleavages within societies. The basic intergroup context of civil conflict is one of exploitation and unequal distributions of resources. Gurr and Duvall found that "stress" was unrelated to civil conflict—by this they meant that shortages or declines in overall values had little effect on intersocietal conflict. It would seem therefore that it is not frustrations *per se* that give rise to turmoil or rebellion, but frustrations engendered by intergroup inequalities.

The analytical preconditions for such intergroup confrontations can be listed. These include the development of an ingroup ideology; this will demand certain values for the ingroup, at present held by the outgroup, and will also suggest ways for the ingroup to gain those values. The strategy for attainment will depend on whether equality is sought with the outgroup or whether the ingroup aspires to total control of the values. The reluctance of the outgroup either to share or relinquish values means the subordinate ingroup is thwarted by the dominant outgroup. This basic intergroup situation will be reflected in the ingroup's ideology, which will contain two elements—an ingroup mythology and an outgroup mythology. This can be illustrated with respect to the black rioters. The aims of the majority were not separatist or supremacist, but were directed towards the achievement of an equal share with the white society (for instance, Marx, 1967; Tomlinson, 1970). Their ideology was two-fold, relating to the ingroup and the outgroup. The ingroup element was embodied in the emphasis on racial pride and black cultural values (Caplan, 1970). This ingroup pride and consciousness enables the ingroup to develop an ideology of increasing expectations:

> The young militants, male or female, no longer accept the fatalistic stereotype that their ghetto existence is a result of their own inherent weakness or inability to improve themselves. Compared with nonmilitants, the riot supporters have very strong beliefs in their ability to control events in their own lives and to shape their own future. (Forward and Williams, 1970, pp. 87–8.)

The outgroup element of the black ideology relates naturally enough to the white-dominated society. It is a matter of debate whether the black ideology conceives as its outgroup whites as such, or on the other hand particular white power groups (Paige, 1970). Nevertheless, a powerful outgroup is perceived and blamed for racial discrimination (Caplan and Paige, 1968). An intergroup situation is developed in which the dominated group develops a positive ingroup ideology, while at the same time challenging the more powerful outgroup. When a subordinate group rebels against its position *vis-à-vis* the dominant group, the rebellion must be understood in terms of differential power and privilege. So long as this differential exists, there will exist either the actuality or the potentiality of an ideology of rebellion. The differential will be resolved if (a) the dominant group shares its privileges with the subordinate group, and the latter is satisfied with this—in this case the intergroup differentiation could cease to exist as an important social force, this being the hope of the civil rights movement; (b) the dominant group and the subordinate group part company and each go separate ways, e.g. at the break-up of a colonial empire, when the subordinate group frees itself from its colonial domination; (c) the subordinate group replaces the dominant group, e.g. a successful class revolution, where a new class takes control of the country as the bourgeoisie supplanted the aristocracy after the French revolution; (d) the dominant group successfully crushes the subordinate, and destroys, at least for the foreseeable future, the possibility of organising resistance—in this case of course the differential has not itself been resolved, but the ideology of discontent destroyed. The first three possibilities are all ways of resolving intergroup differentials and inequalities. Whether a successful dissident movement will achieve (a), (b) or (c) will depend to a large degree on its ideological aims, and also on the actions of the outgroup during the period of revolutionary conflict.

The emphasis of this analysis has been on the status differentials contained in the intergroup situation. Just as the frustration-aggression relationship in the interpersonal situation had to be understood in relation to variables such as status and authority, even more so does the intergroup situation. The importance of such variables in the intergroup context was tacitly recognised by one of the first studies to formalise the concept of relative deprivation; Davis's (1959) concept of relative deprivation is closer to the notions of social comparisons than

Gurr's. Instead of defining relative deprivation purely in terms of individual expectations and gains, Davis holds that relative deprivation follows when an individual compares himself to someone more fortunate. When he compares himself to a less fortunate individual, "relative gratification" is the result. Davis provides an intergroup "analogue" for these interpersonal processes. Comparisons with an outgroup will result in either "relative subordination" or "relative superiority"; thus implicitly Davis recognises the importance of status and domination when considering intergroup relations.

Thus far the revolutionary intergroup situation has primarily been dealt with from the point of view of the rebellious dissident group. However, it is not just the ideological beliefs and actions of the ingroup that are of importance. In an analysis of the total intergroup situation the role of the outgroup must not be neglected. The violent threats of the dissident ingroup will almost certainly produce counter-aggression from the dominant group seeking to preserve its status. A revolution will unleash counterrevolutionary forces, which psychologically are correlates of the revolutionary forces; the counterrevolution will be ideologically directed against an outgroup, which is responsible for, or threatens to be responsible for, ingroup discontent. In the case of the counterrevolutionary group this discontent will focus around the loss of privilege resulting from a successful revolution. If the revolution takes place at a time when the subordinate group is improving its lot, then quite probably the dominant group has already begun to experience a loss of privilege. As a result it might have developed its own ideology of discontent, which will act as the contradictory to the ideology of the rising revolutionary group. Birrell (1972) has illustrated this process with reference to the internal struggle in Northern Ireland; he argues that "reverse" relative deprivation is an important factor in the rise of Protestant extremism between 1964 and 1968. It was just at this time that the Catholics were making definite economic gains and were catching up on the more favourably placed Protestants. The Protestant feeling of loss of privilege gives rise to "reverse" relative deprivation, and this when ideologically articulated, forms a conservative philosophy. Rosenbaum and Sederberg (1974) argue that "unofficial" vigilante groups, supporting the existing status quo, are analogous to insurgent groups, threatening the existing order. They argue that the same theoretical approaches should be applied to the actions of both sorts of group.

   The analysis of counter-revolutionary or counter-rebellious forces is
necessary for an understanding of the total revolutionary intergroup
situation; the movements for social change must be seen in relation
and in opposition, to the movements for preserving existing status
differentials. Tilly (1963) has remarked that "counter-revolutions test
our explanations of revolutions" (p. 30). Even the black ghetto riot is
essentially an intergroup situation, in which the counter-riot forces
exert a significant influence. In this case the most immediate counter-
riot force is the white-dominated police. Their role in the total riot
situation must not be neglected. Marx (1970) has analysed this role
during the disturbances, and comes to the conclusion that the police
definitely saw the situation in intergroup terms: he writes of the
police viewing the riot as a "them" and "us" situation, and of the
belief spreading that:

> . . . they are in a war and all black people are their enemy. As police
> control of the "turf" is effectively challenged and rioters gain control
> of the streets by default, the word may spread . . . that rioters have "beat
> the police". Losing face, humiliated by their temporary defeat and with
> their professional pride undermined, police may have a strong desire
> for revenge and to show their efficacy. (Marx, 1970, p. 49.)

   In this situation one can discern the threat of losing status as a spur
to counter-riot activity. The police feared losing control of the "turf"
to the rioters and thereby having no control or authority in the ghetto
areas. This clearly conflicted with the philosophy that police should
have control and maintain the law in these areas. The intergroup
spiral of conflict has started, with counter-aggression following and
producing aggression. A polarisation of opposing ideologies is likely to
result as the rebellious group reacts to the attempts of the existing
authorities to frustrate their "subversive" goals, and likewise as the
dominant group seeks to protect its position against the dissidents (for
instances of the radicalisation of dissident belief following counter-
dissident intervention, see Hahn, 1969; Adamek and Lewis, 1973. This
account of intergroup polarisation is obviously somewhat oversimpli-
fied—in particular it neglects the role of those who oppose the act of
rebellion, but who do not support the authorities—see, for instance,
Anderson, Dynes and Quarantelli, 1974).

   The present insistence upon the intergroup nature of revolutionary
conflict is quite deliberate, since it will be argued that there are some
important theoretical consequences arising from this point of view. In

particular these consequences relate to underlying presuppositions concerning the nature of political repression and violence; in a very real sense these presuppositions are themselves ideological. To begin with, one can note that, by considering counter-revolutionary action in an analysis of revolution, a number of difficulties are raised for any simple analogy with the frustration-aggression relationship as studied in the psychology laboratory. The assumption behind any straight-forward translation of frustration-aggression theory to mass social phenomena is that it is possible to equate mass social frustration with the behaviour of mass movements of dissidence. This assumption is clear in the writings of Berkowitz (1971 and 1972) and in the Crawford and Naditch (1970) psychological model of social change. However, if counter-revolutionary action is taken into consideration, then it is reasonable to apply the same sort of social psychological principles as were applied to the behaviour of dissidents. Frustration-aggression explanations need not be reserved solely for the behaviour of the opponents of the *status quo*.

Gurr (1970, chapter eight, and 1973) recognises this point and he deliberately draws a parallel between dissident and counter-insurgent behaviour. He notes that revolution can lead to counter-revolution and thereby to an escalation of violence. He bases the link between revolution and counter-revolution upon the psychological premise that "people have an inherent disposition, irrespective of cultural differences, to respond violently to violent attacks" (Gurr, 1973, p. 380). Just as Gurr bases his psychology of the dissident upon frustration-aggression theory, so does he base his psychology of the counter-revolutionary on the same theory. Certainly much of the experimental evidence bears out his "psychological premise"—there has already been occasion to mention some of the numerous studies which have shown that an attack on an experimental subject can lead to an aggressive response. However, the evidence does reveal some limiting circumstances to this "general law". For instance, it has been found that the threat of retaliation can reduce the aggressive response (e.g. Baron, 1971; Shortell, Epstein and Taylor, 1970; Donnerstein *et al.*, 1972), and so can the disapproval of others (Borden and Taylor, 1973). Similarly, vulnerability to a future counter-attack can reduce the aggressive response (Gaebelin and Hay, 1974). Nevertheless, it has been shown that the threat of retaliation may not reduce aggression if the subjects are particularly angry (Knott and Drost, 1972; Baron,

1973). Gurr's psychological premise does seem to be subject to certain eminently reasonable qualifications, relating primarily to the perceived wisdom and consequences of counter-attacking.

The findings from such experimental studies of interpersonal aggression have certain parallels with studies investigating large-scale social aggression. There have been a number of correlational studies in recent years which have investigated the relationship between the coerciveness of governments and the incidence of civil disturbance. *Prima facie* there seem to be two diametrically opposed possibilities. On the one hand, it might be thought that a highly coercive and repressive regime might inhibit all possibilities of opposition. On the other it might be held that its coerciveness might itself encourage violent opposition since more peaceful channels would be closed to its political opponents. The results from the correlational studies have not absolutely confirmed either one or the other hypothesis. For instance, Jacobson (1973) found a zero-order correlation between regime-coerciveness and internal civil strife. Gurr (1972) has provided evidence that counter-revolutionary violence increases civil conflict. This proposition is supported by other sources; for instance Janowitz (1969) argues that the black riots were exacerbated by the civil authorities' use of force. Nevertheless it is reasonable to suppose that there is no one-to-one correlation between regime coerciveness and the occurrence of violent opposition. Just as the interpersonal studies showed that the threat of retaliation sometimes acts as an inhibitor of aggression and sometimes does not, so the same can be the case with wider social aggression.

In this respect, Gurr (1970) posits a curvilinear relationship between regime and revolutionary violence. He hypothesises that there is a "coercive balance" between the forces of the *status quo* and the forces of opposition. A highly coercive regime will be able to maintain its position by force to the extent that its opponents are weak. Similarly, the stronger the opponents the more likely is violent opposition (see also Gurr, 1969). In a similar vein Feierabend, Feierabend and Nesvold (1969) deny that regime coerciveness either absolutely inhibits or encourages internal civil strife. In their view governments at mid-levels of coercion endure the most turmoil. They develop this point in a later paper (Feierabend, Feierabend and Nesvold, 1973) when they claim that other variables mediate the relationship between regime coerciveness and internal strife. For instance they argue that an important mediating variable is the perceived legitimacy of the coerciveness of the regime. If violent acts committed by the established authorities are considered illegitimate, then there is a greater likelihood of violent protest—this is not the case if the actions are considered legitimate. Since the variable of perceived legitimacy of the regime is, by definition, related to the amount of support that exists for the regime the account of Feierabend *et al.* (1973) is in basic respects similar to Gurr's (1970).

There is another aspect in which the accounts of Gurr and of Feierabend *et al.* concur: they both hypothesise that regime coerciveness may inhibit opposition in the short term, but in the long term it increases the likelihood of violent opposition. Once a coercive regime begins to weaken its hold, the forces of the opposition will be correspondingly encouraged and strengthened; thus the ultimate violent showdown will be made more likely. In this sense these formulations would seem to support the aphorism that those who live by the sword will perish, ultimately, by the sword. If this seems to support the original notion that aggression breeds more aggression, it nevertheless does so in a way that takes into account rational strategic considerations. The original "psychological premise" was based upon a motivational model of essentially irrational behaviour. However, more rational elements would seem to account for the lack of a direct correlation between regime coerciveness and incidence of violent dissidence. These elements include common sense tactical notions—for instance, that it is useless to attack a powerful and ruthless opponent if one's own position is weak. Another obvious tactical consideration is that such a ruthless opponent must normally be countered by force, since he will have no scruples against using his own force to crush opposition. In this sense the violent regime will breed violent opposition.

In saying this an important theoretical step has been taken: the relationship between dissidence and aggression has been expanded and placed into a wider context. No longer is the prime focus on the aggression of the forces of opposition. Primarily the application of frustration-aggression theory to social protest concentrated upon the frustrations and aggressive responses of the dissidents. It was argued that this account should be extended to take into account the aggression of counter-revolutionary, or counter-insurgent, forces. However, this extension by itself still leaves the assumption that the first aggressive action is committed by the forces of opposition. Counter-revolutionary violence is seen in this model to be a reaction to revolutionary violence; this latter is held to be the first act in the escalating sequence of aggression followed by counter-aggression. When the coerciveness of a regime is considered another variable is being inserted into the model—aggression committed by the forces of the *status quo* is being viewed as being a determinant of dissident aggression. Rebellious or revolutionary aggression can be seen as a response to institutional aggression—the first blow need not be seen as inevitably coming from the side of the opposition.

In this respect, the extreme amounts of violence shown by the subjects in Milgram's obedience experiments are relevant. These subjects responded to the commands of a legitimate authority and displayed aggression not accounted for by the frustration-aggression framework. Similarly, a crude application of frustration-aggression theory to social movements of opposition omits the aggression committed by legally constituted governments and their agents, and neglects that such aggression, often in the name of "law and order", can be integrally related to dissident violence. It may be no coincidence that Milgram has produced, in his experimental situations, far greater amounts of subject aggression than has been displayed by the angered or frustrated subjects in the usual frustration-aggression paradigms. This could be a case of the laboratory experiments illustrating in miniature a more general feature of large-scale social events. Certainly some researchers have claimed that aggression committed by the *status quo* far outweighs aggression committed by the forces of opposition. For instance, Nardin (1971) has claimed that regimes are responsible for more civil violence than are dissidents. Similarly Lowry and Rankin (1972) have estimated that seventy-five per cent of violence in the history of the United States has been committed by "the forces of legitimate authority and representatives of the establishment" (p. 615).[2]

By restricting attention to the violence of dissidents, a distorted picture of civil intergroup conflict emerges. This distortion is not,

2. Rudé (1974) has calculated the loss of life during the storming of the Bastille. Over 150 members of the Paris crowd had been killed by Royalist forces and Rudé comments that "it is perhaps surprising that the angry and triumphant crowds, pouring through the open gates of the Bastille, did not exact a more complete and indiscriminate vengeance" (p. 93). Out of 110 members of the defending garrison only six were killed.

however, fortuitous, but contains biases in favour of the forces of "order". The ideology of discontent, which articulates the deprivations of the opposition has already been discussed. There is, of course, a corresponding ideology of the *status quo*. One form which this ideology can take is to claim that the forces of dissidence are unreasonably destroying a harmonious society. This ideology, therefore, has an ingroup and outgroup aspect. The ingroup aspect links the interest of the ingroup to "society" conceived as a unified whole, and the outgroup aspect discredits those who threaten this pre-established harmony. There is, however, a formal similarity between such an ideology and the writings of certain frustration-aggression theorists. The assumption of the irrationality of the forces of opposition and the assumption of a pre-existing social peace are both to be found in the applications of frustration-aggression theory to social conflict. For instance, the assumption of a pre-existing social peace is clearly enunciated in Crawford and Naditch's (1970) psychology of social change model. Stages one and four of this sequential model are characterised by social stability, and what disturbs this stability are the actions of the dissident group. Prior actions of the dominant group, and the effects of counter-insurgency are not considered; the aggression is limited, theoretically at least, to the opposition, rather than traced to the social structure which nurtured this opposition. The social structure is assumed to be a static unity; if disturbed it will return by some sort of homeostasis to its state of rest. The "blame" for any disturbance is laid at the door of the dissident.

The normative presuppositions, contained in such a view, should be clear. They become even clearer in Berkowitz's (1971) discussion of the urban riots. He does not seek to relate the riots to the structure of society. Instead he concentrates upon the behaviour of the rioters. He suggests that the police may have acted as aggressive stimuli to the blacks, but does not mention the opposite possibility, namely, that the blacks may have acted as aggressive stimuli to the police. By this omission Berkowitz is discounting the possible relevance of the long history of police brutality against the black community (Marx, 1970). Instead of attempting such an analysis he concentrates upon the situational stimuli which "trigger off" an irrational and impulsive response.

Also one can note that there is a vagueness about the use of the term "aggression". Dollard *et al.* justified the use of the one term "aggression" to cover a multitude of forms of behaviour on the basis of "functional unity" relating to the concepts of catharsis and displacement (Dollard *et al.*, 1939, pp. 52–3). However, it is now possible to discern another use of the term. A riot or a protest demonstration would hardly seem to be "aggressive" in the sense that the Vietnam War is aggressive. Yet there is a tendency in the writings of the social psychologists, investigating frustration-aggression theory, to apply the concept of aggression to the former type of conflict, rather than the latter. The use of the overall ill-defined term "aggression" cannot be justified on the same grounds as Dollard *et al.* justified it, since the topics of displacement and catharsis have not occupied the forefront of recent frustration-aggression research. Instead one can note the comments of Tilly (1973) against writers who have expanded the use of the word "violence" to include almost any illegal act whatsoever. He dubs such writers as "lovers of order and defenders of the state" and comments that in their hands the notion of violence "has little value as an analytic tool but carries great moral weight" (Tilly, 1973, p. 439).

The second assumption in the ideology of order is that the dissidents are in some essential respects irrational. This side of frustration-aggression theory has been commented upon at length. However, the concentration on irrational aggression, linked theoretically to frustration, produces a most unflattering picture of the dissident. When the "revolution of rising expectancies" is considered, one of its main determinants in the view of frustration-aggression theorists is the greed of the dissidents. For instance, Gurr (1970) notes that men's expectations are likely to outstrip their capabilities and that they "are quick to aspire beyond their social means" (p. 58). It is as if the irrational greed of dissidents is what is at issue, rather than a conflict over what constitutes "the social means" and who should stipulate how they should be distributed throughout the society. Avoidable inequalities between social groups or classes are lost sight of if the intergroup nature of civil conflict is neglected for a criticism of the psychology of dissidence.

Berkowitz (1971) writes in a vein similar to Gurr. He states that:

> It could be that the rapid socioeconomic improvements produce more hopes and expectations than can be fulfilled. Hope outstrips reality, even though conditions are rapidly improving for the society as a whole, and many of the people in the society are frustrated. Some such process, of course, may be occurring in the case of our present Negro revolution. (Berkowitz, 1971, p. 185.)

Of course, the central issue is precisely "whose hope" outstrips "whose reality". Social reality is a man-made construction and can be changed by the actions of men. If the hopes of dissidents outstrip the social realities, as defined for them by the forces of order, then it is those realities which they aim to change. It is the conservative who attempts to portray the existing social realities as immutable facts of nature, and who wishes to see the social structure, which has created those realities, remain untouched. Revolutionary ideology, on the other hand, does not aim at adjusting to the present realities and preserving their social basis—the crucial point about revolutionary ideology is that it aims to change reality.

Displacement and intergroup relations

In conclusion to this chapter a few words need to be said about the displacement of aggression following a frustration. Originally the frustration-aggression theory was thought well-equipped to explain irrational outgroup prejudice on the basis of the psychological model of displacement. However, in the foregoing discussion of the social ramifications of the theory, this aspect has been somewhat neglected, in favour of an analysis of social protest and revolution. The previous sections have primarily been concerned with direct aggression, in which subordinate groups have attacked their dominant group frustrators. However, it is now necessary to consider whether and to what extent the displacement of aggression can be said to occur at the level of intergroup relations.

The basic proposition of the intergroup theory of Dollard *et al.* (1939) was that hostilities against ingroup members will be displaced onto outgroup members. In this way intragroup conflict will be turned into intergroup conflict. In essentials their formulation closely resembles that of Freud; both accounts of intergroup relations are based upon a motivational theory which postulates a fixed amount of aggressive energy within a society, and that this energy needs to be discharged if ingroup cohesion is to be maintained. A similar premise has also been encountered in the social theories of Marcuse and Lorenz. All these accounts therefore hypothesise a close link between intragroup and intergroup conflicts. In particular, they assume that intergroup conflict will act as a "safety-valve" to defuse within-group dissension, and any negative ingroup feelings will be displaced onto the outgroup.

From this basic premise a number of hypotheses can be derived. In the first place it is possible to predict that at any one point in time there will be a negative correlation between the occurrence of internal and external conflicts. Secondly, it is possible to hypothesise that, if intergroup conflict acts as a "safety-valve" then the occurrence of international warfare should be predictable from the state of intra-national stability; thus intranational instability at one moment should be correlated with international conflict at the next point of time. Further hypotheses linking the two variables of within- and between-group conflict are possible from the basic frustration-aggression premises. However it is not the present purposes to construct any *a priori* schemata linking inter- and intra-group relations. Rather, it is to show that these two variables are intimately linked in the displacement theory of intergroup relations, and then to consider the empirical evidence concerning these two variables.

The evidence does not, however, support any facile linking of the variables of inter- and intra-group conflict. For instance, Rummel (1963) conducted a correlational study, investigating the relationship between dimensions of inter- and intra-national conflict; his data came from an extensive survey of the behaviour of seventy-seven nations between 1955 and 1957. Tanter (1966) extended this survey by studying national behaviour between 1958 and 1960, and also by correlating his findings with those of Rummel. The findings from these two investigations showed only a small linkage between the two main variables. Tanter's study did suggest that a time-lag could be important: the occurrence of internal conflict to a small degree affects the future occurrence of international conflict. In particular the evidence suggested that internal conflict might be correlated with future diplomatic confrontations.

If these two studies provide only meagre evidence in support of the strong link hypothesised by the displacement theory, then even less support comes from other quarters. Gurr and Duvall (1973) far from finding that intra- and inter-national conflict were negatively correlated, discovered that the probability of external warfare increased with the severity of a revolutionary conflict. Tanter (1969) made a detailed study of American involvement in Vietnam and the incidence of dissident disturbance within the U.S.A. He found, not unsurprisingly, that increasing escalation of the war in Vietnam was positively correlated with increasing internal protests. Thus the international conflict was accompanied by increases in intranational conflict, and in no way could the former conflict be considered a safety-valve for displaced internal conflicts. Brooks (1969) has commented upon the uniqueness of the protests against the Vietnamese war in the history of the U.S.A., and he stressed that the perceived legitimacy of a war is the key variable in predicting the amount of internal opposition. As the escalation of the war in Vietnam was felt to be indefensible by a growing number of American citizens, so the volume of protest grew. Once again, therefore, an hypothesised motivational relationship between frustration and aggression would seem to be in need of a mediating variable such as perceived legitimacy.[3]

Putting together the results from these few studies, a composite picture can be developed which stresses the social, rather than motivational, link between internal and external conflict. The time-lag finding of Tanter (1966) is open to two contrasting interpretations. In the first place it might be argued that internal pressure might force on the government changes in foreign policy which have direct diplomatic repercussions. For instance, prolonged demonstrations may force the ruling powers to break off diplomatic relations with a particular power, or to recall a foreign ambassador. Such a sequence of events clearly does not need to be explained in terms of the displacement of a fixed quantum of aggression. Alternatively, another explanation of Tanter's correlations is equally possible, and this is one which parallels the displacement concept more closely. Governments may possibly create diplomatic incidents in order to divert attention from internal conflicts and to rally dissident forces behind them in the face of a "foreign threat"; the postulated action of governments in this sequence is necessary since it is diplomatic confrontation which Tanter found to be weakly correlated with internal strife, rather than actual full-scale international warfare.

At first sight, this alternative explanation might seem to be easily linked to an explanation based upon displacement. However, there are certain preconditions that must exist for such a governmental attempt at displacing internal conflicts, and these preconditions relate primarily to social factors rather than motivational ones. In the first

3. For a critical review of studies correlating internal and external conflicts, see Scolnick (1974). One of the main criticisms that Scolnick makes is that such studies fail to postulate any intervening variables to link domestic and international conflict.

place the government would need strong control of the dissemination of information throughout the country. Not only would it need the physical control of the instruments of communication, but its messages would also need to be perceived as credible; the potential dissidents must believe statements implying that the country was being threatened by overseas forces. They will need to create the ideological belief in the dissidents that the real cause of the nation's misfortunes lie beyond the frontiers of the country and that unity in the face of imminent peril is paramount. In doing this the government will be attempting to manipulate a cognitive reappraisal of political events, rather than attempting a cathartic displacement of irrational impulses.

One of the essential preconditions for affecting such a displacement of internal protest is that the government should still retain strong powers of control. The operation of the mechanism of displacement can be illustrated by reconsidering the Miller and Bugelski (1948) boys' camp experiment. In this study the authorities, the experimenters, frustrated the boys, and in turn there was some evidence that the subjects may have displaced some aggression onto outgroups. If the authority of the experimenters were well established and the boys had inhibitions against expressing hostility against them, then it is possible that the experimenters could have been in a position to stage-manage a displacement. If, instead of giving no explanation for the frustration, they had blamed some other outgroup for it, then it is reasonable to expect that the boys would have shown strong aggressive reactions towards this outgroup, even if this outgroup were purely fictional. Thus if the authorities had provided certain sanctioned channels for the expression of outgroup hostility, then full-scale scape-goating may have resulted. What should be emphasised is the social and psychological context for such an occurrence: there would have been a frustration caused by the authorities, a certain power relation-ship between the authorities and the subjects (which is accepted by both groups as being legitimate), and the stage-management by the authorities of the role of an outgroup "enemy". In this way the authori-ties would have created a "false consciousness" amongst the subjects. Thus, such a process of stage-managing information would have re-sulted in a false ideological belief. If one then attempts to define such intergroup displacement in terms of the creation of false ideological beliefs, it is important to realise that this use of the term "dis-placement" is essentially cognitive and not motivational.

This discussion of political displacement has concentrated upon the actions of a government or ruling group in creating a false (or displaced) ideology to account for the nation's ills. Bearing this in mind, the hypothesis of Horowitz (1973) can be discussed. Horowitz considers that the frustration-aggression account of scapegoating may have a direct relevance to a particular form of ethnic conflict. He describes a number of instances where provocation by a dominant ethnic group has not resulted in insurrection by the subordinate group, but in an attack by them on a group of equal power. Horowitz cites the case of the Burma riots of 1938. The British colonialists had used force in dispersing a march of Burmese nationalists; however, this did not lead to retaliation against the British, but to an outbreak of rioting against the Indian community. Horowitz argues that, in such cases, the frustrated group is inhibited from attacking their powerful frustrators, and as a consequence takes its aggression out upon a parallel group. He notes that not just any target is chosen, but the aggression is reserved for a previously disliked group, against whom aggressive tendencies were manifest in the first place. For this reason Horowitz refers to such aggression as "cumulative" rather than displaced.

The analogy between Horowitz's account and the experimental evidence is plain. For instance, his concept of cumulative aggression ties in with Berkowitz and Green's (1962) finding that aggressive feelings are displaced onto a previously disliked subject; and the stress on the inhibition against attacking a powerful frustrator fits in with the previous discussion of the role of authority in the Lange (1971) findings. Thus Horowitz does offer an interesting parallel between interpersonal and intergroup displacement of aggression. Also one can note that he does not overlook the ideological nature of cumulative aggression, and that his account does not neglect the wider intergroup context. He firmly relates the phenomenon of ethnic cumulative aggression to intergroup domination and differentials in power. However, it should be emphasised that in calling a particular sequence of events either "displaced" or "cumulative" aggression, no assumptions have necessarily been made about the psychological states of the individual rioters—certainly Horowitz provides no evidence on this account. There need not be an isomorphism between the social sequence of events and the feelings of the individual actors.

To investigate the matter further one would wish to compare those instances where parallel rioting occurs, with those instances, which must be so much more frequent, where insult from the dominant group produces no such violent reaction. Such a comparison might well reveal other mediating variables. For instance, the dominant group might play an active role as an *agent provocateur* in inciting conflict between the two subordinate groups.[4] Alternatively, the role of the ingroup's leadership may be vital—the parallel riot may be a deliberate tactical ploy in order to maintain the level of the group's morale. It is important to remember that Horowitz does not claim that the frustration-aggression analogy vitiates the need for other forms of explanation: he specifically denies that it excludes the possibility of an explanation based upon class (Horowitz, 1973, p. 6). In this respect Horowitz has drawn attention to a phenomenon, which *prima facie* resembles the interpersonal paradigms of aggression-displacement, and which in itself has great intrinsic interest for an account of ethnic relations. As such he would seem to have identified a fertile area for further investigation. But he does not make inflated claims for the frustration-aggression theory as an explanatory tool for complex intergroup phenomena.

In discussing the displacement of aggression in an intergroup context, only one form of displacement has so far been considered—viz. the displacement of discontent onto a third party. An alternative type of displacement is possible, and this type does not involve a third party other than the frustrator and the frustrated. In frustration-aggression theory this form of displacement occurs when the frustrated person directs his aggression against himself. Historically this notion derives from Freud's theories of masochism, and was incorporated into the schemata of Dollard *et al.* Berkowitz (1962) also considered this possibility, but mentions that this particular form of masochism is difficult to study experimentally. One of the few frustration-aggression experi-

4. For instance Pollis (1973) reports that British colonial rule was instrumental in creating ethnic hostilities; he discusses the case of Burma and cites Furnivall (1956) in suggesting that Burmese hatred of the Indians was non-existent before the British colonial administration. This in itself does not imply any deliberate provocation by the dominant ruling group. However Marx (1974) in an examination of the role of *agent provocateurs* in social movements argues that their importance is far greater than had been suspected by many sociologists hitherto. Although it is hard to obtain quantitative and reliable data on a phenomenon, which by its nature is shrouded in secrecy, nevertheless the role of authorities in provoking acts of dissidence and rebellion should not be forgotten.

ments which has approached the problem has been Holmes's (1972) study. Even then the problem was tackled indirectly—Holmes's main interest was in guilt reactions following improperly directed aggression as opposed to guilt following acts of aggression against the frustrator. Holmes defined guilt operationally as the amount of aggression subjects said that they themselves would be willing to accept. This measure could also be taken as a measure of aggression directed against the self; it should be noticed that a guilt reaction is an aggressive reaction against the self, according to Freudian theory. However, masochistic aggression differs from guilt aggression, in that it follows, according to frustration-aggression theory, from an inhibition against expressing aggression towards a frustrator. The guilt reaction, on the other hand, is a consequence of an aggressive act. It is unfortunate that Holmes's study did not contain a condition where the subjects could only aggress against themselves, and not against either the frustrator or an innocent target. Had this been done, it might have been possible to separate experimentally guilt reactions from masochistic aggression. It is to be hoped that some future study will be addressed to this problem.

The social parallels to interpersonal masochistic displacement are somewhat easier to identify. Broadly speaking, one might state that masochistic displacement has its parallel when a subordinate group blames itself for its own discontents. In other words, the situation referred to is one where the dominated group has accepted a fatalistic ideology: instead of an intergroup analysis in which the dominant outgroup is seen as the prime cause of the ingroup's misfortunes, the group has an ideology of self-blame. Of course it is in the interests of the dominant group if this is the ideological belief of the subordinate group members, and the dominant group may do all it can to maintain this ideological false consciousness. The dominant group may continually humiliate the subordinate group, deny its members access to education and social success, and so arrange things such that the behaviour of the subordinate group will seem to confirm their status. The "lower orders" of society will live an unprivileged life and so "justify" their exclusion from the refinements of society. It is the hope of a dominant group that the "lower" strata will accept their station as legitimate. It is quite possible that the "greed" or "quickness to aspire beyond their social means" of low status groups whose lot is improving is due to the collapse of an ideology of self-blame. Once a few gains are made, the belief that the subordinate members cannot and should not aspire to a better life is disproved. The few gains destroy the illusion that the social inequalities are natural and immutable facts of nature. By their initial limited successes the subordinate group is creating a new ingroup ideology and is proving the falseness of the ideology of defeat and unworthiness, fostered by the superior outgroup.

In this sense the social parallel of masochistic displacement is essentially ideological: it refers to the ideology of a subordinate ingroup. There is another way of considering masochistic displacement in an intergroup context. This is to reverse the motivational account of ingroup displacement of aggression onto outgroups. Instead of postulating that ingroup conflicts are displaced onto the outgroup, one could argue that outgroup conflicts are displaced onto the ingroup. Such a situation would arise if the outgroup were strong and there were inhibitions against attacking it. Franz Fanon has adopted this type of motivational model in order to explain some of the facets of colonialism. He gives a vivid description of the sense of powerlessness that arises from the subordinate group's acceptance of the dominant group's ideology. He shows the degrading effects which arise when "the Negro has to wear the livery that the white man chooses for him" (Fanon, 1968). More than this, he adds a motivational premise to his account and suggests that masochistic displacement can occur in an intergroup context at a more irrational level. He characterises the colonial situation thus:

> The settler keeps alive in the native an anger which he deprives of outlet; the native is trapped in the tight links of the chains of colonialism ... While the settler has the right the live-long day to strike the native, to insult him and to make him crawl to them, you will see the native reaching for his knife at the slightest hostile or aggressive glance cast on him by another native; for the last resort of the native is to defend his personality *vis-à-vis* his brother. Tribal feuds only serve to perpetuate old grudges deep buried in the memory. By throwing himself with all his force into the vendetta, the native tries to persuade himself that colonialism does not exist, that everything is going on as before, that history continues. Here on the level of communal organisation we clearly discern the well-known behaviour patterns of avoidance. (Fanon, 1967, p. 42.)

Thus, according to Fanon, the aggression which should be directed against the frustrator is channelled back into the ingroup and gives rise to interpersonal aggression amongst ingroup members.

It is possible however to maintain the hypothesis that inhibition against attacking the dominant outgroup will affect ingroup behaviour without accepting a motivational presupposition. The previous account of displacement of aggression onto an outgroup was intended to show that the motivational premise was unnecessary; the same will be suggested briefly for masochistic displacement. Just as a unified subordinate group presents a potential threat to the dominant group, so a disunited subordinate group is correspondingly less dangerous. If the dominant group can maintain factionalism within the subordinate community then its power base is that much enhanced. Therefore, if an ideological consciousness is a danger, a purely interpersonal mode of action is not. So long as Fanon's natives fight amongst themselves, they are not challenging colonialism, and what is more, they are reinforcing the belief that they are unable to challenge the colonialist. The way forward for them is an ideological analysis of the intergroup situation which would entail a change from an interpersonal mode of action to an intergroup mode.[5]

The transition from an interpersonal to an intergroup mode can be illustrated by an example taken from Rainwater's (1966) description of Black lower-class family life in the United States. Rainwater recounts the experience of a black man working hard and saving his money in order to create a better life for his wife and child. His dreams of a better life are shattered when he loses his job, for refusing to work longer hours for no extra money. He suspects that this is merely a pretext for his dismissal, since his empoyer already had another black lined up for his job—a man who in fact he could pay less. After losing his job the man's family life crumbles, and his wife walks out on him. Rainwater reports that these misfortunes changed the man's political views from moderate to radical, especially with respect to race relations. Rainwater states that "again and again in his comments one can see the displacement into a public, race relations dialogue of the sense of rage, frustration and victimisation he had experienced in his ill-fated marriage" (1966, p. 194).

5. In Fanon's work the motivational premise serves an ideological function. He uses it to justify violence as a cleansing or cathartic force, which revitalises the oppressed ingroup. He provides a revolutionary counterpart of the conservative doctrine that all dissident violence is to be condemned as psychologically irrational. In Fanon's work dissident violence is praised *carte blanche* as a purification. This dangerous doctrine, like its conservative opposite number, is based on divorcing violence from the social context; as a result the motivational premises on which they both rest are untenable.

It would be absurd to claim, as Rainwater seems to imply, that this man's political beliefs were merely a displacement of interpersonal aggression arising from his broken marriage. The man is looking beyond his immediate interpersonal concerns; he sees the issue as one wider than the behaviour of his wife and is questioning the social context in which a hard-working man like himself can suddenly have his world destroyed by an unscrupulous employer. The general point at stake is wider than this particular example, and wider than the field of race relations. It relates to any intergroup situation of domination and to the development by the subordinate group of an ideology of intergroup action, which unites the ingroup to look beyond their immediate interpersonal concerns. It is through the development of an ideology of discontent that an existing system of intergroup inequalities can be challenged.

This line of thinking suggests that the growth of subordinate group opposition marks a change from an interpersonal mode to an intergroup mode of thought and action. If a radical ideology is overtly intergroup, then a conservative ideology, which seeks to prevent social change, might stress the value of the interpersonal mode. It may not be altogether fanciful to link this line of thought to the writings of those social psychologists who attempt in their analyses to reduce social frustrations to individual frustrations. Certainly it has been possible to identify a number of normative presuppositions in their formulations—enough to suggest that their "science" is by no means free from the ideological influences itself or totally neutral with respect to the phenomena it studies.

6

Gaming and Rational Conflict

Until now the main emphasis in this discussion has been on social psychological approaches which have stressed the irrational side of human nature. The psychoanalysts probed the instinctive unconscious in order to elucidate the hidden motivational determinants of intergroup conflict. Personality theorists have sought the locus of negative outgroup stereotypes in the psychological distortions of the prejudiced individual. In a similar spirit the frustration-aggression theorists concentrated upon the impulsive and irrational anger which follows frustrating experiences. These various approaches were broadly criticised for their failure to account for the more obvious cognitive aspects of intergroup relations. It has been argued that large-scale social aggression cannot be adequately explained if the ultimate causal determinants are sought in pre-social irrational impulses. Also it has been suggested that the irrational approach to mass social behaviour often itself entails a bias against forms of social action designed to promote fundamental changes.

In this chapter a more rational approach to the study of intergroup conflict will be discussed. One of the central tenets of Game Theory, and of the tradition of empirical research it has created, is the assumption that humans are rational thinking beings. Even if men are often prone to make errors of judgement, nevertheless it is assumed that such errors can be corrected. In fact it is one of the aims of the gaming approach to locate faulty decision-making and to provide the guidelines for enabling more rational decisions. As such the gaming approach is inevitably concerned with the surface cognitive variables, which tend to be neglected by the theorists of irrational behaviour. Inasmuch as it constitutes a specifically cognitive approach, it presents a theoretical contrast with the approaches which have been discussed in previous chapters.

In examining Game Theory and related gaming approaches it is inevitable that the topic of intergroup relations will not be discussed directly. It was mentioned in the last chapter that the frustration-aggression theorists considered their empirical studies of interpersonal behaviour to be relevant to the study of intergroup behaviour, and that they often hold implicitly reductionist assumptions. The same is by and large true of the gaming researchers. The belief that their work is relevant to problems of large-scale social phenomena is often not explicitly stated. However, the background context for this research testifies to the implicit connection between the interpersonal gaming studies and their potential for elucidating intergroup phenomena.

There are basically two contrasting schools of research workers in gaming research: the "war-gamers" and the "peace researchers". The war-gamers are often employed directly by military establishments to investigate problems of strategy and conflict behaviour. In their case the connection between the study of games on the one hand and the real-life situations of military conflict on the other hand is comparatively straightforward. The peace researchers, however, hope to abolish warfare, rather than make it more efficient. They generally hold the idealistic belief that their research might enable statesmen to avoid the irrationality of large-scale destructive conflict. The implicit connection between their gaming studies and the problems of intergroup relations can be illustrated by considering the *Journal of Conflict Resolution*, which is one of the main academic organs of the peace researchers. This journal has done more than any other to foster the study of gaming behaviour. It is an interdisciplinary journal, which welcomes contributions from all academic fields, with the only proviso that the research be relevant to problems of war and peace. The implication is clear—the research which is regularly published in the gaming section of this journal is considered to relate to group conflict and its resolution.

One of the ironies of the research of the war-gamers and peace researchers is that they often seem to be producing very similar lines of study. Their stated ideological opposition has by and large not always been reflected in their academic work. In the last chapter the importance of the concept of ideology was emphasised for the understanding of intergroup phenomena, and it was also argued that the social psychological theories of mass behaviour can themselves contain substantial ideological elements. These themes will reappear in the discussion of the gaming approach. To start with, the theoretical background of Game Theory and the concept of the rational decision-maker will be considered. Following this there will be an examination of the laboratory studies of interpersonal gaming; the discussion will stress the importance of social variables for understanding gaming behaviour. Finally in this chapter, questions will be raised about the suitability of gaming studies as models for intergroup phenomena, and also about their adequacy for providing the basis for more general theories of human behaviour. The main body of this discussion will revolve closely around the details of the gaming approach and around the experimental research produced by the gaming experimenters. Nevertheless, it is hoped that this will serve as a prelude to more detailed discussions of the implicit ideologies of the gaming researchers themselves.

Game theory and rationality

The primary impetus for studying group conflict through the examination of games came from outside the discipline of psychology. Although many of these ideas central to the theory of games have a long intellectual history (Plon, 1972), the renewed interest in games can be traced to *The Theory of Games and Economic Behaviour* by Von Neumann and Morganstern (1947). Neither of these two authors were psychologists, nor was the psychology of conflict their main interest. In fact their subject matter was not the behaviour of actual people in conflict situations; rather it was the logical possibilities available to hypothetical decision-makers. As such, Game Theory was intended to be a strategic guide, which would demonstrate the most rational and logical decisions for certain sorts of situations. In the words of one of the leading Game Theoreticians, their ideas represent a "depsychologised" decision theory (Rapoport, 1970, p. 3). Although not intended to be a psychological theory, nevertheless Game Theory has had a substantial influence on psychological research in the past fifteen years. In particular it has either directly or indirectly determined the course of social psychological research into conflict behaviour.

In essentials Game Theory is a branch of applied mathematics. Nevertheless some of its central concepts can be extracted from their original complex mathematical expression and described in simple everyday terms. One of the basic ideas is that of the "maximisation of utility" —this is the assumption that the rational decision-maker, or game-player, will try to extract for himself maximum benefit or utility from the given situation. In terms of Game Theory this is virtually a defini-tion of rationality (Luce and Raiffa, 1957; Mazur, 1968). A utility describes how much the outcome of a particular decision is worth to the decider. For instance, an individual might be deciding whether or not to gamble £1 on a bet, which would pay out £7 if he won. In this case the utility for him, if he wins, is £7, and the utility if he loses is —£1. By adopting the principle of the maximisation of utility, the decision-maker will only accept those bets which on average should pay him as much as possible, i.e. give him the greatest possible out-comes or utilities on balance. In the example just cited, the man should accept the bet if the probability of winning is greater than one chance in seven, and reject the bet if the probability of losing is greater than six chances in seven, with all other things being equal.

The gambling situation is a comparatively easy one for Game Theory to deal with. The evaluation of bets is based on the mathe-matical principle of multiplying the expected utility of the outcome by the expected probability of attaining that outcome. Once this is done, it is a fairly standard procedure to determine which bets are worthwhile risks and which are not. The major problems do not arise at this stage, but involve the estimation of the utilities and the proba-bilities themselves. The present interest in Game Theory is focussed on the topic of conflict between persons (and groups), rather than on betting decisions as such. Only the problems of Game Theory relating to the models of conflict will be discussed. For intance, the topic of the measurement and estimation of utilities will be considered—but it will be discussed in relation to attempts to construct models of inter-personal and intergroup conflict situations. Similarly the difficulties of the game-theoretic, or rational approach, to human psychology will be considered in the light of its applications to the study of conflict.

In one sense the pure gambling situation represents an intrapersonal conflict—an individual has his own personal conflict of whether or not to risk a certain sum of money. The conflict revolves around himself and his own decisions. No-one else is immediately involved at this stage. However, if the situation is looked at in a wider context, there is another person involved, namely the person with whom he makes the bet. This person also has had to make a decision—whether or not to offer a bet, and at what odds. If the gamble is looked at from this perspective it ceases to be purely an intrapersonal affair, involving only the would-be gambler; it becomes an interpersonal situation, where the eventual utilities accruing to each side are mutually dependent on their joint decisions. The wins and losses of the punter depend on the prices fixed by the bookmaker; similarly the wins and losses of the bookmaker depend on what bets are made by the punter. In this sort of situation the gains of the one will be the losses of the other; the bookmaker and the punter are in direct competition with one another. In saying this one is excluding all considerations of the social context of gambling. For instance, the overall profits of the bookmaker under nearly all circumstances are greater than the punters', even short-term gains by the punter are in fact usually in the long term interests of the bookmaker. If the overall social context is for the moment set aside, and only the individual bet is considered, then one can view the gambling situation in terms of a direct conflict between the punter and the bookmaker.

This conflict can be seen as a form of game. Game Theory analyses situations which involve the decisions of more than one person; the outcomes accruing to the "players" are dependent on their mutual decisions. Typically a game involves two persons, pitted against each other; there is no *a priori* reason why it should be restricted to two persons, and not involve a larger number. The Game Theory approach is to analyse such situations in order to prescribe what are the best, most rational decisions, for the participants. In the case of the punter and the bookmaker, it will suggest what are the most logical and profitable bets to be offered and accepted. In this case what the punter loses the bookmaker wins, and vice versa. Consequently the joint total gain to both must always be zero. This sort of situation is referred to by game theoreticians as a "zero-sum-game". The players in this sort of game can play the game rationally with only one motive, i.e. to gain as much as possible at the expense of the other player. Collaboration with the other player is irrational; to win the zero-sum game must, by definition, mean defeating the other player.

Not all game situations are of this type. It is one of the contributions of Game Theory that it can uncover the mathematical structure of different sorts of gaming situations. For instance, the mathemetical description of the zero-sum game differs from the mathematical description of those games which do not involve a direct relationship between one player's winnings and the other's losses. These sorts of games, non-zero-sum, can be more complicated. However, Game Theoreticians have discovered that the majority of these games can be "solved" if presented in a certain form. By "solution" it is implied that there is a rational decision for the players, if the games can be described in terms of a fixed number of players having a fixed number of choices. The most common form of game is the 2×2 game, in which there are two players and each can choose one of two moves. The eventual outcomes accruing to each are dependent on both players' decisions, and these eventual outcomes are normally expressed in numerical terms. The situation is essentially a narrow and well-defined one, and within these limits the Game Theoretician can state what is the most logical decision for each player. This solution depends on the famous "minimax" principle, which is an extension of the maximisation of utility principle combined with the principle that the rational player will also try to minimise losses.

Most of the games which can be numerically quantified can be solved by the minimax principle. Such games are referred to as having a "saddle-point", and completely rational players should always arrive at the same joint solutions. However, there are games without such a saddle-point, where there is no obvious solution. Typically these games are called mixed-motive games, because a description in terms of a simple minimax solution would appear unsatisfactory. These are the sorts of games which have particularly caught the attention of the psychologists and which have predominantly been used as a research tool for the analysis of conflict. Above all other mixed-motive games stands the prisoner's dilemma game—this 2×2 mixed-motive, non-zero-sum game has attracted more attention than probably any other single game from the mathematical theoreticians as well as from the social psychologists.

The formal features of the prisoner's dilemma game have been detailed by Luce and Raiffa (1957) and by Rapoport and Chammah (1965). However, it is possible to describe the essential features of this game in ordinary language. Basically it is a situation in which two rational strategies conflict—in this case the individual interest of each player conflicts with their combined interests. The dilemma for each player is whether he should co-operate with the other player to secure maximum joint gain, or whether he should play competitively and risk ending up with less if the other also plays competitively. The game takes its title, and indeed its basic structure, from an old fable about two prisoners, who have been separately arrested for murder. Each is faced with the dilemma of whether to tell tale to the authorities about the other or not. Thus each has to make one out of two choices. They both know that the other has been arrested, but they have no way of finding out whether the other has told the authorities anything or not. If they both implicate the other then they both will be sentenced to life imprisonment because the authorities will have incriminating evidence against both of them. If only one tells tale, then he will go scot free and the other will hang. If both keep quite then neither will hang, but it is possible that the authorities will charge them on some very minor offence. In terms of joint outcome it is obviously best if both keep quiet; the dilemma is that by keeping quiet it is also possible to receive the worst outcome, i.e. being hanged if the other does not also keep quiet. The dilemma therefore can be viewed in terms of whether to risk cooperation or whether to play competitively for the highest stakes.

It is because of the mathematical formulations of Game Theory that the precise structures of these 2×2 games can be elucidated, at least abstractly. It is possible to write out payoff matrices of the outcomes for each player contingent on their joint but independent decisions. Rapoport and Guyer (1966), were able to make an exhaustive list of all the possible types of 2×2 games. This was done theoretically by examining the mathematical relationships between the various types of payoff, quantitatively expressed, within the confines of the 2×2 game. Rapoport and Guyer showed by their Game Theory analysis that there are 78 strategically distinct possible games, including the prisoner's dilemma. In this way the formal properties of different gaming situations can be compared. Rapoport has concluded that Game Theory is more than a prescriptive theory which stipulates the most rational strategies to be pursued under specifically defined circumstances. According to Rapoport it can also lead to a fuller understanding of conflict situations themselves. On this view Game Theory is:

> ... essentially a structural theory. It uncovers the *logical structure* of a great variety of conflict situations and describes the structure in mathematical terms ... The discovery of logical structures of conflict situations

therefore allows a classification of conflicts. (Rapoport, 1965, p. 196, italics in original.)

The implication for the study of conflict and its resolution is clear. If conflicts can be categorised according to their logical structure in the gaming situation, and then be solved, Game Theory might be of help in solving real-life conflicts. If actual disputes between persons and groups are categorised according to their logical structures, then rational considerations, rather than emotional ones, might prevail. Whereas men once had only their instincts and intuitions to guide them, now rationality can be the yardstick. Unnecessary conflicts might be avoided if the expected utilities are calculated beforehand and the principle of minimax used to guide behaviour. These are obviously not trivial and unimportant implications. However, this dream of a rational arrangement of human affairs depends on certain presuppositions. There are a number of questions that need to be answered before one can state with any confidence that the Game Theory approach is of any relevance to the study of actual human conflicts. Such questions include whether actual human behaviour is guided by principles of rationality as postulated by Game Theory. More than this, it needs to be asked if it is possible to order human affairs according to such principles. Bound up with these two problems are questions about the relationship between the narrow and defined conflict situations of the 2×2 game and actual conflicts. If there is little psychological relationship between the two, then the model derived from the narrow situation will be of limited use for analysing the larger one. In fact it could be a definite hindrance, which acts as a smokescreen obscuring the real features of genuine conflict situations. In any analysis of the rational approach to the study of conflict, these questious must be taken into account.

If Game Theory provides a logical framework, then it can be compared to actual behaviour in the gaming situation. In particular, it is possible to use the Game Theory criterion of rationality in order to discover how far people conform to this conception of rationality. An analogy can be made with the psychological study of language. Psycholinguists have made comparisons between abstract models of language usage, as devised by linguists, and actual language behaviour as studied. It is interesting to note that at the same time as the abstract Game Theory models were being put to the test of experimentation, psycholinguists were attempting to compare the "ideal speakers" of linguistic theory (Chomsky, 1957; 1965) with actual speech (see for instance, Green, 1972). Similarly gaming experimenters aimed to discover what was the relationship between the "ideal" players of mathematical Game Theory, and actual flesh-and-blood game players in the psychological laboratories.

The primary question, then, is whether humans actually show the rationality which the ideal player shows in the abstract formulations of Game Theory. The short answer to this question is that by and large they do not. This relates both to individual choice behaviour (Dolbear and Lave, 1967) and to gaming behaviour proper. One gaming study indicating this is that conducted by Messick (1967). Human subjects played a zero-sum game against a computer, which had been programmed to adopt a number of different game-playing strategies. According to Game Theory, players in a zero-sum game should not be influenced by the play of the opponent—they should persist in the optimal "rational" strategy which is obtained from the minimax principle, i.e. they should always choose the solution to the game. Messick's subjects did not adopt this principle but were influenced by the choices of the computer. Messick summarises his results thus:

> In complete accord with previous research on the issue, the study reported here unambiguously indicates that human Ss do not behave in a manner consistent with the minimax theory. The very fact that Ss react differently to different opponents suggests that the determinants of human decision strategies in interdependent contexts are not exclusively those dealt with by the classical theory of games. Specifically, game theory asserts that one's strategy should be a function solely of the payoff matrix. It is a matter of empirical fact that this is not the case. (Messick, 1967, p. 46.)

If actual observed behaviour deviates from the optimal rational strategies, then this could arise from two possibilities: (a) humans try but are unable to make the calculations required in order to achieve rationality; (b) humans do not even attempt to play rationally, but have motivations outside the scope of the Game Theory model. If the former is the case, then the deviations from the "rational" model are due to human frailties and inadequacies, and the Game Theoretician can with justification claim that his models have educative value. A knowledge of Game Theory and its techniques would then help to obviate the errors which humans commonly make in decision-making situations. If the latter is the case, the use and scope of Game Theory becomes inevitably restricted—it refers primarily to abstract humans, and may not help actual humans solve their real non-mathematical affairs. Therefore the crucial question for Game Theory is not so much whether behaviour deviates from the ideal model, but rather, why this deviation should occur in the first place.

If irrationality in game-playing were due to inadequate calculation, then one of the reasons for this could centre around the calculation of the payoffs. It could well be that experimental subjects have been unable to make the necessary mathematical reckoning in order to apply the minimax principle effectively. The time in which they have to make their decisions, and the form of the payoff matrices in the experimental games, may possibly not be conducive to efficient calculation. Therefore one needs to examine behaviour in those situations where the calculations for the subject are not difficult and where the sorts of decisions are not far removed from everyday sorts of decisions. If in such situations there is still a preponderance of irrational decisions, then the "faulty calculation" hypothesis would have to be rejected; one would need to investigate what other motivations, apart from the simple maximisation of utilities, people have in the game-playing situation. This would be necessary in order to determine whether these sorts of conflict situations are perceived in terms quite remote from the Game Theoretic calculations of personal self-interest.

A study by Tropper (1972) fits the requirements of an experiment in which the payoffs are quite clear to the subjects and the method of play a simple one. This experiment is based on a game devised by Shubik (1971). The game is a form of auction, involving two players; however, both have to pay their top bid although only the very highest bidder actually receives the auctioned object. Thus the second bidder is forced to pay for nothing in return. As Shubik (1971) remarked, the conventional Game Theory analysis of this situation is trivial (p. 111); however, the game derives its interest from psychological rather than strategic considerations. Tropper found striking confirmation of this in his operationalisation of Shubik's game. Amongst the objects auctioned were one-dollar bills. In this case the value of the utility to be gained is quite clear, and so was the value of the potential losses, since the subjects made their bids in real money, too. The results were clear-cut—the subjects consistently bid more for the objects than their actual value. Thus the subjects were willing to pay as much as three and a half dollars for a one-dollar bill. Under no circumstances could this sort of behaviour be considered rational in terms of money paid out and money received.

Tropper interpreted his results as demonstrating that the subjects' main motivation was not to secure the best bargains possible in economic terms. It was to pursue victory over the other player, even if such victory is worth less financially than the effort expended in obtaining it. In Game Theory terms, Pyrrhic victories are defeats, but in psychological terms the victory itself seemed to be of prime value. This conclusion is supported by results from other game playing studies. McClintock and McNeel (1967) listed three possible motives for subjects in the game-playing situation: (1) maximising one's own gain; (2) maximising the joint gain to all players; (3) maximising the difference between one's own gain and one's opponent's gain. It is this last strategy which corresponds to the desire to beat one's opponent; when this strategy is pursued in opposition to the desire to maximise one's own gain, then the result can be the Pyrrhic victory. In order to discover whether subjects would pursue such a course, McClintock and NcNeel devised the Maximising Difference Game—a 2×2 non-zero-sum game with little inherent mathematical interest. Experiments using this game have consistently shown that subjects' game playing behaviour is affected by the motive to do "better" than their opponent (e.g. McClintock and McNeel, 1966a; Messick and McClintock, 1968; McClintock and Nuttin, 1969; Marwell, Ratcliffe and Schmitt, 1969; McClintock, Nuttin and McNeel, 1970).

These studies all point to the conclusion that it is not just the maximisation of money or points that motivates subjects in the experimental situation. There is also the social motivation to excel the opponent. This desire would seem to be outside the confines of Game Theory itself. However, it could be argued that these findings do not necessarily contradict the assumption of rationality—all they show is that experimental subjects' utilities are complex and difficult to calculate. The rational model of human behaviour can still be preserved if one states that there is a positive utility in excelling the opponent, i.e. that winning has a value in itself. Any model of human behaviour would have to take into account this value. In other words, social gains must be calculated along with the more obvious monetary gains. The argument would be that if the social utilities are considered, then humans still can be said to base their behaviour on the principle of maximising their gains.

This point of view has been advocated by a number of social scientists; the most notable and influential have been Thibaut and Kelley (1959), and Homans (1961). These writers accept that the basic motivation behind human behaviour is the maximisation of utilities; although these utilities do not have to be financial or economic, nevertheless they rest upon versions of the maximisation assumption. The Game Theory flavour of this analysis can be illustrated by a quotation from Thibaut and Kelley who describe the basic psychological processes that mediate interpersonal relations, and in particular dyadic relations, thus:

> . . . whatever the gratifications achieved in dyads, however lofty or fine the motives satisfied may be, the relationship may be viewed as a trading or bargaining one. The basic assumption running throughout our analysis is that every individual voluntarily enters and stays in any relationship only as it is adequately satisfactory in terms of his rewards and costs. (Thibaut and Kelley, 1959, p. 37.)

Similarly Homans (1961) analyses human behaviour in terms of the exchange of rewards and costs; and he assumes that humans choose courses of action that produce the maximum rewards and the minimum costs.

This application of the minimax principle to general theories of human behaviour raises a number of crucial issues. However, at present, only one minor aspect will be considered; this relates to the usefulness of this kind of approach which describes human behaviour in terms of rewards and costs. Such theories can only be maintained if everything which is valued can be counted as a reward. The problem then is to estimate such rewards. The theories become least tautologous if there is no way of making such an estimation. Just to state that people must believe that they are maximising their rewards, if they act in a particular way, explains nothing, so long as there is no independent way of estimating these rewards. The concept of "reward" is then a vacuous concept, one that is synonymous with "whatever people do". When faced with particular pieces of behaviour, which seem at first sight to contradict the maximisation principle, such as for instance martyrdom and altruism, the rationalist must postulate that there is value or reward for some people in being a martyr or a hero. This is stated simply because people behave in this way and people only behave voluntarily in ways that maximise rewards. The circularity and pointlessness of this sort of argument is obvious and should not need to be laboured.

The crucial problem, then, for any general theory of human behaviour, based upon the principles of behaviour exchange, is the measurement of rewards and costs. Unfortunately for such theorists as Homans and Thibaut and Kelley, there has been no solution to this problem. It has been found possible to assess and quantify utilities in certain restricted laboratory situations. For instance, Ofshe and Ofshe (1970) have been able to present a theory of behaviour in coalition games based upon the maximisation of subjective utilities. This approach has been praised for its success on a theoretical level (Burhams, 1973); nevertheless it should be recognised that it refers to a very narrow range of human behaviour in rigidly controlled experimental situations. Accounts which have attempted to describe more naturalistic types of decision-making in terms of the maximisation of utilities have been altogether less successful; for instance, Patchen (1965) in his critique of Singer's (1963) attempt to describe real life decision-making, has suggested that the concept of "utility" should be abandoned and alternative approaches explored.

In a similar vein, Wiberg (1972) has contended that it has not been possible to assess utilities with any degree of success outside the laboratory situation. He goes further and argues against the plausibility of ever producing meaningful measures of non-trivial utilities. His basic argument is that certain human preferences must inevitably present serious difficulties for any attempt at quantitative mathematical analysis. What is beyond doubt is that no such attempt to date has achieved anything but a very limited success; there still does not exist any ready-made technique of measurement to give body to the theoretical framework of Thibaut and Kelley, and of Homans. The present state of such theoretical positions has been little advanced since their first formulations, especially with respect to the measurement of their central concepts. Thus Abrahamsson (1970) has shown how Homans is forced to admit, because of his theoretical presuppositions, that the same behaviour sometimes has a reward value, and sometimes it has a cost value—and that there is no way, in Homans's schema, of determining whether the bahaviour has a reward or cost value at any particular time, except in observing whether the behaviour in question is performed or not. In this way his explanatory framework is reduced to circularity. Kelley (1968) has openly admitted that lack of measurement produces difficulties; however, he takes the view that it is not the job of social psychologists to devise instruments for measuring utilities, since this would distract them from their proper job of investigating the purely social psychological aspects of behaviour. In practice this has meant that Kelley has tended to use the concepts of reward and cost less in his later writings, and to employ more psychological concepts (for instance, his work on "interpersonal accommodation" and "attribution theory"; Kelley, 1967 and 1968). Therefore in a practical sense Kelley has abandoned any theory of human behaviour based upon a rigid determination of utilities.

The conclusion from this would seem to be that the overall theories of rational human behaviour have little psychological interest on their own. If they do have any interest, it has to be imparted from sources outside the basic Game Theory approach. For instance, Thibaut and Kelley in their analysis use the concept of a "comparative level of reward". People do not act purely in terms of rewards and costs received and given—they also have standards of comparison to assess these rewards and costs. This idea of a "comparative level" is not of itself derived from the rationalist analysis, but has strong affinities with the sociological concept of "reference group" and the social psychological concept of "social comparison".

At present it is sufficient to note the vacuousness of a straight rationalist theory of human motivation. Plon (1972 and 1973) has suggested that although this approach may have little scientific interest, it does contain a great deal of ideological content, and is a natural adjunct of certain conservative economic theories. The rationalist analysis, as it relates to the study of conflict, would then seem to be at an impasse. On the one hand, it has been found that humans react irrationally, and on the other hand it has been argued that it is unsatisfactory to attempt to widen the rationalist theory to encompass this irrationality. Therefore the rationalist model must be seen as having limited value as a psychological theory. From this, it seems there is a short step to the conclusion that its limitations derive from the essential irrationality of humans. The lack of correspondence between maximisation theories and evidence from game-playing experiments would suggest that humans conduct their affairs in an irrational manner.

Such a conclusion, together with its moral overtones, should be resisted. The nature of "rationality" and "irrationality" as defined by the minimax principle should be briefly considered, especially with respect to one area where actual game-playing behaviour would seem to correspond to the prescription of Game Theory. The most frequent gaming situation in experimental gaming research has been the prisoner's dilemma (see, for instance Gallo and McClintock, 1965; Vinacke, 1969; Nemeth, 1970; and Oskamp, 1971, for reviews). The original dilemma has been operationalised and the choices open to the players are expressed in monetary values, rather than prison sentences and hangings. The consistent finding from the experimental research is that the overall level of cooperation is low. In terms of the original dilemma this means that most people choose to implicate the other, and not adopt the cooperative strategy of keeping quiet. Far from learning to act according to mutual advantage during the course of successive plays of the prisoner's dilemma game, there is an increase in competitiveness. Typically the game ends with both players making competitive choices; and once this competitive sequence is started, neither player seems able to break out of it. If only one player tries to break out of the deadlock, then he risks losing even more, if the other continues to play competitively. Thus both players get "locked in" to a mutually competitive strategy, and both are the losers for this. This sort of result is not the product of a particular experimental technique—the basic prisoner's dilemma has been presented to subjects in various different forms without the results being particularly affected (Evans and Crumbaugh, 1966; Pruitt, 1967; Kanouse and Wiest, 1967; and Oskamp and Kleinke, 1970). Also the value of the payoffs has been systematically varied without the end results being necessarily altered (e.g. Wrightsman, 1966; Gumpert, Deutsch and Epstein, 1969; although certain dissenting views concerning the importance of payoff values have been expressed by Gallo, 1968; Slusher et al., 1974; Friedland et al., 1974).

All in all therefore, there has been a considerable amount of evidence to suggest that, in certain sorts of experimental conflict situations, subjects will persist in making mutually disadvantageous responses. This occurs even when the responses concern real monetary rewards. It might be thought that here is a supreme example of irrational human behaviour—irrational in the sense that humans seem consistently to choose to compete with one another instead of being able to combine together for the mutual benefit of both. The players seem to find themselves unnecessarily in conflict within this sort of situation. The prisoner's dilemma might then represent one of those situations where Game Theoretic calculations would provide a solution, and where purely "rational" considerations, efficiently worked out, would obviate the unnecessary conflict.

However, it is just at this point that Game Theory falls down. There is no easy answer to the prisoner's dilemma according to mathematical Game Theory. In fact the mathematical application of the minimax principle to the dilemma reveals that the competitive strategy is the most rational (O'Connor, Baker and Wrightsman, 1972). If both players use the "rational" minimax strategy they will end up by being locked into a joint losing sequence of plays. And this of course is what happens. Subjects therefore act "rationally" in this situation according to game theory, but according to common-sense they would seem to be acting irrationally. The question is whether this paradox can be resolved. Firstly it should be noticed that there have been attempts to improve the basic Game Theory analysis of the prisoner's dilemma, so that the "solution" can prescribe mutual cooperation. However these attempts have been made by extending the mathematical framework of Game Theory, and not by improving calculations within that framework. For instance, Howard (1966) introduced the concept of the meta-game, and Shubik (1970) has argued that this introduction necessitates sociopsychological assumptions about the nature of "plausible threats". Similarly, Shubik's own resolution of the prisoner's dilemma involves the addition of certain economic assumptions (Shubik, 1964 and 1970). It seems that a purely mathematical strategic theory, which makes no assumptions about the psychology of the players or about the economic context in which they play, is unable to prescribe a procedure for both players to achieve jointly maximum gain. If this is the case then the "rationality" of pure Game Theory strategies must be called into question.

The point is that the concept of "rationality" is defined within the confines of mathematical theory—however, humans do not live within the confines of mathematical theory. The real world is infinitely more complex than the mathematical one. The decisions which face humans do not necessarily conform to the limitations of the 2×2 matrix. This can be seen in situations where the prisoner's dilemma has been held to be the underlying model of real life decision-making situations. For instance, the decision facing two nuclear superpowers of whether to disarm unilaterally or to continue nuclear stockpiling can be interpreted in terms of the prisoner's dilemma. In this case the "rational" Game Theory solution would advise both sides to continue building up their nuclear armaments. Similarly Dawes (1973) and Dawes, Delay and Chaplin (1974) have described the decision whether or not to pollute the environment in terms of the prisoner's dilemma matrix; they have shown how the "rational" decision would result in massive pollution. They argue that such an outcome is recommended by Game Theory, because the prisoner's dilemma format artificially restricts the number of considerations, which are taken into account. Consequently the 2×2 matrix oversimplifies the complexity of actual decision-making and its "rational" prescriptions can as a result become distortions.

However it is not merely the case that the gaming analysis oversimplifies by restricting the range of relevant factors. Actual decision-making does not only depend upon the maximisation of utilities, but also involves the beliefs and actions of others. It is illogical and absurd to base one's decisions on the assumption that other decision-makers will react like computers pre-programmed with Game Theory strategies. Wiberg (1972) in a lengthy discussion of this issue has demonstrated that many facets of everyday decision-making call into question the elementary mathematical assumptions of Game Theory. If everyday decision-making were modified to accord with the canons of mathematical theory, then the result would not be a well-ordered existence, with unnecessary conflicts forever abolished. Rather it would entail an incapacity to engage in a number of ordinary activities. The social world is not a neutral mathematical universe. The failure of Game Theoretic strategies to arrive at a commonsense solution to the prisoner's dilemma situation in a controlled laboratory situation is ample proof of that. Even in the tightly controlled laboratory situation, subjects have specifically social motivations. Consequently it would seem necessary to examine the social processes, which affect the subjects' interpersonal interactions in such situations.

Social processes in gaming experiments

By and large experiments using 2×2 mixed-motive games have demonstrated the complexity of human motivations, even within the limits of the controlled laboratory situation. Already mentioned have been the studies which have shown that the subjects are motivated by a desire to excel opponents. Numerous other studies have demonstrated that

social factors are of considerable importance in determining the outcome of experimental conflict situations. It is not just a matter of
subjects coldly and dispassionately applying strategic principles to a
clearly-defined payoff matrix. The subjects take their normal conceptual outlook with them into the laboratory. They do not cease to be
ordinary social beings, prompted by a multitude of different motivations, once they step into the settings engineered by the gaming
experimenter.

First of all, there have been a number of experiments which have
shown the social nature of the gaming situation. An exhaustive review
is not intended; however, certain results will be mentioned in order
to illustrate the general point that although the experimental conflict
situations may be highly contrived and controlled, the subjects themselves are not. The experimental game may have a certain intrinsic
simplicity. However, to gain an understanding of the actual behaviour
in such situations, one needs more than a mathematical analysis. This
is so because it has been shown that the subjects' behaviour in gaming
situations is not merely motivated by the desire to maximise profit or
to defeat their opponent. Other, more social considerations, must be
taken into account. For instance, Kaplowitz (1973) has shown that
ethical considerations affect game play, and that subjects expect their
opponents to follow an equity norm. Baker (1974) concludes from his
study that gaming research generally has neglected the importance of
equitable behaviour and that the existence of an equity norm means
that "economically irrational behaviour may not necessarily be unreasonable behaviour" (p. 316). Also there have been a considerable
number of studies demonstrating that the characteristics of the opponent can affect play, contrary to the rationalistic precepts of game
theory. For example, Baxter (1973) and Knight and Mack (1973) have
shown that the race of the opponent can have an affect on the behaviour of American subjects; Mack et al. (1971) and Mack and Knight
(1974) have shown differences according to the sex of the opponent.
Similarly Swingle and Gillis (1968) have shown that play between
friends differs significantly from play between non-friends. These
examples all reinforce the basic point that subject behaviour in actual
gaming-situations is determined by more than the features of the game
matrix.

The recent tendency in gaming research has been to focus attention
on the social processes within the gaming situation. As O'Connor,

Baker and Wrightsman (1972) have argued: "The PD game (prisoner's dilemma) may not be a rigorously controlled experiment in even the most stringent settings and may not control variables which may have tremendous significance for our understanding of the game" (p. 26). Instead of interpreting the subjects' plays in the game as being evidence for either competitive or cooperative motivations, these authors asked their subjects to indicate their strategies after the game in a questionnaire. The results showed that a considerable number of subjects were in fact neither trying to be competitive nor cooperative —they were experimenting with moves and amusing themselves. As one subject reported "I got tired of flipping the blue, so every once in a while I would flip the red one to make things a little different" (O'Connor, Baker and Wrightsman, 1972, p. 26). Thus the same objective play on the game matrix can have a number of different subjective meanings. The same particular choice might reflect a desire to compete or an effort to stave off boredom. The utilities of the game matrix cannot, therefore, be assumed to be the utilities of the subjects.

The importance of the social context of the gaming experiment has been demonstrated by several investigators. Alexander and Weil (1969) examined the gaming situation from a symbolic interactionist viewpoint—they investigated the meaning of the situation to the participants and showed how the game playing behaviour was affected in changes in social interpretation. They found that both within and between experimental conditions the meaning of the various moves in the game was perceived as altering. The psychological meaning of the situation cannot be said to be dependent on the properties of the matrix alone—the importance of the matrix in the total situation must be considered. Similarly Abric and Kahan (1972) found that subjects were not so much influenced by the actual behaviour of the opponent, but by the image or representation of the opponent. Similar results have been found by Marlowe *et al.* (1966) and Baxter (1973). Other specifically social variables have also been found to affect game-playing; for instance, Meeker and Shure (1969) and Brown (1968) have shown the effects of the presence of an audience on game-playing. Messé *et al.* (1973) have shown the influence of prior non-gaming behaviour on gaming research, and Friedland, Arnold and Thibaut (1974) have shown that the subjects' previous gains affect their gaming choices.

If the gaming situation is to be seen as a social situation, in which the usual social psychological variables operate, then one can inquire as to the nature of the interaction between the subject and his opponent. This would mean looking at the gaming situation in terms of the mutual effects of the behaviour of *both* players, rather than concentrating upon the effects of the mathematical structure of the game on the behaviour of the *individual* player. The situation is then seen as a form of social interaction. This has been effected by manipulating the strategy of the other player in a two person game situation. A number of studies have considered this problem by having experimental subjects playing against a "stooge" or simulated opponent. In such experiments the feedback that the real subject obtains concerning his opponent's responses can be carefully controlled during the course of the game. The original studies which used this technique generally reported negative results. For example, Bixenstine and Wilson (1963) compared the decisions of subjects in a prisoner's dilemma game, when they faced an "opponent", who used a random strategy of 83% cooperative responses, with a subject who used 83% competitive response. Very little effect was found to have been produced by these differing strategies of the "opponent". Similar results were found by McClintock, Harrison, Strand and Gallo (1963) where the opponent used strategies of either 15%, 50% or 85% random cooperative responses.

These results helped to encourage the notion that the crucial variable in the gaming-situation was the game itself. If the strategy of the opponent was an unimportant variable, then maybe the major determinant was the structure of the payoff matrix—the logical features of which could be uncovered by Game Theory. Unfortunately, as has been seen, the Game Theory analysis is limited in this regard. Moreover, subsequent research has shown how important the strategy of the other can be; it has also shown, contrary to the earlier findings, that the opponent's strategy can be of more importance than the formal properties of the game itself. All that studies like those of Bixenstine and Wilson (1963) and McClintock *et al.* (1963) showed was that pre-planned strategies administered in a random fashion did not affect the real subject's choices. In both these experiments the percentage of cooperative and competitive responses was determined in advance and these responses were made regardless of the real subject's responses. In other words, there was no genuine interaction between the "opponent" and the subject. The "opponent" could not be said to be acting in any meaningful sense or attempting in any way to communicate with the real subject. Under such circumstances, it is perhaps not particularly surprising that the subject and the "opponent" did not manage to reach a tacit agreement to both play cooperatively and so increase their mutual joint gain.

Those experiments which have not used rigidly pre-programmed randomised strategies have yielded very different results. Such studies have used "opponents" playing according to contingent strategies; i.e. the "opponent's" choices are contingent upon the decisions of the subject himself. In Sermat's (1967) experiment, using both prisoner's dilemma and "chicken" games, the opponent played a "tit-for-tat" strategy; this entailed making the same response as the subject had made on the previous trial. Under such circumstances Sermat found a high level of cooperation. This finding has been replicated in other studies; it has been sonsistently found that contingent strategies of "opponents" produce significantly more cooperation than noncontingent randomised strategies (e.g. Wrightsman, Davis *et al.* 1972; Wrightsman, Lucker *et al.* 1972; Whitworth and Lucker, 1972). In these studies the strategy of the "opponent" was found to be the crucial determinant of the subject's level of cooperation, as compared to other variables, e.g. the race of the opponent, prior training, philosophies of life, etc. (see also Oskamp, 1970 and 1974).

It is not only contingent strategies of opponents that have been found to affect the play of the real subject. Sudden changes in strategy can also affect game behaviour. For instance, Harford and Solomon (1967) compared two types of changes in strategy: there was the "reformed sinner" who began by consistently playing competitively but then changed to a strategy of cooperation—also there was the "lapsed saint" whose behaviour was the exact reverse; the lapsed saint started by playing cooperatively but then changed to a competitive strategy. The results showed that the "reformed sinner" was particularly effective in eliciting cooperative responses from the actual subjects. Consequently a noncontingent "other-strategy" significantly determined the game-playing behaviour of the real subjects.

Oskamp (1971), in a detailed review of the effects of programmed strategies, came to the conclusion that the strategy of the other was a critical determinant of behaviour if that strategy was either contingent, or as in Harford and Solomon's study contained abrupt changes. The question, then, is why these two sorts of strategies should be more effective in determining behaviour than the noncontingent randomised strategies. The answer to this should be clear from the previous discussion about the meaning of the various plays in the gaming experiment. Put simply, both the contingent and the abruptly changing strategies of the other are meaningful. In the case of the contingent strategy, an interaction of some sort is possible—the subject can affect, and realise he is affecting, the behaviour of the other. In this way there can be some sort of minimal dialogue between the two. The moves themselves can transmit meaning and messages, especially since in the normal game-experiment explicit communication is impossible. This sort of dialogue is what the theorists of conflict behaviour call "strategic interaction"; the game-plays are taken as meaningful communications in themselves and as such are an intergral part of the social interaction between the players (Ladner, 1973).

In the case of noncontingent abrupt changes in strategy, there is also the possibility of strategic interaction. The fact that such changes can be perceived as meaningful can be illustrated by the names that Harford and Solomon (1967) give them. The terms "lapsed saint" and "reformed sinner" are in themselves descriptive and convey certain assumptions about past and present motivation. No such descriptive labels easily suggest themselves for the 85% randomised either competitive or cooperative strategy. One could call the player of such a strategy a "generally competitive/cooperative individual with inconsistent lapses"; but in so doing the problem is highlighted. One cannot trust a fellow who shows such inconsistency, especially when his lapses appear to have no meaning. There must be an element of untrustworthiness and unpredictability about such a player; the question is whether the prisoner in the original dilemma would stick his neck out and risk his life for such a fellow. A negative answer to this question would help to explain the high number of competitive responses in the experimental situations.

If the hypothesis is correct that strategic interaction is an important factor in experimental games, then a prediction can be made. One could predict that as actual communication increases between the players, then so should the strategic interaction decrease. The pronounced effects of the "opponent's" strategy should be diminished by actual interaction. An experiment by Michelini (1971) provides some evidence on this point. In this study the contact between the two players was systematically manipulated—the subjects either had some positive prior interaction, visual contact during the game, the expectation of future interaction, or no contact at all. The results revealed that as contact between the subjects was diminished, the importance of the opponent's strategy increased in its effect on game-playing. It might be concluded that the importance of strategic interaction increases as the possibility of actual interaction decreases, at least in this sort of artificial experimental situation. Certainly prior free communication between subjects can be effective in producing mutual cooperation in situations where individual advantage conflicts with joint advantage, (e.g. the classic experiment of Mintz, 1951). Similarly, closer physical contact between the players can increase cooperation, (Durkin, 1972; Gardin, *et al.,* 1973; Nydegger, 1974), as can communication during the game (Voissem and Sistrunk, 1971; Wichman, 1970).

The trend of the argument in this section has been to emphasise the importance of social motivations and processes in the gaming experiment. It has been stressed that the experimental game is essentially an interpersonal interaction, which the participants impart with their own meaning and significance. The moves in an experimental game do not just centre around the mathematical values of the payoffs. If strategic interaction takes place, and there is every reason to think that it does, then the psychological importance of the various moves needs to be determined. In the course of a game the same move can be seen as, for instance, a concession, a threat, a refusal to cooperate, etc. Whatever it is perceived as, and intended to be, depends on the interpretations of the participants. In a sense, the game is little else than a restricted bargaining situation, in which direct agreements are not possible. Just because the subjects cannot use ordinary language to communicate with one another, does not mean that they do not use their ordinary language concepts to interpret the situation. It should be remembered that these concepts are derived from situations where they are applicable, and where non-linguistic mathematical calculations may be inoperative. The language of bargaining and diplomacy is deliberately subtle and unclear. Shubik (1970) has argued that this subtlety of language invalidates the purely Game Theory approach to the study of interpersonal conflict:

Many of the "plays" and the counterplays in bargaining involve words and gestures whose meanings are often deliberately ambiguous . . . It is precisely the presence of this ambiguity that gives rise to much of the art of "gamesmanship". Skilled negotiators and lawyers thrive on the ambiguity. (Shubik, 1970, p. 191.)

Thus the analysis of game-playing behaviour would seem to be leading away from its origins in mathematical theory and into broader issues of social psychological theory. In this respect it should be no surprise that there has been a proliferation of games used in experimental studies which are not as easily quantifiable as the prisoner's dilemma, "chicken", etc. Such games are not intended to be operationalisations of certain mathematically defined conflict situations as the classic 2×2 games were. For instance the "trucking-game" experiment of Deutsch and Krauss (1960 and 1962) was intended to investigate the role of threats in a bargaining situation. In these experiments the "threats" were not operationally defined in terms of certain mathematical values of the payoff matrix. Rather the threats were based on actions with more immediate psychological impact for the subjects— the blocking of a one-way road which both players have to use in their capacity as make-believe truck drivers. Deutsch and Krauss defined the use of a gate to block this road as a threat, and concluded that the possibility of using threats decreased the likelihood of cooperation. These findings have been debated by Kelley (1965) and Shomer, Davis and Kelley (1966); they contend that the Deutsch and Krauss definition of "threat" prejudges the issue. More recently, Froman and Cohen (1969) have attempted to extend Deutsch and Krauss's findings beyond the trucking-game; also Cheney, Harford and Solomon (1972) have thrown further light on the effects of threats in the trucking-game. In this experiment, subjects were allowed to send different sorts of messages depending on the experimental condition: contingent or noncontingent promissory messages, contingent or noncontingent threatening messages, both or neither.

This more recent trucking-game experiment has not stifled the criticism of the operational definition of the key concept of "threat". Rapoport (1972) in his discussion of the study by Cheney *et al.* criticises all such attempts to operationalise ordinary language concepts in anything but mathematical terms. He argues that such studies reveal:

> . . . the futility of posing hypotheses couched in concepts derived from everyday language, with a view to testing them by behavioural experiments. When such experiments are undertaken, concepts like "threat" or "cooperation" are (implicitly or explicitly) defined operationally in terms of behavioural criteria. In different experiments those criteria are different, so there is ample reason to expect that the results may well point to different conclusions. (Rapoport, 1972, p. 95.)

This point clearly has substance—it would be absurd to build a general theory of cooperation on the basis of the trucking experiments alone. However, Rapoport's own remedy to this problem is drastic. Instead of advocating the study of the social variables as they relate to the overall meaning of each experimental situation, he advocates a rigid operationalisation which would in fact restrict the examination of social variables. His is a resistance to the separation of gaming experiments from their parent Game Theory. He has argued that concepts such as threat must be operationalised in terms of the mathematical structure of the game in order to avoid the confusions which are contained within the ordinary language terms (confusions, it might be added, which could motivate the subjects' behaviour and perceptions). By tying the experimental analysis closer to the mathematical analysis, Rapoport (1968) advocates a restriction of the number of categories of independent variables to be investigated by researchers. Principally, he argues, there should be four basic independent variables which should be investigated in a 2×2 gaming situation: (1) the payoff matrices of the games; (2) the length, or number of plays in a game; (3) subject differences, especially cross-cultural differences; (4) the strategy of the opponent.

Essentially Rapoport's programme would reduce the number of social psychological variables to be investigated in the gaming situation. Such matters as direct communication between subjects, the interpersonal perceptions of the subjects, their interpretations and intentions, etc., would not be the prime objects of study. In fact, as far as possible, they should be rigidly controlled. As has been argued, this would be ineffective if the strategy of the opponent were to be studied, since the strategy is only important as it interacts with the psychological variables. Similarly, complex interactions between these variables and the length of play could be expected, (Kelley and Stahelski, 1970). Also one might wonder what point there is to cross-cultural research in this area, if it is not to see the effects of differing belief systems and their cognitive ramifications on game behaviour. Therefore, if the desire is to get as near as possible to the effects of the "pure" gaming situation on behaviour, uncontaminated by unquantifiable social effects, then these three variables should be excluded.

This is in fact what has been done by Guyer and Rapoport (1972). They refer to the experimental game as an "environment"; they attempt to discover what effect slight changes in this environment have on game playing behaviour. Accordingly they permutated several versions of each of the 78 strategically distinct possible 2×2 games, and had 214 subjects play each of these games once. All variables relating to strategic or other interaction were controlled. The situation was, therefore, as devoid as possible of social psychological variables. However, it could never be totally devoid—it was still part of a social interaction between the subjects and the experimenter. There is no way of knowing whether the results were biased by the subjects' perceptions of the experimenter and the experimental situation. They might have wondered, not unreasonably, given the nature of the experiment, why the experimenters should want to conduct it at all. With this in mind, the findings of Slusher *et al.* (1974) should be mentioned: differences in a single play game were found to depend on whether the subjects played the game at home or in the laboratory. The social variables cannot be excluded, since the experimental situation is itself a social one. Guyer and Rapoport's discussion of their results is without psychological interest. It contains no attempt to relate the behaviour to any psychological principles, let alone any body of psychological theory. The impression gained is that the experiment was a complicated exercise done for its own sake. It was not testing any theoretic points, but simply fact-finding for fact-finding's sake.

For Rapoport, however, this approach is a matter of returning to basics in order to construct a solid foundation. He wishes to build up painfully and systematically knowledge of the mathematically defined 2×2 gaming situation. However, in pursuing this aim, he must inevitably resign himself to the detailed study of minutiae—the claims of relevance to real-life conflicts must be shelved. If the analysis is intended to start from basics, with no assumptions, then the assumption of relevance must be discarded too. This Rapoport is willing to concede. He justifies his study of games for its own sake, and not for any extrinsic value:

> ... there is much to be learnt about the dynamics of interaction in the playing of iterated 2×2 games. It seems desirable to obtain this knowledge by an intensive study of such games in their own right, postponing for the time being the question of how relevant this knowledge may be to an understanding of mixed-motive conflicts in real-life ... The value of the laboratory experiment in the simple context of the 2×2 game is the opportunity it gives for building a systematic theory *of that situation*. What relation that theory will have to real life conflicts (if any) only time will tell. (Rapoport, 1968, p. 469, italics in original.)

Rapoport seems to have arrived at something of an impasse—he neither wishes to relate his gaming studies to real-life intergroup conflicts, nor use them to investigate purely social processes. They are, in his opinion, neither practical tools for those engaged in intergroup conflict situations, nor methods for constructing social psychological theory. It seems as if the gaming studies are to be conducted primarily for their own sake. It might be thought that this is somewhat of a bizarre position for one of the world's leading game theoreticians to adopt, given that game theory, throughout its history, has been seen as a pre-eminently practical branch of mathematics. However, it is hoped that Rapoport's position will become more comprehensible when the implications of alternative views are discussed; the following section of this chapter will consider the implications of those attempts to relate experimental findings directly to intergroup conflicts. It will be suggested that such attempts are not ideologically neutral, but are closely allied to certain normative presuppositions and political contexts. It is Rapoport's political conscience which prevents him from drawing facile analogies between the experimental situations and the real world. His views of the 2×2 gaming situation extend beyond the confines of the laboratory and the features of particular matrices. It is for such reasons that the discussion of the relevance of the gaming studies to intergroup conflict situations will inevitably encompass much wider issues—especially when the studies and the theories derived from them are placed in their ideological context.

The arguments put forward in this section have emphasised the social nature of the experimental gaming situation. In particular, experimental games have been characterised as being forms of interpersonal interaction. As such, the gaming experimenters have not studied directly problems relating to intergroup interaction. In conclusion to this section, a line of gaming research will be considered, which has attempted to investigate intergroup variables in the context of the experimental 2×2 gaming situation. These studies will be discussed critically in some detail and it is hoped to show that they do not succeed in raising the focus of gaming research from the interpersonal to the intergroup. It will be suggested that such experiments are still essentially investigations into interpersonal variables.

There have been a number of prisoner's dilemma studies that have had an intergroup aspect, in that the opponent in the two person-game has been a member of a different social group. For instance, Baxter

(1973) had members of different ethnic groups playing one another, and Wallace and Rothaus (1969) compared the game-playing of pairs of hospital patients from the same ward with pairs of patients from different wards. These experiments were concerned to investigate the effects of existing group membership upon game-playing behaviour—they did not attempt to seek the determinants of group membership *per se*, by using experimentally created groups. The experiments to be discussed here have attempted to take the intergroup interaction one stage back by the use of artificially produced ingroups and outgroups. The advantage of using such artificial groups is that, in principle at least, it is possible to identify and distinguish the various processes that contribute to the genesis of intergroup effects. When subjects from pre-existing real groups are used, such processes have already been markedly developed and so are not, in themselves, amenable to laboratory examination.

Most of intergroup experimental work using the prisoner's dilemma paradigm has been associated with the research of Warner Wilson (Wilson and Miller, 1961; Wilson, Chun and Kayatani, 1965; Wilson and Kayatani, 1968; Wilson and Wong, 1968). Basically all these experiments follow the same experimental design; that of the prisoner's dilemma game involving four subjects. Initially these subjects are split into two teams of two subjects each. The teams play against each other on a prisoner's dilemma game for real money. If the team has won any money in its intergroup play, then the two team members play a similar prisoner's dilemma game amongst themselves to determine how their winnings should be split. Therefore each intergroup trial is followed by an intragroup trial. Comparisons between these two sorts of play permit an analysis of the differences between within-group and between-group interaction. Also in these experiments each subject is asked to rate the other subjects on a number rating-scale; thus perceptions of ingroup members can be compared to perceptions of outgroup members, in order to see whether any intergroup differentiation is accompanied by a cognitive evaluation.

The basic result that has consistently emerged from these studies is that there is a significant difference between intergroup and intragroup game-playing behaviour. The subjects make more competitive choices when playing against members of the other team than when playing against their team-mate. The results from the rating scales also, by and large, reveal a bias in favour of the ingroup—the ingroup member is rated more favourably than the outgroup members, at least on certain of the scales. The results of the actual game-playing behaviour, at first glance, seem to have considerable bearings upon theories of intergroup relations which stress the rational aspects of intergroup conflict. A "realistic" group conflict theory would state that competitive goals should lead to conflict, whether they are individual or group goals; therefore, it would predict that the occurrence or absence of conflict should depend on the formal properties of the situation. With regard to the prisoner's dilemma intergroup situation there should be no more competitive choices in the intergroup plays than in the intragroup plays—the formal properties of the game matrix are identical in both cases. The significant differences in response according to trials must be due to some sort of perception that the one opponent is an ally to be trusted, and the other is an outgroup member to be defeated. The determinants of this differential perception of ingroup members cannot therefore be traced to the objective requirements of the conflict situation. They must, accordingly, be traced to the psychological interpretations and motivations of the participants.

The above line of reasoning would seem to be the obvious conclusion from the experimental results. Nevertheless there are a number of features about the experimental design that make it difficult to draw any clear-cut conclusions. In particular there are certain aspects which seem to militate against interpreting the results in terms of group processes. If the results are fully comprehensible in terms of inter-individual processes, and if the specifically group and intergroup variables are unclear in the design, then the usefulness of these experimental results for an intergroup theory is seriously limited. For this reason a number of critical points concerning these experiments will be made, both with respect to inadequacies in the experimental design and also to alternative non-group explanations of the phenomena.

To begin with, one can consider the most obvious finding from these experiments, namely, that intragroup decisions were more cooperative than intergroup decisions. There is however a major difficulty in comparing these two sorts of decisions in order to isolate the specific effects of inter- v. intragroup effects. This difficulty resides in the fact that the intragroup decisions are individual decisions, made by the subjects completely on their own—whereas the intergroup decisions are joint decisions, about which the two ingroup members have to reach an agreement. This is not a trivial difference because there is a consider-able amount of experimental evidence showing that group decision-making differs from individual decision-making (cf. Moscovici and Zavalloni, 1969), and that such differences have been found to occur in an intergroup context (Doise, 1969). On the whole, laboratory studies have demonstrated that group decisions tend to be riskier than decisions made by individuals on their own (Fraser, Gouge and Billig, 1971); also this "risky-shift" has been found to occur in gaming situations (Blascovich, Veach and Ginsburg, 1973; Imai and Okumura, 1973). Taking this evidence as a whole, there is good reason for raising the possibility that the differences in the intergroup and intragroup decisions found in the Wilson studies might be a function of the number of subjects involved in these decisions, rather than a function of genuine intergroup processes. The intergroup decisions were the joint decisions in this paradigm and they can be construed as the riskier decisions; a competitive play in the prisoner's dilemma game involves attempting the greatest gain, whilst at the same time risking the greatest loss. The cooperative play, on the other hand, is the cautious choice. Therefore the results of the game-play in the Wilson experi-ments can easily be interpreted in terms of risky joint decisions and cautious individual decisions.

It would not be too difficult a methodological problem to separate risky-shift effects from genuine intra- and intergroup effects in this experimental paradigm. Further experimentation could easily control the individual-versus-joint decision-making variable. Thus the objec-tion need not be considered overwhelming and insurmountable. There are however more serious objections that can be raised against a simple explanation of the Wilson results. These objections all derive from the fact that the prisoner's dilemma game does not present a cognitively simple situation for the subjects. It has been suggested that the sub-jects' interpretations of the gaming situation and their effect on game-playing behaviour can be complex. If this is true of the normal two-person prisoner's dilemma game, then so must it also relate to the more complicated inter- and intragroup games of the Wilson situation. The previous discussion emphasised the importance of inter-subject com-munication as a variable that influenced game choices. In particular it was noted that increased communication between players in the two-person prisoner's dilemma game made the possibility of joint co-operation more likely. In the Wilson experimental paradigm there is a differential amount of communication between ingroup members and outgroup members. The ingroup members can communicate together when they make their intergroup choices, but there is no corresponding communication between ingroup and outgroup members. The intragroup choices are between pairs of subjects who have been in communication with one another, whereas the intergroup choices are between two teams who have had no prior communication. Therefore from the point of view of the differences in communication, one would expect greater cooperation on the intragroup choices than on the intergroup choices. The only possible communication between different groups is through the game-playing itself, i.e. through "strategic interaction". In this regard, it is interesting to note that Wilson (1971) has found that the overall amount of intergroup cooperation can be affected by systematically altering the strategy of a fictitious outgroup. This finding suggests that differences in the type, as well as amount of inter- and intra- group interaction, could have a significant bearing upon the results of the prisoner's dilemma intergroup experiment.

The evaluation of the results from Wilson's experiments has been so far concerned with the actual game playing behaviour; it has been argued that the differences between ingroup and outgroup choices are easily explicable in terms of variables not directly related to the intergroup situation. Similar criticisms can be made of the findings that there are differences between the ratings of ingroup members and outgroup members. The results have generally revealed that subjects rate ingroup members' motives more favourably than they rate outgroup members' motives, and that these are the main intergroup differences on the rating scales (Wilson, Chun and Kayatani, 1965; Wilson and Kayatani, 1968; Wilson and Robinson, 1968; Dion, 1973); this finding has not always been replicated (Dion, 1973a). However it is not necessary to interpret this difference in the rating of motives in terms of an embryonic intergroup stereotype; nor need one assume a universal rule of intergroup interaction, that ingroup members are more likely to be trusted than outgroup members. A simpler explanation is possible based upon the differences between intra- and intergroup communication. It is possible that the increased communication between members of the same team allows each to gain greater insight into the other's motives. Not only this, the previous communication was of a cooperative nature, in that they had to combine to perform a joint task. No such prior cooperation is possible in the case of members from different groups, and therefore it is unlikely that the subjects will have been able to gain such an appreciation of the motives of outgroup members.

A further difficulty is that in these experimental situations even the finding of intergroup bias is not completely unambiguous. For instance, the pattern is not that intragroup interaction raises the estimation of ingroup members for each other, and that intergroup interaction is accompanied by a deterioration of attitudes towards outgroup members. In fact Wilson and Miller (1961) and Wilson, Chun and Kayatani (1965) compared ratings of ingroup members and outgroup members before and after the experimental interaction. They found that estimation of both ingroup members *and of* outgroup members rose during the course of the experiment, but that this rise was greater in the case of ingroup ratings than in the case of outgroup ratings. What this means, is that subjects rated outgroup members more favourably after having played against them. This finding is particularly difficult to interpret in terms of a meaningful theory of intergroup relations, especially as Wilson (1971) found that there was a high correlation between ingroup ratings and outgroup ratings: subjects who rated ingroup members favourably also rated outgroup members favourably. Thus ingroup identification does not seem to be accompanied by negative outgroup feelings. In fact a high opinion of ingroup partners seems to be associated with a high opinion of outgroup opponents. Again there is the suspicion that the specific group and intergroup variables might be overlaid by some other variable relating to the game-playing interaction or to the situational determinants; and that this other variable may be the key factor in producing the final experimental findings.

One further example of the complexity of the prisoner's dilemma intergroup situation is provided by the experiment conducted by Dion (1973). This study aimed to test the hypothesis that ingroup cohesiveness would be positively correlated with intergroup discrimination. Such a hypothesis has figured in a number of previous theories of intergroup relations: for instance, in Freud's (1921) theory of intergroup relations, and also in the frustration-aggression formulation of Dollard *et al.* (1939). It is an hypothesis that certainly bears testing in an experimental setting and one that should be examined on a level of group processes, rather than individual processes. In the Dion (1973) study, cohesiveness was operationally defined in terms of perceived similarity of personality characteristics; in the high cohesive groups the subjects were told that they had very similar personalities to their partner, and in the non-cohesive groups they were told that they were totally dissimilar, (there was no inbetween group). The main result from this experiment was that the high cohesive group subjects showed intergroup discrimination, whereas the subjects in the low cohesive groups did not. However, it is unnecessary to explain these results in terms of a general principle of intergroup relations. They are easily explicable in terms of the oft repeated experimental finding that people are attracted to those they think are similar to themselves, (see for instance, Byrne, 1969 and 1971, for reviews of the considerable amount of experimental evidence on this point). In this experiment it is reasonable for the "high cohesive" subjects to feel more positively to each other than to the outgroup members, and also the "low cohesive" subjects should not show a similar pattern of preferences. Dion's (1973) results may be a further demonstration of the experimental effect of similarity-attraction; as such they would seem to be the product of interpersonal processes rather than of intergroup processes.

The Wilson intergroup experiments have been discussed in some detail in order to show that they do not present an exception to the rule that gaming experiments are essentially interpersonal situations. Wilson's experimental results are comprehensible in terms of decision-making effects, interpersonal communication or the similarity-attraction hypothesis. Such experiments can be thought to be an extension of social psychological research into interpersonal influence. As such they fall into the tradition of mainstream social psychological research using the gaming paradigm. It is the relevancy of this interpersonal tradition to the study of intergroup relations, which needs to be investigated. This is especially so since most of the experimental researchers, with the exception of Rapoport, assume the validity of the interpersonal game as a model for wider social processes.

Games as models for intergroup conflict

When considering the problem of the relevancy of the gaming experiment to real-world intergroup conflicts, there is a curious preliminary fact that needs to be noted; behaviour in the gaming situation does not seem to be especially related to behaviour in other social psychological experiments. If the gaming experiment is to be held up as a valid model for mass social phenomena, then the very least that one would expect is that gaming behaviour should be related in some way to behaviour in other similarly artificial and controlled laboratory situations. If gaming behaviour is not generalisable even within the social psychology laboratory, then confidence can hardly be great for generalising outside the confines of the laboratory. At the minimum it would be expected that variables which affect behaviour in the gaming situation should also be the variables which figure prominently in the mainstream of social psychological theory. This would be expected if there were "intimate connections between games and social life" (Coleman, 1966, p. 3). If no such connections can be shown, even to other laboratory studies, then one might well be drawn to Rapoport's conclusions concerning the isolation of the gaming study.

To begin, the relation between the gaming experiment and other social psychological experimentation will be considered briefly. The operative word is briefly, since not a great deal of work has been conducted relating gaming behaviour to other sorts of experimental behaviour. Sermat (1970) noted this deficiency: accordingly, he conducted a series of experiments to test the generality of gaming behaviour within the laboratory situation. It must be stressed that the issue is not the one often raised by the critics of the experimental method in social psychology, namely, that the results do not generalise to the outside world. For the moment, the issue is the much narrower one of generalisation between laboratory paradigms. Sermat correlated behaviour in the Prisoner's Dilemma game and Chicken game with behaviour in two other experimental interpersonal situations. One was another game—the Paddle Game, modelled fairly closely on Deutsch and Krauss's trucking game—and the other was a dyadic discussion task concerning the interpretation of pictures. What especially interested Sermat was whether subjects who were either extremely cooperative or extremely competitive in the Prisoner's Dilemma and Chicken games would behave similarly in the other two situations. The results revealed some differences between the high cooperators and competitors (as measured by behaviour in Prisoner's Dilemma and Chicken games) in their performance during the Paddle Game. However, few differences were forthcoming in their behaviour in the dyadic discussion task. Sermat came to the general conclusion, on the basis of his results, that broad generalisations from gaming behaviour to other sorts of interpersonal behaviour were unwarranted.

This conclusion is in contradiction to the general tenor of the work of Kelley and Stahelski (1970) in which an attempt is made to link gaming behaviour to Kelley's (1967) attribution theory. To summarise Kelley and Stahelski's position: they claim that people can be classified as belonging to one of two basic types—the cooperative or the competitive. These types represent relatively stable personality traits, which manifest themselves in game playing behaviour, and in particular in the two person non-zero-sum games investigated by Kelley and Stahelski (a similar approach is also adopted by Moore and Mack, 1972). Not surprisingly the prediction is that competitive persons will be more competitive and cooperative persons will be more cooperative. More than this, Kelley and Stahelski claim that there are differences in the way that competitors and cooperators perceive the gaming situation, and that these differences affect the pattern of interaction in a two-person game. In particular, the competitive person thinks that others are likewise competitive, and therefore in his play he acts on the assumption that the other will play competitively too. On the other hand, the cooperator is more willing to recognise that others can be both competitive and cooperative, and is therefore more flexible in his strategies of game-playing behaviour. Expressed in this way, Kelley and Stahelski's theory seems quite reasonable. In a sense it seems to be saying little more than that people expect others to play these games of minimal information in the same way as they themselves do. The rigidly competitive person expects others to be likewise rigidly competitive and the more flexible person expects others to be similarly flexible—and they interpret the moves of others in the light of these assumptions. These hypotheses cannot be said to be particularly surprising, given the lack of direct communication in the normal 2×2 game situation; nor are misperceptions in such situations particularly startling in themselves. Similarly it could be expected that people think others will behave like themselves; and given that the subjects have only two choices of action, it then becomes an easy matter to divide them into a two-way classification of cooperators and competitors.

The interest in Kelley and Stahelski's theoretical formulations is not for any potential insights that they might afford into the gaming situation *per se*. It is that they relate their two-way classification of game-playing behaviour to the wider issue of styles of personality. The two basic styles of personality can be roughly summarised by stating that the competitor is a dogmatic, unyielding and authoritarian type of person, generally unwilling or unable to perceive any ambiguity or heterogeneity in the world. On the other hand the cooperator possesses the reverse traits—he is generally tolerant, undogmatic, non-authoritarian and not bothered by ambiguity and heterogeneity. Thus the authoritarian is the person who carries his own prejudices into actual conflict and competitive behaviour, whereas the non-authoritarian is less prone to be competitive. The locus of competitive behaviour is placed in the individual's basic personality rather than in any interpersonal or situational factors. This line of thinking provides the possibility of a *rapprochement* with the personality theories of "authoritarianism" and "dogmatism" which view intergroup relations in terms of the prejudiced individual (see chapter four).

It is of course simple to test Kelley and Stahelski's hypothesis—personality scales can be administered to subjects in game-playing situations, in order to discover any correlations between behaviour and personality. It is no surprise that such a simple procedure should have been attempted numerous times—the surprise is that no consistent results have been yielded (see Terhune, 1968, 1970; Baxter, 1972, for reviews of studies correlating personality variables with game-playing behaviour). Kelley and Stahelski (1970) admit that this line of research has not been too successful and that the correlations that have been found "are not as strong or consistent as we might like" (p. 83). In a similar vein, Baxter (1972) has commented that "such findings, or lack of consistent positive findings . . . have been very disturbing and frustrating to many psychologists" (p. 100). The conclusion would then seem to be that the linking of game-playing behaviour with styles of personality is still at the stage of hypothesis and search rather than an established fact (Mack, 1972). Firm connections have not been identified unambiguously, although it may be possible to uncover certain subtle and complex relationships (Wrightsman *et al.*, 1972, pp. 104–106). Certainly the evidence is not substantial enough to support a general theory of interpersonal relations, let alone a wider theory of prejudice and conflict behaviour.

Similarly, there are difficulties with studies which attempt to correlate game-playing behaviour with the personality or life styles of different subject populations. For instance, Pilisuk *et al.* (1971) compared cooperation in a Prisoner's Dilemma game and personality variables of "hippy-type" students from Berkeley with army cadets. Amongst other things the results of this experiment indicated that the Berkeley students were less dogmatic in personality and more cooperative in game playing than the military cadets. However, before one can start to draw any meaningful conclusions about the interrelationships between personality, population and game-playing variables, one would first wish to know exactly how personality and population differences relate to each other in this particular case. More than this, one would wish to know how these variables relate to a wide range of experimental gaming situations, especially whether cooperation was a unitary dimension in such situations. Also of course one would want to know whether there is, as is quite likely, any difference in behaviour between Berkeley students and military cadets in their reactions to experimental situations *per se*, regardless of whether they were gaming or not; for instance, it is conceivable that differences between the behaviour of the two populations in experimental conditions might have nothing to do directly with cooperation or competition. The impression to be gathered from such studies is that the gaming experiments have by no means been integrated into personality or social theories as they stand at the moment—consequently, the social psychological knowledge of the variables affecting gaming behaviour has not been advanced particularly far in that direction.

Despite the lack of correlation between game-playing and other forms of behaviour, there have been claims that the gaming conflict situation can in some way function as a model for real-world intergroup conflict. Too often such claims have not been directly expressed, but nevertheless they have been, as it were, an implicit backdrop to much of the gaming research. This backdrop can be adduced by the fact that many gaming experiments have been described in terms normally reserved for actual large-scale group conflicts. For instance, Pilisuk *et al.* (1965) refer to different strategies of game-playing behaviour as being either hawkish or dovish—an obvious and deliberate reference to differing American attitudes to the Vietnamese war. Similarly, elsewhere Pilisuk and Rapoport (1964) refer to "disarmament" in the context of a two-person gaming study. In fact this is only one instance of many; references to disarmament and escalation are legion in gaming research reports. The experimental designs deliberately attempt to reproduce certain features of the cold war situation. It has been mentioned that the Prisoner's Dilemma can be interpreted as a model of the arms race between the U.S.A. and the U.S.S.R. In the same way, the Game of Chicken can be said to mirror nuclear confrontations such as the Cuban crisis. Similarly the emphasis on conflict "resolution" in such studies is by no means accidental—the implication is that the gaming study can have something to contribute to the factors which might underlie the preconditions for world peace. However, it is one thing to use such global metaphors in order to describe experimental games, and quite another matter to justify the use of such metaphorical language, especially when the metaphor unites two such disparate phenomena as a contrived experimental game and mass group conflict.

To probe further into the nature of this metaphor, the standpoints of two leading social psychologists will be considered. The positions of Morton Deutsch and Harold Kelley will be discussed for a number of reasons. Firstly, they are both eminent and respected social psychologists, and therefore cannot be said to represent minority or particularly unorthodox approaches within their academic discipline. Also both have expressed their basic orientation to their subject matter with clarity. Thirdly, it is instructive to consider any similarities that they might have in their basic approach because it cannot be said that their social psychological theories present a common front. The debate between these two authors concerning the nature of the trucking-game experiments has already been mentioned. Plon (1969–70) has argued that this difference represents an underlying ideological difference—Deutsch takes the position of the "dove" *vis-à-vis* the Vietnam war by denouncing the efficacy of threats, whilst Kelley takes the opposing "hawkish" stand. If there is such an ideological debate between the two, then it is true to say that it takes place primarily at the level of the experimental investigation into gaming behaviour. In this case both writers can be said to share the common assumption that the laboratory person-to-person conflict situation is relevant in some way to the real-world conflict situation. What this "relevance" consists of will be considered, in order to show that behind the assumptions of Deutsch and Kelley is concealed a particular social theory, which determines, to no small degree, their theories of conflict.

To begin with, it can be noticed that there is inevitably a strong element of reductionism involved in any claim that the simplified laboratory experiment can serve as a useful model for real-world conflicts. Obviously the varied and complex phenomena which exist in the real world have to be simplified and reduced in order to fit the narrow confines of the laboratory situation. This sort of reduction is inevitable for any sort of psychological experimentation which tries to reproduce real-world phenomena. However, in the case of Deutsch and Kelley it is possible to be more precise about the nature of their particular brand of reductionism. Essentially what both Deutsch and Kelley, along with most other gaming researchers, assume, is that intergroup processes can be reduced to interpersonal processes. Their model for actual intergroup conflicts is not so much laboratory intergroup conflicts, as laboratory interpersonal conflicts. Thus there is a common assumption behind their research programmes that the variables which determine intergroup conflict can be identified and understood by looking at interpersonal conflict situations.

The elements of this form of reductionism are clearly expressed in the writings of Kelley and Deutsch. In Kelley's case there is a clear statement of his reductionist orientation at the start of his book *The Social Psychology of Groups* (1959), written in collaboration with Thibaut.

> Because the existence of the group is based solely upon the participation and satisfaction of the individuals comprising it, the group functionalism becomes an individual functionalism. The ultimate analysis then is in terms of the vicissitudes of individuals as they try out various adaptations to the problems confronting them. (Thibaut and Kelley, 1959, p. 5.)

In other words group phenomena can, for the purpose of study, be considered as individual phenomena. Consequently, Kelley concentrates almost exclusively on dyadic interaction. In *The Social Psychology of Groups* there is in fact a chapter devoted to groups larger than the dyad—this chapter discusses the triad. The authors state that "the consequences of the dyad-to-triad transition are used as a basis for speculating about the effects of increasing group size in general" (Thibaut and Kelley, 1959, p. 191). Likewise in his present research, Kelley still focuses on problems of interpersonal interaction, and dyadic interaction especially. His recent theories of Prisoner's Dilemma gaming behaviour have already been mentioned (Kelley and Stahelski, 1970). He still holds the view that there is an essential isomorphism between interpersonal and group processes. For instance, he has expressed the view quite clearly that the experimental interpersonal situation can offer good insights to the student of larger real conflicts (Kelley, 1968). It can do this because there is a basic similarity between the two sorts of situation; the interpersonal experimental situation can demonstrate "the essential properties" (Kelley, 1968, p. 409) of the real intergroup situation.

Similarly Morton Deutsch's research interests have been directed towards the interpersonal aspects of conflict. Without adopting the rigid reductionism implied in Thibaut and Kelley's definition of a group, Deutsch nevertheless emphasises the similarities between group and individual processes. He writes of a "real conceptual similarity" between the processes (Deutsch, 1969a, p. 1091; cf. also Deutsch, 1962a and 1962b). He specifies what the nature of this conceptual similarity is—Deutsch particularly sees similarities between nations and persons, in as much as they can perform the same tasks. The same terms can be used to describe the behaviour of nations as can be used to describe the behaviour of individuals: "I am asserting that nations as well as individuals acquire information, make decisions and take actions, and that they will act in similar ways under similar circumstances" (Deutsch, 1969a, p. 1091). In another and earlier article Deutsch describes his own version of reductionism in the following manner: "I assume there is some merit in viewing nations, like persons, as behaving units in an environment and in conceiving of international relations in terms somewhat analogous to those of interpersonal relations" (Deutsch, 1962b, p. 390).

It should be stressed that neither Deutsch nor Kelley holds that these assumptions can be undeniably demonstrated, or that they rest upon a set of proven facts; they operate as heuristic guidelines. Kelley (1968) expresses the hope that his form of social psychological research will prove useful to the understanding of intergroup conflict; and in a similar vein Deutsch (1969a) admits that he can offer no guarantee that there is in fact a close correspondence between the real world and the laboratory. It is his hope that insight can be gained from the laboratory situation, and that this insight will eventually contribute to the "welfare of man" (Deutsch, 1969a, p. 1092). To see whether in fact this hope is justified entails examining in greater detail the grounds for, and consequences of, this reductionist position.

Firstly one can note certain difficulties in treating the individual and the group as isomorphic. Traditionally in social psychology these difficulties have been referred to collectively as the "group mind fallacy". This fallacy specifically concerns the attribution of mental predicates to social collectives; for instance, the fallacy covers such assertions as "the crowd was angry", "the people were depressed". By themselves such statements suggest that a collective itself has a mind and feelings over and above those of its individual participants. This is obviously a fallacy—the group has no mind of its own, nor emotions beyond those of its members. Consequently, for such statements as "the crowd was angry" to be meaningful, there must be some way of translating them back into descriptions of the mental processes of the individuals who make up the collective; for instance the translation could be "the majority of those in the crowd were angry". If the mental predicates cannot be translated into statements concerning the mental states of individuals then the group mind fallacy is in danger of being committed.

Deutsch specifically denies that he is committing the group mind fallacy (Deutsch, 1969b, p. 37, and 1973, p. 7). *Prima facie* he seems to be coming close to it, when he refers to nations taking decisions and acquiring information. To avoid the fallacy he would have to provide ways of translating such statements into statements about the way that particular individuals in the nation take decisions and acquire information. This would involve at least a minimal amount of social analysis into the social structure of particular nations. For instance to say that "England decided to go to war in 1939" does not entail that some abstract entity termed "England", over and above any individual Englishman, took a decision to go to war. Nor does it imply that all Englishmen took such a decision; it means that certain specifiable individuals in certain specifiable positions of power took a particular decision. However, when Deutsch writes of nations deciding, he does not offer any way of translating this sentence into individual terms; he does not offer the implied social analysis of power relations and power structures which would be involved in such a translation.

In other words, if it is accepted that he does not intend to commit the group mind fallacy, then there is an omission in Deutsch's equation of interpersonal and international processes—this omission refers to the lack of some sort of social analysis which would make the interpersonal metaphor meaningful. Nor is this a minor point; it will be suggested that this lack of social analysis, which characterises the work of Kelley as much as that of Deutsch, is not just the result of psychologists attempting to investigate their own area of specialisation as impartially as possible, without trying to trespass on the areas of other disciplines. On the contrary, it will be suggested that by their neglect of social analysis such researchers are in fact upholding a particular social analysis. It is therefore hoped to bring to the fore some of the assumptions behind this reductionist approach and also certain wider implications of these views. In particular it will be suggested that the stress on interpersonal decision-making and the neglect of analysis of the social context of decision-making within a particular society, has the effect of confirming the power and legitimacy of existing decision-makers. This of course militates against the notion that such a science of social psychological processes is by definition free from value assumptions concerning the nature of society.

If the research traditions, in which social psychologists like Deutsch and Kelley operate, stress the role of decision-making in intergroup conflict situations, then so do two other branches of study which are offshoots from gaming research, namely, studies of interpersonal bargaining and simulation studies of conflict. Like the traditional social-gaming study, the simulation study reduces intergroup phenomena to interpersonal phenomena. In such a study, the participants play the role of some real-life decision maker. The sorts of simulations of prime interest here are those which are intended to mirror real intergroup conflict situations, especially international conflicts (e.g. Guetzkow *et al.* 1963; Crow, 1966; Zinnes, 1966). Typically the participants play the part of some national leader. There are built into the situation certain constraints on his possible courses of action; these constraints are intended to reproduce the real life constraints of national leaders, (for example, the security of his power-base at home, the efficiency of communication between leaders, the amount of national resources at his disposal, etc.). As a result the simulation of international conflict revolves around the decisions and interactions between national leaders—these are the dependent variables in such studies. Such studies rest upon the reductionist assumption, i.e., that the essentials of inter-group conflict situations can be studied by looking at the interpersonal relations of those involved in the conflict, especially those involved as decision-making leaders. A similar assumption is made by studies which directly link interpersonal bargaining with international relations (e.g. Sawyer and Guetzkow, 1965). It is implied that the "behaviour of nations" can be identified with the behaviour of national leaders; in this way intergroup relations can be studied by concentrating upon the interpersonal relations between such leaders.

This reduction of intergroup variables to the interpersonal ones characterises the studies of both the war-gamers and the peace researchers. In both traditions of research interpersonal games have figured widely. It would be true to say that most of the studies discussed so far can be classed under the general rubric of peace research. Nevertheless there is not a great theoretical divide between the two traditions. For instance parallels can be drawn between the psychological theories of Thibaut and Kelley (1959) and of Homans (1961) with the strategic theories of the war-gamers. It has been mentioned that the psychological theories can be seen as extensions of the principle of the maximisation of utility. As such they have been criticised on the grounds that they portray humans as being economists or small-time businessmen (Moscovici, 1972; Plon, 1972). Such theories assume that individuals will seek the maximum possible advantage for themselves, and also that it is rational to attempt to maximise utilities. These assumptions are shared by the narrow theories of the strategists, who have produced guides for militarist thinking (e.g. Schelling, 1960; 1966). In these works the businessman is replaced by the military commander or politician, whose maximum utility is derived from outsmarting opponents.

As in peace research, the study of interpersonal games has figured largely in military research (Wilson, 1970). The connection between research into war-games and the U.S. military complex has been well documented (Horowitz, 1963 and 1970). This connection has not merely produced numerous gaming studies, which have been classified as confidential material and so are unobtainable to the average student. It has also affected directly or indirectly the traditional academic research institutions (see particularly Horowitz, 1970). Moreover, war games have been frequently used as part of schemes for strategic training. Wilson (1970) has revealed the importance of simulation studies in such training schemes. However, the simulation study is not confined merely to the military. Davis (1966) discusses whether social psychological research is "relevant" to real life; one of the points he makes is that simulation studies provide valuable training for actual decision-makers. If the simulation study has an educational purpose, then one might express doubts about the value of studies like that of Zinnes (1966); in this study schoolchildren accurately re-enacted (or were taught to play) the parts of European statesmen, making the decisions leading to the First World War.

In the following chapter it will be suggested that the interpersonal reductionism, espoused by both the war-gamers and the peace researchers, prevents a critical social analysis. Their concentration is upon the actions of decision-makers as models for intergroup relations; because of this, large-scale social processes are reduced to questions either concerning cost-efficiency or to psychological problems. The war-gamers tend to take the former stance and the peace researchers the latter. Since the peace research tradition will be discussed more fully later, a few words about the nature of the war-gamer can be mentioned. In particular he is concerned with the gaining of strategic advantage and with the details of efficient administration. The wider ethical and human issues tend to escape his notice. Chomsky (1969 and 1973) describes the "backroom boys" of the Pentagon, with respect to their administration of the American involvement in the Vietnam War. His study of the Pentagon Papers (1973) reveals the full depth of the military mind. There is the obsession with administrative questions and a refusal to consider the effects of decisions in anything but the logic of cost-efficiency and strategic advantage. According to Chomsky the "Pentagon Papers are a study of decision making, nothing more", and they only discuss decisions "in terms of military success and cost" (1973, p. 26).

Although the strategists work from premises about efficiency and military advantage, it should not be thought that their bureaucratic thinking is in itself ideologically neutral. Chomsky discusses in detail their underlying ideological presuppositions. Similarly, Pilisuk and Hayden (1973) refer to the "core beliefs", which form the background of U.S. military thought. The point is that the narrow cost-efficiency logic does not exist in some ideological vacuum—bureaucratic thinking implies the existence of a bureaucratic structure, whose social, political and economic functions can be analysed. In the same way the theories of decision-making which are based upon considerations of strategy must be applicable to decision-makers who occupy particular social positions within definable social orders. By reducing the intergroup to the interpersonal the war-gamer excludes these wider questions. It will be suggested that the peace researcher can similarly neglect broader issues by his adherence to the reductionist model. He tends to seek the locus of irrational behaviour in the breakdowns of interpersonal behaviour; in this respect he does not attempt an investigation of the ideological roots of rationality. In the following chapter, the ideological bias in certain social psychological traditions of peace research will be considered. By this it is hoped to extend the present discussion of the gaming situation to broader issues relating to the topic of ideology in the context of intergroup relations.

7

Group Ideology

Ideology in conflict research

It is the purpose of the present chapter to continue the discussion of gaming and conflict research. In this section the ideological presuppositions and implications of this line of research will be considered. From this basis, it is hoped in subsequent sections to widen the discussion by examining the general nature of ideology and false consciousness. In this way no definite distinction is being made between ideology as a bias in social scientific investigations and ideology as a phenomenon to be studied by the social sciences. It is maintained that ideological bias within a social scientific discipline can be part and parcel of the wider ideology which affects large-scale social processes. The scientific enterprise, then, is not to be seen as something over and above the rest of society, but is itself a product of social processes.[1]

The traditions of the war-gamers and the peace researchers were mentioned in the previous chapter. In discussing the ideological influences in conflict research the main emphasis will be on the peace researchers. Although the peace researchers have never had the funds or facilities which have come the way of the war-gamers (Wilson, 1970) their work has attained a certain eminence within the academic community. Moreover it has achieved a considerable influence within the discipline of social psychology. When considering the ideological implications of this line of research much of the discussion will centre around the work of Morton Deutsch. His views are certainly not those of the hard-headed strategic school of militarists; rather they represent the liberal conscience of America. His work also contains some of the chief

1. For a discussion of how ideological bias can operate within psychological research, see Innes and Fraser (1971).

characteristics of the conflict research outlined in the previous chapter, namely, an underestimation of ideology as a social variable, a reduction of intergroup conflicts to interpersonal conflicts and an absence of any systematic social analysis. It will be suggested that all in all his approach constitutes a highly ideological analysis of social phenomena.

One of the most immediate consequences of reducing intergroup conflicts to interpersonal conflicts is that the theories used to describe such conflicts can be phrased exclusively in interpersonal terms. The social psychological theories of conflict lay great emphasis on such variables as perceptions and misperceptions, channels of communications, threats etc. All these variables can affect the course of interpersonal interaction, and therefore by implication can affect intergroup relations. For instance, laboratory experiments, such as Deutsch's trucking game, can reveal that players misperceive the intentions of their opponents, or that partial and/or incomplete communication can lead to a worsening of relations between the two participants. Because such a situation constitutes the basic model for the real-life intergroup situation, the same factors are assumed to operate in actual group conflicts. Thus Deutsch (1969a, 1969c and 1973) refers to the possible factors which can result in either "co-operative or competitive processes" of interaction, and these factors are to a large extent dependent upon the psychological states of the participants. He comments that "the presence or absence of conflict is never rigidly determined by the objective state of affairs" (Deutsch, 1969c, p. 9).

If the root of conflict is not to be found in the objective state of affairs, then according to Deutsch it should be sought in the subjective states of the participants. In this regard Deutsch puts considerable stress on the role of misperceptions and misunderstandings in the development of competitive processes. There are two essential assumptions underlying this: (a) that the competitive processes are something undesirable and that one should aim at achieving cooperative processes; and (b) that men would live together in peace and harmony if they could only understand one another. The liberal optimism implied in such a statement underlies Deutsch's entire theoretical approach. He advocates that individuals should learn to give and take, and to attempt to see the other person's point of view. Specifically Deutsch decries the use of threat as an appropriate way of achieving one's objectives; threat in Deutsch's view leads to an ever-increasing vicious spiral of threat and counter-threat. The obvious reference is to President Johnson's policy of escalation of the Vietnam War, of which Deutsch was a critic. To combat this vicious spiral, a benevolent co-operative process is needed, by which friendly and trusting attitudes on both sides can be mutually reinforcing. This involves not being blinded by one's own dogmatic point of view. This last point is a theme which will reappear in the discussion of the conflict research; it is part of the general distrust and downgrading of ideology inherent in this approach to the study of intergroup relations.

The above is a distillation of some of the more essential strands of Deutsch's thinking over the past ten years or so. The important thing to be observed is that pride of place in his analysis of conflict is given to psychological variables such as attitudes and dispositions. Conflicts are abstracted from their social contexts; the crucial variables hypothesised to determine such conflicts are ones derived essentially from interpersonal psychology. Cooperation and competition are the product of cooperative and competitive attitudes, and the problem is to enhance the cooperative attitudes, in order to avoid that *bête noire*, conflict (there are however in Deutsch's more recent formulations certain exceptions to the general negative value attached to conflict which will be considered below). Given this basic orientation, the differences between Deutsch's approach and the present approach start to emerge. In chapter five it was argued that intergroup revolutionary conflict was comprehensible only in terms of the underlying ideologies; these in turn are derived from the underlying social conditions between the revolutionary and counter-revolutionary groups. Deutsch (1973), on the other hand, considers ideology as something that is produced as a consequence of revolutions. For instance, he refers to the egalitarian philosophies that became prevalent *after* the French and Russian revolutions (pp. 101–2). To admit that these ideologies may have been instrumental in causing revolutions might mean legitimating revolutionary conflict as a means for achieving social justice, which would be at variance with the general negative values assigned to conflict.[2]

2. It is interesting to note that in the final chapter of Deutsch's book *The Resolution of Conflict* he writes of the necessity of discontented unprivileged groups indulging in "consciousness-raising" tactics. It can be argued that his discussion of the tactics open to unprivileged groups contradicts his general theoretical orientation; he can be interpreted as implicitly suggesting that such groups must become ideologically cohesive and must threaten aggressively the powers that be. For detailed discussion of this possible contradiction within Deutsch's theory see Billig (1975).

The abstraction and reduction of conflict entails that conflict situations between actual groupings are to be analysed apart from any economic considerations, which might determine the context of the conflict (see Plon, 1973, for detailed arguments on this issue). Economic considerations are played down in favour of psychological ones. If economics are mentioned it is as a psychological motive to maximise gain; in this way questions of economy are reduced to the interpersonal along with other considerations. The emphasis in much of Deutsch's research is on ways of reducing conflicts between opposing desires for gain in zero-sum type situations. For instance, in the Deutsch and Krauss (1960, 1962) trucking-game experiments the stress is on solutions to the mutual benefit of both participants. Similarly the series of studies by Thibaut into interpersonal bargaining has focused attention upon those situations where a conflict of interest can be modified by the development of some sort of agreement between the two parties, concerning the allocation of a fixed sum of money (e.g. Thibaut and Faucheux, 1965; Thibaut, 1968).

This general trend of considering conflicts in terms of psychological variables derived from the abstracted interpersonal situation is what Plon (1973) has termed *"l'installation de la psychologie au poste de commandement"*. This form of reductionism postulates that social psychology, above all other social sciences, provides the ultimate key to the understanding of intergroup conflicts. The major factors that determine intergroup relations, according to this view, must inevitably be the psychological states of the participants, and this in practice means the psychological states of the decision-makers or group leaders. In this way Deutsch is able to give an account of the Vietnam war in terms of the psychological processes that combine to create a vicious competitive spiral. According to him, the Vietnam war is a paradigmatic example of how misperceptions amongst decision-makers can cause such a spiral, which escalates through "the process of unwitting involvement" (Deutsch, 1969c, p. 18). In this way Deutsch locates the prime cause of the Vietnamese conflict in errors of judgement made by decision-makers. Because of his equation between such decision-makers and their nations, he is able to talk about America stumbling into the war (Deutsch, 1969c and 1973). He also discusses the way that America could have extricated herself from the conflict by turning the vicious circle into a benevolent circle. This would involve a change of attitudes: America must show a willingness to trust in the other side, by offering solutions that would leave intact the self-esteem and honour of all sides, the Americans, the Vietcong, the North and South Vietnamese (1969c, pp. 56–7). In this way Deutsch reduces the Vietnamese war to a series of psychological problems. Its origin and its solution are expressed in terms of people understanding or misunderstanding each other, showing respect or disrespect for each other's self-esteem. Who exactly these people are is not quite clear, but the implication is that they are the national leaders and diplomats.

Deutsch's account of the Vietnam war can be contrasted with Chomsky's (1973). Chomsky discusses the theory that it was only foolishness or misunderstandings that embroiled the U.S. in the war. This according to Chomsky is a naïve and unsatisfactory explanation, in that it leaves unanswered too many questions concerning American intervention in other parts of the world:

> To mention only the simplest: Why were the policy makers always subject to the same form of ignorance and irrationality? Why was there such a systematic error in the delusional systems constructed by post-war ideologists? Mere ignorance or foolishness would lead to random error, not a regular and systematic distortion: unwavering adherence to the principle that whatever the facts may be, the cause of international conflict is the behaviour of the communist powers and all revolutionary movements within the United States are sponsored by the Soviet Union, China, or both. (Chomsky, 1973, p. 68.)

In this way Chomsky can identify an ideological pattern underlying the so-called "mistakes" and "misunderstandings" of a succession of American decision-makers, military leaders and politicians. This renders the mistakes comprehensible; but more than this, it renders them predictable. Because an ideological pattern of thought is identified, instead of a series of individual errors, it becomes possible to enquire about the social context of the ideology. An ideological group does not and cannot exist in some sort of socio-historical vacuum. The ideology must be a response and also a way of creating certain social conditions for the ideological group. In particular, the ideologies can be manufactured in the course of struggles within a society; and an ideology can be deliberately spread as false consciousness by a group in power.

Given this, it becomes a proper question to enquire about the social context of the ideology, outlined by Chomsky, which is shared by the power groups in America. Chomsky himself offers an answer to this question and he links the spread of the anti-communist ideology to the defence of economic interests. The needs of capitalist production have ensured, according to Chomsky, that the American people should be maintained in a bellicose state of anti-communism, and that periodic conflict is necessary in order to preserve the capitalist economy. In this account the ideology of anti-communism is a prime example of the spreading of a false consciousness. Other accounts that link the U.S. military machine with economic interests can be found in Barnet (1969), Melman (1970), Pilisuk and Hayden (1973) and Stevenson (1973). These works all give differing views on the nature of the relationship between the military machine and the processes of capitalist production; nevertheless by their approach they enable a link to be made between a particular group ideology and the economic interests that produce and maintain such an ideology.

In the interpersonal approach questions are not raised about the ideological purpose of the positions of various protagonists in a conflict. There is no attempt to underpin the interpersonal model with any description of the way in which societies operate. Questions of social and economic organisation are not raised. All is reduced to the operations of diplomats and decision-makers. In this way social movements cannot be understood. The criticisms of Brewster (1969) concerning Rapoport's analysis of the Vietnamese situation can be applied with as much force to Deutsch's analysis. Brewster makes the point that the only question to be raised in such an analysis is why the Americans have been fighting in Vietnam; the question why the Vietnamese are fighting in Vietnam is not considered. Of course, to attempt to answer such a question would stretch the interpersonal abstracted model to the limit. This is the case, because, it will be suggested, the interpersonal abstracted model is a theory inherently critical of social movements which threaten the *status quo*.

So far it has been argued that Deutsch's approach is designed to avoid any genuine attempt of social analysis. Generally speaking, within the traditions of American social psychological research into conflict situations, questions of economic and social organisation are not raised. If they are it is either in a narrow frame of reference which precludes serious analysis, or alternately, it is in a way which reveals the underlying political presuppositions of this approach. An example of the former approach is provided by Robinson and Snyder (1965). These authors specifically discuss the topic of decision-making in international relations—typically, given the tenets of the abstracted interpersonal approach, they talk about international decision-making in terms of the personalities of the decision-makers, and the nature of the decisions to be made. They also include, rather untypically, a third sort of variable which relates to social organisation—"the organisation of decision-makers". However, this does not refer to the social organisation by which decision-making groups are related to the rest of their societies, and the particular interests that the decision-making groups represent. Instead it refers to the narrower matter of the organisation of institutions and groups which have the power to decide. The power itself is accepted as a given; there is no attempt to explain how it is maintained and in whose interests it is maintained. Other examples of this approach can be found in Alger (1965), Holsti (1970), and Siverson (1973).

When these questions are raised, the implicit social analysis of the interpersonal approach becomes more apparent. It is true to say that these questions are not often directly broached in this line of research. One instance however is the article by Katz (1965), in which he takes a wider view than most social psychologists; in this article he attempts to relate national decision-making to the social organisation and functions of the modern nation state. In doing this, he lists three functions of the modern nations state. These are, according to Katz: (1) to achieve internal integration; (2) to maximise favourable input-output ratios (that is, to achieve economic expansion); (3) to afford protection from outside enemies. Katz's main theme is that in the modern bureaucratic state, affective and emotional ideologies are replaced by more pragmatic and task-orientated attitudes. This is, according to Katz, something to be welcomed since it facilitates successful resolutions of conflict. Katz is here stating a belief which runs through much of the conflict research, namely, that ideological commitment impedes conflict resolution. Nevertheless, he argues, in the modern state there is less of a tendency for ideological emotionality to get in the way of the smooth running of society.

This thumbnail sketch of Katz's views reveals several features. Firstly, his description of the modern nation state closely fits the description of a modern capitalist society. Economic expansion is seen as a major function of the state; whereas neither economic stability nor economic justice are considered. Having detailed this fact, Katz does not go on to develop the consequences of this economic function. He does not suggest that the pressure for continual economic expansion might be instrumental in the creation of certain ideologies. In particular, he does not suggest that this continual economic expansion can influence the form of his third factor, i.e. determine who the enemies of the state are. In other words he does not consider that the economy of the "modern nation state" could determine and be determined by the ideological beliefs of its members, in particular, those who wield the power within such a society. This is outside his frame of reference because Katz denies the existence of ideology in the modern nation state. It is pragmatic and logical to seek economic expansion, and the methods to achieve such expansion are themselves ideologically neutral—at least this is the implication. Moreover, if it is being denied that ideology functions in such a state, then it is also being claimed that the intellectual apologia for that society is also hard-headed and value free. If this is so, then Katz's own social analysis of the functions of modern bureaucracy is also free from any ideological content—it is merely a non-ideological defence for a non-ideological society.[3]

Katz (1965) by considering questions relating to the functions and organisation of the modern nation state, allows a glimpse of the social theory which underpins the reductionist approach to the study of conflict. A clearer picture of this implicit social theory can be gathered by returning to the ideas of Deutsch. In particular, the flavour of this theory can be adduced by considering the implications of that ubiquitous term "conflict resolution". Deutsch believes that his research might in some way contribute to the resolution of conflict, and by implication, the establishment of a peaceful order. Plon (1973) has effectively detailed the values inherent in this abstracted notion of conflict and its resolution. Basically, Deutsch, and others sharing his approach, consider conflict to be an evil that should be avoided. Specifically, international conflict could be avoided if honest and open approaches were adopted by the world's leading statesmen.

3. In this respect Mannheim's (1972) views on bureaucratic thinking are illuminating. He wrote that "the fundamental tendency of all bureaucratic thought is to turn all problems of politics into problems of administration" (p. 105). The bureaucrat conceives of society as a static system and he regards "revolution as an untoward event in an otherwise ordered system". Today, over forty years after Mannheim wrote that warning of the bureaucratic mode of thought, we witness military juntas, seizing power in order to "put right the muddles of politicians" and to restore "normal" government. The net result of such "non-political" order is invariably a repressive brutality against the junta's opponents.

It is Deutsch's hope that fair and straightforward communication would go a long way to alleviate international tensions and conflicts.

Similarly Deutsch hopes that intranational conflicts can be peaceably resolved. Intranational conflict is, according to Deutsch, harmful because it attacks the stability of society. Plon has argued that theorists like Deutsch tend to contrast the terms "society" and "conflict", with the implication that a society is something that is essentially an harmonious integrated unit. Here one can note that Katz's first function of a society is to promote internal integration. Similarly Deutsch defines the primary functions of a leader to be "creating and maintaining a sense of unity despite the existence of divisive individual interests" (Deutsch, 1962c, p. 282). On this account, the term "society" represents some cohesive unit, whose cohesion is to be protected against disruptive influences. In this, there is a strong resemblance to the presuppositions of the frustration-aggression theorists, whose work was reviewed in chapter five. Both view society as being essentially an harmonious unity, and that conflict within this unity is harmful and therefore to be avoided.

If conflict within society is viewed negatively, then any prescriptions for reducing conflict are bound to reinforce the pre-existing harmony of society. The diagnoses of conflict must not strike at the roots of the social structure. However, if the basic structure of society is seen as the cause of intrasocietal conflict, then any resolution of that conflict might entail a radical alteration of the basic structure. As was argued in chapter five, vested interests do not readily forgo their social privileges and revolutionary violence is integrally related to legitimated societal violence. Thus the peace researcher finds himself advocating solutions to intrasocietal conflicts which do not threaten the fabric of the social structure, rather than advocating a more revolutionary solution which might promote just the sort of conflict which he hopes to avoid. The upshot is that the peace researcher recommends non-structural changes to intrasocietal conflicts, and his recommendations are inevitably conservative in that they do not threaten the position of entrenched controlling élites.[4]

---

4. A fuller discussion of some of the values implicit in peace research is given by Eide (1974). Although recognizing the limitations and presuppositions of the 'psychological' approach, Eide does nevertheless consider that a wider, non-conformist, social analysis is possible within the tradition of peace research.

Deutsch has on a number of occasions recognised the influence of Fisher on his theories of conflict. Conservative presuppositions are clearly discernible in the writings of Fisher (1964 and 1969), who advises how conflicts should be "managed". He argues that the ideological element should be removed if possible from the conflict situation—there should consequently be "issue control". Similarly, Fisher argues that conflicts should be "fractionated", i.e. divided up into as many small parts as possible. The net result of these two policies is to diffuse any challenge to existing power structures. It is clearly in the interests of entrenched power groups that ideological movements, questioning the existing bases of power, should be controlled and the challenging issues not be raised seriously. Similarly it is in the interests of the *status quo* that any challenge should be confined to comparatively trivial areas. Given the nature of the policies of "fractioning" and "issue control", it would seem that the advice from conflict theorists such as Fisher has an inbuilt ideological bias. Perhaps it should be no surprise that conflict theorists, as has been pointed out by Deutsch (1969c), should have addressed their advice almost exclusively to powerful and privileged groups.

In his more recent publications Deutsch has modified his position; he no longer offers an outright condemnation of all forms of conflict but has introduced the notion of a constructive conflict as opposed to a destructive conflict (1969c and 1973). Constructive conflict can be a force for social progress and as such Deutsch's modified formulation is better equipped to deal with problems of social change and intergroup relations than his original. The distinction between constructive and destructive conflict is essentially psychological. Deutsch (1973) defines the two in terms of the participants' perceptions: a conflict is destructive if the participants feel dissatisfied with their outcomes and it is constructive if they feel they have gained as a result of the conflict. The constructive conflict is resolved by trusting attitudes and honest communication, whereas the destructive conflict is characterised by threats and counter-threats. Competitive processes are properties of destructive conflicts and cooperative processes are properties of constructive conflicts. Generally these processes are self-fulfilling; "cooperation breeds cooperation, while competition breeds competition" (1973, p. 367). Deutsch calls this his "crude law of social relations" (p. 365).

Deutsch uses this framework to discuss numerous different conflict situations. Although his perspective is psychological and his key concepts refer to participants' feelings and perceptions, nevertheless Deutsch incorporates certain basic values into his analysis. To illustrate this, Deutsch's discussion of class conflict and capitalist society will be considered. In his analysis Deutsch shows again his bias against ideology and his support for existing socio-economic structures; more importantly from a theoretical point of view, Deutsch suggests that future constructive conflict solution might depend on economic variables rather than psychological ones. This suggests that his framework might contain certain internal inadequacies.

Deutsch (1969b and 1973) claims that Marx's ideas have been refuted by the development of capitalism. Instead of the increasing polarisation between bourgeoisie and proletariat predicted by Marx, there has been, according to Deutsch a constructive solution to class conflict. The working class has benefited from capitalist development and industrial disputes are resolved peaceably and cooperatively. Deutsch does not consider the possible alternative thesis that differences in relative wealth might be increasing (e.g. Miliband, 1973; Westergaard, 1973), nor does he mention that references to a future "relative pauperisation" are to be found in Marx (e.g. *The Economic and Philosophical Manuscripts of 1844*).[5]

Deutsch (1973) concedes that the "constructive solution" of class conflict has not been achieved without destructive violence (for instance, he specifically mentions the accounts of Roberts, 1969; and Taft and Ross, 1969). He claims that this violence was due to oversights on the part of management and was therefore a human error rather than economic inevitability (1973, p. 96). The constructive approach would not have stood in the way of unionism. Just as the

5. Deutsch's interpretation of Marx is by no means the one universally accepted by Marxologists. The thesis that Marx predicted a polarisation between the working and capitalist classes, with the former becoming increasingly impoverished, is only one of a number of interpretations of Marx's writings. For instance, Ossowski (1963) suggests that Marx's analysis of capitalist society involves more than a simplistic dichotomy of two classes. Nicolaus (1969) argues that Marx predicted a growth in the intermediate middle class. In an excellent discussion of these problems, Friedman (1974) claims that Marx's scheme is essentially continuous, rather than dichotomous, and he denies that Marx unequivocally predicted bipolarisation as a necessary precondition for a proletarian revolution. Consequently, one should be wary of undocumented claims, such as those made by Deutsch (1969b and 1973) that subsequent history has refuted basic components of Marx's analysis.

U.S.A. blundered into the Vietnam war, so too did management blunder into violent opposition to the principles of trade unionism. Marxists are sometimes accused of portraying history in terms of simplistic plots by "wicked" capitalists against "good-hearted" workers; nevertheless Deutsch's framework seems at times to lead him into personalised generalisations of precisely this sort. In terms of his own model there is the problem how the early destructive attitude of management was changed into the constructive later attitude; such a change would *prima facie* seem to be a contradiction of his crude law of social relations.

Although Deutsch does not specifically seek the ideological origins of certain perceptions and misperceptions, nevertheless his analysis is not totally psychological; his arguments are augmented by economic assumptions. For instance, economic expansion is seen as one of the variables which has allowed class conflict to become institutionalised and cooperative (1973, p. 97). Similarly there is the assumption that the maintenance of this cooperation depends on an expansionist economy. If this is the case then the desired atmosphere of mutual trust and openness may not be dependent on the good will of the participants but might also be governed by external market forces. This might be true of future economic developments; so might it have operated in the case of past conflicts. For instance the "misperceptions" of the destructive bosses might have been a direct consequence of an economic condition demanding immediate profit maximisation.

Deutsch's views can be further illustrated by considering a document which he has included in three of his works (1969b; 1969c and 1973). Entitled *Causes of Industrial Peace* this document according to Deutsch shows how disputes can be settled. Not surprisingly, in view of Deutsch's endorsement, there are recommendations for mutual trust and confidence. More important from the present point of view is the condition that there should exist no serious ideological incompatibility between management and the workers. This lack of incompatibility involves that "the union fully accepts private ownership and operation of the business" (quoted by Deutsch, 1969b, p. 47). In other words, peaceful cooperation in industrial matters is only possible if the workers renounce any socialist beliefs they might hold and recognise the capitalist owners of industry as their rightful employers.

Deutsch, therefore, does not dispute one of the basic tenets of the Marxist analysis of capitalist industry—that one class owns and oper-

ates the means of production and that the other class sells its labour to
that class. This is implicit in the document. What Deutsch seems to be
arguing is that, when everybody recognises that this is the right and
proper state of affairs, then there will be no serious destructive conflict.
In order to achieve this recognition on the part of the workers, Deutsch
says that it will be necessary for owners and management to make a
number of small concessions to their work forces. It should be noted
that Deutsch is offering advice to the powerful group. Deutsch re-
assures the industrial owners that giving concessions will not undermine their basic interests: ". . . power and prosperity are like information in some respects; it does not necessarily get lost by being given
to those who lack it" (Deutsch, 1969b, p. 56). Thus Deutsch is advocating that owners of industry should consolidate their class interests by
offering certain concessions; industry will still remain in private hands
and the profits will still accrue, if "trusting and open" owners concede
a pay claim here or a holiday bonus there. Trust will continue so long
as the work force recognise the rights of the owners to own and do not
impede the constructive workings of industry with any socialist
ideology.

The ambiguities in Deutsch's framework are revealed when he
deals with constructive social conflicts. Deutsch (1973, chapter five)
specifically focuses upon constructive intergroup, rather than interpersonal, conflicts. Such conflicts arise when an underprivileged group
seeks to improve its position within a particular social structure rather
than overthrow that structure. A prime example are American ethnic
minority groups who have been excluded from economic and social
power but who nevertheless uphold the basic "American dream" (see
for instance Marx's, 1967, description of black attitudes and the
Gutierrez and Hirsch, 1973, study of Chicano attitudes). In such cases
the underprivileged groups should seek to impress privileged groups
so as to increase "the likelihood that those in power will be responsive to change" (Deutsch, 1969c). This situation resembles Gurr's
(1973) definition of "reformist violence" in which efforts are made to
persuade the powerful to make changes. Deutsch offers the underprivileged advice; he warns against emotional reactions of rage (1969c,
p. 35) but recommends techniques of ridicule and embarrassment
(1973, p. 397). The underdog (referred to by Deutsch as Acme) should
communicate openly with the power that be (Bolt) and should also
show appreciation of Bolt's difficulties.

The problem is what Acme should do if Bolt fails to be impressed by all this good intent. Deutsch offers two significant pieces of advice to Acme: he should make "a statement of the negative harmful consequences that are inevitable for Bolt's values and objectives if Acme's wishes are not responded to positively" and he also should make "an expression of the power and resolve of Acme to act effectively and unwaveringly to induce Bolt to come to an acceptable agreement" (1973, p. 392). To put the matter bluntly Acme must threaten Bolt.

Deutsch however does not describe these two prescriptions as "threats". To do so would contradict his argument that he is providing a recipe for constructive conflict resolution. Threats are properties of destructive conflict; according to Deutsch's framework they "tend to elicit more resistence than do positive sanctions such as promises and rewards" (p. 389). The have-nots have no rewards to offer the haves, and if their promises of future good conduct are brushed aside they have no alternative but threats. Deutsch seems to recognise this implicitly at least, however he fails to see that this conflicts with his own theoretical assumptions, that such behaviour must lead to mutually dissatisfying destructive conflict. The fact is that even reformist causes have to be pursued with a certain amount of vigour if an underprivileged group is faced by an unyielding and unreasonable enemy. If such conflicts are to be called "constructive" then it must be on the basis of values unrelated to the immediate perceptions of the participants, (for a fuller discussion of Deutsch's theoretical framework see Billig, 1975).

It would seem therefore that Deutsch's attempt to distinguish between "good" conflicts and "bad" conflicts on the basis of psychological criteria has led to certain inconsistencies. He would seem faced with the alternatives of either referring to the black civil rights movements as instances of destructive conflict or of recognising that ultimately the distinction between "destructive" and "constructive" conflicts will have to be drawn on political rather than psychological criteria. His stop-gap solution of denying that threats are really threats would theoretically seem to be the least satisfactory solution.

The implications of Deutsch's approach to intergroup conflict have been spelled out at some length. His more recent formulations might be an improvement on his earlier blanket condemnation of conflict. However, this newer formulation also highlights some of the consequences of framing what are essentially political judgements in psychological terms. Deutsch's support for black civil rights is not predicated upon the psychological dispositions of the blacks but is based upon anterior standards of equality and justice. In the same way his analysis of capitalism and his belief that continuing economic expansion will be the key variable in future constructive conflict resolution is derived from a wider analysis than psychological dispositions. Despite these underlying assumptions, the focus of attention is directed upon what are basically interpersonal variables such as communication or trust; the explicitly political, as well as the historical, are correspondingly neglected.[6]

"Trust" and "communication" are not abstract acts. They take place in specific contexts for specific purposes. To give all trusting actions the stamp of approval would in certain circumstances be self-contradictory for Deutsch. It is possible for trust to be used strategically for ends which Deutsch would not consider constructive. Henry Kissinger in his book *Nuclear Weapons and Foreign Policy* (first published in 1957) argues that bargaining, trust and communication are necessary strategies if one is engaging in a limited war. He contends that efficient channels of communication between enemies are indispensable and that it is crucial not to misperceive the enemy's intentions (p. 171 and pp. 203ff). In such a case the variables which Deutsch associates with constructive conflict would be used to engage in the sort of conflict (i.e. the Vietnam war) which he considers destructive. It is true that Kissinger argues that trust, etc. will prevent a limited war escalating into an unlimited one. However, Kissinger does not use this argument to show how conflicts might be reduced but on the contrary shows how they might be efficiently conducted. It is precisely because warfare can be contained and limited that he advocates it as a useful instrument of foreign policy. Limited warfare is, according to Kissinger, the

6. The gaming approach consistently leads to a neglect of historical analysis. An example of this is provided by Lumsden (1973) who described the situation in Cyprus in terms of a 2×2 prisoner's dilemma game. The two players are the Greek and Turkish communities who both have a choice of two alternatives. The implication is that the destiny of the island is solely in the hands of the islanders. Foreign intervention, including invasion, is neglected. Moreover there is no analysis which might trace the historical roots of Greek and Turkish sentiments and thereby provide a key to the development of the present crisis. An historical analysis might involve other parties; for instance Pollis (1973) relates the development of Cypriot ethnic identities directly to the policies of the British colonial administration.

form of conflict "which enables us to derive the greatest strategic advantage from our industrial potential" (p. 155).

In this way Deutsch's variables of "trust" and "communication" can find themselves in the strategist's handbook, despite the fact that Deutsch's intentions might have been to formulate a non-strategic model of conflict. Much of the impetus for his theories came from a reaction against what has been called the "zero-sum mentality" which affected American strategists of the cold-war era. Their approach was based on viewing all situations as zero-sum games to be won at all costs. Horowitz (1970) has suggested that such theorists provided "scientific" justifications for American foreign policy. An unwitting connection between gaming theory and strategic thought might still exist in the post-cold war era; one might conjecture that, as Deutsch was developing his models of trust, not altogether dissimilar notions might have been current in strategic circles. Deutsch's own opposition to the policy of strategic warfare in Vietnam would make any such congruence of ideas all the more ironic.

Rapoport in his work has shown a far greater awareness than Deutsch of the potential connections between gaming research and strategic thought. In the previous chapter Rapoport's own research was described as being something of an intellectual dead-end. It should not be thought that this is due to any lack of imagination; rather it is the product of his determined opposition to the strategic approach and his refusal to embrace the ideological implications of certain gaming theories. Rapoport's book *Strategy and Conscience* (1964) was explicitly written as a polemic against the militarist thought of strategists like Herman Kahn and Thomas Schelling. His concern for peace research has not however led him into a simple-minded advocacy of the virtues of trust, honesty and general niceness. He recognises the need for social analyses which stretch beyond the interpersonal model. Consequently he has sought to delineate the limitations of gaming research (Rapoport, 1960, 1964 and 1974). He firmly distinguishes between "games" and "debates". Debates, unlike games, involve a conflict between ideas; Rapoport specifically argues that viewing all conflicts as games leads to a neglect and a downgrading of ideological conflicts. Similarly he fully acknowledges that the gaming framework cannot encompass revolutionary conflicts, in which the prevailing order of society is rejected. A fight for social justice involves more than a strategical game of "winning" a pre-arranged prize. Thus Rapoport states that the gaming approach "is not equipped to analyse asymmetric, structure-orientated conflicts where the 'actual' issue is neither the conflicting nor coincident interests of the conflicting parties, but the *structure of the system* in which they are immersed" (1974, p. 236, italics in original). Similarly he notes the need for wider social analysis in order to understand the organisation and functions of intergroup conflicts. More than this, Rapoport recognises the possible practical implications of such an analysis:

> . . . the investigation of the war machine and its connections would involve social or political action, and would probably make necessary the enlistment of people outside the research community. (Rapoport, 1970a, p. 286.)

In this way Rapoport avoids many of the strictures which have been aimed at gaming research. Nevertheless it would seem that Rapoport's concern with the social context of gaming research has inhibited his own activities in this sphere. As a consequence Rapoport's work has become somewhat divorced from the mainstream of gaming and conflict research.

In conclusion to this section a few comments can be made upon the current social psychological approaches to the study of intergroup behaviour, based upon the gaming and frustration-aggression traditions of research. The ideological implications of both approaches have been discussed in some detail as well as the underlying reductionist premises. These two approaches have dominated the social psychological study of conflict in the past fifteen or so years. It may seem surprising that no serious attempt has been made to integrate these two separate research traditions. Perhaps the reason is that they are complementary rather than opposing traditions. To illustrate this the two approaches can be loosely combined into a general composite picture reflecting certain dominant themes. This picture is not intended to represent the work of particular individual theorists but can be said to emerge from an accumulation of countless studies.

At first sight it might be thought that the two approaches are irreconcilable because they start from different theoretical premises. The gaming approach starts from the premise of rationality whereas frustration-aggression theory starts from the opposing premise of irrationality. However this difference is not crucial because there is a curious division of labour between the two approaches, which ensures they do not contradict one another. They are usually applied to separate types of phenomena. The gaming approach is designed primarily to apply to the behaviour of international diplomats and politicians. Frustration-aggression theorists tend to apply their models to social movements of discontent.

This division of labour together with the different theoretical premises creates an overall picture with clear ideological implications. The assumption of irrationality ensures that the theorist places a distance between himself and the phenomena he studies. For instance one frustration-aggression experimentalist, Baron, seems to categorise protests and ghetto riots as "tragic instances of collective violence" (1971a, p. 240). The mood he expresses is far different from the mood expressed by protestors and rioters; for them the tragedy lies in the reasons for the riot or protest not in their own actions which are optimistically designed to end the tragedy. The premise of rationality, on the other hand, emphasises the similarity between the researcher and his phenomena. Disagreements, including those between theorist and politician, are seen to be due to misunderstanding not to any qualitative difference in nature or mood. It may be of significance that when Deutsch breaks the implicit rules of this division of labour and offers "rational" advice to discontented groups, his theoretical model is faced with certain contradictions. This might suggest that the "social psychological picture" of conflict contains its own internal logic; the construction of a different picture is not to be achieved merely by extending the scope of existing theories. If this is so then a more radical theoretical reappraisal would be necessary.

The general picture can be summarised crudely as follows: aggression caused by those in power is the result of unfortunate personal errors, which have arisen out of a sad lack of mutual trust and open communication. On the other hand aggression caused by dissidents is the product of impulsive and irrational urges. In this way, legitimated aggression tends to be viewed as the product of individual mistakes, whereas insurgent aggression is caused by the unreasoning nature of those challenging the *status quo*. Thus two different sorts of psychological explanation are offered for the two types of phenomenon. The reductionist assumptions of both approaches also ensure that no deeper social analysis is needed. In particular the reduction of social phenomena to individual or interpersonal problems insulates the social psychologists from making any suggestions for basic structural social changes. Since the locus of social aggression is either in the unfortunate errors of otherwise well-meaning statesmen or in the irrationality of the discontented, the social psychologist will as a result find no need to make any radical critique of society. In this way an ideological defence of the *status quo* can be propounded under the guise of a "neutral" science.

The consequence of this division of labour between the frustration-aggression theorist and the conflict theorist is an ideological double standard. The actions of governments are not related to the wider social context. In particular the American political-military complex escapes fundamental criticism for the American involvement in Vietnam, and the relations of this complex to the economy go unnoticed by the social psychologist. The irrational massacre of civilian populations and the calculated destruction of a whole country are due to the blunders of a few individuals, but with good will all round matters can be put right. Anger at the actions of such a government and protest against inequality becomes, according to the social psychological picture, an irrational reaction to individual frustrations.

The above criticism of the "social psychological picture" is intentionally harsh. If social scientific investigation were confined to the laboratory investigation of certain interesting, but ultimately trivial, phenomena, and if it had no effect on wider social trends, then perhaps a harsh critique would not be altogether justified. However, the net result of the academic social psychological picture is that radical social criticism becomes muted just where it might be supposed to be strongest, namely, in those university departments supposedly investigating the structure of society. More importantly, it ensures that a new generation of social scientists will be produced, who will not question accepted ideological standards. That the Western military establishment employs a considerable number of social scientists is undeniable. Their role is not merely confined to war-gaming research; there has been an increasing involvement of trained social scientists in devising techniques of counter-insurgency, brainwashing, "pacification", and in generally facilitating the interests of economic and military interests (among the growing literature on this topic, see for instance Horowitz, 1967; Chomsky, 1973b; Porter, 1973; Shallice, 1973).

This is not to say that individual social psychologists have facilitated such processes by their particular experimental programmes. In fact it is part of the present aim to shift the focus from individual analysis to a social examination of ideology. This means accepting the social psychological assumptions as being themselves ideological products of their time. In the following sections the present conception of ideology and its relation to group and intergroup contexts will be outlined. In conclusion to this survey of what has been called the "social psychological picture" one might say that it stands indicted by its failure to develop any radical critique of social phenomena. Because of its basic spirit of empiricism, it has often concealed conservative presuppositions and has not functioned as an ideological opposition to received standards.

The concept of ideology

In the versions of psychological reductionism discussed previously, the trend has been for historical, economic and political matters to be reduced to psychological processes; this is true whether such processes be unconscious motivations or conscious perceptions. In this way subjective variables are seen as the prime determinants of social phenomena. In calling for an explicitly social analysis of ideology, an opposition to this form of subjectivism is being made. The intention is not to reduce social phenomena to the subjective, but on the contrary to emphasise the essential relatedness between the objective and the subjective. To this end it will be assumed that ideologies are first and foremost social creations, which depend on objective social factors for their existence. In turn the objective factors both create, and are themselves determined by, the subjective variables. The relationship between the objective and the subjective will thus be characterised as a dialectical one, and the basic dialectical nature of human society will be stressed. It is from the writings of Marx that the present conception of ideology will be developed, and it is hoped that this will allow the sort of critical social enquiry which is stifled by orthodox social psychological theory.

In most experimental social psychological studies economic variables are almost by definition excluded. *Prima facie* economic variables might be thought to be examplars of what can be called "objective factors". The importance of economic factors in social organisation should not be underestimated, just because experimental studies in social psychology have tended to ignore this aspect of group relations. Different forms of economic production and organisation, the division of labour, the development of ruling groups not involved in the actual processes of production, etc. can all be said to be of direct relevance to the social psychological study of actual group relations within their particular historical contexts. The effect of economic variables upon psychological ones is true for undeveloped societies as much as for the developed ones. This point can be illustrated by mentioning the correlational study conducted by Barry, *et al.* (1959). These research workers looked at child-rearing practices in 104 undeveloped societies with subsistence economies. They divided these societies into those whose economies required a high accumulation of food resources and those with a low accumulation of food resources. Their results indicated a significant difference between the child-rearing practices of these two sorts of societies: those communities with high accumulation taught their children to be individualistic. From this the authors conclude:

> ... a knowledge of the economy alone would enable one to predict with considerable accuracy whether a society's socialisation pressures were primarily toward compliance or assertion. (Barry *et al.* 1959, p. 59.)

This study indicates with clarity the importance of a society's economy to its psychological forms. If one took the economy as the objective factor and the attitudes and social practices as the subjective factors, then it might be thought that definite advances might be made by an interdisciplinary methodology which sought to correlate the two types of variables, similar to the methods used by Barry *et al.* In this way correlations might be sought from disciplines like economics, or even the sociology of formal structures, with more subjective or psychological phenomena. However, it will be suggested that more is needed than the mere collection of interdisciplinary correlations—such data needs to be interpreted. To do this there is need of more than a mere methodological integration; an integration is also needed at a theoretical level. Such an integration would need to characterise the interrelations between the "objective" and the "subjective" variables.

No such grand design is to be attempted here; however, a few remarks germane to any integration of the objective and subjective factors are in order, if only to make clear some of the assumptions underlying the present approach to the problem. Firstly, it can be admitted that the distinction between objective and subjective may in itself be misleading. It could well turn out to be a product of the present non-integration of the phenomena in question; for instance, one might surmise that the phenomena of social structure, group ideology and intergroup hostility do not in fact break down into methodologically neat parcels of "objective" and "subjective" factors.

To assume that they do is to run the risk of divorcing all these variables from the specific forms of human activity from which they arise.

This last point needs amplification. The so-called objective variables should not be understood as betokening entities that somehow exist over and above the everyday activities of humans. If certain economic or structural variables are held as determining certain social processes, then the practical reality which underlies these variables should still be examined. To characterise them as "objective" and to claim that the social analysis is complete once these variables have been identified, is to leave unanswered a number of important problems. Primarily the questions relate to the way in which particular economic or social structures have been developed and are in fact developing. The "objective" facts of social systems are created and maintained by human activity. Analysis of the different forms of this activity is still required.

The dialectical relationship between the objective and the subjective factors was previously mentioned. In its simplest form this phrase can refer to the basic way in which human beings collectively are able to create for themselves their own objective social reality and how this in turn conditions their own subjectivity. In other words, human activity creates certain forms of society and social organisation, which come to be recognised as an objective permanence. In turn this takes on a life of its own, i.e. such activity is objectified (cf. Berger and Luckman, 1967, for a theoretical description of these processes). There is also the corresponding process of "subjectification", which is a necessary concomitant of objectification—the objectified forms of human activity then determine the subjective consciousness of the actors, and shape their outlook upon the world. Their particular social creation becomes the way the world is for them. The way that their society is objectively constituted determines conversely how it is subjectively constituted. Both arise from the practical activity which underlies, maintains, and in a very real sense *is* the society.

The important point to be gathered from this very brief outline is that the processes of objectification and subjectification are both inherent in social activity. The implication of this is that human thought and actual social activity are closely and inevitably interrelated. By activity, all forms of social intercourse are implied, but especial emphasis can be placed upon what may be called for all societies essential activities, i.e. those that relate directly to the mode of subsistence of its members. In more developed societies this activity will refer to those forms connected with the production of its material products. Thus one would expect the particular economic organisation of a society to affect its particular forms of thought.

Given this preamble into the dialectical notions of objectification and subjectification, one then is in a position to make certain presuppositions about the concept of "group ideology" and the social importance of the concept. In the first place, the obvious point arising out of the preceding discussion is that group ideologies cannot be examined on their own as abstracted entities: they are human products which are developed by specific human activity. They do not issue forth from some sort of social vacuum. If one can assert that a particular group's ideology is the product of the activities of that group, then one can further assert that an intergroup ideology will arise out of a definite relationship between groups. Not only this, the ideologies themselves, or the forms of thought, will both refract and in turn determine the activities of the group and its intergroup relations. In this way the assertion can be made that the group ideology will be closely wedded to what, for the sake of convenience can be termed, the objective activities of that group. Having outlined briefly these basic presuppositions, more can be said about the present conception of the concept of ideology, and the relationship of this present conception to other formulations. In the first place the differences between the present use of the term and its use in much current social psychological writing can be noted. Already outlined and criticised have been the ideas of those social psychologists, notably Deutsch and Katz, who have considered ideologies as some sort of irrational barrier to peaceful intergroup coexistence. This conception obviously differs from that suggested here; the present position views ideologies as necessarily a part of group functioning, and not some unfortunate offshoot which should be avoided if possible. In the work of Deutsch and Katz this necessary connection is not perceived because their basic theoretical orientation is reductionist. Their notion of ideology is essentially an individualistic one, and refers to ideologies for people rather than ideologies for groups. Thus the notion is removed from the social context of group and intergroup phenomena.

In the reductionist social psychological account, an ideology is something that, above all else, orders and organises an *individual's* perception of the world. An illustration of this is afforded by Frank (1967):

he lists a number of synonyms for "ideology", which he claims all stand for the same basic phenomenon, e.g. "reality world", "assumptive world", "image", "belief system", etc. Whilst Frank recognises that these concepts are all relevant to such global problems as international relations and warfare, he nevertheless interprets them from the standpoint of individualistic psychology. He writes that "these questions are . . . best approached from the standpoint of the contexts, functions, and maintenance of individuals' world-views." (Frank, 1967, p. 87.) In essence, then, his approach is to extract the group significance from ideology (or world-view, to use his favourite term). Consequently he divorces an ideology from its functions and origins as a social and inter-individual creation; instead he examines ideology in relation to the hypothetical isolated individual. The social and group importance of ideology is passed over in favour of the important "psychological functions for individuals" that ideologies possess (Frank, 1967, p. 110).

Similarly a series of experimental investigations by Daniel Druckman into ideology can be mentioned (e.g. Druckman and Zechmeister, 1970; Druckman, 1971; Zechmeister and Druckman, 1973). Instead of seeking a wide-ranging examination of the concept of ideology these studies reduce ideology to a matter of interpersonal bargaining. In the light of the previous discussion on conflict research, it should come as no major surprise that the basic hypothesis of Druckman's experiments is that ideological commitment impairs the chances of "successful" conflict resolution. In a theoretical paper, Druckman and Zechmeister (1973) describe their position: "When contending positions in a conflict of interest are derived explicitly from opposing ideological orientations, the conflict will be more intense than when the link between competing positions and ideological orientations is not made explicit" (p. 453). Druckman's experimental situation involves pairs of subjects who have to come to an agreement about the allocation of money to be spent on a hypothetical social relief project. In the "non-ideological conditions" the subjects are given information of a purely factual nature to guide their discussions. In the "ideological" conditions the issues to be discussed are deliberately linked to wider questions. In using "ideology" in this way. Druckman is divorcing the concept from a group context. His definition of an ideological conflict is close to Aubert's (1963) notion of a value dissensus (see Druckman and Zechmeister, 1973, especially pp. 450–52). The important point about this definition is that an ideological conflict can refer to any dis-

agreement between two persons over any value. It would seem un-
remarkable that individuals find it harder to collaborate if they
disagree about basic issues, than if they have similar beliefs. In this line
of research the context of the collaboration, or decision-making, is
ignored; other experimental investigations have, to be sure, compared
subjects making decisions for themselves and when they are acting as
group representatives (e.g. Lamm and Kogan, 1970; Lamm, 1973).
However, the point is that in Druckman's concept of "ideology" the
term becomes virtually synonymous with any strongly held belief,
which is not of an obviously factual nature. In this way the ideological
is reduced to matters of interpersonal or individual psychology, and the
social context of the belief becomes essentially irrelevant.

This individualism runs through the predominance of social psychological theories and research on attitudes and belief systems; primarily what is studied are attitudes and belief systems of individuals.
This can be illustrated by briefly considering probably the most important, and certainly the most fertile, social psychological approach
to the study of attitudes in recent years—the theories of attitude consistency or dissonance (e.g. Festinger, 1957, 1964; Osgood and Tannenbaum, 1955; Rosenberg, 1960 and McGuire, 1960 for seminal formulations of this approach). This research tradition is based around variants of the proposition that an individual does not like to hold conflicting beliefs, and as a consequence wishes to attain a harmonious
and consistent outlook on the world. Whichever of the many formats
of this theory is taken (whether it be balance, congruity or dissonance
theory, etc.), the basic starting-point is the individual and the cognitive
processes that affect him. These processes are deemed to be fundamental psychological processes that operate, no matter what is the
social and historical context.

There would seem to be little point in documenting the individualistic flavour of this line of research into belief-systems and the social
psychological problems arising from them. Any brief look at the major
texts in this tradition would confirm this view. More important perhaps are those few studies which do not conform to this individualistic
approach and which attempt to widen the scope of the balance
approach. Because of the present emphasis on the necessary interrelatedness of group and ideological processes, attempts to widen the
scope of balance theories merely by multiplying their individual
effects cannot be considered as representing a satisfactory group

approach to the problems of attitudes. Mandelbaum (1968) attempts to interpret historical problems in the light of dissonance theory, but is forced to admit that the theory is best equipped to deal with problems of intellectual history and changes in accepted scientific theories. Thus the theory would seem most apt for explaining, in a very simplistic way, the reasons why particular scientists and thinkers come to reject received dogma, and why they search for new paradigms of thought. Any attempt to relate these shifts in scientific thought to changes in social and economic history must inevitably be outside the confines of balance theory, at least as orthodoxly considered. It is, of course, precisely in order to tackle such questions, or to provide a framework in which they can be tackled, that the close connection between ideology and group processes is being stressed.

Before leaving the topic of balance theories, two studies which do attempt to situate the theory in a group approach can be briefly mentioned. Firstly, Festinger *et al.* (1956), in a classic study, did attempt to study processes of dissonance reduction in an actual group situation—this was in their study of a religious group. However, here the focus of attention was upon the individual group members, rather than on examining the group *per se* and its relation to the wider social context. More important from the present point of view is the discussion by Campbell and LeVine (1968) which links cognitive congruity theories with intergroup relations. Without hypothesising the underlying mechanisms, these authors apply the formal principles of congruity theories to intergroup attitudes; they attempt to specify under what circumstances groups will hold positively-valued outgroup images, and under what circumstances they will hold negatively-valued ones. The limitations of such a procedure can be illustrated by considering the central tenet of individualistic dissonance theory; this is that people will seek some sort of internal harmony by altering their attitudes. When applied to the intergroup context, this assumption implies a theory of group behaviour that is both reactionary and unsatisfactory. The implication is that a dominated group will not fight against its domination, but will attempt to reduce dissonance by changing all its aspirations to liberty:

> When a population has imposed upon it economic or political structures that entail compliance to a new set of organisational demands entailing an alteration in boundaries between groups or statuses, then group labels and stereotypes will be altered so as to be concordant

with the newly established boundary condition. (Campbell and LeVine, 1968, p. 561.)

In other words any colonised group will accept its fate passively in order to achieve a concordance within the colonial situation. This view is based on a false premise, namely, that groups seek concordance, or to use more social terms, social stability. The desire for social change, to alter the structures of domination, is of course a powerful factor in intergroup relations. The struggle for liberty by a dominated group is achieved by formulating a defined ideology that seeks to overcome the received group situation. Any congruity theory of intergroup situations which accepts the *status quo* power relations as an inviolate given cannot offer an account of the dialectical relationship between the intergroup situation and the intergroup ideology; in particular it will not relate them to processes of social change.

To begin with, a clearer formulation of the concept of "ideology" is necessary. The differences between the present position and that normally taken by social psychologists investigating attitudes and belief-systems have been outlined. It is therefore in order to detail the similarities between the present approach and that of others. The present approach is derived from the formulations of Marx and Mannheim: two writers, whose works have tended to be overlooked by orthodox social psychologists, but whose writings contain some of the essential building-blocks for a social psychological analysis of group ideologies.

The clearest statement of Marx's conception of ideology is contained in *The German Ideology*, written in collaboration with Engels. In this work he argues that philosophical and abstract systems of thought cannot be properly understood if they are considered apart from the social conditions out of which they have arisen. The particular object of Marx's attack here is German Hegelian philosophy which interprets the world in terms of Pure Thought, divorced from the material conditions of life. Marx and Engels outline their basic premise in contradistinction to this viewpoint: "We set out from real, active men, and on the basis of their real life-process we demonstrate the development of the ideological reflexes and echoes of this process". (Marx and Engels, *The German Ideology*, p. 47, 1970 edn.) Although *The German Ideology* starts out as an essay in critical historiography, it nevertheless contains important discussions of the concept of ideology, not only with respect to German nineteenth century philosophy, but also

in relation to wider issues in intergroup relations. In this way Marx
and Engels remove their discussion from the particular form, to formulate a more general account of the genesis and functioning of group
ideology in the actual material life of social groups.

Of particular interest are those passages in *The German Ideology*
which relate ideology specifically to the intergroup context. Marx and
Engels connect ideology to the intergroup situations that exist *within*
societies, rather than those that exist *between* societies. Their basic
contention is that a society's dominant ideology reflects or echoes the
interests of the ruling group within that society: "the ideas of the
ruling class are in every epoch the ruling ideas, i.e. the class which is
the ruling *material* force of society, is at the same time its ruling *intellectual* force" (Marx and Engels, 1970 edn., p. 64, italics in original).
Thus the ideology of the dominant group is used to maintain its
superiority over subordinate groups. In this, the dominant group will
often contain ideological specialists, whose profession is to uphold the
material power of the group by formulating ideological justifications.
Often, claim Marx and Engels, there is conflict between the intellectual and practical wings of the dominant group, but these conflicts
should not disguise a basic commitment to the maintenance of their
group's dominance. The relevance of this analysis to certain trends in
social psychological theory should be apparent; just as some theorists
present their formulations as non ideological, objective, neutral truths
of science, so Marx and Engels maintain that the ruling class "has to
give its ideas the form of universality, and represent them as the only
rational, universally valid ones" (1970 edn., p. 66). Marx and Engels
relate the concept of ideology to the group context out of which the
ideologies are produced. They look beyond the manifest content of
the ideology in order to discover its relation to the actual and material
processes that underly it. Thus they can relate group ideologies
directly to the theory of classes and class struggle; they trace the history
of ideology in Europe from feudal to bourgeois ideology and through
to the revolutionary ideology of the proletariat. In this way ideologies
are seen as products of particular human groupings and the relations
between such groupings have to be understood in this context of group
relations.

Like Marx, Karl Mannheim also espouses a non-reductionist approach to problems of ideology. In his book *Ideology and Utopia*, first
published in 1936, Mannheim makes a number of points that bear

directly on the present discussion of the issue. In the first place he steadfastly opposes the approach which reduces ideologies to problems of individual psychology. He argues that ideologies should not be examined purely in terms of their overt meaning, their underlying significance should be sought. Two different sorts of underlying conditions can be discovered and these correspond to two different sorts of ideology. On the one hand there is, what Mannheim called, "particular ideology". This is an ideology that operates at an individualistic level, and corresponds to the normal modern social psychological conception of "belief system". The underlying conditions relating to the particular ideology are the motives, intentions and personality of the individual. They concern the reasons why a particular individual recommends a particular ideological position. However, according to Mannheim, this is a superficial and narrow conception of ideology. He criticises those who do not look beyond the particular ideology to see the wider social significance; this criticism should be borne in mind by all those social psychological research workers and theorists, who today show no inclination to transcend the individualistic approach:

> Since the particular conception never actually departs from the psychological level, the point of reference in such analyses is always the individual. This is the case even when we are dealing with groups, since all psychic phenomena must finally be reduced to the minds of individuals. . . . If we confine our observations to the mental processes which take place in the individual and regard him as the only possible bearer of ideologies, we shall never grasp in its totality the structure of the intellectual world belonging to a social group in a given historical situation. (Mannheim, 1972 edn., pp. 51–2.)

It can be seen that Mannheim offers a critique of the individualistic reductionist approach to problems of ideology. It is therefore no accident that a social psychology which examines intergroup relations in terms of "particular ideologies" (i.e. belief systems of individuals), should arrive at answers phrased in individualistic terms. Thus Deutsch, especially in his earlier theories, starts from the premise that intergroup phenomena can be reduced to interpersonal phenomena, and his theoretical analyses are built around the psychological motivations of the participants of the intergroup conflict. This work affords a prime example of an approach limited to the problems of particular ideology, and not touching on the more important problems of "total ideology". To advance beyond the particular ideology, Mannheim argued, it is necessary to examine the wider social situations of groups themselves, and not be restricted to looking at the actions of particular members within those groups. The total ideology is of necessity allied to the group situation and corresponds to the German word *Weltanschauung*, or complete social outlook of a group. In this sense, the concept of ideology does not refer to a coincidence between the contents of individual belief-systems, as is implied in the reductionist analysis. If the concepts of ideology and group are analytically connected, then one can assert that the existence of an ideology presupposes the existence of a social group to share and uphold that ideology. The reverse proposition that the existence of a social group presupposes the existence of a group ideology, it will be argued, is of a different order and cannot be upheld, at least in the same way.

Both Marx and Mannheim relate a group's ideology to the material activity of that group. There are, however, a number of differences between Marx and Mannheim in their concept of "ideology". Both endow the concept with a critical edge. Marx uses the term in his critique of all pre-proletarian modes of thought—the success of the proletarian revolution would, in his view, mark the demise of ideology. Mannheim, on the other hand, faced with the results of actualised proletarian revolution, distinguished between ideologies and utopias. Ideology, in his account, designated the thought of an existing social structure, whereas utopian thought aimed to transcend the existing order. Thus the ideology was the product of a dominant social group, and utopian thought is confined to ascendant or revolutionary groups. Utopian thought is changed into ideological thought when the ascendant group attains a position of power; as a result there is always the possibility that "the utopias of today may become the realities of tomorrow" (Mannheim, 1972, p. 183). However, the change from utopia to ideology, according to Mannheim, involves substantial changes in the group's thought and "what was originally in absolute opposition to historical reality tends, now, after the model of conservatism to lose its character as opposition" (1972, pp. 222–3).

Mannheim could be interpreted as either stating a tautological truth, or making an assumption about the course of all revolutionary movements. On the one hand he could be stating that once a revolutionary group attains power, it must cease overthrowing the existing order and commence its task of reconstruction. This much is true, almost by definition. If, however, he is implying that all revolutionary forces must tend to conservatism and cease to be a dynamic instrument of social change, then he is essentially making an assumption of a political nature about the limitations of revolutionary activity. Because no such assumption is intended in the present work, Mannheim's distinction between ideology and utopia will not be maintained. Instead the term "ideology" will be used to cover the thought of conservative power groups as well as that of revolutionary dissident groups. It will not be assumed *a priori* that some sort of permanent process of revolution cannot be instituted, which does not of necessity culminate in the establishment of a new dominant power élite.

In applying the term ideology to encompass the outlook of all major social groups the present use must necessarily differ from narrower uses of the term. For instance, ideology is sometimes taken to refer to the customs and rituals of particular individual institutions, rather than applying to the wider social framework in which such institutions exist (for instance, see Garnier's (1973) analysis of the "ideology" of a military academy). The present use is wider than Apter's (1964) conception of ideology; Apter concentrates upon ideology "binding the community together" and helping to "support an élite and to justify the exercise of power" (p. 18). The opposite functions of ideology are correspondingly neglected. A different conception of ideology is provided by Shils (1968) who sees it as a "relatively systematised or integrated body of thought" (p. 66). Similarly, Geertz (1964) conceives of ideology as a developed creation, which he likens to model-building. However, the present position is to place more emphasis upon the social functions of ideology, than upon its form.[7] Mannheim (1972, pp. 206f), noted that conservative thought had less need than revolutionary thought of systematic theory, because the conservative does not attempt to justify the *status quo*, but to present it as the natural state of affairs. Therefore a lack of systematisation should not be taken as indicating an absence of ideology; rather the social functions of this lack of systematisation should be sought. In this respect, Litwak, Hooyman and Warren (1973) concluded from their study of "middle-American" attitudes that a lack of systematic integration neither demonstrated a lack of ideology nor a lack of rationality.

In order to understand the social significance of an ideology there is a need to look beyond its subjective meaning, and to place it in its

7. cf. for instance, Chabat's (1973) distinction between "constructed" and "applied" ideology.

group, or intergroup, context. This can be illustrated by considering in abstract the phenomenon of polygamy. It would be possible to describe in intricate detail the polygamous customs of a particular tribe, paying attention only to the subjective meanings of those customs. However, to give an account of polygamy as an ideology, it would be necessary to consider the wider social context. For instance, Cohen and Middleton (1970) have suggested that polygamy is impossible unless a tribe has a ready supply of women, and that it is practised as a consequence only by groups who can exploit or dominate other groups. Thus the ideological significance of a polygamous practice will be related to this intergroup context, and can be seen as a means by which the dominant group will attempt to perpetuate its dominance.[8]

Similarly it is possible to place an over-emphasis upon the subjective meanings of participants in social movements without attempting to relate such movements to the wider context. For instance, Wilson, J. (1973) explicitly aims to give the concept of "ideology" a wider significance than that given it by Marx (p. 93). Thus, he deliberately divorces the ideological from the economic; however, the result is that he often seems to be examining social movements as isolated entities, concentrating on their internal structures and exotic beliefs, and consequently neglecting their wider significance. An example of this is contained in his discussion of the West Indian Pentecostal sects in London (cf. Calley, 1965); these are discussed as social units in their own right and there is no mention that it was rejection by white religious institutions that forced the West Indians to form their own sects (Hiro, 1973). By concentrating upon the given forms of the social phenomena, the wider intergroup context is forgotten—in this case the context includes white racism and black community development. As a consequence ideology is given a narrower, not wider, focus.

The present conception aims to connect ideology with social power and threats to power, especially in an intergroup context. An ideology will reflect that intergroup context, and the subjective meanings will bear strong traces of the objective situation. In this respect, Lichtheim (1974) states when discussing the Caesars' doctrine of *imperium* that

8. The precise relationship of polygamy to intergroup conflict is almost certainly more complex. For instance, Ember (1974) has found a strong correlation between polygamy and mortality in warfare, which suggests that polygamy may be a response to an unbalanced ingroup sex-ratio, which is itself a consequence of intergroup conflict.

"no ruling class can function without a creed" (p. 25). The ancient heritage of the *imperium populi Romani* was used to justify and legitimise the empire of Rome. Similarly, a belief in the inherent differences between different peoples became part of the ideology justifying British imperial ambitions in the nineteenth century (Kiernan, 1969; Bolt, 1971; Pollis, 1973). Maquet (1961) writes of the premises which underwrite all cultures and which link the cultural superstructure to the economic and political infrastructure. In the culture of Ruanda, studied by Maquet, the dominant ideological premise was the belief in the essential inequality of all social groups. This ideology was the product of a divided society, in which one social group had mastery over another. The "premise of inequality" underscored the total cultural superstructure built around this dominance. Similarly racist ideology in South Africa perpetuates and arises from a system of extreme intergroup exploitation and must be understood in terms of intergroup power differentials (Wilson, W. J., 1973).

If intergroup ideology is seen in this wide perspective, then there can be no simple separation of factual and normative elements. In the ideology, fact and value will be inextricably linked, just as theory and practice will inevitably be confused. This can be illustrated by considering a hypothetical example. If two societies are continually competing for the same scarce resources and have as a result built up a long history of intergroup rivalry, then one would expect their intergroup ideologies to reflect this basic economic situation (see, for instance, Mack and Snyder, 1957, proposition 48; LeVine and Campbell, 1972, p. 36). In particular each group will form a stock of beliefs, which explain, characterise and thus determine the other group as the traditional enemy. This theme will run throughout the intergroup ideology. If the characterisation of the outgroup as an "enemy" is a value-laden judgement, then it should be recognised that it arises out of the historical fact of scarce resources, and similarly determines that fact in the future. In terms of existing intergroup relations, the outgroup is the enemy, and the negative traits attributed to the enemy will be confirmed and reinforced by this pattern of intergroup relations. Thus within the ideological structure, the fact and the value combine to form the actual whole.

In this sense a group's history will contain a fusion of factual and value-laden statements and itself be an ideological creation; this ideological element is explicitly recognised by certain historians (e.g.

Carr, 1961; Jones, 1972). The ideology will become self-fulfilling: the fact will determine action, which will in turn ensure more similar facts—at least until the ideological system is defeated. In this respect the "facts" of ethnic differences accepted by the British imperialists (and supported by the science of anthropology, cf. Lewis, 1973), determined colonial policy; as a result ethnic differences were substantiated and imperialist exploitation ideologically justified (Pollis, 1973). In the same way the Western educational system presupposes "facts" of innate differences in intellectual ability; consequently persons of widely differing abilities are "produced" by the system and social inequalities are validated. In this way differences in wealth are justified on the basis of differences in innate ability. It is because of this ideological fusion of the so-called facts and the wider political and economic structure that there is much concern about the present re-crudescence of scientific racism and about the ideological purpose of the "facts" produced by Eysenck, Jensen and others (see: Rex, 1972; Rose, Hambley and Haywood, 1973; for a discussion of the errors and ideological bias in the arguments that genetic differences validate social inequality, see Chomsky, 1973b, chapter five, pp. 132 ff). The history of ideologies should teach us to be suspicious of "neutral" facts which purport to show inherent differences between different social groups, especially when these facts are advanced at times welcome to the forces of domination and exploitation.

This emphasis upon the links between facts and values in ideo-logical formulations is at variance with the conceptions of mainstream social psychological theory. In most formulations, attitudes are pre-sumed to be composed of distinct elements. A glance at some of the leading textbooks on the subject would confirm this impression. Thus Krech, Crutchfield and Ballachey (1962) define attitudes as systems by which individuals organise their feelings, cognitions and action ten-dencies (p. 139); similarly, Secord and Backman (1964) define attitudes as "certain regularities of an individual's feelings, thought and pre-dispositions to act toward some aspect of his environment" (p. 97). In a more recent textbook, Aronson (1973) too maintains the distinction between the evaluative and cognitive aspects of attitudes; he writes that "an opinion that includes an evaluative and an emotional com-ponent is called an *attitude*" (p. 86, italics in original). Likewise there have been empirical attempts to separate these theoretically distinct components (e.g. McGuire, 1960b; Peabody, 1968).

However, this separation of the affective and the cognitive has not been without its critics within social psychology (e.g. Kelvin, 1970). There has been increasing evidence that an individual's attitudes are not the summation of discrete affective and cognitive components (e.g. Sherif and Hovland, 1961; Eiser and Stroebe, 1972, for descriptions of some of the empirical evidence). If this is the case with attitudes considered from an individualistic point of view, then it is also true of attitudes considered as ideology. One of the clearest ways to demonstrate the social psychological complexity of intergroup attitudes is to look at the ways in which children acquire the intergroup attitudes prevalent in their culture. By investigating the stages by which children learn their full ideological picture of the world, the various strands of the ideology itself can be distinguished. For instance, it has been shown that intergroup attitudes in the west are learned at an early age (Proshansky, 1966), especially when these attitudes concern racial groups (Milner, 1971 and 1973; Pushkin and Veness, 1973). In the case of children, it can be shown that cultural values attached to groups may be learned before any specific knowledge of those groups. Tajfel and Jahoda (1966) showed that British children had marked and uniform preferences for other countries without knowing anything about the nature of these countries; similar results were also obtained by Stillwell and Spencer (1973) who also showed that children's intergroup attitudes can be based upon a fragmentation of facts and values. Experiments on American children have revealed that reaction to black and white objects can reflect the racial attitudes of the wider community, and thus intergroup attitudes are generalised to "neutral" objects not connected with the intergroup context (see Stabler and Johnson, 1972, for a review of this line of research).

As a result it is possible to distinguish various aspects of intergroup ideology in the developmental processes of children. In this respect it has been possible to separate the child's affective preference from any factual knowledge which he might have. However, this distinction, which can be held for children, should not be taken as implying that the very same distinctions can be easily drawn with respect to full-scale adult ideologies. In fact the reverse could be upheld—it is through examining the development processes that one can appreciate how the various strands of ideological intergroup thought are combined to form the total adult picture. The fragmentation demonstrated in the attitudes of children is only possible because these are

ill-formed. The adult ideology involves a complex interrelation between fact and value; it is dialectically related to the social structure
and intergroup context in which the adult lives. It is the social forms
of this ideology that determine the degree to which the ideology
functions as a means of preserving or changing the social structure.

Ideology and false consciousness

One of the themes running through the preceding discussion has been
that a group's ideology reflects the objective situation of the group. It
has been asserted that the ideology arises from the practical activity
of the group and is as a result dialectically related to future activity.
Having assumed this, it might be thought that an analysis of the set
of beliefs held by a group would be sufficient to reveal its objective
condition. In other words, if the subjective reflects the objective condition, then the objective will be contained, in all essentials, in the
subjective beliefs. As a result, the social scientist might concentrate
purely upon the subjective elements of ideology and these would lead
him inevitably to the objective elements. According to this reasoning,
one would expect to discover whether or not there were power élites or
dominant classes within a particular society, merely by examining the
ideological beliefs current in that society. If there were a broad con-
census of opinion that there were such élites or dominant classes, then
the social scientist would admit their existence, otherwise they could
not be said to exist. In this way, the objective structure of society, as
defined by the social scientist, would be contained in the beliefs of the
society's members.

However, it is to avoid such a subjectivist approach that the concept
of "false consciousness" is introduced into the present analysis. It is not
assumed that the relation between the objective and the subjective is
in any way a simple one. To speak of the subjective reflecting the
objective explains little unless the nature of this reflection is in some
way specified. A simple interpretation of this "reflection" might posit
that a dominant group will always have an ideology which stresses its
superior position and a subordinate group an ideology which stresses
its inferior position. However, such a simple interpretation would rest
on the unwarranted assumption that all groups have the same power
to create their own ideologies, and that one group does not shape the
ideology of another group. To assume this would be to lose the critical

edge of Marx's concept of ideology and to neglect his assertion that the ruling ideas in any age are the ideas of the ruling class. In other words, under certain circumstances, the ruling group will have the power and resources to shape the ideology of the subordinate group. The purpose of such an ideology will not be to explain the inferior status to the subordinate group in a way that will be most beneficial to its interests. It will not aim at reflecting the underlying objective reality in so far as that ideology is based upon inequalities which can be altered; nor will it demonstrate the material conditions by which the alterations can be made. The purpose of the ideology will be to perpetuate the system which maintains the intergroup inequalities. One way in which this can be effected is by obfuscating the objective conditions which underlie the pattern of intergroup dominance. For instance, the ideology of the ruling group may aim to minimise or conceal the actual intergroup *divisions* within the society by emphasising, for instance, a national wholeness. On the other hand the ideology might stress a multiplicity of various group divisions, and thereby conceal a major division. In either case the objective class division would be concealed behind a false consciousness of other intergroup divisions.

In stipulating this, a wedge has been driven between the underlying material conditions and the group's ideological superstructure. As a result it becomes necessary to investigate closely the processes by which an ideology is shaped and maintained, for the ideology may function to conceal, rather than reveal the objective infrastructure. In this sense the ideology can be said to function as "false consciousness". It is therefore possible to interpret the notion of false consciousness with respect to the intergroup situation; in this respect it refers to a subordinate group's ideology which is determined by the dominant group, in such a way that the objective conditions of society are concealed or misrepresented. By assuming the possibility of false consciousness, one can then allow for the non-isomorphism of ideology and group activity. In particular, the presence or absence of an ideological consciousness cannot by itself be said to determine the nature of the social structure. The present position is in agreement with C. Wright Mill's assertion that the problem of classes is not to be solved on the issue of class consciousness alone (Mills, 1963, p. 317). The absence of any developed class consciousness does not necessarily imply a classless society. As such, studies which equate class conflict with class consciousness must be seen as an oversimplification. For instance Morris and Jeffries (1970) conclude that the topic of class conflict can be forgotten because their sample of American respondents showed little or no class consciousness, at least in the traditional meaning of the term. By recognising the possibility of false consciousness the existence of a social group need not be identified solely by the existence of group consciousness; as a result a more critical social analysis becomes possible.

Similarly the relation between objective and subjective factors is not to be revealed by any simplistic correlations. For instance, recent studies have attempted to correlate objective social status with subjective social status (for example, Hodge and Treiman, 1968; Jackman and Jackman, 1973). Such studies are presented as tests of "Marxist" hypotheses, and they do this by correlating the degree to which people identify themselves with the upper, middle or lower classes with their earnings, education, private wealth, etc. The first thing to notice about such studies is that they generally exclude the very wealthy. Secondly, the "objective" variables are considered as independent continua and are not allied to any dynamic model of society. As a result they merely reveal that people who have more wealth or education than others tend to consider themselves as different from others. Because of this there is no identification of objective power groups within the society, and thereby no analysis of the way in which the society operates, regardless of subjective group identifications. If the problem of subjective group identification is not isomorphic with the problem of the existence of objective groups, then there is no reason why objective factors should be assumed *a priori* to consist of independent continua.

Having established theoretically the distinction between the existence of a social group and the existence of a group consciousness, it is then possible to make a further distinction; namely between those groups whose ideology accurately reflects their material conditions and those groups whose ideology represents a false consciousness. The former will be referred to as groups-for-themselves and the latter as groups-in-themselves. Since false consciousness has been here related to an intergroup context, one might say that the problem for any subordinate group is to free itself from its imposed ideology and to develop its own true consciousness. Revolutionary group activity can represent the process by which a group-in-itself becomes a group-for-itself. Because of the definition of false consciousness in terms of intergroup dominance, the dominant group might be thought to be, by definition, a group-for-itself: it will have developed its own ideology which will reflect and thereby function to preserve its position of dominance. However, a more detailed analysis would reveal the over-simplifications of this formulation. In particular it oversimplifies the processes of social change. For instance, the simple assertion that the dominant group is a group-for-itself would need to be substantially qualified to cope with those situations in which its power is being seriously threatened. In this respect Mannheim (1972) noted that con-servative thought only articulates itself under attack; as such it con-stitutes a counter-ideology and Mannheim states that "conservative mentality discovers its *idea* only *ex post facto*" (p. 207). It may well be the case that a threatened and declining dominant group may formu-late an ideology which fails to serve its own interests; and what is more, this ideology may fail to represent the objective material conditions which are threatening to bring about the dominant group's downfall. In this respect a false consciousness may well be a possibility for a dominant group whose interests are under attack and which is in the process of becoming a group-in-itself from a group-for-itself.

The foregoing is merely a hypothesised theoretical sketch. Obviously the concepts mentioned would need to be sharpened considerably and their interrelations specified in much greater detail, in the course of describing actual intergroup situations. Nevertheless it can be stated that, by placing the concept of false consciousness in an intergroup context, the stress is upon the power of a ruling group to construct an ideology that represents its own interests. Wirsing (1973) in his com-parative anthropological study of primitive societies, found that the political power of a governing elite was positively correlated with its control of information within the society. The same process can be observed in our own Western capitalist democracies, which, according to general belief, function to create consensus from freely competing interest groups. However, Murdock and Golding (1973) have shown how economic vested interests have virtual control over mass-communi-cations and that this commercial control affects content such that "all information is ideology" (p. 226). Similarly, Miliband (1973) and Sal-lach (1974) have noted how capitalist interests ensure an ideological bias in favour of the *status quo*. This bias is not so much achieved by direct censorship, but through the continual presentation of only one broad ideological picture and by limiting the area of discussion to particular topics within the existing structure, rather than allowing a discussion of that structure itself. Thus, Sallach writes of "the suppression of alternative views through the established parameters which define what is legitimate, reasonable, sane, practical, good, true, and beautiful" (1974, p. 41). In this way dominant interests can affect the ideologies that are disseminated, and also the ideologists which are neglected—if these are to be disseminated, then they need to seek and create other channels.

In a sense the present conception of false consciousness is a relativistic one; the ideology of a ruling class can be seen as a false consciousness, not as far as their own interests are concerned, but as far as the interests of the ruled are considered. The consciousness is not false in an absolute sense, but is false for a particular social group. However, having stressed the relation of false consciousness to intergroup domination, at least for present purposes, it should be emphasised that no simplistic social psychological critique is being intended. In particular, no psychological assumption about the motivation of a dominant group is maintained. For instance, it might be assumed that the false ideology of a subordinate group is being supported by the deliberate deceit of the dominant group. In other words, the psychological assumption would be that the existence of false consciousness implies the existence of a deliberate intent to deceive.

However, the problem of conscious deception is not a major issue with respect to false consciousness. Mannheim's distinction between the particular and the total ideology is of relevance here. Mannheim specifically related the problem of deceit to the particular ideology, which is concerned with essentially interpersonal aspects. He states that the particular ideology embraces "all those utterances the 'falsity' of which is due to an intentional or unintentional, conscious, semiconscious, or unconscious, deluding of one's self or of others, taking place on a psychological level and structurally resembling lies" (1972, p. 238). Questions of deceit and personal motivation do not strictly apply to the total ideology, which provides a complete picture of reality. An individual can deliberately tell a particular lie, but a whole social group cannot in the same sense be said to live a total life of lies, at least not intentionally.

To be sure, interpersonal deceit can be instrumental in maintaining and transmitting a false consciousness. This interpersonal deceit, however, does not replace the total ideology, but operates at the intersection between the particular and the total. This intersection exists at the centre of political power within a group. To illustrate this, one can consider the deceit of political leaders. Chomsky (1973a) and Porter (1973), have shown how the deceit of U.S. politicians has enabled lies about the political situation in Vietnam to spread through the American mass-media: the deliberate deceit of the leader is only operative if his lie is seen as reality. Thus honesty and dishonesty only relate to a limited sphere of action on the part of political leaders; the way their words are distilled and transmitted by the mass media and political "experts" ensures that the issue is wider than that of interpersonal deceit. The newspaper reporter, the television commentator, the political pundit, together with their public, are not necessarily wittingly engaged in a deceitful operation, for the lie is becoming changed from the particular to the total. As the lie is spread, it is altered from, as it were, private property to public property.

Similarly social psychological experiments have shown that communicating information can by itself produce a belief in the information, (e.g. Janis and King, 1954; King and Janis, 1956); the dissemination of content can therefore determine personal belief, and in this respect the prevalance of false consciousness must be a wider problem than the prevalence of personal dishonesty. There is no contradiction in a false consciousness being earnestly and sincerely transmitted. In the same way, folklore and popular belief may originate from the cynical lies of political leaders. The news media may serve to propogate and exacerbate popular prejudice. Knopf (1974) in her study of the racial bias in the twentieth century American press, discounts the suggestion that racist misreporting is the product of a deliberate conspiracy by newspaper editors. Rather, she concludes that the spread of racist myths arises out of the structure and function of the press within American society.

It is one matter to make a theoretical distinction between false and true consciousness, and between the group-for-itself and the group-in-itself; it is another matter to maintain such distinctions in an actual intergroup context. Certainly within the social psychological laboratory there is no major problem. False and true consciousness can be operationally defined in terms of any experimental deceit; since deception is a common feature of social psychological experimentation (Kelman, 1968 and 1972), the distinction might possibly have some methodological, as well as theoretical, advantage. Previously in the discussion of the intergroup experiment conducted by Miller and Bugelski (1948) the operation of a limited form of false consciousness was described. However, there would be little point in retaining theoretical concepts that could only apply to experimental situations. Such concepts must also be applicable to the real world, which the experiments are supposed to illuminate in some way.

If false consciousness can be unambiguously identified in the experimental situation, the real world nevertheless is not so simple. There is no abstract and absolute standard, which can resolve intergroup conflicts; this notion will be considered and rejected in the following chapter. By the same logic, one must reject the notion that there exists some litmus test that can distinguish true consciousness from false consciousness. The idea that such a test could exist conflicts with the relativist nature of false consciousness, at least as the term is being used in the present context. The distinction between true and false consciousness must itself be an ideological one; since ideology arises from practical activity, the distinction in any important matter must inevitably be a practical one likewise. Thus competing analyses of a particular context of intergroup relations will produce competing definitions of false and true consciousness. Rigorous empiricism will not settle the issue, since more is at issue than discoverable empirical facts. To stipulate what is false consciousness means more than an empirical investigation of the present—it also involves a commitment to the future.

This commitment to the future can be seen clearly in the case of subordinate groups-in-themselves. A false consciousness will be seen as an obstacle to the group's progress to becoming a group-for-itself. It will be assumed by those who categorise a particular view as false consciousness that the group is able to realise itself and achieve its own liberation. Such an assumption cannot be derived from a purely "neutral" factual study of the present and the past. Similarly those ideologues on the other side, who might deny the possibility of the group attaining its own realisation, are making a commitment to the future. The denial of a possibility is just as much an ideological commitment as its avowal. Since the ideological commitment can itself be an obstacle to achieving the future, and likewise because it can also contribute positively to its attainment, the distinction between true and false consciousness must inevitably be a practical matter. Thus Mannheim (1972) asserted that it is only in retrospect that it is possible to distinguish between realisable and unrealisable ideologies, because at the time they "are buried under the partisan conflict of opinion" (p. 184). The practicality of truth was something that Marx, above all, stressed. This is the basic message of his *Theses on Feurbach* (Marx and Engels, 1968 edn.); and in the second thesis he clearly states the principle that it is through practical activity that man demonstrates the truth of his thought.

The main issues to arise from this discussion have centred around ideology and the intergroup context; also it has been stressed that distinguishing true from false consciousness involves in itself an ideological commitment, both to the present and to the future. In the course of this discussion purely psychological matters have been somewhat pushed to the background. This has been deliberate since it is the present position that the social psychological variables, affecting intergroup relations, only operate within a wider social context. It might perhaps have been simpler first to have discussed intergroup conflict from the point of view of the commitments of the group members. Certainly the processes by which a group-in-itself becomes a group-for-itself are not lifeless rearrangements of economic variables, but involve the hopes, fears and beliefs of individuals. The processes also require that such individuals should identify their group and show a commitment to it. The topic of group identification will be discussed in following chapters, but it will be emphasised that any such commitment or identification must depend upon the wider social context and its underlying objective features. To forget that is, from the present point of view, itself a false consciousness which intellectually prevents a critical social analysis.

8

The Context of Intergroup Relations

The concepts of ideology and false consciousness have been outlined on a theoretical level. It is now necessary to apply these concepts to specific issues which arise in the social psychological study of intergroup relations. This chapter will focus on a number of different issues relating to large-scale social processes. Amongst the topics to be discussed will be the role of third parties in intergroup conflicts, social movements, ethnocentrism and group goals. Although the subject matter of this chapter will be somewhat diffuse, it is hoped that there will be a conceptual unity in the discussion of these various issues. In particular the various subsections will be linked by the underlying theme that social psychological variables need to be set in the wider context of intergroup relations.

Ideology and neutrality

If the ideological beliefs of two opposing groups arise out of the intergroup situation, then one must also enquire about the ideological basis of any third-party which attempts to mediate between the two conflicting parties. It will be suggested that although a third-party can act impartially with respect to certain issues, there is no guarantee of social neutrality. In fact neutrality in a strict sense is impossible; the third-party is part of a wider social system and whatever claims to impartiality it might have are derived from its social position.

The role of the third-party can be considered with respect to experimental investigations of bargaining. In most social psychological experiments the role of the experimenter himself tends to be neglected.

He is considered as some sort of neutral fixture in the situation. The previous discussions of the frustration-aggression research pointed to the importance of the social role of the experimenter in the laboratory situation. He is an integral part of the social situation of the experiment. If this is the case then the normal bargaining experiment involving two opposing subjects is in reality a three-party situation. The most obvious counterpart in real life to the experimenter is some sort of ideologically impartial third-party, who stands aloof from the details of the conflict between the two parties. The role of the experimenter can be illustrated by considering the bargaining experiments of Thibaut, (e.g., Thibaut, 1968; Thibaut and Faucheux, 1965; Thibaut and Gruder, 1969). In contradiction to the Deutsch and Krauss trucking-game experiments, this series of studies was designed to demonstrate that the power to disrupt a given relationship can lead to the development of certain conflict "solutions"; in this case the adoption by both parties of certain contractual norms that regulate the conflict. However, it has been pointed out by Murdoch and Rosen (1970) and Gruder (1970) that one of the crucial factors in the development of such contractual norms is the behaviour of the experimenter himself. The contractual norms are not spontaneously developed by the subjects, but have to be explicitly suggested by the experimenters or some other "neutral" third party. The ways in which a third party intervenes in a bargaining situation can materially affect the possibility of agreements (Erickson *et al.* 1974).

The role of the experimenter in the situation can be further clarified by considering what exactly he does. In the Murdoch and Rosen (1970) study the subjects were engaged in a trading relationship, in which each wanted to score as many points as possible. If they scored a certain number of points, they would qualify for an actual monetary reward. However if they both traded competitively, then neither would score anywhere near enough points to hope to qualify for the monetary payment. The experiment was designed to see under what circumstances the subjects would accept the contractual agreements presented to them by the experimenter. Thus the experimenter had both the subjects literally working for him with the promise of reward for the "best" of them. The method of payment was therefore designed to divide the subjects against one another. Also the experimenters watched over every move made by the subjects by monitoring their entire conversations. If this situation is intended to be a model or an illustration of certain real-life processes, then one has to ask what sort of situation it resembles. Certainly it does not seem to model the normal bargaining situation between two moderately free-agents: the crucial role of the experimenter is left out of the picture if this is the model. Rather the situation suggests something like a prison-work-camp, designed to achieve maximum control, maximum work output and minimum security risk. Also the experimental situation might be compared to a work situation with a most barbarous system of exploitation and management control.

This example from bargaining experimentation illustrates the fact that, within the experimental situation, the experimenter does not function as merely some neutral fixture with no psychological relation to the behaviour of the subjects. If the experimenter is considered as some sort of neutral figure standing over and above the experimental subjects, then it becomes a short-step to saying that in real-life it is possible to find such neutral god-head-type figures. If this is the case then it is possible to hope for *deus ex machina* solutions to intergroup problems; consequently one might hope to establish institutions that could function as such third-party conflict-resolving agencies, rather like large-scale impartial umpires to disputes. In the context of the experimental situation this can be done operationally—for instance, Vidmar and McGrath (1970) use the impartial experimenter to judge what has and what has not been "successful" negotiating behaviour. However, this example shows by implication the factors that the successful third party must possess. Basically these boil down to the third party either possessing a certain power over the disputants—in the case of the experimenter, his power in his laboratory is usually undisputed; or the third party should be accepted as a legitimate authority by the disputants—subjects in an experimental situation normally also accept the legitimacy of the experimenter. These two factors often accompany one another; for instance, in organised sporting contests the competitors usually accept the referee or umpire as the right and proper authority for judging disputed issues within the contest; also the legitimated authority of the referee or umpire is backed up by the power of the sporting organisation. Thus players who dispute a referee's decision or undermine his authority may easily find themselves in conflict with the powers that administer the sporting tournaments.

The sporting illustration shows two sides to the third-party's function. On the one hand he must be accepted as legitimate—this in the normal course of events implies that he is impartial with respect to the exact details of the dispute. On the other hand he must be backed by a certain power in order to function as an effective third party. It is in considering this power basis that the idea of a strict ideological neutrality of the third party must inevitably be modified, for the third party does not, and cannot, exist in some sort of social vacuum divorced from the social context of the disputants. The distinction between these two sides of the third party's authority has been made by Young (1967) in his book on the role of third parties in international affairs. Young makes a distinction between the impartiality of a third-party, which he argues is essential to successful intervention and the neutrality of the third-party, which he states is a contradiction in terms:

> It is reasonable to expect substantial impartiality from a third party. But the very fact of intervening in a crisis at all makes strict neutrality virtually impossible to attain. (Young, 1967, p. 82.)

In other words the third-party must be impartial as to the precise details of the dispute in question, but cannot be neutral as to the social context in which the dispute occurs.

The lack of neutrality of the third-party can be considered with regard to the power relations between it and the other two parties. In particular the third-party must be in some position of power in order that its recommendations should have some effect. This fact, within an intergroup context, is implicitly recognised by Deutsch (1969c) who welcomes the use of third-parties to "encourage a resolution" to a conflict. Third-parties can force less powerful conflicting parties to end their dispute. Deutsch regrets that the U.S.A. is unfortunately too powerful to be able to sample the benefits of third-party intervention by some superior power:

> We in the United States are in the unfortunate position that relative to our prestige and power there is neither a disinterested third party nor an international community that is powerful enough to motivate us to accept a compromise when we think our interests may be enhanced by the outcome of a competitive struggle. (Deutsch, 1969c, p. 19.)

In this way the third-party should preferably be a stronger party than the other two. Baker (1974) has shown in an interpersonal experimental situation that the third-party will cease to be impartial if his own interests are seriously threatened. It is all too easy to postulate the existence of powerful and impartial third-parties in a spirit of optimism—the actual reality of such third parties needs to be examined, especially in an intergroup setting.

The unsatisfactory nature of postulating an abstract third party can be seen with reference to two notions for establishing world peace. The first notion is one that is expressed on the interpersonal level, and therefore suffers from all the defects of the interpersonal approaches to intergroup phenomena. Gerard's (1961) suggestion of a third-party to mediate international disputes basically revolves around the existence of an object, rather than a person. He suggested that the world could be rid of international deception, if all political leaders had to submit to a lie-detector to verify their various utterances. Quite apart from the fact that this idea reduces intergroup conflict once more to the diplomatic game, the inherent naïvety of the idea should be transparent. The lie-detector would have to be operated by someone; there would have to be ways to ensure that people believed and accepted its findings. In other words there would need to be some sort of social organisation to administer the detector. Most notably this would involve some sort of agreement between the powers willing to submit to such a procedure. Gerard raised the suggestion with respect to confrontation between the U.S.A. and the U.S.S.R. However, one can assert that before the leaders of these two countries could agree to such a humiliating experience there would have to be a considerable degree of policy agreement between the two. If such an arrangement were feasible, it could only work under conditions of considerable détente, for instance, where both sides agreed to divide the world into mutually exclusive zones of influence. In this case, both would wish to respect and preserve such an arrangement. However, the lasting peace would be rudely shattered by any grouping which objected to such imperialistic designs, and therefore objected to the lie-detector, which would no doubt have become the ritual symbol for this arrangement of dominance.

The second third-party notion to ensure international peace is the idea of a world government. This idea is by no means a new one. The hope for an eventual world government or higher authority which would mediate peaceably between nations was instrumental in founding first the League of Nations and later the United Nations. This form of thinking underlies the idealistic book by Clark and Sohn, *World Peace Through World Law* (1960); in this work the authors

detail the ways and means of achieving the state of affairs described by
its title. The ideal state of affairs, according to Clark and Sohn, would
be a world government possessing legitimate authority over and above
individual nations. However, in order for such an institution to have
any cutting-teeth, it must be endowed with powerful enough resources
to make sure that its laws and prescriptions were obeyed. Quite apart
from the practical difficulties of establishing such an authority, it
should be noted that the world government becomes analogous to a
national government; and as Claude (1962) has effectively argued such
an authority would be liable to insurrection from below. The establishment of a national government certainly does not preclude that country
from revolutionary and counter-revolutionary struggle. So likewise the
mere establishment of a world authority will not of itself make re-
dundant ideologies of discontent that lead to revolution. In a percep-
tive comment Reardon and Mendlovitz (1973) mention that as a precondition for any world law there needs to be some economic justice
so that dissident elements would not feel the need to threaten the
world order (p. 160). The authors do not give any clue as to the means
of achieving, and the social nature, of this economic justice.

Thus the intervening third-party does not automatically become
some sort of absolute arbiter of rationality and fairness. Under certain
circumstances the two conflicting parties may decide, or be forced, to
submit their differences to the third party. But this does not mean that
the third party has gained some sudden access to ideologically neutral
truths, with which all disagreements can be ended. The temptation
to believe this is strong, if the third-party is a social scientist. However,
a belief in the validity of social scientific methods should not obscure
wider social relationships. In particular it should not hide the relationship of the research worker to the protagonists in the conflict which he
is investigating. The assumption that the research worker is a neutral
third-party seems to lie behind a good deal of applied conflict research
(e.g. Blake, Mouton and Sloma, 1965; Doob, Folz and Stevens, 1969;
Walton, 1970; Lewicki and Alderfer, 1973). Nevertheless by his presence in a conflict situation, the researcher becomes an active participant.

An instance is provided by industrial conflicts. It should come as no
surprise that unions are on occasions suspicious of the "neutral" research workers hired by management, and that this suspicion should be
based upon a realistic appraisal, rather than on emotional and irra-

tional feelings (see particularly Brown's (1973) and Friedlander's (1973) criticisms of the Lewicki and Alderfer (1973) study of a labour-management dispute, in which the intervention of the conflict researchers was rejected by the union officials for being biased towards management). The conflict researcher's belief that a particular conflict *ought* to be solved is itself an ideological belief, which will rest upon certain presuppositions concerning the ideal relations between the two conflicting parties. It is possible for him to be impartial in his execution of this belief, within the socially-defined limits of impartiality in the particular context. However to go further, and claim any sort of absolute neutrality is little more than self-delusion; this belief will be shattered each time one of the conflicting parties rejects the structure by which the third-party was introduced into the conflict. It is when the basic structures of a social relationship are challenged, that the ideological background to a supposed neutrality is revealed.

Social movements and psychological explanations

The present argument has strongly stressed the need to develop a conception of ideology which is not derived from the principles of either individual or interpersonal psychology. The reductionist viewpoint must necessarily neglect the link between an ideology and the wider group or intergroup social context. In this section a particular variant of social psychological reductionism will be briefly considered. This variant of reductionism is far more subtle in its assumptions than the forms which attempt to reduce all social phenomena to "basic" psychological principles. It is not a general reductionism of all forms of social behaviour; on the contrary it reserves its reductionist explanations for breakdowns in organised social behaviour and for the emergence of mass movements.

Variations of this development of the reductionist viewpoint can be found in a variety of social scientific disciplines. Its influence can be observed in social psychology (Toch, 1966), political science (Kornhauser, 1960), social history (Cohn, 1970), sociology (Smelser, 1963) and anthropology (LaBarre, 1971). It is not the present intention to give detailed documentation of the notion that mass social movements are the result of the existence of certain states of mind. Rather it is hoped to give the general flavour of this approach. What is stressed in this form of reductionism is the contrast between periods of social stability and those historical periods of turmoil and disruption, in which mass social movements arise. When institutional structures break down and established social supports are fragmented, then individuals become isolated. This state of isolation is said to predispose people to certain varieties of mass social behaviour, which otherwise would not occur. It can be seen, therefore, that this form of reductionism does not consider the isolated individual to be the prime cause of "normal" social phenomena, but only of "abnormal" social events. In fact it could be said that this approach confines its reductionism for those occasions when society itself has been reduced. Under such conditions the psychology of the isolated individual becomes the determinant of historical forces.

For instance, Kornhauser (1960), concentrates upon, what he calls "the atomised individual" as the prime force in mass movements. The basis for such movements is, he maintains, the individual cut off from stable roots and unintegrated into the mainstream of society. It is from the breakdown of stable group identities that the "mass man" emerges. From this he deduces that mass movements are not composed of persons with traditional class identities. Thus Kornhauser states:

> . . . mass theory looks to the breakdown of class identities as a critical process whereby people are freed to form new ties based on the commonly shared plight of mass men rather than the mutually exclusive plight of class men. In short, this approach finds in mass men the shock troops in large-scale efforts to overturn democratic orders. (Kornhauser, 1960, p. 181.)

Kornhauser sees the breakdown of class identities as the critical process in the formation of mass movements; Toch (1966) similarly views mass movements as providing individuals with answers for their particular problems, including the problems that follow the disruption of established orders. Cohn (1970) in his detailed account of millenial movements in the Middle Ages, advances a similar conclusion to that of Kornhauser—for Cohn the root cause of millenial movements was the collapse of the traditional feudal society. The breaking up of traditional social bonds brings in its train the atomised individual occupying a marginal social position. These rootless individuals lie waiting for "a *propheta* to bind them together in a group of their own" (Cohn, 1970, p. 282).

When the established social order has collapsed and mass movements are rife, it is easy to offer psychological explanations for the appeal of such movements. Cohn (1970) likens the millenial movements he studied to mass paranoia, and LaBarre (1971) calls the crisis cult a "paranoid autistic response" (p. 8). Similarly Smelser (1963 and 1972) refers to the individual psychological predispositions of the members of mass movements, (see, for instance, Weller and Quarantelli's (1973) criticisms of Smelser's psychological reductionism). Kornhauser (1960) postulates a link between the marginal alienated status and the psychological consequences of this alienation in terms of Adorno *et al.*'s (1950) characterisation of the authoritarian personality. There is no need to pursue the matter in any great depth, in order to make the general point that such theorists are prone to assume individualistic psychological explanations in their descriptions of mass movements. They take the breakdown of existing social order as their starting point; they then trace the genesis of mass movements through the isolation of the individual and his attempts to recreate a social order —this isolation being a key variable that predisposes the atomised individual to put his faith in bizarre and somewhat "fantastical" social movements.

In chapter four it was argued that there are certain dangers in employing individual psychological theories of personality to explain large-scale social events. However, it is possible to link the basic assumptions of the limited form of reductionism to general social psychological principles. In this respect Tajfel and Billig (1974) hypothesised that under conditions of cognitive uncertainty and/or instability people will restructure their cognitive outlook in order to restore a greater amount of order and certainty. They will therefore be more responsive to the influence of others, and consequently more liable to form group affiliations, which will provide them with the necessary social supports. Tajfel and Billig basically draw on two lines of social psychological evidence to justify this notion. Firstly, Schachter (1959) found that anxious individuals seek out others in a similar predicament to themselves. Secondly, the autokinetic experiments of Muzafer Sherif can be used to support the basic hypothesis linking uncertainty to the formation of social groups. Sherif (1936) found that subjects were significantly influenced by others when judging an uncertain stimulus. Moreover, Sherif and Harvey (1952) demonstrated that this tendency was enhanced when the general experimental situation was made more confusing and the subjects were made anxious in ways bearing no relation, at least *prima facie*, to the autokinetic stimuli. Tajfel and Billig summarise this work by surmising that "anxiety and/or uncertainty can give rise to the development of cohesive ingroups". They go on to state that "it appears as if the formation of such ingroups and the social support which they afford their members diminish the insecurity experienced in the experimental situation" (Tajfel and Billig, 1974, p. 162). In this way an ingroup might provide some sort of "psychological refuge" for the uncertain and isolated individual (Kohler, Miller and Klein, 1973).

The wider social scientific analyses and the particular experimental approach of the social psychologist might be thought to have converged; taken together they provide a unified picture of the formation of mass social movements, based upon a limited form of reductionism. The social psychological hypothesis that uncertain and/or insecure individuals seek cognitive and group support could be said to complement the theory that atomised and isolated individuals provide the basis for mass movements. It will nevertheless be suggested that this general picture of mass social movements is incomplete and that the social psychological evidence does not support the hypothesis of Tajfel and Billig. Moreover it will be suggested that this approach to the study of social movements contains certain inherent difficulties.

Firstly the experimental evidence does not altogether bear out this hypothesis, at least in its present formulation. The assumption behind the hypothesis is that when there is some sort of breakdown of cognitive structure, certain general psychological principles can be said to operate—these principles are primarily directed toward building up a new cognitive structure, but they also predispose the individual to seek out and place reliance on others. Alexander *et al.* (1970) have criticised the classic autokinetic experiments of Sherif, and have suggested that Sherif's original explanations for his results need to be substantially modified. In particular they criticise the tendency in Sherif's work, and in social psychology generally, to offer "universal organismic" explanations of social behaviour. Such explanations are based upon general laws of psychology which are held to be true for all individuals, regardless of social and cultural situation. The explanation of group affiliation on the basis of subjects' inability to endure cognitive uncertainty, is a prime example of a universal organismic explanation. Alexander *et al.* (1970) have criticised the details of Sherif's experimental situation, arguing that the results are not due to the subjects lacking any cognitive structure to interpret the experimental situation. On the contrary, they claim that during the experiment subjects have a definite set of cognitive expectations, and that these expectations relate to the way they expect the experimenter wishes them to respond. By altering this expectation, Alexander *et al.* (1970) were able to reverse the results of Sherif's original autokinetic experiments. Thus the convergence of judgements found by Sherif (1936) and by Sherif and Harvey (1952) and by many other experimental psychologists since then, need not be thought of as a means by which subjects impart meaning to an uncomfortable cognitive vacuum. The subjects do not enter the experiments with their minds as a *tabula rasa*; on the contrary, they have quite definite expectations. The experimental situation cannot be presumed to reveal subjects to be acting according to "basic" psychological principles, uncontaminated by social or cultural factors.

Moreover the organismic hypothesis linking uncertainty and/or anxiety with group membership received no experimental support from Tajfel and Billig (1974). In a deliberately artificial intergroup situation created in the laboratory, these authors compared the intergroup feelings of subjects who were familiar with the general experimental situation with those who were unfamiliar and presumably more anxious and uncertain. In contradiction to the basic hypothesis, they found that it was the less anxious subjects who showed the more ingroup identification and who produced the greatest amounts of negative outgroup bias. Thus within the confines of the Tajfel and Billig experimental situation, the hypothesis that anxiety and/or uncertainty would lead to ingroup affiliation was disconfirmed.

If there are difficulties with the detailed experimental evidence, then there are certain objections which can be raised with respect to the wider theoretical position affecting real-life social processes. In the first place, the hypothesis that atomised individuals constitute the core of social movements conflicts with much of the empirical evidence, especially that concerning contemporary political movements (Orum, 1974). In chapter five, some of this evidence was mentioned when the ideological character of protest movements, and of the Black urban riots of the 1960s in particular, was emphasised (e.g. Marx, 1967; Caplan and Paige, 1968; Caplan, 1970; Moinat *et al.* 1972). The picture of the Black rioter to emerge from these studies is not of an isolated and alienated individual—on the contrary the rioter appears to be better integrated into the Black community and to be more highly educated than the non-rioting ghetto resident.[1]

The wider theoretical position also encounters difficulties of a more general nature. It can be objected that such writers as Cohn, LaBarre, Kornhauser, etc. make too great a distinction between social change and social stability. In their formulations there is the implication that mass movements arise as a consequence of the disintegration of a stable social order. In this respect, their views resemble those of the frustration-aggression theorists who have extended their psychological analyses to cover wider social phenomena. A similar critique can be made of the hypothesis of the "atomised protester" as was made of the frustration-aggression position. According to both views, it is assumed that complete stability proceeds complete change. There is, however, an alternative way of describing social processes of change and stability that does not contrast the two as exclusive conceptions. For instance, it is possible to detect changes and internal stresses within the so-called times of social stability; this leads to the possibility that the stability might be a function of the quality and rate of social changes rather than of their complete absence (Coser, 1956; Wilson, J., 1973). Thus social conflict need not be confined to particular times of what seem to be unusual social activities, but can be a more general phenomenon. This conception of social change can be illustrated by the metaphor of scientific change—a comparison which, in fact, LaBarre (1971) makes in his discussion of crisis cults. In that article, LaBarre compares the messianic cult to Kuhn's (1962) conception of a scientific revolution. Kuhn had contrasted periods of normal scientific activity with periods of revolutionary scientific activity. During the periods of normal science, there are accepted paradigms of thought, which remain unchallenged. During the revolutionary period, these paradigms are seen to fail and new scientific theories are proposed to replace the previous paradigm. One of these theories typically becomes generally accepted, and so is adopted as the new paradigm. After this, there is a reversion to the calmer days of normal scientific activity. In the same way LaBarre says the crisis cult arises when the more traditional modes of thought become unsatisfactory. If successful, the crisis cult may then

1. In his analysis of the eighteenth century Paris "mob", Rudé (1964 and 1974) comes to a similar conclusion. His examination of the documentary evidence suggests that it was composed mainly of respectable artisans rather than the "degenerate riff-raff" which right-wing propagandists have luridly described. Nor, according to Rudé, was the London "mob" much different.

be established as the new paradigm of social thought, and lose its revolutionary character. Thus to parallel Kuhn's (1962) distinction between normal and revolutionary science, there are periods of social stability and social change. However, it should be noted that more recently Kuhn himself has been forced to modify his position and acknowledge that the periods of so-called normal science themselves consist of the testing and rejection of theories; he now argues that the activities taking place in such periods do not qualitatively differ so much from the activities occurring during the more hectic revolutionary periods (Kuhn, 1970: see also Toulmin, 1967 and Stephens, 1973). In the same way the periods of comparative social stability need not be thought of as some sort of golden era of peace and harmony—the stresses and conflicts may be present and significant, although not in the spectacular manner associated with the times of rapid social change. This latter approach does not insist on a complete distinction between stability and change. Societies are not viewed *a priori* as unified wholes; but the social, political and economic contradictions within societies are recognised.

If the sharp distinction between times of social stability and social change is rejected, then it is possible to draw an analogy with the experimental evidence. Sherif (1936) and Sherif and Harvey (1952) drew an implicit distinction between their subjects' normal cognitive interpretations, and those they employed in the experimental autokinetic situation. However, Alexander *et al.* (1970) has suggested that this distinction is a spurious one, and that the subjects' perceptions of the experimental situation are a continuation of their normal day-to-day outlooks. Similarly, the rise of mass social groups need not be seen as evidence for the breakdown of social order, but their genesis can be interpreted in terms of past social processes. In particular it becomes possible to interpret social movements in an intergroup context, instead of an individual context. If "normal" social structures can be said to contain actual or potential group conflicts to a greater or lesser degree, then emerging social movements can be understood in the light of these intergroup situations. The so-called breakdown of established order may, on this account, be no more than the struggle involved in the toppling of an established dominant group.

This can be illustrated with regard to the period studied by Cohn (1970). The power of the mediaeval feudal lords was being threatened by the emerging urban bourgeoisie. Not only were new economic and political interest groups being formed to challenge the older interest groups, but the feudal lords, because of their weakened power, were unable to exert the same degree of control over their erstwhile subjects. As Cohen points out, the millenial movements occurred during a period of revolutionary intergroup conflict, whose political and economic determinants cannot be described merely in terms of individual psychological processes. Cohn (1970) expresses it thus:

> When, finally, one comes to consider the anarcho-communistic millenarian groups which flourished around the close of the Middle Ages, one fact is immediately obvious: it was always in the midst of some much wider revolt or revolution that a group of this kind emerged into daylight . . . (T) he mass insurrection itself was directed towards limited and realistic aims—yet in each instance the climate of mass insurrection fostered a special kind of millenarian group. As social tensions mounted and the revolt became nation-wide, there would appear, somewhere on the radical fringe, a *propheta* with his following of paupers, intent on turning this one particular upheaval into the apocalyptic battle, the final purification of the world. (Cohn, 1970, p. 284.)

Cohn seems to be distinguishing between two different sorts of social movement—the one being part and parcel of realistic intergroup conflicts, and the other being an unrealistic fantastical social movement arising out of the breakdown of normal social order. In a similar vein one can note Kornhauser's (1960) distinction between the mass movements of marginal men and actual class conflicts.

The "anxiety and/or uncertainty hypothesis", thus, seems only suited to the unrealistic sort of mass movement, and not to those mass movements which realistically reflect their social position. Another way of stating this is to say that the hypothesis cannot explain the genesis and actions of groups-for-themselves, but only those of groups without any marked degree of political consciousness. For those lacking such consciousness an individualistic psychological explanation is offered. This would imply that there is a qualitative difference between dissident groups involved in an intergroup conflict with a defined political ideology of discontent, and those whose ideology would appear to be fantastical. There is however evidence that suggests that even the fantastical group may not be so politically naïve as might be thought. Thompson (1963) has detailed the political backgrounds of such movements as the Luddites and the followers of the latter-day *propheta*, Joanna Southcott. He describes such seemingly irrational movements in relation to the general working-class struggles of England in the eighteenth and nineteenth centuries. Nor does he require a different form of explanation to account for the varieties of working-class ideologies which were developed during this period. In his account there is no neat separation of those that arise out of individual psychological states and those that genuinely reflect political and economic struggles. Similarly, Watson (1973 and 1974) has analysed the Black Muslim movement in the U.S.A. and the Ras-Tafarians of Jamaica. At first sight, both these movements would appear to be religious-based dreams of utopia—with the Black Muslims looking forward to the refounding of the lost nation of Islam and the Ras-Tafarians to a repatriation in Heile Selassie's Ethiopia. However, Watson argues that both these movements contain strong political ideologies, and that these are ideologies that need to be understood in relation to the intergroup context of white racism. Although criticisms can be raised against these movements for their analysis of racism and their strategies of improvement for oppressed peoples, these movements should not be dismissed as being the products of individual psychological problems. Specifically Watson writes of the Ras-Tafarians that "individual psychology cannot explain the kinds of problems which their existence poses" (1974, p. 331). Watson goes on to analyse the Ras-Tafarians in terms of the class structure of Jamaican society and the Rastas' rejection of white cultural values.

The trend of this discussion is that the "anxiety and/or uncertainty hypothesis" would seem to entail a firm distinction between two sorts of mass social group—namely, between the sort of social movement realistically engaged in an intergroup struggle and the sort of fringe group destined for disappointment and failure. The implication is that this distinction is a methodological one; it implies that the fringe social movement should be reduced to the psychological state of its participants, whilst the realistic movement needs to be investigated in its full social context. The danger of this approach is that it is easy to concentrate on the so-called "lunatic fringe" movement at the neglect of the total social context, which enables the existence of such movements.[2] More importantly, there is the danger of underplaying the

2. It is also possible to neglect social processes within "lunatic fringe" movements by concentrating upon the psychological characteristics of the individual members. Wallis (1974) distinguishes between cult movements which do not have defined structures and sects, which have more formal organisations

connections and similarities between the "lunatic fringe" and the more realistic social movement (in this regard Thompson's 1963 (chapter two) criticisms of Cohn's *Pursuit of the Millenium* can be cited). This is especially the case if the distinction between the two sorts of social movement is made on the basis of their ideology. In making this distinction, reference is being made to the difference between the group-in-itself and the group-for-itself. The present approach stresses the practical nature of a group ideology, especially in an intergroup context; as a consequence the way in which a group-in-itself transforms into a group-for-itself is a practical social problem. It is not *prima facie* one concerning the psychological health of its individual adherents; social analysis should not be substituted for an *ad hominem* argument, based on the psychological characteristics of the individual group member.

Social structure and ethnocentrism

One of the main themes to emerge from the preceding discussions has been that exclusively psychological approaches to the study of intergroup relations must necessarily be limited. They inevitably confine their attention to subjective variables at the expense of objective variables. In this section an approach which seems to combine objective and subjective variables will be discussed. This approach has stemmed from the research of certain anthropologists—LeVine and Campbell (1972) have referred to the intergroup theories which have been derived from this approach as "social-structural theories of conflict in anthropology" (p. 43). In essentials this approach is based upon correlating the social structure of the ingroup with the attitudes which ingroup members hold about outgroups. It is on the basis of such correlations that anthropologists have hoped to elucidate some of the determinants of intergroup conflict, as well as to document the extent

---

built around a recognised leadership, and describes the processes by which the cult can be transformed organisationally into a sect It would be absurd to explain the change from the "individualistic" cult into the "authoritarian" sect in terms of underlying personalities, since the same individuals are often involved in both the individualistic and authoritarian stages of the movement. It is possible that cults might tend to attract different sorts of persons than do sects; nevertheless the internal developments of such movements cannot be explained solely by a psychological reductionism.

and significance of the phenomenon of ethnocentrism. Consequently the present discussion will encompass not only issues concerned with the social-structural theory of intergroup relations, but will also lead on to some of the issues related to ethnocentrism.

At face value the social structural approach would seem to correspond to what was being recommended previously, namely, that theories of intergroup relations should specifically attempt to investigate the dialectical interplay between objective and subjective factors. One might characterise the social structural features of an ingroup as being "objective" variables, and the intergroup attitudes of the ingroup members as being "subjective variables". Correlations between these two sorts of variables, then, might be thought to constitute a serious attempt to develop a genuinely dialectical approach to the study of the intergroup context. However, it will be argued that the issue is not so simple as to be resolved by making the sorts of correlations suggested by the social structural theorists. In particular it will be suggested that their focus upon structural variables is somewhat restricted.

The social structural theories of conflict can be identified with the empirical research of Murphy (1957), Murphy and Kasdan (1959). Thoden van Velzen and van Wetering (1960) and Otterbein (1968). On a theoretical level the position has been advocated by LeVine and Campbell (1972) and especially by LeVine (1965) who draws together his own anthropological field work with that of Murphy into a comprehensive theoretical position. The bare essentials of this theory can be summarised briefly by stating that two different forms of social structure give rise to different sorts of outgroup attitudes and relations. These two different forms of social structure are: (a) the pyramidal segmentary structure, which is a divisive form of ingroup arrangement; and (b) the cross-cutting structure, which is an internally cohesive form of ingroup structure. The theory states that different outgroup attitudes become the cultural norm depending upon whether the society is internally divisive or cohesive.

The initial evidence for this position came from Murphy's (1957) study of social organisation which existed in the Mundurucú (a Brazilian Indian tribe) in the nineteenth century. The most notable feature of the Mundurucú social organisation was that it was matrilocal, i.e. after marriage the men lived with the families of their wives. This often entailed that the bridegroom had to move to another village. Thus the tribe consisted of a high proportion of men who resided in one settlement, but had their own kin groups in a different settlement. Murphy argues that, in such a community, all internal feuding and aggression has to be under strict control. If internal conflict were not strictly controlled, the situation could easily arise where men found themselves in the centre of a conflict between two loyalties—their kin group and their residential group. Murphy summarises the situation thus:

> Conflict had to be rigorously suppressed, for if men became arrayed in overt violence along lines of residential affinity, it would pit patrilineal kin against each other and destroy the very fabric of the kinship society. (Murphy, 1957, p. 1030.)

As a consequence all aggression was displaced outwards into members of other tribes. The Mundurucú were famed as particularly aggressive warriors. Their warfare against neighbouring tribes was not for gain or for territorial reasons. The Mundurucú waged war for sport, and any non-Mundurucú (or *pariwat*) was considered a legitimate object for attack. Murphy concluded that this clearly defined and stable pattern of outgroup hostility was a means of preserving a particular social structure, which was especially vulnerable to internal disintegration because of cross-cutting loyalty ties.

The social structure and the outgroup attitudes of the Mundurucú can be contrasted with those of the Bedouin Arabs (Murphy and Kasdan, 1959). Unlike the Mundurucú the Bedouins do not emphasise an overall tribal loyalty which is contrasted with clearly defined outgroup enemies. The Bedouin social structure is based upon a hierarchy of ingroups, ranging from the immediate family to the wider ethnic group. Feuds and disputes are liable to occur at any level of this hierarchy. For instance, a Bedouin at one moment may be conducting a feud against another family in his village, whereas at another time these two feuding families may combine to conduct a feud with the families of a neighbouring village. There are no harmonious ingroup relations within the community, but instead there are continually shifting antagonisms and loyalties. Ingroups and outgroups are not stable definitions, but are defined anew depending on the current conflict. As a result, when the tribe is taken as a whole, ingroup conflict and discord is a common occurrence. Unlike the case of the Mundurucú, this is possible without threatening the stability of the social structure. The Bedouin society is not based upon cross-cutting ties and a matrilocal organisation. On the contrary, it is patrilocal and endogamous within small patrilineal groups, which become socially isolated with no cross-cutting or dual-membership loyalties occurring amongst the men.

LeVine (1965) compared the studies by Murphy (1957) and Murphy and Kasdan (1959) with his own researches into two Kenyan tribes, the Kipsigis and the Gusii. The former resemble the Mundurucú, in that they have a "cross-cutting" social structure and well-defined out-group "enemies". The Gusii on the other hand resemble the Bedouins —there is not the same clear-cut dichotomy of the social world into friends and enemies. Similarly their social structure is based upon a hierarchical pyramid of group loyalties. Further evidence for the relationship between matrilocality as a social structure and internal peace come from several correlational studies (e.g. Thoden van Velzen and van Wetering, 1960; Otterbein and Otterbein, 1968; Otterbein, 1968; Ember and Ember, 1971; Divale, 1974). Although not directly tackling the problem of ingroup structure and outgroup relationships, these studies nevertheless give credence to the general conclusion that the variable of matrilocality/patrilocality can determine intergroup attitudes and the choice of outgroup "enemies".

Such is the data which forms the background of the social structural theory of conflict. LeVine (1965) interprets this data in a way that connects the social structure-intergroup conflict relationship to socialisation processes. Murphy (1957) on the other hand, explicitly makes the link between the variables of social structure and outgroup attitudes in Freudian terms. He writes of hostility in Mundurucú society being displaced onto outgroups. Thus the hostility that the Mundurucú displayed towards all outgroups served as a "safety-valve" institution. Murphy's Freudianism is not confined merely to the topic of intergroup relations—he has also interpreted the cultural symbols of the Mundurucú in terms of their sexual symbolism (Murphy, 1959). However, there are two immediate questions that arise from the theoretical positions of LeVine and of Murphy concerning their interpretations of intergroup phenomena. These are: (a) whether the linkages hypothesised to exist between structural variables and intergroup variables can be legitimately described in Freudian terms; and (b) what sort of societies can be analysed in terms of the social structural theory of conflict. With regard to the second of these questions, one would especially wish to know whether the same principles operating with small-scale societies, such as those studied by Murphy and LeVine, can be applied to large-scale developed societies.

Some of the issues involved in answering the first question have already been discussed, when it was argued that it is extraordinarily difficult to identify the workings of the individual unconscious in any social or group situation. This is not to deny that such processes do not operate, nor to deny the psychological reality of the unconscious. One should be especially wary of denying the possibility of unconscious motivations affecting the social customs of small-scale societies. This is not because the inhabitants of such societies are more primitive or unsophisticated than the inhabitants of modern large-scale western societies. It is purely and simply that the two sorts of society differ in their size. LeVine (1965) specifically states that in a preliterate society intergroup conflict is often conducted at a face-to-face level. Given this, he writes, "an expectation of close correspondence between the motivational state of the population and the patterns of intersocietal action is entirely reasonable" (LeVine, 1965, p. 47). No more will be said on this particular matter as it relates to small-scale societies. However, it can be argued that even if the Freudian interpretations of small-scale social behaviour are not *a priori* untenable, they are unsatisfactory when applied to large-scale societies. Nonetheless, the relevance or irrelevance of the Freudian interpretation of the social-structural conflict theory does not settle the basic issue concerning the theory itself: this is whether it can be applied to the larger societies, or whether it is restricted to particular types of social organisation to be found in preliterate social groups.

LeVine states that the theory is relevant to the modern large-scale society and in particular to developed nation states (1965, p. 45). He also draws conclusions from such studies about methods of diminishing international tensions and warfare. In particular, he points to the moral that cross-cutting ties can lead to a reduction of tension. Although it has been found only to lead to a reduction of ingroup tensions at the expense of increasing outgroup hostilities, LeVine nevertheless suggests at the end of his article that this particular form of social organisation need not inevitably lead to outgroup divisiveness. He anticipates and hopes for a time when the world as a complete whole will develop cross-cutting ties; if this could be achieved, he argues, then world unity could be achieved and international conflict be eradicated. This idea is not developed by LeVine; the mere fact that he suggests it, however, is sufficient to illustrate that he considers the anthropological studies to be relevant to problems of international conflict and world peace.

In attempting to discover the valid range of the social-structural theory of conflict, as expressed by LeVine and Murphy, there is one salient fact which must be emphasised: this is that all the evidence which has been put forward to support the theory has been gathered from societies with no centralised government. The Mundurucú, the Bedouins, the Kipsigis and the Gusii all share the distinction of being stateless societies. This is an important point, since the present discussion on intergroup relations has concentrated upon power relations and patterns of subordination and dominance within societies. The question is whether the same conceptual framework can be adopted when looking at the pre-literate stateless society as the more complex modern state.

The first obvious way of approaching this problem is to examine those pre-literate societies which do have a central government. The results of Otterbein's (1968) study are of particular relevance here— he correlated data from 50 societies in order to determine the correlates of internal warfare. His results indicated that there was only a correlation between patrilocality and internal warfare for those societies without a centralised government; for those societies with a government there was no such relationship as hypothesised by the social structural theory of conflict. It seems that the connection between social organisation and outgroup behaviour found to exist amongst the Mundurucú, the Bedouins, the Kipsigis and the Gusii only occurs in other stateless societies.

If the social structural theory, as formulated at present, has only been found to apply to societies without a centralised government, then this must severely limit its application to complex societies. The present analysis has stressed the importance of governing groups and élite authorities in the formation of intergroup images. The same analysis in terms of false consciousness and internal power relations is of course irrelevant to those societies without internal intergroup divisions based on vested interests. LeVine (1965) touches on this problem in a passing remark. He comments upon the "fantastic group images" that are sometimes produced in an intergroup situation: "superordinate groups sometimes maintain them as a rationalisation for keeping other groups in subjection" (p. 49). However, he does not develop this point, nor does he use it to illustrate the differences between the outgroup images of pre-literate stateless societies and those societies based upon antagonisms between superordinate groups and subordinate groups. LeVine does not mention the possibility that different concepts may be necessary to investigate the antagonistic society than are used to describe societies free from organised vested interests and domination.[3]

The conclusion could be advanced from the data of preliterate societies that not only is "kinship structure" related to outgroup attitudes, but also, and probably more importantly, so are political structures. The kinship structures only appear to be important variables where there is no stabilised governmental structures. The existence, then, of a governmental structure, (or maybe a governing élite) would seem to affect the nature of outgroup ideologies over and above any particular arrangement of family and kin groupings. If this has been found to be the case in small-scale societies, then one can wonder how much more true this must be of more developed societies, where subordinate-dominant groupings and vested group interests have been developed to a far greater extent. This is not to contradict flatly the notion that there might be certain connections between the anthropological descriptions of small-scale societies and intergroup relations on a larger scale—but it does suggest that the social structural theory as it now stands is not directly applicable to the large-scale society with internal divisions. Nor does this contradict LeVine's hope that worldwide cross-cutting ties might ensure a more peaceful world. But what it does imply is that such cross-cutting ties could only be effective to this end in a world where conditions of group dominance had been abolished. Translating this into terms relevant to the modern industrial society, one might say that cross-cutting ties might possibly be useful for preserving a classless society, but they are no means of eradicating class divisions and antagonisms.

The social structural theory of conflict would seem to have a restricted range; in particular it confines itself to the examination of kinship

3. A modified form of the cross-cutting hypothesis has been tested with respect to the international alliances of modern nation-states. Wallace (1973) correlated the occurrence of international warfare with the patterns of international alliances. In particular he wished to discover whether cross-cutting patterns of alliances would inhibit the outbreak of warfare, as compared to a polarised pattern of alliances. No direct evidence, however, was found to link the cross-cutting pattern with international peace.

systems in simple pre-literate societies, without attempting to link
such systems specifically to political or economic variables. The influence of political organisation on the matrilocal/patrilocal variables,
at least as far as it affects intergroup relations, has already been mentioned. Similarly these variables have been found to interact with
economic factors: for instance, Ember and Ember (1971) have found
that the connection between matrilocality/patrilocality and internal/
external conflict is significantly affected by the way necessary subsistence labour is divided. In this way the economy of the preliterate
society can be said to be directly linked to the relationship between
social structure and intergroup conflict. As such it would seem to be
too narrow to equate social structure with kinship structure and to
ignore the effects of political and economic variables on intergroup
attitudes, even with the preliterate society.

   This last point can be illustrated by considering the problem of
ethnocentrism. Campbell (1965) and LeVine and Campbell (1972)
link elements of the social-structural theory with a particular theory
of ethnocentrism. Clearly the evidence about segmentary systems of
shifting alliances and conflicts means that any straightforward theory
of ethnocentrism is in need of modification. The classic statement of
ethnocentrism was made by Sumner (1906). He summarised its basic
proposition thus:

> Each group nourishes its own pride and vanity, boasts itself superior,
> exalts its own divinities and looks with contempt on outsiders. Each
> group thinks its own folkways the only right ones, and if it observes that
> other groups have other folkways, these excite scorn. (Sumner, 1906,
> p. 13.)

   However, if the boundaries of group loyalty are continually shifting
then there can be no simple ingroup identification and outgroup disparagement. The doctrine of ethnocentrism would seem to be unsuit-
able, as formulated by Sumner, to cope with the fluid loyalties of the
segmental pyramid form of society. In their discussion of ethnic boundaries, LeVine and Campbell (1972, chapter seven) draw attention to
the fact that societies are seldom clearly defined entities, sharply de-
marcated from surrounding communities. They refer to the "ethnic
mosaics", which characterise the overlapping similarities of neighbouring groups. They claim that the anthropologists of the last century
overemphasised the unity and separateness of less complex societies. In
fact such anthropologists often interpreted pre-literate societies in

terms of their own nationalistic assumptions, and consequently their anthropological theories are closely connected to imperialist ideologies (cf. also Cohen and Middleton, 1970; Goddard, 1973 and Lewis, 1973, for discussions of the relation between anthropological theory and imperialism).[4] In contrast to the early anthropologists, LeVine and Campbell (1972) claim that tribal societies are not small nation states, but are less distinct and bounded entities, for which the classic assumption of ethnocentrism cannot be upheld. They list five sorts of common phenomena, which contradict the anthropological assumptions of distinct ethnocentric socio-cultural units: (a) territorial interpretation of ethnic communities; (b) disagreements about ethnic categorisations; (c) interaction across ethnic boundaries; (d) continuous variation in cultural and linguistic characteristics; (e) shifts in ethnic identity and culturally defined life-styles.

Nevertheless, Campbell (1965) and LeVine and Campbell (1972) do not altogether reject the notion of ethnocentrism; instead they reformulate the theory by linking it to an evolutionary framework. They recognise that sharp and stable boundaries are not universal characteristics of social systems, but claim that they do tend to be characteristic of more recent and developed societies. Consequently they claim that boundedness and political development may have an adaptive advantage in the process of social evolution: "sharply bounded political organisations displace ones with unstable or unclear boundaries through the selective propagation of adaptive forms (LeVine and Campbell, 1972, p. 111). The development of national states is the national outcome of this evolutionary process. According to LeVine and Campbell, nationalism "represents an advance over earlier forms of ethnocentrism, in the sense that it obtains the more intense and broad responsiveness of a large population to the state leadership" (p. 112). In this way LeVine and Campbell outline the adaptive virtues of the politically strong national state. Also they are able to explain exceptions to the classic ethnocentric hypothesis as being inferior forms of development, which will be replaced or modified in the natural course of social evolution.

LeVine and Campbell's evolutionary theory can be seen as an

4. It can be noted that a number of non-western anthropologists claim that contemporary western anthropology reflects racist and neo-colonial assumptions (e.g. Hsu, 1973; Sathyamurthy, 1973). As a consequence, it cannot be said that the relationship of anthropology to imperialism is a purely historical problem.

attempt to derive a theory of intergroup relations from an analysis of general systems. It should be stressed that the theory refers to the evolution of social systems themselves and not to the genetic make-up of individuals within particular social systems. Campbell (1965) lists three basic requirements for any theory of social evolutionism. These are: (*a*) the occurrence of variations, (*b*) consistent selection criteria and (*c*) a mechanism for the preservation and propagation of positively selected variants. Requirements (*a*) and (*c*) are in themselves relatively non-controversial. One might assume that in all societies there is some modicum of variations in individual behaviour and the possibility for social innovation. Also it is reasonable to presuppose that certain variations can become cultural norms and be transmitted inter-generationally by socialisation procedures, etc.

It is the assumption that there are consistent selection criteria that poses the greatest problem. The particular issue refers to the existence of criteria which selectively produce well-bounded, discrete social systems. LeVine and Campbell suggest that there are two types of criteria. The first is based upon the principle of least effort or convenience which predicts that "it is easier in terms of human information processing if boundaries of different types coincide rather than overlap" (1972, p. 111). This criterion is essentially a psychological one, derived from processes of individual psychology. As such it should apply equally to all levels of societal development. Consequently a drift towards bounded social systems should be evident in politically underdevelop societies as well as developed ones. If this reasoning is correct then one might predict on the basis of this criterion that among stateless societies a matrilocal social structure with defined ingroup boundaries would be more "convenient" than a pyramidal segmentary system with shifting ingroup-outgroup loyalties. Also a trend from the pyramidal segmentary system towards defined boundaries might be expected. However, the evidence does not suggest that matrilocality and defined intergroup boundaries is the norm for successful surviving stateless communities. In fact it would appear to be a comparatively rare exception. Divale (1974) estimates that such societies are deviations from the normal pattern of patrilineality and internal divisiveness (p. 77). There would not therefore seem to be universal pressure for boundedness, which would give rise to a predominance of discretely bounded social systems over less discrete systems.

LeVine and Campbell's second type of selection criterion is based

upon intergroup processes rather than individual ones. They hypothesise that a well-bounded and centrally organised social system is
better equipped to deal with military threats from outgroups. Consequently intergroup conflict, arising from intergroup competition, will
place a positive adaptive value on boundedness. In this respect it is
interesting to note Divale's explanation for the existence of matrilocal
societies. He argues that matrilocality is a response to intergroup conflict. When a society is forced for economic or military reasons to
migrate into a new area it is liable to change its social structure to
matrilocality in order to minimise internal conflict between fraternal
interest groups. By so doing it will be better organised to cope with
hostile indigenous groups. Divale supports this idea by showing a significant correlation between the variables of matrilocality and migration. He quotes Murphy as suggesting that the Mundurucú had mi-
grated and shifted to matrilocal residence in the first half of the
nineteenth century. Matrilocality is only one means of achieving
internal cohesion; the development of a strong central authority is
another means. It might be presumed that if a group is large, centrali-
sation might be more efficient both from a military and political point
of view. Ember, C. R. (1974) provides some evidence on this point; she
has found that the correlation between migration and matrilocality
tends only to occur amongst smaller societies. Given this, there would
seem to be a case for arguing that intergroup conflict situations can
act as selection criteria for well-bounded, politically developed communities.

   In stating this it should be recognised that the development of any
rudimentary form of political system must be related to economic
development. Maquet (1961, chapter five) argues that an economic
surplus is a necessary precondition if a society is to develop from a
loose tribal arrangement into a state. A subsistence economy by definition cannot support a central authority, one of whose functions is
to collect some form of tax or tribute. It would seem entirely appropriate therefore to extend the evolutionary argument to cover economic
as well as political development. It could be argued that surplus
economies have a greater chance of surviving economic crises, whether
produced by natural or social causes; consequently they would have a
greater social adaptedness.

   LeVine and Campbell, however, tend to divorce political development from economic development in their account of the evolutionary

argument. Moreover their argument stretches beyond a simple comparison between states with and without political structures. They suggest that one particular form of political development has had an adaptive significance throughout history. The national state is the end product of the evolutionary process and is seen as the "most evolved, or perhaps only pure form" of ethnocentrism (1972, p. 112). The selection criteria which produce this form are consequently considered to have an ahistorical consistency. However, it will be suggested that alternative accounts of societal development would seem to be every bit as reasonable if other systems, apart from state systems, are considered.

It had been noted that LeVine and Campbell stress that many small societies do not possess the most evolutionary adaptive features. It is also true that not all developed nation-states are internally cohesive units, with uncontested ethnocentric traditions. LeVine and Campbell mention that many contemporary nations are troubled by ethnic divisions which threaten national unity. They do not then proceed to draw the conclusion that the existence of such states contradicts the evolutionary argument. Instead they contend that strong super-powers enable weak states to continue surviving, and that this testifies to the unevenness of the evolution towards ethnocentrism. There is in this line of argument a concealed implication, which LeVine and Campbell do not themselves draw; this is that the "protection" of weak states by the powerful is somehow a potentially dangerous interference with the laws of social evolution.

The facts would seem to suggest that the ethnocentric well-bounded society is the exception rather than the rule, despite the fact that the processes of social evolution have been operating for countless centuries. Most undeveloped societies are not discrete systems, and the contemporary international scene reveals numerically more "weak" nations than super-powers (this ignores for the moment the fact that the super-powers themselves may have serious internal divisions). It would therefore seem strange that social evolution has not produced an overwhelming preponderance of well-adapted societies, and that the so-called non-adaptive societies have shown a remarkable capacity for survival. This casts doubt on LeVine and Campbell's assumption that there are consistent selection criteria and that intergroup conflict can be seen as probably the most crucial criterion. One might hypothesise that under certain economic conditions, for instance, extreme scarcity, competition might act to produce boundedness and that diffuse and non-integrated societies might be a prey to more cohesive neighbours. However, under other economic conditions one might assume that the establishment of trading relations and intergroup contact might be more conducive to social growth; in such situations it might well be the rigidly xenophobic community that is at a disadvantage and fails to develop its economic and military potential. This would imply that there could be a complex interaction between economic and political factors in social development. Certainly it has been argued that contemporary international relations cannot be understood if the emphasis is purely on state-systems. Non-state systems which transcend national boundaries, such as economic and ethnic relations, must be considered (Burton, 1974). It is by no means clear that all economic conditions place a survival premium on ethnocentrism. For instance, it can be argued that the development of international surplus accumulation, as realised in advanced capitalism, requires a less parochial form of ethnocentrism for its smooth operation. The general point is that LeVine and Campbell's intergroup selection criterion is essentially a social criterion, which must operate in a social context and be subject to social changes. If an ingroup and outgroup both simultaneously develop along the same parallel lines, then the intergroup constraints operative at one level of development may be inoperative at another. To insist that the intergroup situation always favours the development of the state system would *prima facie* seem to reify that system and run counter to the most obvious facts of the matter.

LeVine and Campbell's evolutionary argument carries with it certain tacit assumptions about the future course of social development. They imply that the future contexts of intergroup relations will not be qualitatively different from past or present conditions: the national state will continue to have adaptive utility. This can be contrasted with the classic Marxist account of social development. Whereas LeVine and Campbell stress the growth of outward symbols of ingroup cohesion, Engels in *The Origin of the Family, Private Property and the State* emphasises the origin of ingroup divisions. If the development of a political structure and the growth of a national consciousness can be associated with the production of an economic surplus, so also can the division of labour and the beginnings of social exploitation:

> Under the given historical conditions, the first great division of labour, by increasing the productivity of labour, that is wealth, and enlarging

the field of production, necessarily carried slavery in its wake. Out of the first great division of labour arose the first division of society, into two classes: masters and slaves, exploiters and exploited. (Engels, 1968, edn., p. 579.)

If this "first great division" is also accompanied by the development of a political state, then the following paradox emerges: the psychological unity of a society is accompanied by the development of an objective division. This paradox is easily comprehensible if one analyses the ruling group's or faction's ideologising in terms of false consciousness. The development of a rudimentary form of ethnocentrism may be seen as a form of political displacement, which cloaks within-group divisions. The paradox is resolved if it is claimed that the actual society is itself paradoxical. Where the Marxist interpretation fundamentally differs from the social evolutionary viewpoint is that the Marxist interpretation predicts that under given historical conditions the objective divisions will become too great to support the psychological unity. In these circumstances the factors that support ethnocentric nationalism will be broken and a qualitatively different pattern of group relations emerge. By postulating the historical constancy of the national state, the proponents of the evolutionary argument neglect the possibility that underlying objective conditions may, under certain circumstances, be the precursors for a further development of economic, political and social forms.

The present analysis, in contrast to that of LeVine and Campbell, stresses the actual and potential divisions within complex social groupings. In this respect, the hypothesis of ethnocentrism should be examined for its generality throughout developed social groups. There has been a considerable amount of evidence that attitudes generally favour one's own national group—for instance, the ethnocentric perspective has been found in a number of cross-cultural studies on children's attitudes (Lambert and Klineberg, 1967; Tajfel et al. 1970; Jaspars et al. 1972). However, it is not the case that ingroup favouritism accompanies all forms of group membership. In the complex industrial society the individual belongs to more than just a national group. There is a good deal of evidence suggesting that members of disadvantaged groups, and disadvantaged ethnic groups in particular, do not share the general ethnocentric outlook. On many tests the members of such groups have shown significant outgroup biases and have devalued their own group. For instance, Morland (1966) and Goodman (1964) found this when they tested Black American children. Milner (1971 and 1973) found similar results with his sample of West Indian and Asian immigrants' children in Britain; and Vaughan (1964) has reported such outgroup preferences amongst Maori children in New Zealand. In all these cases the minority group is held in low esteem by the dominant (white) culture, and it can be said that to a certain degree the children of the minority group have absorbed the majority values. The result is the acceptance, either partially or wholly, of an ingroup ideology which reflects the ingroup's disadvantaged status.

Prima facie this would seem to be an exception to the rule of ethnocentric favouritism. Nor is there any reason to suppose that these exceptions should be confined specifically to ethnic minority groups. If the disadvantaged group were in fact the majority group and were denied all political and economic power within a particular society, there is reason to suppose a similar state of affairs would emerge, especially if the dominant group maintained an ideological control as well. Similarly, the acceptance by a group of an ideology that to some degree justifies their exclusion from most avenues of power, need not be confined to ethnic groups. In this regard it is easy to point to the example of women in the western world, who have accepted an inferior status for centuries, although in fact constituting a numerical majority in the population. In a like vein, Miliband (1973, chapter eight) has suggested that the education system in capitalist countries aims at forcing working class children to accept their own unfitness for education, and fosters the notion that they themselves are responsible for their own failures. In all these cases there would seem to be some measure of acceptance by a subordinate group of the ideology of unworthiness, by which the dominant group is able to maintain its privileged position. As such, these ideologies of domination do not constitute unfortunate exceptions to the general rule of ethnocentrism, but must be seen as part and parcel of intergroup situations of dominance—at least those situations in which a counter-ideology of discontent has not yet been formulated by the subordinate group.

The exceptions to the ethnocentric hypothesis seem to imply a complete social stability and neat differentiation between social groups. They seem to justify the assumption that people will passively accept whatever social identities it is their lot to receive. They will then identify with this received social group and despise all other groups. Nevertheless, the situation is by no means so simple.

The wholehearted acceptance of the dominant group's ideology would not seem usual for the subordinate group. Thus Maquet (1970) is able to describe how the Hutu rebelled against their long-standing domination by the Tutsi—he mentions that their status as second-class citizens in Rwanda must have built up a vast amount of bitterness and discontent, which of course would be incomprehensible if the Hutu had accepted without question the Tutsi ideology of basic inequalities. Similarly, the revolts by disadvantaged minority groups has demonstrated that such groups have not accepted ideological premises that justify their disadvantaged states. For instance, McCann (1974) has described how the Catholic Northern Irish community were fully aware of the injustices they suffered under Protestant Unionist rule; however, before the civil rights movements their discontent was not channelled into effective social movements. In the same way, Negro "subservience" in the United States prior to the mid-twentieth century is not to be explained by assuming that the blacks adopted the racist values of white culture as a form of false consciousness inhibiting black protest. Nobles (1973) has attacked the thesis that the Negro Americans have shown "self-hatred"; similarly Moinat et al. (1972) have stated that emerging black consciousness as a political force is not the product of a sudden rejection of negative ingroup stereotypes—rather it is the product of an increasing awareness of the means to remedy inequalities, whose injustices have long been resented.

In these instances it should not be thought that the dominated group will passively accept the false consciousness, which is disseminated by the superior group and which alienates the subordinate group from its true interests. To postulate such a passive acceptance is to adhere to a model of social processes, which neglects the possibility of social change. Essentially it would assume a functional and static model of society, which emphasised the "functions" of a negative ingroup identification for adapting the ingroup to its inferior status, rather than detailing the ways in which such a status can be changed. However, it might be assumed that the ideological values, created by the dominant group, rarely mirror exactly the experiences and situation of the subordinate group. Ideological slogans about the value of "justice" and "liberty" can have little meaning for a group that daily experiences injustices and oppression. The group may not have articulated an ideology of discontent for itself, but this does not necessarily mean that it wholeheartedly accepts the "official" views of the dominant group. Rather, the ideology of the dominated group can be seen as being in a state of tension, which reflects its own dominated status and also its possibilities for future freedom. In this way, it is not a question of whether the group's ideology is based either on feelings of self-hatred or upon positive estimations of self-worth; rather these will be two elements which will be derived from two different ideological sources. The former will be seen as derived from the false consciousness, which serves to perpetuate the rule of the dominant group, whilst the latter will arise more directly from the subordinate group's own experience. These two ideological elements will reflect divisions within the group between "the uncle toms" and "the rebels", each according greater importance to one or other element. However, as the group progresses to become a group-for-itself the false consciousness will be correspondingly weakened, as the group's "positive" ideology is successful. Thus the uncle toms will be swept along by the tide of success and the former false consciousness, which only partially mirrored the group's experience, will become totally discredited. The dominant group will note the "greed" and "unreasonableness" of the emergent group-for-itself as it rejects the premises, which have served to justify the dominance. If the material conditions, which supported the dominance, crumble, then a new pattern of intergroup relations emerges.

In this way the ideology should be evaluated according to its social functions rather than according to its particular elements. Given the stress upon the social creation of ideology with respect to intergroup relations, it should be no surprise that isolated beliefs can have widely different ideological meanings in different intergroup contexts: thus Van den Berghe (1967) reports that Black South Africans have rejected the attempts by the White government to foster indigenous African culture—this being seen by the Blacks as an attempt by the Whites to create internal dissensions and also to foster the racist myth. Therefore Africanisation is seen as a form of false consciousness, created by the dominant group for the subordinate group with the purpose of perpetuating existing inequalities. The situation is the opposite to that occurring amongst American Blacks who have re-discovered their African heritage. In this case, pride in things African has sprung directly from the group's own ideology and is not the creation of an alien group wishing to preserve its dominating position.

The argument has once more returned to the topics of group ideology and false consciousness. It has been maintained that attempts to relate particular structural variables to intergroup relations should also take into account the wider political and economic context. This is especially crucial with respect to potential ingroup social divisions. In a similar vein, the arguments against the hypothesis that ethnocentrism is evolutionary adaptive stressed the need to consider underlying objective trends. The hypothesis was criticised for being essentially ahistorical and abstract, and also for overemphasising the social unity of the modern national state. In contrast the present discussion sought to emphasise the divisions which can exist in the politically developed society. By retaining the concept of false consciousness and by relating it to the wider social context, a general hypothesis of ethnocentrism is resisted. Instead, on both an intellectual and a political level of analysis, ethnocentric attitudes are not to be accepted at their face value, but it is necessary to question their social and ideological basis.

Competitive and superordinate goals

In this section an explicitly non-reductionist approach to the social psychology of intergroup relations will be discussed. As such, it raises a number of the key problems concerning intergroup processes and the development of group identification in an intergroup context. The approach is based upon the work of Muzafer Sherif. Both his empirical and theoretical research on intergroup relations bear the marks of his opposition to reductionist social psychology. Sherif makes this quite plain in his introductory section to his book *Group Conflict and Cooperation*. Here he states that:

> . . . characteristics of functional relations between groups cannot be deduced or extrapolated solely from the properties of relations that prevail among the members of the group itself. (Sherif, 1966, p. 12.)

It is not that the intergroup situation itself has to be examined, as opposed only to the study of ingroup processes, it is also that the method of study itself must not be reductionist. His approach is formulated explicitly in opposition to those personality theorists and frustration-aggression researchers who have placed their own researches at the core of intergroup problems. He states that personality disorders or individual frustrations cannot be held to account for intergroup phenomena (Sherif, 1966, p. 6). If those individualist approaches are rejected as unsatisfactory, then a more holistic orientation must be adopted. Sherif expresses it thus:

> We . . . must consider both the properties of the groups themselves and the consequences of membership on individuals. Otherwise, whatever we are studying, we are not studying groups. (Sherif, 1966, p. 62.)

In other words, to construct a social psychology of intergroup relations, the phenomena themselves must be studied at their own level and not be reduced either to problems of purely group psychology or to problems of individual psychology.

Sherif's own theoretical formulations and his empirical research are in basic accord with the approach advanced so far, at least inasmuch as Sherif disavows reductionism. The differences between Sherif's position and that suggested here will become apparent as the discussion proceeds. For the present it can be noted that there is a substantial agreement concerning the essential methodological premises— both as these relate to the necessity of a non-reductionist analysis and to the importance of studying the relations between groups over and above their own internal properties. It will be argued that Sherif's approach enables him to pose questions concerning the objective and subjective factors involved in intergroup relations. Moreover, Sherif is able, at least in theory, to commence an analysis of the interrelations between the objective and the subjective. Nonetheless it will be argued that Sherif himself does not undertake a deep enough analysis of these problems, and that his interpretations of his own empirical findings can profitably be reconstrued.

To begin with, Sherif's own researches can be considered. This will be done for two basic reasons—first and foremost Sherif's own theory of intergroup relations has been developed as a direct consequence of his empirical findings and his theory should therefore be discussed in conjunction with his research. Secondly, the research itself is a veritable *tour de force* and an important landmark in social psychological research into intergroup relations. The richness of the results, as well as Sherif's own methodological skill and organisation, ensure that the research will bear re-examination and re interpretation. In this, Sherif's original experiments are in need of theoretical understanding rather than any empirical replication or modification.

Essentially Sherif has based his theoretical formulations on the results of three similar observational studies conducted in boys' summer camps in the late 1940s and early 1950s (Sherif and Sherif, 1953; Sherif *et al.*, 1961). The first two of these three studies follow the same basic design and the third contained certain modifications to be discussed later. The subjects were normal, healthy white American boys who spent two weeks or so in a summer camp, run by Sherif and his associates. They were completely unaware that their behaviour was being observed or that the camp itself was in fact an outdoors social psychological laboratory. As far as they were concerned it was a normal routine summer camp. In reality, the camp did differ from the ordinary, in that the camp authorities deliberately organised the camp activities so that a number of hypotheses concerning the genesis and course of intergroup rivalry could be tested.

The experiments were divided into different stages, during which Sherif examined different facets of group and intergroup behaviour. During the first stage of the experiment the subjects were brought to the summer camp and became acquainted with one another and with the camp itself. During this stage all activities were campwide—the boys ate, slept and engaged in organised pursuits all together as a group. Their friendship choices and their patterns of interaction were noted by the experimenters and/or camp-leaders. After about a week, the boys were split into two distinct groups—care was taken to separate close friends and to place them into opposing groups. The camp-leaders told the boys that it would be simpler to organise the camp activities if they were divided into these two groups. From then on, their daily life revolved around the groups. The communal activities ceased; the groups had separate bunkhouses, ate separately and engaged in separate pursuits. During the course of this stage of the experiment, Sherif reports that definite ingroup customs and hierarchies evolved; in a sense the boys developed their own group cultures. Thus, during the stage two, the features of the ingroups were consolidated.

During stage three of the experiment the two groups were placed in competition, one with the other. Sporting tournaments were organised; the camp chores were arranged on a competitive basis, such that the better group was awarded points for excelling the other. The points were to be part of an overall competition, with prizes for the members of the victorious group, when the series of tournaments had been completed. During this stage of intergroup competition, Sherif and his associates noticed a rapid and dramatic deterioration in intergroup relations. Negative outgroup stereotypes were developed and actual overt hostilities between the two groups were not infrequent. The boys could be said to have formed two distinct warring factions; solidity and cohesion within the groups were established, but the distance between the two groups was vast.

In the last of his three experiments, Sherif introduced a fourth stage. He was evidently troubled by the ease with which he had created intergroup hostility and therefore sought to find means by which such hostility could be diminished. Sherif himself was by no means happy with the idea of sending the boys home from their summer holiday filled with a strongly developed antipathy towards an artificially created outgroup. Therefore he arranged that, during stage four, situations should arise that were the obverse to the group competition of the previous stage. Basically what happened in this stage was that the two groups were placed in situations in which they had to combine their efforts in order to achieve some goal mutually desired by both groups. For instance, they had to combine to pull a broken-down food-truck, and had to pool their financial resources in order to purchase a film-show for the whole camp. These situations were ones in which the members of the two hostile groups had what Sherif termed "superordinate goals". Such goals he defines as "those that have a compelling appeal for members of each group, but that neither group can achieve without the participation of the other" (Sherif, 1966, p. 89). The results showed that during this stage of the experiment there was a decrease in intergroup tension and hostility—Sherif found that the boys once more made friends across the group divisions, something that had not occurred since stage one.

That, then, is a basic outline of the main results from Sherif's boys camp experiments; from these results Sherif formulated his theory of intergroup relations. The essence of the theory can be simply stated— it is that competitive goals cause intergroup conflict and that superordinate goals give rise to intergroup co-operation. As such it obviously fits in well with his own empirical results, and with those from the few replications which have been conducted (for instance, Blake and Mouton, 1962; Rabbie, et al. 1974). On the other hand there is a certain barrenness to the description of the theory, as just portrayed. In a sense, Sherif's formulation would seem obvious—conflict will develop when people have conflicting goals and co-operation will be the outcome of complementary goals. That much seems reasonable, but disappointing as a theoretical formulation. However, because Sherif has phrased his theory in group terms, rather than individualistic ones, it becomes possible to extend this basic idea in a number of directions. It should not be thought that Sherif himself has undertaken such a systematic extension of his theoretical notions; in fact his theoretical statements have unfortunately remained comparatively undeveloped. This does not of course vitiate the need for such an extension; in attempting this, there will, initially at least, be some convergence with Sherif's views, although the present discussion will aim at progressing beyond Sherif's analysis.

Sherif's own explanation and description of his results focuses upon the goals held by the participants, and in particular the goals which are determined by group membership. In this he could be said to be concentrating on subjective factors involved in intergroup relations; "goals" as such refer to the shared perceptions and motivations of the group members. In this way, they can be viewed as referring to shared states of mind, and thus to subjective factors. Whereas certain social psychological theorists of conflict resolution were previously criticised for reducing complex social events to subjective factors, the same criticism cannot be levelled at Sherif. Their reduction was possible because initially they reduced group conflict to individual conflict— Sherif on the other hand does not take this step. His concentration on subjective factors does not betray a basic error in his theoretical orientation, but rather an incomplete analysis of the phenomena in question. Especially, it shows that questions relating the objective to the subjective have not been posed, although they can be raised, given his original theoretical premises.

Because Sherif formulates his notions of competitive and superordinate goals in terms of groups, it becomes possible to ask questions about the development of these goals within an intergroup context. The existence of such goals need not be taken as the final step in the theoretic analysis of intergroup situations. Instead of using such group goals as final explanatory concepts (and it should not be taken that all of Sherif's descriptions imply that this is what he in fact does), they lead to certain fundamental problems in the analysis of intergroup relations. The immediate question, and one that can be asked with direct relation to Sherif's own experiments, is "by what processes and under what circumstances do these subjectively felt goals arise?" This basic question can be posed in a slightly more formal way by enquiring under what objective social conditions do groups subjectively develop superordinate and competitive goals. In short, what relations are there between group beliefs and goals and the objective situations in which groups find themselves?

Sherif's own experimental situations can provide a useful starting-place; in answer to such questions, a simplistic explanation can be given concerning the boys' camp findings. One could say that, by putting two groups in a competitive situation, the development of competitive goals is encouraged; and conversely putting groups into a co-operative situation encourages the development of superordinate goals. In other words, one could attempt to seek the locus of such group goals in features of the intergroup situation itself. In relation to the boys' camp experiment, one could point to the *institutionalisation* of competition which could have led to the competitive goals. In his experiments Sherif established formally competitive situations and organised tournaments—he built them into the fabric of the daily camp life. The institutionalisation of conflict could therefore be held to be the prime cause in the developing of the subjectively held goals. In proposing this, one is also able to go part of the way in explaining the relative ineffectiveness of superordinate goals, as opposed to competitive ones. Sherif found that the superordinate goals of stage four of the final experiment did not eradicate the intergroup hostility, although they diminished it. It could be argued that, had the superordinate situations been as formalised and institutionalised in terms of the camps social structure, then the intergroup tensions may well have been dispelled more effectively. As it was, the co-operative situations resembled chance accidents rather than vital features of the camp life.

In proposing this, the discussion has inevitably focused on the relation between the social structure and the intergroup goals of the group members. Translating this into the terminology which has been employed in previous chapters, we are faced with the problem of the relation between social structure and group ideology. The discussion of the institutionalisation of competition highlights the roles of institutions in social structures. Since institutions, in the social sense, are not god-given entities but human products, one can ask of any institution in an intergroup situation: what groups have effectively established that institution, by what ideologies is the institution maintained, and what groups are directly and indirectly involved in its maintenance? Thus the central question can be approached: in whose interest is the institution?

If answers to some of these questions are sought in relation to Sherif's experimental situations, then some rudimentary analysis of the social structure of those situations is required. Analysis of the structure with relation to these questions reveals, on the one hand, a fairly simple objective social structure, but on the other hand a certain complexity with regard to the interrelations between this structure and the more subjective social psychological variables. In attempting to find out in whose interest the institution of competition was, one has to face one of the most glaring, and yet neglected features of the whole situation: the one group in the boys camp with a definite vested interest in the institution of competition and the "semi-institution" of group co-operation was, in fact, neither of the two groups of boys. It was the third group—the experimenters/camp authorities. The importance of this group to the total social structure of the boys camp should need little explanation. However, this importance should not blind the social psychologist attempting to evaluate the interrelation of group goals and intergroup structure, and allow him to overlook the obvious.

This third group, the experimenters, is the social group which creates the other two groups—giving them their social meaning and their social reality. This group constitutes the legitimate authority in the camp. Whether or not to include Sherif himself in this group is somewhat problematic; he was not an obvious authority but was disguised as Mr. Mussee the caretaker, and as such hardly accorded much respect by the boys. However, one can leave aside his own "marginal" status. Previously, in the discussion of more traditional laboratory experiments in social psychology, it was found to be necessary to include the role of the experimenter himself in order to attain an overall analysis of the situation. Just as the experimenter in certain laboratory situations is an important variable, so in this case are the camp authorities crucial to the dynamics of Sherif's boys camp investigation. This is, of course, in accord with the previous discussion (p. 174) of the Miller and Bugelski (1948) experiment. Like the Sherif studies, the Miller and Bugelski study was conducted in a boys' camp which had been adapted for experimental purposes. Similarly, the re-evaluation of that experiment stressed the role of the experimenters as an independent social group within the experimental situation. The essential intergroup cleavage in that study, it was argued, was between experimenters and subjects; and this cleavage was discussed in relation to the concepts of group ideology and false consciousness. It will be suggested that Sherif's experiments present an analogous situation.

Firstly, the nature of the two groups of boys in Sherif's boys camp experiments should be specified. The groups are artificial in the sense that they do not represent a spontaneous development, but were deliberately created. However, they are real in the sense that they had a strong psychological reality for their members. These groups certainly fall under Sherif's definition of a "group" (1966, p. 62). He stipulates that a group is a collection of individuals that (a) stand in status and role relationship with one another, and (b) possess explicitly or implicitly a set of norms or values. Quite obviously the boys' camp groups qualify under both these counts. However, during stage one of the experiment *all* the boys in the camp could be said to constitute a group —a group which was divided by the experimenters. Not only this, the total group during stage one also functioned within an intergroup context, the outgroup being of course the camp authorities. The fact that relations between these two groups were harmonious and mutually accepted should not conceal the fact that essentially the camp itself presents an intergroup situation. Also in a real sense this intergroup division persists throughout the time when the intergroup differences between the boys occupy prime attention. The role of the experimenter/authority group during this period will be considered in some detail.

The original account of Sherif's results highlights the importance of institutionalised competition, and states that no intergroup hostility between the two artificially created subgroups should be discernible before the advent of this competition. This account predicts that no intergroup hostility should occur in stage two, but should appear with the onset of stage three of the experiment. Nevertheless, a closer look at Sherif's data reveal a more complex state of affairs, with a greater interrelation of variables than the original account suggests. In examining the situation in greater detail, the focus of attention will be on the second experiment; Sherif's (1953) detailed report brings out the points which will form the basis of the present discussion.

Sherif presents in detail what occurred after the boys had been split into two groups, the Blues and the Reds. They develop during stage two an ingroup consciousness which not only results in the formation of ingroup structures and rituals, but also entails a conscious renaming process—the Reds became the Red Devils, and the Blues styled themselves as the Bull Dogs. More important from the present point of view is that during this stage the preconditions for intergroup hostility are developed. For instance, the boys dubbed ingroup members, who mixed with their former friends from the outgroup, as "traitors". This implies that the groups were not merely building themselves as strong cohesive social units, but were doing this in contradistinction to their perceived outgroup. There is more evidence that these ingroup developments of structures were in fact taking place in a conscious intergroup setting. For instance, when the Red Devils were decorating their hut, they refused to have any blue decorations or insignia—blue being the adopted colour of the Bull Dogs. Sherif also reports that the boys made spontaneous intergroup comparisons; for example, they made remarks like "our pond is better than theirs". In this way it can be seen that the development of "cultures" within the respective ingroups was occurring all the time with reference to the outgroup. It was as if the boys wanted their group to be distinct, but comparable to the other group—comparable, of course, in a favourable light.

Interesting in this respect are the findings from the final boys' camp experiment (Sherif *et al.* 1961). This experiment was different from the other two in that there was no stage one. The boys never formed one overall group, but came to the camp separately in two different groups. In fact, for a while they were unaware of the presence of the other group. At this time they were obviously developing their ingroup "cultures" completely in isolation from the unknown outgroup. However, the mere discovery of the other group had a profound effect on the boys. Sherif writes that the reactions of the "Rattlers" (one of the groups) were altered by the discovery of the "Eagles" (the other group): "from that time on the outgroup figured prominently in their lives" Sherif, 1961, p. 94). Thus even in this situation with no prior acquaintance, the mere existence of the outgroup affects the internal development of the ingroup, before the institutionalisation of competition.

One particular incident, which occurred in the second experiment, can serve to illustrate the intergroup nature of the ingroup developments during stage two. It also provides an example of the role of the camp authorities in the situation. Sherif (1953) writes of a territorial dispute between the two groups concerning the extent to each group's own domain. The upshot of this dispute was that the boys attempted to set up clearly defined boundaries between their territories. However, this led to a certain amount of skirmishing between the two groups; the camp authorities then intervened to put an end to this intergroup hostility, and the two groups were separated. Sherif describes it thus:

> Since this conflict between the two groups was occasioned by their being in proximity with one another, it was necessary to reduce further opportunities for contact between them at this stage. (Sherif, 1953, p. 258.)

In this quotation the importance of the authorities is clear, especially in relation to the amount of intergroup hostility between the two groups of boys. Sherif's conclusion concerning stage two is that there was no "consistent day-to-day hostility between the groups" (Sherif, 1953, p. 267). This finding is, of course, to be contrasted with the hostility displayed in stage three. However, the lack of hostility in stage two should be interpreted in the light of the statement that the camp authorities deliberately acted to prevent any such hostility, and separated the groups when such an outbreak appeared imminent.

The importance of the authority groups role in restricting any intergroup hostility in stage two can be seen when the institutionalisation of conflict is examined in greater detail. The institutionalisation of competition is, of course, a crucial feature in Sherif's theoretical description of his experiments and is the corner-stone of his account of this sort of intergroup situation. Quite obviously, organised competitions do not arise in some sort of social vacuum, but are created by specific people or groups in specific situations. In the case of the boys' camp experiments, the simplistic explanation would state that the authority group created the competition, and this in turn gave rise to the resulting intergroup hostility. However, this account does not do justice to the depth of intergroup feelings amongst the two groups of boys themselves, and the significance of these feelings for a theoretical description of the institutionalised competition.

Sherif (1953) reports that during stage two, before the establishment of competition, both groups repeatedly asked the camp authorities if they could hold sporting competitions between themselves. These requests were turned down by the authorities. In fact, the eventual competition was introduced to the boys as if the authorities had agreed to accept their requests and had finally been persuaded to allow intergroup competitions. A similar desire for competition can be discerned in the behaviour of the boys during the third experiment. In this experiment these competitive feelings can be traced to the mere discovery of the presence of an outgroup. Sherif *et al.* 1961, wrote:

When the presence of another group was definitely announced, the Rattlers immediately wanted to challenge them, and to be the *first* to challenge. Performance in all activities which might now become competitive (tent pitching, baseball, etc.) was entered into with more zest and also with more efficiency. Since the efforts to help "all of us" to swim occurred after this, it is possible that even this strictly in-group activity was influenced by the presence of an out-group and a desire to excel it in all ways (Sherif *et al.* 1961, pp. 94–5, italics in original).

Given this, one can interpret stage two, before the institutionalisation of competition, as being a time when the boys actively wish for such competition. The intergroup feelings of rivalry cannot be attributed to some sort of competition which has not yet in fact been arranged. The desire for such an arrangement has to be explained. The role of the authorities can be seen in this one respect as a restraining one—during this stage they are concerned to prevent open skirmishing and the establishment of competitive tournaments. One could summarise the situation by stating that, if the authority group, having established the two subordinate groups of boys, were then to disappear from the scene, the subordinate groups would have instituted their own competitions. The resulting end-product would then have resembled the intergroup hostilities of stage three. There is, of course, no gainsaying that the resulting competition could have substantially differed from the well-organised activities administered by the authorities during stage three.

In this discussion of Sherif's boys camp experiments, two, not unrelated features, have emerged. In the first place there has been an emphasis on the role of the authority group in what has been described as being essentially a three-sided intergroup situation. In the second place it has been stressed that the rivalry between the two boys groups existed in some form or another before the institutionalisation of the competitive tournaments. Both these two features necessitate a re-evaluation of the original account of these experiments. The first factor suggests that the experimental results should be interpreted in terms of a wider social context than that offered by this account. In particular it suggests that the overall power relations in the total situation should be examined in far greater detail. The second factor suggests that the relationship of what might be termed as the psychological variables to the variables of social structure are of a more complex nature than that posited by the simplistic model; the social structural variable of competition cannot be held to be the pure and

312   INTERGROUP RELATIONS

simple cause of the extreme negative outgroup perceptions recorded at the end of stage three.

Sherif's experiments have not been discussed merely for their own sake. The deficiencies in simple explanations of these phenomena have been stressed because of the theoretical issues that can be raised. The experiments were not conducted as intellectual exercises in their own right, but Sherif explicitly hoped to illustrate and understand processes that occur in real-life intergroup situations (see, for instance, Sherif, 1966, for a lengthy discussion of this issue). If this is to be the case, then it is imperative to attempt as full an interpretation of the controlled experimental situation as possible. The simplistic account has been criticised, and thus the limitations of applying this account to the real-world should also be demonstrated. Frank (1967) for instance, applies the theory derived from Sherif's experiments to illustrate real-world phenomena and uses the experimental findings to illustrate international processes between the United States and the U.S.S.R. (cf. also, Klineberg, 1962).

Basically Frank is not so much concerned with the genesis of intergroup hostility, his interest is quite understandably upon its prevention. For this reason he concentrates upon superordinate goals rather than the competitive goals. The moral he draws from the experiments is that superordinate goals can be effective in reducing international tensions; and here he particularly refers to the nuclear arms race, and the nuclear stockpiling of the more powerful nations. He is therefore dealing with situations involving national groupings which have no one superior dominant group above them. He correctly dismisses the view that the establishment of such a superior group could maintain peace by effectively controlling individual nation states. Here he has in mind the idea that the United Nations, or some such similar organisation, could hold the peace between rival nuclear powers—at least a U.N. which is geared purely and simply to policing the world: "No domestic government consisting only of a police force and judiciary and having only punitive powers could long survive; to win their citizens allegiance, governments must perform positive services, and maintaining order is only one" (Frank, 1967, p. 227).

Given this, Frank advocates that the leading nations should set up for themselves some sort of superordinate goals. He accepts the basic premise that the establishment of superordinate goals would be a positive step towards reducing intergroup tensions. Specifically, he advocates that the international superordinate goals should be of a scientific or technological nature. He proposes that the U.S.A. and the U.S.S.R. should co-operate on space and anti-pollution research programmes. In this way, he writes, a mutual interdependence could develop, which would evaporate the present mutual distrust (Frank, 1967, pp. 252–3). Such ideas are not new: the views of Storr (1964) were discussed in chapter three, and it is interesting to note that a Russian scientist, Pokrovsky (1962) has advocated similar programmes. Pokrovsky did not use the term "superordinate goals", but he expressed the basic notion in advocating the establishment of geophysical research projects as a way of building harmonious East–West relations. The basic question, then, revolves around the social context of such superordinate goals. Just as the goals in the boys' camp experiment, whether superordinate or competitive, were shown to interrelate with other factors in the total social situation, then similarly superordinate goals in the real world cannot be considered purely in the abstract.

   In stating this, it is assumed that superordinate goals and competitive goals do not by themselves constitute the basic determinant of intergroup relations. If these two concepts are stressed to the exclusion of all others, then the resulting theory will inevitably neglect what can be called the more objective factors involved in intergroup relations. To illustrate this point Frank's example of East-West relations can be considered, and the implications of his proposed superordinate goals discussed. In the first place, it should be noted that since Frank outlined his ideas, some of his proposals have become fact, and also there has been a general détente in East-West relations. The problem that must be first considered is a simple one: are these superordinate goals, or joint American-Russian scientific projects, a cause or an effect of the general diplomatic détente between the two nations? The answer should be obvious—to claim they are the cause would be absurd and would preclude any serious investigation of the relations between these two nations. In the experimental situation superordinate goals can be established by the experimenters overnight, and if the actions of the experimenters are discounted in the theoretical analysis of the situation, then it will appear that these goals have spontaneously appeared and themselves affected the future course of events. No such description is possible in the case of the real-world situation. The establishment of joint scientific projects by the leaders of the U.S.A. and the U.S.S.R. was the product of considerable diplomatic activity which could only have taken place once the cold war pressures had eased.

Similarly, these projects will not themselves prevent any renewal of hostile intergroup relations—in fact one could surmise that they would be one of the first casualties if the cold war atmosphere were renewed. To understand the shifts and changes in American-Russian relations since the last war would involve looking at the economic and political factors that determine the nature of both countries. Concentrating upon the symbols of the various stages of their relations is no substitute for more detailed analysis. Similarly, to advocate solving intergroup conflicts by establishing superordinate goals means, in effect, to ignore looking at the actual properties of the groups themselves and the ways in which they relate. When Frank recommends superordinate goals as a means of diminishing intergroup tensions, he is arguing in a similar vein to those conflict theorists, discussed previously, who concentrate on the outward signs of intergroup conflict. In doing this they fail to analyse in depth the intergroup situation.

The establishment of superordinate goals *per se* should not be held as a social advance. The inhabitants of the world are not the automatic gainers from joint co-operation by the leaders of the world's super-powers. The power relations within and between groups need consideration. It must be stressed that Sherif himself does not advocate the blind establishment of superordinate goals; he is aware of the need to consider the total social context. He does not present them as some magical machination that will ensure automatic peace and goodwill. He explicitly states that superordinate goals "are not 'devices' to be manipulated in dealing with intergroup tensions. They must arise from the relationships between groups in a fashion so compelling that they can be recognised within each group" (Sherif, 1966, p. 147). Here, Sherif seems to admit that intergroup goals (this applies to competitive as well as superordinate) are themselves the products of the intergroup relationships. Given this, they should be studied with regard to that relationship, and should not be taken as the prime determinants of the nature of that relationship.

Blake *et al.* (1964) discuss superordinate goals in a similar manner to Sherif, in their book *Managing Intergroup Conflict in Industry*. The basic thesis of this work is that intergroup tensions can be resolved if both groups adopt a joint problem-solving approach. The similarity between this idea and Sherif's notions of superordinate goals is manifest—in fact, the book is dedicated to Sherif, and Blake has spent much time verifying Sherif's ideas in an industrial setting. Like Sherif, Blake *et al.* discount the notion that superordinate goals can be simply manipulated to achieve harmonious relations. Similarly, they do not develop this issue further into a wider social analysis. They discuss the inefficacy of superordinate goals between groups without "a new culture in which to view and understand each other" (p. 111). They illustrate their ideas with an example of conflict between the chemical operations department and the maintenance services in a chemical plant. The plant manager set both groups a joint goal concerning the costs of production. Under such circumstances, the authors comment, the superordinate goal led to an intensification of intergroup hostility, not to its reduction.

Blake *et al.* view the attitudes of the participants as the crucial factors in the success or failure of any superordinate goal. Important though these may be, such attitudes should nevertheless be investigated in relation to the social context, and in particular to the power relations between the various groups involved in the situation. In this respect their industrial example resembles the boys' camp experiment in that there is a third-party authority group—in the industrial example this is represented by the plant manager. The power of this authority should be considered an important variable in determining the success the authority has in establishing goals for superordinate groups. Blake *et al.* do not report on the power of the plant manager in their example. It is reasonable to expect different results, if the two subordinate groups were faced with redundancy and little hope of future employment, had they failed to comply with the superordinate goal. Likewise, if in the past they had achieved a certain measure of autonomy from the hierarchy, then one could expect a greater resistance to an imposed superordinate goal. The implication is that the power relations within the industrial setting, and also within the wider society, must be considered—the superordinate goals by themselves should not be abstracted from this wider context.

The necessity for considering these wider social relations can be illustrated by returning once more to the original boys' camp experiments of Sherif. In terms of what has been called the simplistic explanation, these experiments serve as illustrations for the two-party intergroup situation. However, in the present re-interpretation of these experiments the three-party nature of the situation is underlined;

attention is focused on the original distinction between the camp authorities and the boy subjects. This leads to the possibility that the truer real-life correlate of these experiments is not the relations between two national super-powers—it is those situations in which the old Macchiavellian adage of *divide et impera* is appropriate. This adage is of course advice to a ruling group as to the means of preserving its power. It relates to those situations where the ruling group can further its own interests by creating divisions and hostilities between its various subjects.

Such a situation is, of course, a prime example of what has been called "false consciousness". The superior groups are not seen by the subordinate groups as the prime cause of their dissatisfactions; these subordinate groups also see themselves as separate groups without perceiving, or at least giving due weight, to their common group membership *vis-à-vis* the ruling group. It would be quite wrong to push the analogy between this situation and the boys' camp too far. The camp authorities can hardly be thought of as exploiting tyrants! Nevertheless it must be noted that they had a definite interest in dividing their subjects (and, in fact, in restraining any intergroup hostility until the moment that was opportune for themselves). The competitive and co-operative goals that were adopted by the boys all bear evidence of the influence of the authority group. Likewise, no amount of superordinate goals between the Red Devils and the Bull Dogs, or between the Rattlers and the Eagles, would eradicate the basic division between the experimenters and the subjects. Similarly, no amount of superordinate co-operation between two units in an industrial concern will blur the existence of more basic divisions within the industry, if these exist. For instance, if the industry is run for the employer's profit this will conflict with the wage demands of the employees; co-operation between different units within the industry will not eradicate the contradiction between the employer and the employees.

The "divide and rule" interpretation of social intergroup situations dovetails with the notion of false consciousness. In order to examine the boys' camp situation further it then becomes necessary to see whether any features of it can be described as "false consciousness". In the Miller and Bugelski (1948) boys' camp experiment it was possible to characterise certain aspects of the experimenters' actions as establishing a false consciousness in their subjects. Likewise it is possible to do this with regard to features of the Sherif experiments. To begin with, one can consider an especially blatant incident which occurred in the second of the three experiments and is reported by Sherif and Sherif (1953). This represents the most pronounced outbreak of actual hostility to have occurred in any of the experiments.

Sherif and Sherif describe how a tea party was arranged after the organised competitions had been completed. At this stage, one of the groups had been declared the victors and the other the vanquished. The authorities arranged the tea party so that half the refreshments would be battered and damaged, although still edible. It was also arranged that the losing group should be the first to arrive at the party. This group, without any prompting, helped themselves to the undamaged portions of food. By the time the other group arrived, there were only the damaged portions left. Not unreasonably, they thought that their food had been damaged by their rivals in some fit of pique —they did not consider that the culprits were in fact the camp authorities. As a consequence the already existing intergroup hostility was enflamed even further and actual fighting broke out. This was only stopped by the authorities with great difficulty, and Sherif reports that there was a definite danger of the boys inflicting serious injury; at one point, in fact, knives were thrown.

The machinations of the third party authority group are quite evident in this outbreak of intergroup hostility. They are especially relevant in relation to the establishment of the mistaken belief in the victorious group that their party refreshments had been damaged by the other group. The importance of this belief in the whole incident should be apparent. However, this damaged-food episode does in a sense only constitute a minor addition to the main findings of the Sherif experiments. A fair degree of intergroup hostility already existed without this provocation, and similarly the "effectiveness" of the provocation could not have occurred without this background of pre-existing intergroup hostility. Such indeed was its effectiveness as an experimental manipulation that Sherif did not repeat the exercise, not wishing to stir up such extreme reactions again.

If this incident is a peripheral finding, then the question becomes whether false consciousness can be identified in the main experimental phenomena. In order to answer this question, one can in turn pose further questions which cannot be answered properly without empirical data. One can ask whether the groups would have behaved in the same way, would have developed the same ingroup and outgroup perceptions, and would have unquestionably accepted the authority of the camp leaders, had they been aware of the experimenters' intentions and manipulations. Although this is an empirical question for which there is no immediate data, one can ask it with reference to particular features in the experiments. For instance, one can wonder whether the behaviour of the boys would have been different, if they had known that after stage one the authorities were deliberately splitting up close friends—and they were doing this to see whether these friends would turn on each other. This question can be phrased in personal terms: two of the boys in the 1953 experiment, who came to the fiercest blows in the course of the intergroup fighting, had formerly been the firmest of pals. Would their subsequent enmity have developed had they known that they were being purposely separated in order to see whether their spontaneous close friendship would persist?

If the answer to these questions is "no", then one might hypothesise that one of the preconditions for an effective policy of "divide and rule" is the spreading of an intial false consciousness; in particular, this false consciousness should avoid the realisation that the authority group is operating such a policy. Conversely one might speculate whether a "true consciousness" is sufficient to prevent the smooth operation of such a policy. With relation to the boys' camp experiments these are of course empirical questions. In the final experiment, it is true, the operation of any processes of false consciousness may be much more limited; in this experiment there was no separation of close friends since the two groups arrived at the camp separately. Just as much intergroup hostility was discovered in this final experiment. This of course suggests that the role of false consciousness may be of a restricted nature.

Whether or not this is the case with regard to these specific experiments must inevitably remain an open question. It is hoped that this discussion has shown that Sherif's experiments do in themselves raise a number of theoretical issues. Of course, it should be borne in mind that it is experiments, and not actual intergroup conflicts, which have been discussed. Therefore, the problem arises of deciding how much the experimental conflict mirrors the real world. Certain aspects of this problem have been touched upon in the present discussions of Sherif's work, and it is a topic to which we shall return.

In pointing out the importance of the authority group, and the effects that this group had upon the experimental results, it should be noted that no criticism is being levelled at the methodology of Sherif's experiments. His results should not be dismissed as some trivial experimental manipulation, just because the experimenters affected the results by their actions. There is currently much debate in social psychology concerning the so-called "experimenter-effect" (see, for instance, Rosenthal, 1966; Orne, 1962; Friedman, 1967). Typically this debate is conducted at the methodological level and experimenter-effects or influences are seen as troublesome artifacts which confound experimental data, and which threaten the validity of the experiment *per se*. This methodological debate should not act as a smokescreen concealing theoretical debate. The point is not to deny that the experimental authorities had any effect on the results, nor to dismiss the results because of this, but to recognise both the effects themselves and the theoretical importance of these effects. If the goal of experimental research in the area of intergroup relations is to produce intergroup situations composed only of equal groups, then this will preclude any serious study of superior groups. The experimental situation, by virtue of being an implicit intergroup situation, in fact provides an excellent opportunity for examining processes between groups of unequal power. To ignore this inequality of power and such matters as false consciousness is to attempt to construct a fictional social psychology in which all groups have approximately equal power.

Having said that the total social context of intergroup relations must be considered, it then becomes necessary from the present point of view to state what are the most striking of Sherif's findings. If the present re-interpretation of his series of boys' camp experiments is accepted, then the key theoretical issues relate to the actions of the third-party authority group and the potential spreading of a false group ideology. There is also one empirical feature in Sherif's findings worth emphasising: this is the development of intergroup rivalry and comparison *before* the establishment of the institutional competition. It was hypothesised that this rivalry might even have been strong enough to have produced some form of institutionalised competition, were it not for the restraining hands of the experimenters. Sherif in his descriptions of his data and in his theoretical formulations seems to have played down this aspect, and concentrated upon the intergroup hostilities that occurred after the establishment of the organised competition.

This aspect of Sherif's findings raises questions about the contexts in which group identification develops. The implication is that *overt* intergroup competition is not a necessary condition for intergroup attitudes. A laboratory experiment conducted by Ferguson and Kelley (1964) demonstrated likewise that institutionalised competition is not a necessary condition for rudimentary intergroup effects—in this experiment pairs of *ad hoc* laboratory groups worked separately but within sight of one another. The experimenters explicitly gave the subjects no instructions to compete, but it was found that even in the absence of such instructions the subjects developed competitive intergroup feelings. They consistently overvalued ingroup products and undervalued outgroup products. Ferguson and Kelley state that post-experimental discussions with the subjects revealed that the group members "defined the situation as one in which they wanted to excel the other group in their productions" (p. 227).

This complements the finding from the final boys' camp experiment that the mere discovery of another group was sufficient to alter the ingroup's way of life and to produce intergroup competitive feelings. Under such circumstances intergroup identification preceded any rational intergroup competition; in fact the identification could be interpreted as a desire to create a situation in which competitive behaviour would have a rationality. If the presence of an outgroup, in certain cases, is a sufficient condition for the development of intergroup identification, then there could be a number of theoretical implications. For instance it contradicts the notion that contact between groups will suffice to diminish intergroup prejudice. The evidence for the "contact hypothesis" shows that contact can either increase or diminish negative group relations depending on other circumstances (Amir, 1969; McClendon, 1974). It also runs counter to LeVine and Campbell's (1972) idea that the psychological principle of least effort can act as a selection criterion for ethnocentrism. This would imply that group identification and distinctiveness will evolve as a consequence of ingroup processes, and will not necessarily be dependent on intergroup processes. The results of Sherif *et al.* (1961) suggest that ingroup development can be radically determined by the presence of an outgroup. It is of course unwise to extrapolate from an experiment conducted with American schoolboys to the historical development of isolated pre-literate tribal societies. What is suggested, however, is that the nature and social background of intergroup identification need to be examined. In particular there should be an investigation of group identity and its relation to the development of distinct group categories. The discussion in the following chapter will be directed toward these topics.

9

Social Identity and Social Categorisation

In this chapter the nature of group identity will be discussed, and the major burden of emphasis will be placed on linking the concept of social categorisation with that of social identity. Since the immediate subject matter will be that of identification, it is inevitable that the subjective factors related to group phenomena will be the main topics. This is not to belittle the importance of what have been termed the objective factors. On the contrary, it will be argued that a full under-standing of the subjective factors must entail considering the objective factors relating to the group situation. However, since this enquiry is a psychological one, the subjective implications of group identification must be considered as a starting point. This in turn involves the dis-cussion of groups and their composition, as defined not in terms of their objective positions, but in terms of their subjective importance. Thus, when the term "group" is used in this chapter, it will refer to the group whose members share an awareness of a common social identity. In this respect, the twin concepts of the subjective group and identification are analytically linked.

To begin with, one can make a few general remarks about the nature of social identification. It can be broadly characterised as the process by which any individual is bound to his social group and by which he realises his social self. It is to be noted that social identification is here called a process, rather than an act. This is deliberate —by referring to identification as a social process it is hoped that the social nature of this concept is stressed. It is part of the present argument that identi-fication is not an individual act which takes place within the indi-vidual's psyche and which can be understood purely in terms of intra-individual psychological processes. It is inherently a social process; it involves more than just the individual. The concept is a transitive one, i.e. there has to be an object, as well as a subject, of identification. One does not identify *per se*, but one has to identify with something or someone. In particular, when the identification is with a social group, the process is a complex dialectical one—the social group, under many conditions, is an active agent ensuring that the identification takes place and transforms the individual. It is not just a matter of the individual passively receiving the object of his identification into his own subjective consciousness. The process of identification does not take place in some sort of a social vacuum; it occurs in a definite social historical context at a definite time. As such it is related, and can be said to mediate, the two key social processes that underwrite the history of any society—the processes of social stability and social change. In terms of social stability, the concept of identification refers to those processes by which the individual embraces the social groups into which he was born. It is the process by which he comes to define himself in terms of his nation, social class, religious group, etc. and to accept their position in the social order of things as defined to him by his teachers. In other words, this involves the somewhat passive acceptance of certain normative group standards, whose ideological flavour is directed towards maintaining the existing social order. However, there is an alternative side to the process of identification; this is where the group, with which the individual identifies, has itself an ideology of social change and upheaval. Also on an individual level, the process should not be thought of as the mere acceptance of received standards. The process can be said to contain more creative functions, and include instances where objects of identification are actively sought outside the received standards. Just as there are groups that adopt revolutionary ideologies as well as groups who accept a particular *status quo*, so there are individuals who rebel against received standards of conduct. The concept of identification should be wide enough to embrace these group and individual manifestations of social change and stability.[1]

1. In this respect it can be mentioned that the majority of research into "political socialisation" neglects factors relating to social change. It portrays children as passive recipients of accepted ideologies, and assumes that there is a general ideological consensus within the society at large. For critical discussions of the theoretical and methodological short-comings of such research, see Connell (1972); Connell and Goot (1972–73).

The process of identification is not some mysterious act which needs to be examined using the armoury of depth psychology. To do this would mean ignoring the crucial social implications of the process. The present point of view is to concentrate on some of the more obvious facets of social identification. In this regard the present position does not seek to elucidate one common inner psychological process that all the members of a group have undergone, as some sort of psychic initiation rite. It will be argued that the psychological unity of subjective groups is not, at least initially, to be explained in terms of the psychology of its individual members. There is a level at which group identification can be studied in its own right. As a starting-point to such an inquiry the present approach concentrates upon the social categories, or overt linguistic expression, which is part and parcel of any social identification. In particular, two aspects of social categorisation will be emphasised. These two aspects refer to the way in which a social category in itself divides the world into X's and non-X's, and the ways in which the category is integrated into a wider ideological picture. In this way a social category can be said to effect a social differentiation as well as an ideological integration.

The dual nature of categorisation (that it separates reality into X's and non-X's), was appreciated by Freud himself. This is shown in his essay *The Antithetical Meaning of Primal Words* (Vol. 11, 1910). In this he discusses the idea of the German philologist, Karl Abel, that the earliest forms of words had twin meanings, i.e. they expressed both a positive and a negative meaning. For instance, the Egyptian hieroglyphic *ken* meant both strong and weak. Freud argued that such double-meaning words are paralleled by dream thoughts, which do not distinguish between positive and negative meanings. In dreams, he concludes, there is a regression to an archaic mental state, where the positive and the negative are bound together in one whole. He argues that modern linguistic concepts have developed through the progressive distinction of contradictories and contraries—nevertheless, these concepts will bear traces of their archaic origin and thus "our concepts owe their existence to comparison" (Freud, 1910, Vol. 11, p. 157).

If this idea is related to social categories, it suggests that the concept of ingroup and outgroup are indissolubly bound together. Freud attempted to relate this connection to a phylogenetic account of the workings of the inner mind. However, a simpler approach is possible, which concentrates upon the surface phenomena of the process of categorisation. It is feasible that the act of categorisation might by itself be an important variable in the determination of ingroup–outgroup attitudes. The results of the Sherif *et al.* (1961) boys' camp experiment and the Ferguson and Kelley (1964) laboratory study, discussed in the last chapter, suggest that the mere existence of an outgroup can under certain conditions significantly affect ingroup processes and intergroup attitudes. Such intergroup effects cannot be said to be the product of deep intrapsychic processes, but relate to the more obvious social aspects of group division and interaction. In the same way Freud's own feelings of Jewishness contain important social dimensions. In the preface to the Hebrew edition of *Totem and Taboo*, and again in his address to the Society of B'nai B'rith in Vienna (1926, Vol. 20), Freud recognises his Jewish identity, but admits his inability to explain the nature of this identification. His feeling of Jewishness was not based upon any shared beliefs or similarities with his fellow Jews. Clearly there were deep-seated reasons for his consciousness, and his relations with his own father may well have been crucial in this respect (Bakan, 1958). However, the social consequences of this identification should not be forgotten. The concept of Judaism has a historical and social significance both in relation to Jews and to non-Jews. This significance must exist as a reality distinct from the intrapsychic dramas of those who might come to share this social identity. In this respect Freud speaks of the intellectual freedom which his Jewishness gave him; he writes that he never felt obliged to please the "compact majority" (1926, Vol. 20, p. 274; see also *An Autobiographical Study*, 1925, Vol. 20, p. 9). In an obvious sense the social role of the Jews as a permanent minority outgroup in European history, together with the historical reality of anti-Semitism, combined to create this feeling, over and above any personal unconscious motivations Freud might have had.

Consequently the present approach stresses the inherently social nature of linguistic categories, and especially categories denoting social groups. The social category is first and foremost a division of people by people, rather than an expression of individual psyches. Group categories, and the social identities which they create, do not arise spontaneously by themselves; they are the products of social activity in specific historical contexts. As such the language which expresses resulting social identities should not be taken as an absolute non-reducible fact of group behaviour. The social identities, which a group ascribes to itself and to other groups, are necessarily part of a wider ideology. Just as the whole ideology can be described as reflecting the group's practical situation, so also can those parts of the ideology which refer to ingroup and outgroup identities. Even if one concentrates upon the subjective group, and the social means by which a group mediates its own subjectively perceived social unity, it is still possible to relate such subjectivity to the objective group position. This is so because the process of group identification is essentially a social process, dependent on a particular ideological and social context.

Social basis of language

The present approach, then, is to look at the social psychological significance of social categories. Since such categories are in themselves linguistic structures, it will be necessary to make a number of preliminary points concerning the social nature of language itself. Inevitably this entails a deviation from the main topics of social categorisation and social identity. However, this is necessary because the philosophies underlying certain approaches to the study of language can have implications for the meaning of group categories. The discussion will concentrate on the idea that the existence of a linguistic category is sufficient to imply something about the nature of what is categorised. Specifically this idea assumes that a category which divides the world into X's and non-X's implies that all X's share a common property which distinguishes them from all non-X's.

If this idea is correct then it would follow that social group categories mirror essential differences between different groups of humans. It would suggest that there is truth behind the stereotyped thinking that all members of a particular class, race or nation possess a distinguishing characteristic which marks them off from members of all other classes, races or nations. As such this line of thought lends itself to theories of fundamental national or racial characters which embody the "essence" of the nation or race.

The basic linguistic idea has been called the doctrine of "nominal essences". Historically it has been associated with the philosophy of John Locke who asserted that "between the *nominal essence* and the *name* there is so near a connection that the name of any sort of thing cannot be attributed to any particular being but what has this essence" (*Essay Concerning Human Understanding*, 1960 edn., p. 270, italics in original). This doctrine is still current in contemporary psychology.

The phraseology may have changed but the assumptions are basically unaltered. In its current form the doctrine asserts that categories are formed by the abstraction of common stimulus elements from a variety of stimulus patterns (see for instance, Hull, 1920, for a classic statement of this position). In this way concepts are defined in terms of actual, or perceived, stimulus similarities and such similarities constitute the "nominal essence". For instance, Bourne (1966) offers the following definition:

> . . . a concept exists whenever two or more distinguishable objects or events have been grouped or classified together and set apart from other objects on the basis of some common feature or property characteristic of each. (p. 1.)

Archer (1966) offers a similar definition; for him a concept should be treated as "the *label* of a set of things which have something in common", (p. 37, italics in original). Wallach (1958) reverses the definition and defines judgements of similarity in terms of categorisations; despite this reversal the net result is similar in that the two variables (stimulus similarity and categorisation) are linked *a priori* (a fuller discussion of this issue is contained in Billig, 1972).

The reason for linking these two variables stems from an individualistic approach. Categories are analysed purely in terms of the individual subject and the underlying principles are derived from individual psychology. Typically these principles refer to processes by which the subject orders and patterns incoming stimulus information. The overt response, or use of a category, is then defined in terms of hypothesised individual processes and these include the arrangement of similar and dissimilar stimuli.

This approach is unsatisfactory as it stands for two basic reasons. In the first place most ordinary language concepts are not labels for sets of things which have something in common. In the second place the individualistic approach cannot offer an adequate explanation of the social nature of language. The existence of common concepts within a linguistic community must be seen as the result of a happy accident; the individual members of the community must have all abstracted the same stimulus elements from their array of stimulus information. Given the vastly different experiences of people who can understand and communicate complex concepts one with another, this can be nothing short of a miracle.

These difficulties do not arise if one assumes at the outset that language by its nature is inherently social. Like Wittgenstein (1953) one might deny the plausibility of a "private language" and assert language to be a "form of life" (remark No. 241). By doing so the practical nature of language is emphasised. For example, Wittgenstein described a language consisting solely of commands uttered by a builder to his assistant. The significance of such a simplified language lies in the practical nature of its words, not in the abstracted stimulus qualities they might be hypothesised to represent.

Certain similarities can be noted between the approach of Wittgenstein and Marx concerning language. Marx too considers language a public and social phenomenon. He dismisses the notion of a private language: "Production by an individual outside society . . . is as much of an absurdity as is the development of language without individuals living *together* and talking to each other" (*Grundrisse*, 1973, p. 84, italics in original). The practical activities of everyday life determine language and thereby thought since "language *is* practical consciousness" (Marx and Engels, *The German Ideology*, 1970 edn., p. 51, italics in original).

When this perspective is taken it is no longer necessary to equate categorisation with similarities of referents. The isolated individual is no longer the ultimate creator of natural language; on the contrary, language is a social product which is handed down to, and transformed by, successive generations. The individual uses it as he might do any tool. If the social nature of language is stressed there is not the same compulsion to reduce linguistic phenomena to neat stimulus-response paradigms. The untidiness of linguistic categories can be admitted.

The content of a linguistic category is not to be confused with the psychological processes of learning that concept. If this distinction is maintained then it is possible to look at categories to see if they in fact do operate in the way that the doctrine of nominal essences suggests. A brief examination would suggest that the doctrine is refuted by the empirical facts of language use. For instance, Wittgenstein examines the structure of ordinary language and finds no evidence for the sort of nominal essences which Locke and later psychologists postulated. He discusses whether there is something common to all "games":

> Don't say: "there must be something common, or they would not be called 'games' "—but *look and see* whether there is anything common to them all.—For if you look at them you will not see something that is common to *all*, but . . . we see a complicated network of similarities over-

lapping and criss-crossing. (Wittgenstein, 1953, remark No. 66, italics in original.)

Consequently by adopting an empirical stance of "looking and seeing" Wittgenstein is drawn to a different conclusion than the doctrine of nominal essences.

Similar conclusions are drawn by Vygotsky (1962). He found that young children are unable to handle logical concepts, but tend to think in "complexes" and "collections". The objects which are categorised under a complex or collection are not related to one another in a simple logical manner and there is no one stable principle, by which objects are categorised as either belonging to the class in question or not belonging to it. Vygotsky goes further and notes that many ordinary language (or adult) concepts have the same structure as childish complexes and collections. His conclusions are strikingly similar to Wittgenstein's "networks of similarities". Vygotsky develops the point by suggesting that such untidy or nonlogical concepts are an integral part of linguistic change: "if we trace the history of a word in any language, we shall see, however surprising this may seem at first blush, that its meanings change just as in childish thinking" (pp. 72–3). Words "pick up" new meanings and their semantic structure becomes more complicated. This feature is part and parcel of the adaptability and practicality of language itself.

Experimental results using isolated subjects and restricted artificial concepts also suggest that concept use and perception of similarity may be separate variables. For instance Deese (1967) starts from presuppositions contained in the doctrine of nominal essences. He equates categorisation with "grouping" and he defines grouping as occurring only "whenever objects, events and ideas are perceived as containing something in common" (pp. 519–20). However his experimental findings reveal the awkward fact that many subjects were able to group objects together under a category without perceiving any similarity between the objects. Because of his presuppositions he is forced to explain this behaviour as being the product of some sort of erroneous mental operation; he talks of some "slippage" which must have occurred. There is the implication that this behaviour is incorrect rather than a normal instance of language usage. It might be argued that certain forms of intellectual analysis require one to attempt to redefine concepts as far as possible in terms of similarities and to consciously reduce "slippage". However this form of analysis is only one of the countless tasks of language, and itself implies that concepts are vague.

The conclusion of this argument is that by adopting an empirical approach to language one does not need to assume that the existence of a linguistic category entails that all instances of that category share one trait in common. With respect to social categories, it means that one does not need to make any *a priori* assumptions about the traits of group members simply because there is a group label which can and is applied to all of them. Any such inferences must be based upon empirical investigation. Under certain circumstances this approach could have important practical consequences which might be different from the consequences of the nominal essence approach. The social approach would imply that political and social categories used by any group would have to be investigated on their own merits. Their use could be accepted or rejected depending on practical and empirical considerations. One would not feel constrained to assert that simply because such categories are used the world must conform to their linguistic structure. The search for true, as opposed to false, consciousness consists to no small degree in the rejection of impractical and fallacious categories.

The social approach is better suited than the individual approach to examine the ideological features of language. It is not the overt expression of ideological sentiments, which is of relevance here, so much as the covert expression of ideology in the language itself. Thus Wittgenstein's rudimentary language between the builder and his assistant is composed of commands, which in themselves reflect the social relationship between the master and his servant. The language composed entirely of commands is the linguistic expression of a hierarchical social order. Similarly Vygotsky's approach enables one to link processes of linguistic change with processes of social change. In this regard Fishman, Ferguson and Gupta (1968) have shown how the growth of national consciousness in developing countries is often accompanied by a deliberate emphasis on the national language. Fellman (1973) has also suggested that the national languages of former colonies reflect their material and intergroup status. The language is often underdeveloped like the country itself, and relies on words and expressions from the language of the erstwhile colonial master. In this respect the linguistic dependence mirrors the economic dependence of neo-colonialism. A final example of the way a language in itself can reflect the group situation, is taken from fiction. Orwell's novel *1984* shows how the lack of linguistic concepts, rather than their presence, can have ideological significance. He describes the state of Oceania, ruled by the inner party members, according to the ideology of Ingsoc. One of the means by which they attempt to maintain complete political control over the outer party members is through the language of Newspeak. The vocabulary of Newspeak was so designed that dissident thoughts were impossible to formulate in the given concepts. The language "differed from almost all other languages in that its vocabulary grew smaller instead of larger every year. Each reduction was a gain, since the smaller the area of choice, the smaller the temptation to take thought" (Orwell, 1961 edn., p. 254). Thus the political control of the inner party members is reflected by the linguistic control they possess over Newspeak. In this example, Orwell illustrates neatly the relation between linguistic change and social change, and how a language itself can serve an ideological purpose. These are issues that will be returned to later, with relation to the creation and maintenance of social labels. Before that, it is necessary to elucidate the nature and psychological significance of social categories.

Uses of social categorisation

The upshot of the previous discussion is that the existence of a particular linguistic label does not of itself imply that everything that is called by that label must necessarily share some common property or quality. To illustrate this point further, Kurt Lewin's (1948) discussion of the Jews as a social group will be considered; in the course of his discussion, the issue of what constitutes a social group is raised. Lewin's answer to this question provides a good introduction to some of the problems involved in elucidating the nature of social categorisations.

Lewin reaches the same general conclusion that Wittgenstein and Vygotsky arrived at in their analyses of non-social concepts: namely, that there was no one central feature about all those who have called themselves, or have been called, "Jews" throughout history. Thus the Jews, and by implication the members of any major social group, could not be said to possess a common essence which was peculiar to all members of their group and not to be found in the members of any other group. Lewin generalises from his example of the Jews to dismiss the notion that similarity between group members can be the crucial variable determining the existence of social groups. Nevertheless, he does not leave the matter there, but goes on to declare that the constitution of social groups is based on a different principle, other than similarity between members. This other principle is based upon the notion of interdependence. Lewin expresses it thus:

> . . . it is not similarity or dissimilarity of individuals that constitute a group, but interdependence of fate. Any normal group, and certainly any developed and organized one, contains and should contain individuals, of a very different character. (Lewin, 1948, p. 165.)

> It is not similarity or dissimilarity that decides whether two individuals belong to the same or to different groups but *social interaction or other types of interdependence*. A group is best defined as a dynamic whole based on interdependence rather than on similarity. (Lewin, 1948, p. 184, italics in original.)

Having come to the conclusion that groups are not based upon the similarities between their members, Lewin seems to be casting about for some other criterion of group membership. The thinking behind this seems to be that if similarity is not the key variable, then there must be some other key variable to account for the subjectively felt unity of social groups. Therefore he offers the notion of "interdependence of fate". In the second of the two passages cited above, he even seems to be offering "social interaction" as a possible defining characteristic of group membership. This, however, would seem to be completely unrealistic. Applied to Lewin's chosen example, it is patently not the case that all Jews since Abraham have been in contact with one another. The variable of social interaction may be a sufficient defining characteristic for certain small-scale laboratory groups (see for instance Homans's (1951) definition based on behavioural interaction), but it is clearly inadequate to deal with actual groups existing in a historical situation.[2] The importance of large-scale national, ethnic, religious, class groups, etc. extends beyond the realm of face-to-face interaction situations. However, Lewin offers no further formal, or even informal definition of "interdependence of fate". Without any explanation of what this concept means in terms of actual group phenomena, it must remain somewhat vacuous—by itself it adds nothing to the study of group and intergroup processes.

2. In fact there are good reasons for doubting whether the variable of social interaction provides a good basis for defining the small experimental group. For instance, DeLamater (1974) in his discussion of the problems of defining small experimental groups argues that other variables need also to be taken into consideration.

Two attempts to give further substance to Lewin's concept of inter-dependence of fate can be mentioned, since they afford a certain in-sight into the problems of group definition. Firstly, Rabbie and Hor-witz (1969) investigated the effect of "interdependence of fate" upon intergroup perceptions in a laboratory experiment of intergroup re-lations. There were three experimental conditions in which ingroup members were said to have interdependent fates—in these groups, the ingroup members either *all* received a valued reward, or *all* the members of the outgroup received the same reward. The results of this experiment showed that the division of rewards on a group basis in an intergroup situation, produced strong intergroup attitudes. This can be compared to the control conditions in which there was no division of rewards on a group basis and consequently no intergroup attitudes. However interesting Rabbie and Horwitz's results are, they are, nevertheless, only tangentially related to Lewin's problem. Rabbie and Horwitz have operationalised the concept of interdepend-ence of fate such that it stands for the equal allocation of group out-comes in an intergroup situation. Nevertheless it is clear that equality of material outcomes cannot be taken to be a defining characteristic of group membership. The existence of societies, cultures and small groups with palpably unfair distribution of material rewards contra-dict the idea that Lewin's interdependence of fate can be understood in this way. Rabbie and Horwitz's operational definition of inter-dependence refers to an empirical question concerning the amount of intergroup identification occuring within certain sorts of group struc-ture. Such structures cannot be taken as being universal characteristics of all groups, or even of all laboratory groups.

Campbell (1958) discusses the problem of group membership with relation to what he terms "common fate". Although he derives this notion directly from Gestalt principles of perceptual organisation, it nevertheless does resemble Lewin's concept of interdependence of fate. Unlike Lewin, Campbell gives an operational definition of his concept of common fate. It stands for a mathematical relationship which determines the degree to which any two entities are situated at the same locus during a given period of time. This can be applied to human social groupings, and the hypothesis is that members of such groupings will have higher "common fate coefficients" with each other than they will have with non-members. In this, Campbell is providing a sophisticated mathematical tool which in fact relates the concept of interdependence of fate to a large degree with that of social interaction. Two persons in continual social interaction will have a very high common fate coefficient. However, it must be noted that Campbell puts forward this method for determining the existence of groups as only one of a number of possible measurements. It is quite easy to imagine groups where the coefficient of common fate would be a bad predictor of membership. For instance, hierarchical social orders within a given society might have a low internal common fate coefficient and a high intergroup coefficient—masters may have more day-to-day interaction with their servants than they have with other members of their master-class. If the common-fate coefficient were to be the only determinant of group membership then one would be forced to deny the reality of such classes or groups. This would be misleading both in terms of objective and subjective groups. Objectively the masters would constitute an actual social and economic group, and psychologically they might also identify themselves as a communal group.

The conclusion from the above would seem to be that social categories like "Jews" should be treated linguistically in the same way as Wittgenstein analysed "games", i.e. there should be no overall assumption of similarity between instances of the concept. However, such a conclusion would be premature. There is one crucial distinction between a social categorisation and a non-social one. This difference can be simply expressed by saying that the instances of a social categorisation can identify with their label, whereas the issue of identification does not arise in the case of the non-social category. A social categorisation can be "reflexive" in that it can alter and determine the self-conception of what is categorised. There is not the possibility of this interplay between the linguistic category and the referent of the category in the case of non-social objects. Therefore to posit a network of similarities between group members is obviously only half the story, if those group members themselves feel a more compelling sense of unity—and especially if this compelling sense of unity is a major social force.

This feeling of similarity might in its starkest form be associated with the label of group membership, rather than any traits or significant social fact underlying the label. Freud (1926, Vol. 20) considered himself a Jew, and identified strongly with the Jewish tradition, but was greatly perplexed about the actual content of this identification. In a sense one might say that firstly there is a social identification that follows the acceptance of a social category as defining in some way the self. The process of social categorisation might entail a feeling of oneness with others who have likewise accepted the same social category. This identification could exist over and above any actual common similarity between members of the category, although it might be a major factor in determining any future creation of group similarities.

Social evidence for this comes from Moerman's (1965 and 1968) studies of the ethnic identification of the Lue, a tribe living in Southeast Asia. Moerman (1968) asked the Lue what it was that differentiated them from their neighbours the Yuan. From his questioning he derived a list of 30 traits. He found that the majority of these traits referred to customs that were no longer practised, or to features that in fact the Lue shared with the Yuan. Thus the Lue seem to use their ethnic identification similarly to the way in which Deese's subjects handled non-social categories. The concepts can be handled in a practical manner without there being a strict logical base to their use. In the case of the Lue ethnic identification, there seems to have been definite reflexive effect following the social use of the ethnic category. Moerman reports that the ethnic label is not used inductively—the Lue do not look for the relevant criterial traits and then decide whether or not to apply the category. In fact, reports Moerman, the perception of common traits follows the use of the category. He explains:

> To put it baldly, once a native decides to give some person an ethnic label, he finds some traits which that person has that can be used to demonstrate that the label has been correctly applied. (Moerman, 1968, p. 164.)

Nor is this a phenomenon restricted only to "natives"—much of the burden of Moerman's argument is directed towards the point that anthropologists themselves use ethnic categories in the same way as the so-called primitive Lue. The evidence from experimental studies of linguistic behaviour seems to support the generality of this. This points to the broad conclusion that the use and acceptance of a social label itself is a worthy topic of investigation, over and above the criterial attributes claimed for any such label. Not only this, the label itself might possibly be an important factor in the processes that mediate social identity, especially in an intergroup situation.

One of the consequences of stressing the non-inductive nature of social concepts is that it allows an understanding of processes involved in the creation and maintenance of a false consciousness. If social categories are not created necessarily as a consequence of perceived similarities, then it is possible for powerful groups within a society to create social labels for subordinate groups that obscure their true situation within that society. The social label need not be a logical outgrowth of the realities, or even the perceived realities, of the situation. In fact the labels might serve the purpose of obscuring such realities. The effect of the social acceptance of such labels might in fact be to confirm in actuality their substance. As Moerman (1968) pointed out, one of the consequences of the social identification is the justification and demonstration of its applicability. In this respect the social reality can be made to conform to the false consciousness, and the position of the powerful group legitimated. Other consequences of this will be considered later in this chapter.

For the present, attention will be confined to certain remarks concerning the social origin and social use of group categorisations. Quite obviously there are an infinite number of social categories possible, only a small percentage of which are in fact realised in social practice. Also, not all existing social categories need be used equally. At times some categories assume a greater importance than others. In modern western societies social groupings based on class or ethnic identification assume a far greater importance than division of persons into blood-groups or by zodiacal sign. The importance of a social category will be related directly to its social usefulness, and this can clearly vary from social context to social context. Thus Moerman (1968) when assessing the nature of the category of "Lue", found it necessary to ask three separate questions: not only did he ask "who are the Lue?", and "what is a Lue", but also "when is a Lue?". In many societies people have multiple identities and group affinities and there is a variety of social labels which they can apply to themselves. It is not a matter of caprice, which label is applied and when, but this itself is determined by social contexts and the social meaning of those labels.

So far only broad outlines concerning the social nature of the categorisation process have been given. There still remain problems concerning the psychological effects of categorisation and its ideological implications. Basically these will be discussed with respect to the two processes, which have been said previously to describe the functions of a linguistic category: namely, differentiation and integration. These two processes can be characterised in the following manner: (a) differentiation refers to the discrete divisions of a continuous universe, effected through the medium of linguistic categories; (b) integration refers to the way in which one linguistic category is related to a network of other categories. Such processes can be said to be integral features of any linguistic category, but they are especially important when considering the significance of social categories. It is through an understanding of the processes of differentiation and integration that an understanding of the psychological force of intergroup stereotypes can be gained. In the following sections the differentiation process as it relates to social categories will be discussed in some detail, together with a line of laboratory experimentation, which has attempted to relate social differentiation to intergroup relations in deliberately contrived situations. After considering the psychological studies of differentiation, the ideological integration of social categories will be considered.

Differentiation and social categorisation

By its nature a linguistic category will divide the world into what are instances of that category and what are not. In stating this, little, if anything, of a psychological nature is presupposed. The real question for the social psychologist is how this differentiation actually occurs and what its psychological effects are. Following on from the discussion of the social nature of categories, one can assert that categories are primarily a matter of social convention. By this it is implied that they reflect the social world rather than some external reality without any social mediation. To illustrate, one can mention the considerable work conducted by "ethnoscientists". Such anthropologists have studied the different ways in which cultures categorise the world. For instance, much emphasis has been placed on the different classificatory systems of colours, plants, animals, kinship systems, etc. employed by various cultures (see for instance the pioneering work of Conklin, 1955; 1964). If one considers the colour spectrum, it is obvious that the objectively continuous wavelength spectrum can be parcelled up into discrete categories in any number of ways. Brown (1965) compares the British division into six basic categories with the Shona of Liberia who employ four categories, and the Bassa of Rhodesia who have only two colour categories. Obviously, neither British, nor Shona, nor Bassa system is any more correct than the others—they are merely different ways of introducing discontinuity into an otherwise continuous dimension. Why a particular category system is best suited in one particular culture and not another is a question that refers to the history and the nature of the culture. What is a simpler matter is that such category systems are socially based, and that if colour categories are to be used, then the spectrum must be divided into segments to correspond to those categories.

One consequence of the division of a continuum into discrete entities is that the resulting entities are psychologically separated. Thus the Englishman will consider the colour "blue" as distinct from "green", whereas the Bassa will tend not to, since both are subsumed under the one Bassa category of "hui". The implication, then, is that the imposition of a system of categories onto an objective continuum will have certain psychological effects, relating to the perception of the instances of the categorisation. For instance, Liberman *et al.* (1957) found that subjects could distinguish sounds from different phonemic categories more easily than they could sounds from the same phonemic category; they did this, although the differences between the same-phoneme sounds and the different-phoneme sounds were identical in terms of the objective physical criteria of spectographic patterns. Similarly Lantz and Stefflre (1964) found a correlation between the codability of colours and the ease with which such colours can be recognised. Thus, like Liberman *et al.* Lantz and Stefflre demonstrated that there are definite cognitive effects following the division of an objective continuum into discrete categories.

Tajfel (1957, 1959 and 1969) has developed a theoretical position that accounts for such cognitive effects of categorisation. Basically he states that the effect of a categorisation is the exaggeration of differences between instances and non-instances of the categorisation. Also, he argues, there is a minimisation of differences between instances of the category. The effect of the category is to enhance differences between X's and non-X's, and to underplay any difference between X's. The division of the colour spectrum into discrete categories causes a cognitive distortion, which results in the shades within a colour boundary seeming more alike than the shades across a colour boundary. Direct evidence for this theoretical position comes from an experiment by Tajfel and Wilkes (1963). In this experiment the subjects had to estimate the length of eight lines. In the control condition the lines were presented to the subjects without any labels, but in one of the experimental conditions the four longest lines were labelled with an "A", and the four shortest with a "B". The presence of these labels was shown to affect the subjects' judgements—the experimental subjects tended to underestimate the differences between the lengths of lines within each category, and also they tended to exaggerate the differences between the two categories. Thus they tended to overemphasise the difference between the shortest of the "A" lines and the longest of the "B" lines, whereas differences within categories were underestimated.

Similar results were found in a study by Campbell (1956). Unlike the Tajfel and Wilkes study, Campbell did not use stimuli that formed two distinct categories—his stimuli were nonsense syllables, which, in terms of their phonetic structure, formed two overlapping similarity groups. The subjects were shown the syllables one at a time, and each syllable was associated with a position on a blank piece of paper. It was arranged that the syllables from each of the two similarity groupings should be associated with different sides of the paper. After being given a number of training trials, the subjects were presented with the syllables on their own and had to estimate their associated position on the blank sheet. The results paralleled those of the Tajfel and Wilkes study. The subjects tended to group the syllables into two distinct groups; and to exaggerate the differences between the associated positions of syllables from different groups, and to underestimate the variance within the two classes.

In the Campbell study it seems as if the subjects were finding a distinctiveness, based upon a classification, even though the categorised stimuli in fact overlapped objectively. It seems that a complex stimulus environment is simplified into neat discrete categories. Evidence for such a process in the real world, as opposed to the artificial laboratory situation, comes from the anthropological study of Leach (1966). Two contradictory trends can be noted in the present discussion on categorisation processes. On the one hand it was argued that categories in natural languages are often based on complex networks of meaning —on the other hand it is now being suggested that categories bring a certain cognitive simplicity to complex environment. Given this basic complexity allied to a simplistic function, it is inevitable that there should be certain stimuli that become difficult to classify in terms of a simple dichotomous category. For instance, an object may contain features that characterise it both as an X and a non-X at the same time; it may thus straddle the gap that attempts to distinguish neatly between the X and the non-X. It is towards such marginal objects that Leach (1966) directs his attention. He follows the structuralist assumption of Lévi-Strauss (1966 and 1969) who asserted that the key concepts in any culture are essentially binary. Examples of the binary oppositions that make up such key concepts are we/they, holy/profane, big/small, etc. According to Leach this is too simple—it ignores the problem of instances that fall between the discrete binary categories. Leach examined animal categories in English and Kachin (a Tibet-Burman language) and concluded that such marginal entities become the focal point for cultural taboos:

> If A and B are two verbal categories, such that B is defined as "what A is not" and vice versa, and there is a third category C which mediates this distinction, in that C shares attributes of both A and B, then C will be taboo (Leach, 1966, pp. 39–40).

Thus the clear-cut binary distinction is saved. Exceptions are treated as something special and venerated, or even, in the case of certain taboos, not mentioned at all. The exception, then, is removed from the plan of everyday living and the dichotomous categorisation left unrefuted by factual exceptions.

Applying these general principles to social categorisations, one can predict that intergroup perceptions will tend to minimise differences between the members of any one social group and exaggerate intergroup differences (Tajfel, 1959, 1969). One might postulate a basic continuum of human differences which is parcelled up into discrete social groups, in a similar way to the colour spectrum. When this occurs, certain differences within an "ethnic mosaic" will become emphasised and certain differences minimised. Examples of intergroup exaggeration can be given. In an experiment conducted by Secord, Bevan and Katz (1956), it was found that highly prejudiced subjects tended to perceive Negro skin colour as being darker than it was. These subjects to whom the category of black-white was obviously a significant one, tended to exaggerate the blackness of Negroes, and hence the differences between blacks and whites. Similar findings relating to height have been reported in an anthropological study of Ruanda by Maquet (1961). The society of Ruanda was composed basically of two ethnic groups, the Tutsi and the Hutu (there was a third, the Twa, who form only a very small percentage of the population). The Tutsi were the dominant group and were in fact physically taller on average than the Hutu. However, Maquet reports that this physical distinction was emphasised in the culture of Ruanda, and was believed to be greater than it was in fact. Thus the social intergroup categorisation is accompanied by an exaggeration of intergroup differences.

Tajfel has attempted to relate these notions to the development of intergroup identities in an experimental research programme (e.g. Tajfel, 1970; Tajfel *et al.* 1971; Billig and Tajfel, 1973; Tajfel and Billig, 1974). This research primarily concentrates on the differentiation aspect of social categorisation as it relates to intergroup relations in contrived laboratory situations. The basic attempt is to separate experimentally the differentiation aspect from the integration aspect and to discover the effects of social categories which are in themselves meaningless. Tajfel *et al.* (1971) pose the basic question underlying this line of research in the following way: "Can the very act of social categorisation, as far as it can be identified and isolated from other variables, lead—under certain conditions—to intergroup behaviour which discriminates against the outgroup and favours the ingroup?" (p. 151).

The findings from Sherif *et al.* (1961) and Ferguson and Kelley (1964), which suggest that the mere existence of an outgroup may be sufficient to produce intergroup behaviour, have already been mentioned. The classic social psychology experiment of Hartley (1946) suggests that outgroup discrimination could occur against meaningless and unreal outgroups, and that intergroup behaviour may not be dependent upon any realistic intergroup conflict. In Hartley's experiment, it was found that the subjects gave stereotyped outgroup responses to two fictitious national categories, inserted in a list of genuine national categories. This experiment has been replicated more recently by Hall (1968) although there have been criticisms of the original study (e.g. Fink, 1971). These experiments suggest that under certain circumstances negative outgroup bias might be generalised to cover all outgroups *qua* outgroups, i.e. that the important factor is the outgroup category by itself, rather than any meanings attached to that category. However, it would be wrong to divorce biases against outgroups from identification with ingroups; the existence of a sharply delineated outgroup presupposes also a sharply delineated ingroup. In the case of Hartley (1946) the outgroups may have been fictitious, but the ingroup certainly was not; the subjects all belonged to actual national groups which must have served as a comparison against which to judge outgroup attitudes. So even if the particular outgroup may have been bogus, the ingroup identification cannot have been. The research question, that follows from these experiments, is whether any sort of meaningful intergroup differentiation will occur if both the ingroup and the outgroup are in some sense artificial categories. In other words can an inherently meaningless intergroup situation be created in a laboratory setting?

Rabbie and Horwitz (1969) and Rabbie and Wilkens (1971) provide two experimental studies, which suggest that social categorisation by itself is insufficient to produce intergroup effects. Both were primarily interested in testing other hypotheses concerning intergroup interaction: Rabbie and Horwitz (op. cit.) were concerned with operationalising Lewin's concept of "interdependence of fate" in a laboratory study of intergroup processes, and Rabbie and Wilkins (op. cit) had their main interest in the effects of the anticipation of future interaction upon ingroup and intergroup processes. Both studies, however, contained control groups relevant to the study of social categorisation in an intergroup setting. These control conditions were identical in both studies. The control subjects were randomly divided into two groups of three subjects each—the "blue group" and the "green group". The groups were seated at opposite sides of a table and all the subjects worked on their own at several tasks, and then were asked to rate the members of their own group and the members of the outgroup on several personality-rating scales. The results from these rating-scales did not reveal any ingroup bias: the subject did not rate the ingroup members more highly than they rated the outgroup members. It seems that the subjects ignored the group categorisations when they made their responses. Rabbie and Horwitz (1969) concluded from this that "group classification *per se* is insufficient to produce discriminatory evaluations" (p. 272).

There are, however, reasons for thinking that Rabbie's conclusion may in fact be restricted and that his control conditions have not shown that categorisation on its own is incapable of producing an intergroup effect. In the two control conditions there was no possibility of the subjects displaying actual intergroup behaviour; all that they had to do was to rate perfect strangers on certain scales in what they thought was a study of impression-formation. Tajfel *et al.* (1971) and Turner (1974) have discussed the procedure of these control groups in some detail and have argued that, in this experimental setting, the variable of categorisation was not in any way made relevant to the dependent variable of the rating scale. Therefore Tajfel *et al.* and Turner conclude that these experiments do not constitute by themselves a clear-cut disconfirmation of the notion that social categorisation can affect intergroup relations.

In order to test this hypothesis, the Tajfel research programme created experimentally groups which were as minimal as possible. These groups lacked most of the attributes associated with real groups. There was no face-to-face interaction between the subjects, no knowledge about other group members, no utilitarian value to be gained from ingroup identification. Subjects were merely told that they were in a particular group—the dependent variable in these minimal group studies was whether, having been assigned group membership, the subjects would give more money to unidentified and anonymous ingroup members than to unidentified and anonymous outgroup members. The original experiments (Tajfel (1970), Tajfel *et al.* (1971)) showed unequivocally that subjects did identify with their minimal group classifications to the extent of showing significant ingroup favouritism. It was found that such ingroup bias occurred just as much when the minimal groups were based upon a trivial criterion of membership (underestimating or overestimating dots) as when the criterion was based on a value-dimension (good or bad performance on the dot guessing task).

This basic finding has been replicated on a number of occasions (e.g. Billig and Tajfel, 1973; Tajfel and Billig, 1974; Doise and Sinclair 1973; Doise *et al.* 1972; Turner 1973). The study by Billig and Tajfel (1973) showed that such intergroup effects cannot be interpreted in terms of the interpersonal hypothesis of similarity-attraction (Byrne, 1969 and 1971). In this experiment an attempt was made to separate the variable of categorisation from any presumed similarity between members of the same group. In previous minimal intergroup experiments the subjects had been categorised on the basis of some defining attribute, however trivial. As a consequence, the resulting intergroup bias could be understood in terms of similarity-attraction. In order to test this information Billig and Tajfel separated the variables of interpersonal similarity and social categorisation in four experimental conditions. These conditions were as follows: (*a*) social categorisation with interpersonal similarity, as in the minimal intergroup experiments just described; (*b*) social categorisation without similarity—the subjects were divided into explicitly random groups; (c) similarity without categorisation—subjects could make the monetary choices on the basis of interpersonal similarity, but there was no mention of "groups" at all; (d) no similarity and no categorisation—this was merely a control condition. The results showed clearly that the dominant variable in this situation was social categorisation. Interpersonal similarity had some effect on the subjects' choices, but not nearly as much as the variable of social categorisation. In terms of the original hypothesis behind the minimal intergroup studies the key condition of this study is (b)—the social categorisation without similarity. In this condition the subjects showed ingroup bias even though the groups were made totally meaningless; group membership of either "group W" or "group X" was determined by the toss of a coin, there being no similarity criterion between group members. This condition and its replication by Billig (1973) seem to have demonstrated that the mere division of experimental subjects can produce intergroup discrimination in favour of the ingroup, at least in this sort of artificial laboratory setting.

These experiments can be said, then, to constitute a baseline for producing experimental intergroup discrimination. The explicitly random groups in the Billig and Tajfel (1973) and Billig (1973) experiments, would seem to be about as minimal a group as is possible. By increasing the importance of functions of these minimal laboratory groups it has been possible to increase the intergroup effects, i.e. by working up from the baseline and introducing further variables, which are normally associated with groups. Rabbie and Horwitz (1969), Rabbie and Wilkens (1971), Rabbie et al. (1974) found that intergroup bias could be increased if minimal groups expected interaction, or received group-based outcomes. Similarly, Doise et al. (1972) found that an increase in ingroup favouritism accompanied the anticipation of both competitive and co-operative intergroup interaction. Doise and Sinclair (1973) found a similar effect when the groups were categorised in terms of existing and meaningful categories. Therefore, even though ingroup favouritism can be said to occur as a result of minimal group categories, it nevertheless increases with the reality of the categories; as such it bears witness to the importance of the integration process as well as the differentiation process.

In these experiments the existence of ingroup identification is inferred indirectly from the occurrence or non-occurrence of ingroup favouritism. If a subject awards more money to his own group members than to the members of the other group, then he can be said to have identified with his own group. An experiment by Turner (1973) has thrown light upon the strength of this identification in the minimal group situation. This experiment contained conditions in which the subject could award money for himself. However, when he awarded money for himself he was also awarding money for another. It was so arranged that there would often be a clash of interests—that awarding more for the self would mean awarding less for the other. This experiment investigated whether there were conditions under which subjects would show less selfishness when the other was an ingroup member than when he was an outgroup member. It was found that where subjects only had to award money to themselves and another, the group classifications made scant difference—all choices were equally selfish. It was as if the categories "I-other" had replaced the categories ingroup-outgroup as regards determining choices. However, the interesting finding was that ingroup preferences were found if the subject had to complete the self-other payment matrices *after* having shown ingroup favouritism in a minimal intergroup situation in which he had been dividing rewards between two other people. Once the subjects had identified with the ingroup and made meaningful intergroup responses, this ingroup identity seemed to continue. Not only this, the identity was strong enough to make subjects award money against their own personal interest in favour of a fellow group member —something they were not prepared to do for outgroup members. Thus Turner's (1973) experiment suggests that the ingroup identification, found in these minimal intergroup situations, can under certain circumstances be strong enough to replace more individualistic orientations.

Before attempting to assess the theoretical implications of these studies, the methodological criticism of Gerard and Hoyt (1974) should be mentioned. They claim there is a methodological flaw in these studies: the subjects are faced with a forced-choice situation, in which they have to favour either an ingroup member or an outgroup member. Gerard and Hoyt argue that it is not surprising that ingroup favouritism results, since the subjects are given little else on which to base their decisions. The implication is that if the forced nature of the choice were taken away, the resulting ingroup favouritism would disappear. It is interesting to note that Fink (1971) has made a similar

criticism of Hartley's (1946) experiment, which showed significant outgroup bias against fictional outgroups; when Fink made a neutral response category available to the subjects, the negative outgroup valua-
tions disappeared. Thus with relation to the minimal intergroup situation, the question is whether the situation is a forced-choice one, and,
if it is, whether this materially affects the resultant ingroup favouritism.

However, Gerard and Hoyt are wrong in assuming that the standard
minimal intergroup situation is in fact a forced-choice one as described. It is not the case that subjects, by the nature of the task, have
to choose between either showing ingroup favouritism or showing
outgroup favouritism, and that these are the only two responses available to them. It is also open to the subjects to respond in terms of
fairness, which many of them do, or in terms of attaining as much as
possible for all subjects, regardless of group membership—this strategy,
being one that is not commonly used. The standard minimal intergroup
situation is not a forced-choice situation in which group favouritism
must be demonstrated. If this is true of the basic situation, then there
are also certain experimental manipulations which have produced
conditions with even greater response possibilities. If, in such conditions, there is significant ingroup favouritism, then the forced-choice
methodological criticism cannot still be upheld, as explaining away
the experimental results. Firstly, the experimental condition in the
first experiment conducted by Tajfel et al. (1971) can be mentioned
—in this experiment in the "value" condition the subjects were divided
into groups on the basis of good and bad performances on the preliminary tasks. Consequently it was open to the subjects not to show
ingroup favouritism as such, but to have rewarded merit, by awarding
the money to the "better accuracy" guessers. There is evidence that a
strategy of rewarding merit is adopted under similar circumstances,
when there is no explicit categorisation into groups (Chase, 1971). In
this study, which was essentially interpersonal rather than intergroup,
Chase found that her subjects consistently awarded the money to the
good judges, who they considered had "earned it" and had "deserved
it" (Chase, 1971, p. 60). Another experiment also testifies to the reality
of rewarding merit as possible strategy—this is the study by Wilson
and Miller (1961), in which winning teams in the prisoner's dilemma
intergroup game were rated more highly than losing teams. The
strategy of rewarding merit therefore does seem to be a viable one;

the point is that in the Tajfel *et al.* value condition it was a very possible strategy, but was not employed by the subjects. Also, the results from the Chase study suggest that it was the explicit group categorisation, which influenced subjects not to reward merit but to show ingroup favouritism.

The effects of two other experimental manipulations become difficult to explain according to the forced-choice critique. Firstly there is the result by Turner (1973) that under certain circumstances subjects will adopt the ingroup-outgroup categorisation rather than following a strategy of self-versus-others. In this situation subjects will adopt the strategy of ingroup favouritism at the expense of the more obvious and more profitable strategy of self interest. Similarly the forced-choice explanation cannot account for Billig and Tajfel's (1973) result that there is a greater likelihood of subjects showing intergroup favouritism, rather than using interpersonal similarity to affect their responses. If it is true that the subjects would be equally responsive to any way of allocating the rewards, then an experimental situation stressing interpersonal similarity should have as much affect as a situation stressing intergroup division. The Billig and Tajfel findings pointed to the greater potency of the social categorisation variable over the interpersonal variable. Given this finding, and those mentioned above, one can state that the basic minimal intergroup situation is not in itself a forced-choice situation. Not only this, when experimental manipulations provide more alternative ways of responding the ingroup favouritism does not necessarily disappear; and lastly under identical conditions ingroup favouritism can be shown to be a much more powerful response than interpersonal attraction to similar others. All in all, the forced-choice methodological criticism of the minimal intergroup situations does not appear to have reduced the resulting ingroup favouritism to the status of an artifact.

If the methodological critique is rejected, then it is still necessary to evaluate what, if any, theoretical significance these artificial minimal group experiments might have. An early explanation of the resulting bias was in terms of a hypothesised "generic norm" of ingroup favouritism (Tajfel, 1969 and 1970; Tajfel *et al.* 1971). For instance, Tajfel (1970) refers to a "generalised negative attitude towards outgroups" (p. 136). Stated in this form the concept of a "generic norm" of ingroup favouritism would seem to resemble the ethnocentric hypothesis. In the previous chapter the simple thesis of ethnocentrism was criticised, and the same criticisms could equally well apply to any explanation based upon the concept of a generic norm. In particular such a thesis does not deal with the negative identifications of certain disadvantaged groups and fails to relate such group identities to the wider ideological context.

It should be noted that Tajfel has abandoned the "generic norm" hypothesis as an explanation of the minimal group situation. His more recent position concentrates upon the importance of social comparison processes, both with respect to the narrow experimental situation and to the dynamics of large-scale intergroup phenomena. The social comparison framework has been outlined, in articles by Tajfel (1972) and Turner (1975). Neither article is intended to be a completely rigorous and fully developed theoretical structure—rather they are presented as the first steps towards a theory of intergroup relations, and this fact should be borne in mind in the following discussion of the explanation. In essentials the approach by Tajfel (1972) and Turner (1975) represents an attempt to incorporate the variables of social comparison, social categorisation and social identity in a general description of intergroup processes. Arguments have already been offered here concerning the close connection between the variables of social identity and social categorisation, so this aspect need not be discussed in any further detail. The focus of attention accordingly will be on the relation of these two variables to the third variable—that of social comparison.

Both Tajfel and Turner take as their starting-point Festinger's (1954) theory of social comparison processes. Festinger's theory essentially concerned the social comparisons made by individuals and not by groups. As such his theory is situated at the level of interpersonal processes. Essentially, Festinger's theory of social comparison asserted that individuals have a drive to evaluate themselves in terms of other people; in other words, they are motivated to check their own abilities and opinions with reference to the abilities and opinions of others. Thus their standards are primarily social ones, not objective physical ones (cf. however, Tajfel's (1972) criticism of this distinction drawn by Festinger). This drive to compare oneself with others has, in Festinger's formulation, a special characteristic; individuals desire to be at least as proficient as those they compare themselves to, particularly when these comparisons relate to individual abilities. Therefore individuals are motivated to test their own abilities *vis-à-vis* those of others, but they will do so in a way that does not threaten their own self-esteem. This second part of the hypothesis, relating to the preservation of self-esteem, determines which targets will be selected for comparison. There will be a tendency for individuals to compare themselves to others of equal ability or of slightly lower ability. They will not compare themselves to those of infinitely greater ability than themselves as this would damage their own self-esteem. This represents the essential features of Festinger's motivational theory of inter-individual social comparison processes; in passing, it can be noted that Festinger does offer the qualification that this describes the way individuals behave "in Western culture" (Festinger, 1954, p. 124).

At first sight, Festinger's social comparison theory would seem to be an unpromising basis for constructing a theory of intergroup processes; it is basically an approach pitched at the level of interindividual processes, rather than at specifically intergroup processes. The research arising from the theory has likewise been interindividual (e.g. Wheeler, 1966; Wheeler *et al.* 1969; Samuel, 1973). Also, the social comparison theory bears all the traces of being a universal organismic theory, notwithstanding the one qualification by Festinger, mentioned above. The fact that social comparison processes are represented as stemming from motivational drives implies that these processes operate regardless of cultural setting. There is no point to postulating the existence of a drive unless it is assumed to be culture-free and a universal characteristic of mankind. As such the social comparison theory can be seen as attempting to describe basic non-social processes that are the crucial determinants of social phenomena. In the same way, Festinger's theory of cognitive dissonance (Festinger, 1957) which can be seen as being a development of the social comparison theory, is essentially a non-social universalistic theory, (detailed criticisms of this and other universalistic non-social approaches can be found in Harré and Secord, 1972).

Both Tajfel and Turner attempt to remove certain of the key notions of Festinger's social comparison theory away from its orientation towards the drives of pre-social individuals; theirs is an attempt to transplant the theory into an explicitly social context, that can operate to illuminate certain intergroup processes. Firstly it should be noted that the connections between social comparison theory and other more social theories have previously been commented upon. For instance, Pettigrew (1967) draws parellels between social comparison theory, and the notions of comparison level, reference groups and relative deprivation. There has already been occasion to criticise in detail descriptions of relative deprivation that are phrased in individualistic terms (see the previous discussion of the work of Berkowitz and Gurr). Nevertheless, it was also argued that it is not necessary that such a concept should be individualistic—it can also be socially related to matters relating to group ideology and group relations. Runciman (1966) distinguishes between "egoist" and "fraternalist" deprivation. The egoist deprivation is essentially individualistic, in that it refers to the deprivation an ingroup member feels regarding the status of possessions of his fellow ingroup members. The fraternalistic deprivation is, on the other hand, essentially an intergroup process in that it reflects a group's concern about its status with regard to other groups.[3] Similarly it is possible to make a distinction between egoist and fraternalist processes of social comparison. If such a distinction is drawn, then it can be said that Festinger (1954) concentrates almost exclusively upon egoist comparisons, whereas Tajfel (1972) and Turner (1974) specifically aim to develop some of the fraternalist implications of social comparison theory.

The essentials of Tajfel's and Turner's account of intergroup relations can be outlined in the following way: every social group attempts to achieve and preserve a positive social identity, and such an identity is always achieved in contradistinction to an outgroup (the reasons for this last assertion have been mentioned in the previous discussion of social categorisation and social identity). Tajfel and Turner both elaborate further on the notion that a social category marks a group off from a particular outgroup, and they state that such a social category is useless unless the ingroup can be compared to the outgroup upon a particular dimension, or number of dimensions. What is more these dimensions will be important for the maintenance of the ingroup's identity and so will become value-laden and intergroup distinctions will be made on these dimensions. Just as Festinger (1954) postulated that social comparisons will be unidirectional as positive identities are sought and achieved, so Tajfel and Turner postulate that a similar trend of group comparisons will be found, as the ingroup attempts to establish a positive social identity in comparison with an outgroup.

3. See also Vanneman and Pettigrew (1972) for a comparison of "fraternal" and "egoist" deprivation with respect to race relations.

Two brief points can be made about this account of intergroup processes. The first is that the achievement and preservation of ingroup identity must be seen as primarily an ideological process, if there is to be no backsliding into individualistic reductionism. Positive group identity must refer to the ideological beliefs which a group produces, and not to beliefs that the individual members happen by chance to arrive at due to a coincidence of individualistic psychological processes. The second point is that the theory carries with it certain similarities to the generic norm, or ethnocentric approach, discussed previously. Like the generic norm approach, there is the assumption that every social group will attempt to view itself positively and view outgroups negatively. However, the social comparison approach represents a more sophisticated theoretical development from the generic norm approach, and it avoids some of the criticisms that were made of the latter approach. In particular, the social comparison approach does not assume social stability, but also can provide an account of the dynamics of social change. It postulates that social change will occur when a positively valued identity cannot be attained by a group. When there is a glaring inequality in favour of the outgroup along some dimension of comparison, there will then be pressure from the ingroup to change the values of that dimension or to change the dimension of comparison. Turner illustrates an ingroup change of the dimension of comparison, by citing the experiment of Lemaine (1966). In this experiment two groups of children both were required to build a hut, but one of the two groups was deliberately hampered in this task and so could not build as good a hut as the other group. The handicapped group then attempted to create a different standard of comparison between the two groups, other than hut building. Tajfel illustrates the process of value change by referring to the Black Power movement's attempts to create a positive social identity for the Blacks by altering the negative value, which had been placed on blackness, into a positive celebration of blackness. In this case the same dimension of intergroup comparison is retained (that of skin-colour), but the values attached to that dimension are changed.

Before the wider implications of this approach are discussed in any detail, its relevance to the minimal intergroup experimental findings will be mentioned. Turner gives a full account of the relation between the social comparison approach and the experimental results. The details of his analysis will not be entered into here, especially as they relate to the particulars of the various experimental designs. Basically, he argues that the ingroup favouritism, found in the minimal intergroup situation, is a *means* for the subjects to achieve positively valued group distinctiveness, rather than being a *product* of such a distinctiveness. He argues that it was only by awarding more money to the ingroup that the subjects could achieve a positive ingroup identity in terms of the social categories provided by the experimenters. Thus the social identity is achieved through showing ingroup favouritism, rather than ingroup favouritism following from the acceptance of social identity. However, the way in which comparative and categorisation processes operate in the minimal experimental situation may be by no means a simple matter. Much more experimentation is needed before one can state with any degree of certainty how these processes may combine to produce the ingroup bias that is commonly found in this experimental paradigm. Tajfel *et al.* (1971) found there were no differences between positively-valued, negatively-valued, and neutral-valued social categories, these might be expected if ingroup favouritism were a consequence of positive and negative values. Rabbie *et al.* (1974) has shown that weak groups under co-operative circumstances develop a stronger positive identity than strong groups, whereas the reverse is the case under competitive conditions. In this way the definition of the situation may interact with comparison and categorisation variables. This implies that ingroup favouritism may not be the result of a simple desire to achieve a positive social identity, but may also have inter-connections with other variables in the intergroup context. Certainly neither Tajfel (1972) nor Turner (1975) present their theoretical outlines as being more than tentative guidelines for future investigations; both recognise the need for much more experimental evidence before the minimal intergroup situation can be fully understood and its theoretical implications established.

If there is need for a greater integration of variables at the level of experimentation, then also there is need for the social comparison explanation to be more fully integrated with wider theories of social processes. Its stress on group identity can be criticised for not sufficiently detailing the connection between such identity and ideological factors as they relate to the objective positions of groups. This can be illustrated by referring to the processes of social change described by the social comparison approach. Primarily these refer to the process by which dimensions of social comparison are altered and also to the process by which the values attached to the dimension are altered. As such, the approach is describing changes in ideological conceptions, or cultural changes, rather than changes in actual intergroup positions. The implication is that if a group has a negative self identity then it needs to change this identity. However the origin of this negative identity needs also to be established, and the conditions that have given rise to it must be changed as well. It is pertinent to mention the criticisms by Staples (1973) against those Blacks, who view Black liberation merely in terms of cultural expression, and not economic and political liberation as well. Similarly any theory of social change in an intergroup context which concentrates upon changes in group perceptions, cannot do justice to the political elements of social movements. If group ideologies are the outcome of the group's objective social situation, then changes in group ideologies must also take into account changes in that objective social situation.

The negative "self-images" of the Blacks in America, which were allegedly prevalent before the Black liberation movements of the middle twentieth century, should neither be attributed to personal failings of individual Blacks, nor to the collective failure of the Blacks to find new dimensions of comparison or to change the value of black skin colour (cf. Nobles, 1973). Black liberation is not to be achieved merely by the coining of slogans such as "Black is beautiful" nor by the adoption of "Afro" clothes and hair-styles. The crucial facts of political and economic submission are left untouched by such cultural manifestations on their own. The way forward for an oppressed group is through the articulation of an ideology of discontent which reflects and crystallises their opposition to the forces that oppress them. Thus intergroup domination is not resolved by changing the surface factors of the intergroup ideology, but changing the realities of that domination by means of an ideological consciousness that leads to effective political action. In the construction of such an ideology, previously held values concerning the negative worth of the ingroup must obviously be discarded, but this in itself is not enough. Similarly, it is not enough to describe the processes of intergroup change by reference merely to the changes in ideology, without account for the origin and purposes of these changes as social facts.

Given this, it is possible to characterise under certain conditions the processes of "dimension of comparison change" and "value of comparison change" as processes of social control rather than as genuine processes of social change. Thus a dominant group could maintain its position of dominance by manipulating the ideology of the subordinate group to provide such changes. This would be a strategy of warding off real challenges to its position of dominance, by providing sops to the dignity of the oppressed group without materially altering the status of the oppressed group. This is why Black cultural nationalism, devoid of any political analysis, has been attacked as being in the interests of those who control white racism. As such it would constitute a variety of false consciousness, which prevents the group acting as a group-in-itself. Similarly it is possible to characterise the mere acceptance of particular social categories as being evidence for false consciousness. If a dominant group maintains its position through a policy of divide and rule, the crucial social change, as far as the real interests of the subgroups is concerned, is not to be gained from the achievement of a positive subgroup identity. There is need to enquire as to the origin and function of these subgroup categories, and to realise that these categories themselves, and the resulting social identities, are mechanisms of social control. If both subgroups manage to transcend these categories, it will be through an analysis of their situation *vis-à-vis* the dominant group, rather than through balancing self-esteem by selecting the "right" targets for comparison—in such a case one must necessarily enquire for whom such targets are right.

It is therefore necessary to place any fraternalist comparisons within the total intergroup context. If they are abstracted from the total context, including the material conditions that underlie the intergroup relations, it is possible to come to the paradoxical conclusion that a particular positive self-identity of a social group serves that group ill. One should therefore be wary of any assertion that all social groups have some sort of desire to achieve a positive social identity—since this is taking the origin and continuation of that group as a group for granted. It may be the case that people, or at least the majority of them, wish to belong to groups that provide a positive social identity, just as they wish to avoid subjugation to alien forces. Nevertheless, a positive social identity is not something that occurs abstractedly apart from a social ideology and structure. As such one should be careful not to place undue emphasis on this one aspect of the social creation of ideology. This might lead to the cynical, and unwarranted conclusion, that one can keep people happy by giving them their positive value and their dimension of comparison.

Social categorisation and ideological integration

The minimal intergroup experiments have attempted to investigate the differentiation aspects of social categories in isolation from any more meaningful group or intergroup structures. However, the social context of this minimal process of intergroup differentiation should not be forgotten. Previously it was suggested that Wittgenstein's rudimentary language between the builder and his assistant reflected the social hierarchy which determined the relationship between these two individuals. So too, the social origin and function of the minimal intergroup categories should be examined. It is not the case that the social psychology experiment represents a totally vacuous situation, in which only the "official" dependent and independent variables have any significance. As was discussed in the previous chapter, such situations are often part and parcel of wider social processes. In this respect the minimal intergroup experimental situation is no different.

An alternative methodological criticism to the one made by Gerard and Hoyt (1974), can be advanced. This line might concentrate upon the role of the experimenter in the minimal group experiment. It could be argued that the experimenter invites intergroup responses from the subjects by stressing the group categories. Criticisms along these lines have been suggested by Chase (1971) and Deutsch, Thomas and Garner (1971). Deutsch (1973) states that the laboratory intergroup effects will not be found unless the group categories are "utilised by a prestigious authority" (p. 69). This may be thought of as some sort of experimenter-bias, which in a sense trivialises the experimental results. It might be held that the prestigious authority (the experimenter) is demanding that the social categories be used by the subjects; and of course the experimental situation is so designed that the only meaningful way of using the categories is to show ingroup favouritism. Therefore the social categories might be thought of as some sort of demand characteristic which predisposes the subjects' responses in terms of ingroup identification.

In many respects this is true; however, the important point is the theoretical implications of such demand characteristics. On the one hand they may be thought of as invalidating the experimental results, and that the influence of the experimenter should, in some way or other, be eliminated from the experimental situation. However it would be absurd to attempt to eliminate the influence of the experimenter from such an experimental situation, which is deliberately set up by the experimenter and administered by him. Also, the form of experimenter influence is not a trivial one; it is not as if the experimenters have given the subjects a particular order and the subjects obeyed it. Rather, as has already been shown, one of several response possibilities has been used by the subjects in a situation specifically designed by the experimenters. Instead of invalidating the results, the role of the experimenter seems to define the sort of theoretical problems, to which the minimal intergroup experiments can be addressed. These problems relate to the power of a prestigious authority to create group divisions, which can be counter to the objective material interests of those who are so divided. These experiments do not describe situations, in which groups have been spontaneously created by their members and which reflect the needs of those members. The group categories and their acceptance by the subjects represent an embryonic form of false consciousness. Thus questions can be asked about the minimal conditions under which an authority can create a false consciousness based upon a group identification (Billig, 1973). The minimal group experiments can be seen as a non-obvious attempt to provide certain answers to this question.

If the above line of reasoning is accepted, then it becomes unreasonable to try to eradicate the influence of the experimenter *a priori* from the situation. On a theoretical level this becomes tantamount to stating that problems of embryonic false consciousness should not be studied in a laboratory intergroup context. Whatever methodological justifications are offered for this, the theoretical consequences are untenable for social psychology. Not only would this restrict social psychological theorising, but it would also prevent a *rapprochement* with a branch of sociological theory, which has made distinct advances in the past ten years or so. It is not just social psychologists who have investigated the process of social categorisation—the labelling process is also well-known to the sociologists investigating the behaviour of deviant groups (e.g. Becker, 1963; 1964; Lemert, 1967). Such writers have tended to concentrate upon the social category of "deviant" and have investigated the ways in which certain groups of people become classified as deviant. Although this approach has tended to have this comparatively narrow focus of attention, it nevertheless has raised some general theoretical issues. In this more general application a similarity with the present approach can be discerned; this is true especially in relation to the social nature of the categorisation, or labelling process, and the social nature of social identity.

Becker formulated what has become known as the labelling theory of deviance. This approach concentrates upon the social processes that produce deviants—it is explicitly opposed to those theories of deviancy that stress any particular personal quality which deviants might be said to possess and which mark them out from all non-deviants. As such there is an affinity with the previous discussion, when it was argued that the existence of any category does not imply the prior similarity of all those subsumed under that category. The reasons for the emergence of a particular social category are themselves social, and any subsequent similarities found between all the members of a social category can well be a direct result of the use and production of that category. According to Becker, once collections of individuals are branded as being "outsiders" or different from the mainstream of society, they will then react in a way that conforms to this category, and will live up to their reputation. The details of the stereotype will vary in different instances, for example, the stereotyped behaviour of a homosexual will differ from that of a drug-addict etc. What is similar is the general process by which the deviant once labelled, will come to identify with the socially described stereotype. On a general level this can lead to the creation of new deviant groups by society, simply by classifying large numbers of people as deviant. This in part will assure that their behaviour will in turn become deviant. Young (1971) in his discussion of marijuana drug-takers has commented how mythical public stereotypes will in fact be self-fulfilling; there is, in his words, a "translation of fantasy into reality" (p. 44).

The approach by the labelling theorists represents an attempt to trace the social origin of certain social categories. By and large, the deviant groups are compared to the rest of so-called normal society, which in fact has created the social phenomena of deviancy itself. This comparison is in itself obviously an over-simplification, but it does highlight an issue, which is crucial to the understanding of the genesis of social categories. This issue relates to the power relations in which the social category is evolved, and by implication to the power relations that result from the use of the category. In the case of the label of deviancy, one can generally hypothesise a gross inequality of power between those who fashion the label and the group which is being labelled. One labelling theorist has commented:

By and large, labels are most easily affixed to those who are without the power effectively to resist a particular definition, and labels are most likely to be used by those with the power (and the need) to define power-less groups in society as deviant in some specific sense. (Taylor, 1971, pp. 158–9.)

Taylor, then goes on to illustrate this general point by referring to those young active soccer supporters, who become labelled as "thugs" and "hooligans", and who have "little power to resist the attribution of these and similar labels" (p. 159).

Consequently one can say that the origin of the deviant group has to be understood in an intergroup context, in which the non-deviant and more powerful group exerts its power by creating the category of deviance. There is no reason why this general formulation should be the unique property of deviant-non-deviant intergroup relations. As Davis (1972) has argued, much of the research into deviancy labelling has been restricted to an over-exclusive emphasis upon esoteric sects; the result has been that the wider implications for more general descriptions of social control processes have been neglected. The fact is that the creation of deviancy labels is only one form of the general process of the creation of social categories. Also the creation of deviancy labels is only one form of intergroup inequalities in power. The social creation of social labels stretches beyond the so-called deviant groups in the society. What however the deviancy research does demonstrate is that the creation of such categories is integrally bound up with the power relations that exist in the intergroup context. It also demonstrates that where unequal power relations exist, the creation of such categories can be used as a form of social control; a possible example of this is provided by Bentley (1972), who shows how a local government can pursue a racist policy through the manipulation of social categories. Likewise Schervish (1973) suggests that the labelling perspective should be widened to account for political processes, and in particular to study the way in which political groups negotiate their group identities. By their narrow focus, the labelling theorists are neglecting a wider and more critical social analysis, and in so doing they are revealing their own conformist assumptions (Thio, 1973). The general conclusion would seem to point to the importance of societal power relations in the dynamics of the creation of social identity, and also that the subjective factors created by such an identity are socially related to the objective factors that underlie their creation. Thus the socially created group stereotypes will mirror the power relations within and between social groups, and will also reflect the changing patterns of such relations (see for instance, Wilson, W. J., 1973, for an account of the power basis of race relations).

The preceding discussion might be taken as implying that the objective conditions in some sense set the stage for the psychological factors involved in the creation of social identity. Neither the social label itself, nor the group ideology it mediates, nor any processes of fraternalist comparison contained in that ideology, can be understood in isolation from one another or from the objective conditions under-lying the intergroup situation. Even in the experimental situation, in which productive economic factors are of necessity eliminated, the power relations between the experimenter and his subjects must be taken as the fundamental *mise en scène*—this last point has been dis-cussed with relation to the particularities of the minimal intergroup experimental paradigm. This is the framework around which all the other experimental variables in this situation must operate. It must not be overlooked because of its obviousness; nor for different reasons should it assume the status of some sort of unwanted contamination.

If the power relations in the intergroup context set the stage for the more psychological variables of social identification, then they also can determine some of the more physical properties of the intergroup situation. These properties can refer to the pattern of group and inter-group interaction, and to the actual physical situation of the group. This point can be illustrated with reference to the minimal intergroup situation, and also it can show the potential and actual interaction of this variable with the other variables. As has already been mentioned, the minimal intergroup experimental situation presents the subjects with a conflict of interest—between their material interests as subjects and the experimenter-defined social identities. One of the interesting features of these experiments is the way that this conflict is revealed in the remarks of the subjects. When the subjects are given the instruc-tions all together in the same room, as likely as not one of them will ask the experimenter how they should award the money. On being told that it is up to them how to award the money, it is common for one of the subjects to say out aloud words to the effect that "it's quite easy— give as much as possible". Whereupon the other subjects will smile in assent, quietly deriding the naïvety of the experimenters. However, when they have to award the money on their own, often isolated in individual cubicles, they rarely give as much as possible. When separated one from another, they would seem to be more vulnerable to the categories of the experimenter and less likely to assert their own collective self-interest as a group.

Billig (1973), has found that by increasing the communication between the subjects the authority of the experimenters can be weakened in this sort of situation. In this way the isolation of the subjects may have been in itself an important factor in determining their false consciousness. Nor is this isolation socially neutral; it is directly produced by the authority group and as such relates to the differential in power relations. An analogy between this situation and real life social groups can be offered. It might be thought that it is no coincidence that working-class movements, such as trades unions, have developed a tradition of group solidarity which has its physical, as well as emotional, manifestation. Thus, in trades union movements, there is an emphasis on mass meetings and mass actions, in which decisions are taken as a result of a public show of hands. Under such circumstances intimidation by the stronger group, the industrial owners and/ or management, becomes less of a danger. It is not surprising that some of the most vociferous demands for secret balloting of all decisions within the trades union movement come from those outside the movement who have most to gain from any internal weaknesses. The strategy of divide and rule may not only refer to the subjective division of the subordinate group into separate factions, but may also refer to an actual physical separation.

In this way, the actual process of differentiation, as effected by social categories, must be related to other social processes. The previous discussion of the social nature of linguistic categories should serve as a warning against talking about categorisation processes in the abstract. In particular the category will be integrated into a wider linguistic and ideological system—the process of differentiation is only one of the characteristics of these processes. Consequently the differentiation of the minimal categories in the intergroup experiments has to be related to the social context of the experiment itself. Two other examples of social differentiation were mentioned at the start of the previous section. The prejudiced white subjects in the experiment of Secord et al. (1956), exaggerated the differences between black and white faces. Similarly the Tutsi of Ruanda exaggerated the physical differences between themselves and the Hutu (Maquet, 1961). In both cases the differentiation was a feature of a wider ideology—the Secord *et al.* subjects held the belief in the racial inferiority of Blacks and the Tutsi adhered to the "premise of inequality", which Maquet argued, underlay their social culture.

The basic point is that social categorisations do not arise in a social vacuum, but are integrated to serve particular ideological ends. This point has been emphasised by Rex (1969), in his discussion of the concept of "race". He argues that the concept of "race" is not just a method of classifying human beings of different types—in fact racial categories cannot be scientifically justified on such grounds: rather the category is linked to certain ideological positions and intergroup situations. Nor is this particular social category unique in this respect; in general, social categories are more than mere labels of differentiation:

> We do not . . . rest content with merely labelling the various forms of social interaction in which we engage, any more than we rest content with a world of discrete physical things. We grope after some kind of anchoring or validating principle which explains why things are and why they should be so. Myth and theology, ideology, philosophy and science all provide us with systematic ways of meeting this need. (Rex, 1969, p. 150.)

In other words, categories do not merely differentiate objects; the categories themselves are also integrated with other categories of meaning and with social practices. Thus the various category systems uncovered by ethnoscientists should not be considered by themselves, but their integration with other linguistic structures must also be recognised. It is one of the achievements of structuralist anthropology to have demonstrated the internal unity of the cognitive worlds of other cultures (Lévi-Strauss, 1966; 1969). Such cognitive worlds do not consist of a series of independent classification systems; on the contrary, there are interlocking and overlapping structures that can only be properly understood in terms of one another. The limitations of merely identifying a classificatory system, without attempting to integrate it with other structures of meaning, can be illustrated with an example from Wallace and Atkins (1960). These writers discuss the English kinship classification system, and make the point that the words "father", "dad", "daddy", "pop" and "old man" all have the same referents in an objectively defined kinship paradigm. However, these words have different connotations; to explain such differences it is necessary to go beyond identifying their referents in the kinship relation. It would be necessary also to explore their semantic meaning and elucidate their connections with other linguistic structures.

In the case of social categorisations this integration with other networks of meaning is particularly important for the creation of ingroup and outgroup stereotypes. As Rex notes, it is not just the categorisation itself that is the crucial factor, but also the meanings attached to such a categorisation. Just as the subjects of the Secord *et al.* study exaggerated the differences between black and white faces, so in a similar study by Secord (1959) the subjects attributed stereotypic judgements to Negroes regardless of the shading of their skin colour, i.e. light-skinned Negroes, perceived as Negroes were judged by the white subjects to have the same stereotyped traits that dark-skinned Negroes were presumed to possess. The traits were attached to all who fell within the category of "Negro". The process of differentiation is attached to a differential integration with other traits or characteristics to produce the full-blown group stereotype (for a fuller discussion of these issues see Tajfel, Sheik and Gardner, 1964; Tajfel 1969a).

The network of connections used to describe the ingroup will be different to those used to characterise the outgroup. Similarly, the term used to denote the social categorisation will itself inevitably be associated with other linguistic structures. Sometimes this can have importance for the pattern of intergroup relations. Thus Gergen (1967), Williams and Stabler (1973) and Stabler and Goldberg (1973) have pointed out how in English the term "white" is associated generally with positively valued meanings and the term "black" with negative meanings. This association, occurring within the semantic structure of the English language, could well be an obstacle to the elimination of racial prejudice. In this, the English language may be reflecting a history of colonial exploitation and racial bigotry, and it is possible that a change in race relations may be accompanied by changes in linguistic usage.[4]

4. There is the possibility that the equation of "black" with negative meanings and "white" with positive meanings may have a wider cultural significance. Wagatsuma (1967) has detailed such a connection to exist in Japan prior to any contact with the Western World, and Bastide (1967) has linked this symbolism to the historical development of Christianity. Gergen (1967) and Williams and Stabler (1973) suggest that such symbolism may have arisen out of man's fear of the dark. However, it would be mistaken to posit this symbolism as a universal and unchanging element in all cultures: the ideology of negritude and Black Power is a deliberate and successful attempt to forge a new symbolic connection for Black peoples.

The example of the Tutsi and Hutu of Ruanda demonstrated how an intergroup division can lead to a perceptual differentiation. This example was taken from a society which was based on an extreme case of intergroup domination. One might hypothesise that where one group dominates another and attempts to justify this on the basis of an ideology of superiority, as did the Tutsi, then the superior group will attempt to create as wide a social differentiation as possible. In this respect Nazi propaganda emphasised the physical differences between the "dark" Semitic races and the "blond Aryans"—also it is not without significance that they forced the Jews to wear the distinguishing yellow star of David. In a similar vein, the British imperialists always maintained a wide social distance from their subject populations; Kiernan (1972), writes that it would have been unthinkable for them to have worn "native" dress in the way that the Dutch did in the East Indies. The British imperialists saw themselves as superiors bringing civilisation to inferior races, whilst the Dutch saw imperialism more clearly in terms of economic profit to be gained. Thus they, unlike the British, were content to exploit the subject populations in an equal alliance with the traditional rulers, and as a consequence such a wide social differentiation was not maintained (Kiernan, 1972, p. 91 ff).[5]

In a situation of intergroup domination, this process of differentiation on the part of the dominant group can be used to perpetuate the ideology of domination, as a result, this gives rise to further domination and differentiation. An example of this relationship between domination and differentiation is provided in the history of the savage domination of the Spartans over the numerically stronger Helots. Oliva (1971) reports that the Spartans regularly used to force the Helots to consume alcohol, so that the youths of Sparta could witness the "wanton debauchery" of the Helots and, by contrast, reaffirm their own abstemious virtue (p. 45). By this custom, the Spartans were emphasising the distinction between their own morality and Helot "immorality" and thereby confirming the ideology which justified and perpetuated their own dominant position. In this way the young Spartans were regularly furnished with "proof" of the inferiority of the Helots. A contemporary analogy of this situation is the South

5. Differences in dress can also be used to emphasise status and power differentials within social groups. For discussions of the uses of uniforms as symbols of interpersonal power, see Joseph and Alex (1972) and Bickman (1974).

African government's continual exploitation and impoverishment of the African population, and thereby continually "proving" the inferior development of the African.

The picture that a group forms of an outgroup is not an unchanging fact of nature, but a product of the intergroup situation and is liable to change as the situation changes. Sinha and Upadhyaya (1960) measured Indian students' attitudes towards the Chinese in February 1969 before the border dispute. The Indians considered the Chinese then to be friendly, progressive, honest, brave and cultured. By December the climate of international relations had changed, and the Indian students were now calling the Chinese aggressive, cheaters, cruel, warmongering and stupid. For changes in the ethnic stereotypes of American college students the results of the classic study by Katz and Braly (1933) can be compared to the findings of Gilbert (1951) and to those of Karlins et al. (1969). Such studies show how the traits and values associated with a certain categorisation can be changed. They point out gross changes, but in order to discover what mediates these changes, it is necessary to look more closely at the categorisation process and its differentiation and integration functions, especially as these relate to changes in ingroup stereotypes.

Research by Zavalloni (1973 and 1973a) has demonstrated that an ingroup identification need not be a simple process, but can contain a number of potentially conflicting facets. In particular, Zavalloni distinguishes between a personal identity and a social identity. It is possible for a person to see himself as a member of a group, but not see himself as possessing all the traits that he associates with the average ingroup member. Where the personal and the group trait identifications correspond to one another, Zavalloni states that the social identity is *egomorphic*, but a lack of egomorphic identity does not imply a damaged self-concept. A person may consider himself to be an atypical member of his group if he is one of the minority within his group who are working to change certain aspects of his group. Thus, in Zavalloni's research, radical French and American students identified themselves only with certain aspects of what they took to be features of their respective national groups. They also perceived themselves to be members of a subgroup within their national group and ascribed different characteristics to this subgroup than to the rest of the national group. In Zavalloni's terms, there was a substantial difference in the ways in which these radical students characterised "we, the French/

Americans" and "They, the French/Americans". The ascribed traits depended on the nature of the categorisation—whether the larger non-egomorphic ingroup, or the smaller egomorphic ingroup was being characterised. In the one case the subjects were differentiating themselves from the wider ingroup and in the other case they were identifying themselves with it. But even in the former case they were not denying membership of that group.

The important point to note from the work of Zavalloni is that it is possible to describe the process of identification with a social group without at the same time denying the reality of processes of social change. She is able to describe the social identity of those who are actively attempting to change the nature of their social group. The lack of an egomorphic identity in a substantial population of a particular group can act as a sign for a significant movement for social change. Such persons are rejecting the accepted stereotypes of their group, and are in some respects forging a new group identity. In saying this, one should be particuarly careful not to imply that social change consists of nothing more than the re-evaluation of traits associated with a group categorisation. Social change implies more than altering the perceived integration of the group label with other categories. The radical French and American students of Zavalloni's surveys wish to affect basic political changes in their respective countries; ideological changes without the more basic structural changes would be pseudo-changes. In a similar vein, the Black liberation movements in America have been attempting to alter the traditional stereotype of the Negro; however, stereotyped beliefs, for example, that the Negro is lazy and unwilling to work will not be destroyed unless the conditions that have given rise to the ideology of racism are changed. In this case the stereotype was directly related to the economic conditions, in which Black Americans have been grossly underpaid and denied regular employment.

Social change can concomittantly produce a change in the ideological traits associated with a social categorisation. If social change can affect the integration of a social categorisation, so then also may it affect the differentiation produced by a group label. The reasons for asserting this are based more on indirect evidence than on clear-cut findings. In the first place there is evidence that differentiation increases when subjects use a categorisation that is important for them (Tajfel and Wilkes, 1963a). Therefore if people accept that a particular categorisation is the right and proper one in a particular circumstance, then there will be an increased differentiation between instances and non-instances of the categorisation. The reverse of this can also be maintained—if people, for some reason, are forced to use a categorisation they deem to be inappropriate, then there will be a corresponding decrease in differentiation. Evidence for this comes from a study by Eiser (1971); in this study subjects had to rate attitudinal statements, which were labelled. When the labels were acceptable to the subjects, there was greater differentiation between the statements they agreed with and those they disagreed with; when the labels were unacceptable this differentiation was significantly reduced. Thus one effect of the rejection of a particular label could be a reduction of differentiation. This might be presumed to occur, if there are no possibilities for changing the connotations or avoiding the use of such a label. In time, one might predict, the loss of differentiation would lead to the loss of usefulness of the label and perhaps its ultimate obsolescence.

An intergroup illustration of the foregoing can be provided by considering a situation where a dominant group maintains its dominance by a strategy of "divide and rule". Thus the subordinate group is split into two subgroups. If these two subgroups begin to see through the false consciousness which keeps them divided, they may then start to reject their subgroup categorisations. They will then cease to emphasise differences between themselves, and thus blur the distinctions created by the subgroup categorisation. However, so long as the dominant group maintains its actual political power, the two subgroups may still be forced to maintain their subgroup identities and labels, as a sign of their submission so to speak. But once they cease to believe in the false consciousness, the labels will lose their power of differentiation. No doubt, if the two subgroups combine to defeat the dominant group, they will reject entirely their former status, and the erstwhile subgroup label will become obsolete. It will have served its purpose for the former dominant group, and with the dominant group's overthrow, there will be an overthrow of its ideological tools of dominance. Under such circumstances, the processes of social change could lead to changes in the psychological differentiation effected by the social categories. In point of fact, such changes would inevitably be accompanied by profound ideological changes, which would affect both the differentiation and integration functions of the relevant social labels.

In this way the psychological effects of social categorisation can be seen as being directly related to the intergroup situation. The creation of a particular group ideology and social identity is wedded to the underlying social conditions. In the hypothetical situation just described, the subordinate groups reject the social analysis of the dominant group; this interpretation of the social structure involved at least three major social categories—the category of the dominant group and those of the two subordinate groups. In rejecting this, the subordinate groups adopt, and thereby identify themselves with, a dichotomous social distinction, between themselves as one group and the dominant group as the other group. In this way the challenge to the dominant group is mediated by a change in ideological conception from three basic social categories to two categories.

In his book *Class Structure in the Social Consciousness* (1963), the Polish sociologist Ossowski discusses the various different typologies of categories that can be used to describe social reality. He compares the dichotomous conception of society with multi-category descriptions of social reality and he describes the situations in which the dichotomous conception will be used. He argues that there are essentially two separate circumstances, in which the dichotomous conception will be employed, functioning either to preserve an existing power élite, or forming the basis of an ideological challenge to the *status quo*. Ossowski argues that the dichotomous conception will be used by a privileged class if its privileges are firmly established and there is a sharp and impenetrable distinction between it and the rest of society. In such cases the dichotomous description of social reality will further the interests of the privileged and will be "an expression of their effort to increase the distance between their class and all the others" (p. 35).

The example which Ossowski offers of a ruling group establishing a dichotomous conception of society is that of the Polish nobility after the sixteenth century. They viewed society as being composed of two classes: those who gave orders (themselves) and those who obeyed (their subjects). However, the dichotomous conception may be an exception for ruling groups. Previously, there has been occasion to mention four regimes that would seem to satisfy Ossowski's requirements of being based upon entrenched and impenetrable ruling classes: the ancient Spartans, the Tutsi of Ruanda, the British imperialists and the white South Africans of today. In none of these instances is the ruling groups' conception of social reality strictly dichotomous. The British imperialists adopted a strategy of "divide and rule" in their administration of the empire: consequently the colonies tended to have social structures based on more complex divisions than the simple British/ native distinction (Pollis, 1973). In Sparta the social order was trichotomous, with the Periokoi forming an intermediate group between the Helots and the ruling Spartans. Similarly, in Ruanda, a third social group existed—this was the Twa, despised equally by the numerically larger Tutsi and Hutu. In contemporary South Africa, there is a basic four-fold social division of ethnic groups: the Whites, Blacks, Coloureds and the Indians.

It may be the case, therefore, that Ossowski somewhat overemphasised the extent to which entrenched ruling groups will employ a strictly dichotomous conception of social reality. However it is also Ossowski's point that the oppressed classes will tend to use the dichotomous conception, and thereby view society as a simple antagonism between rulers and ruled, masters and slaves, poor and rich, oppressors and oppressed, etc. Ossowski contrasts the Marxist and bourgeois interpretation of capitalist society: for the Marxist, capitalism is founded on the essential antagonism of the two major classes—proletariat and bourgeois. On the other hand the capitalist view is based upon a system of gradations which blurs the distinction between worker and capitalist. Nor is this fortuitous; the Marxist dichotomy, like previous dichotomies made by oppressed groups, constitutes a challenge to the status quo, whereas "the propaganda disseminated by the ruling class is opposed to sharp divisions in the mode of perception of the social structure because it is opposed to the idea of the class struggle" (Ossowski, 1963, p. 36).

Disputes about the way social reality is to be categorised are more than disputes about words. Wider practical implications will be involved. What may appear to be a linguistic controversy about the nature and definition of a particular class in a particular society may under certain circumstances be translated into a genuine social controversy; in such a case the disputants will have to act on the basis of their words. Ossowski stresses the social importance of semantic conventions and disputes. In any dispute if we wish to understand "the essential difference between the standpoints involved . . . we should seek this in their incompatible views about reality or in their divergent aims" (1963, p. 171).

If this is accepted then social analysis is one of the primary tasks of any group. This analysis should include accounts of the ways different groups relate to one another, and ultimately to the ways the individual does, and should, relate to his group. The obligations and freedoms permitted to the individual will be contained in the analysis, as well as an account of how well present obligations and freedoms match a stated ideal. If the match is sufficiently imperfect this does not mean that each individual should in isolation take his own remedial action. Except in very special situations this would lead to no improvement. What is required is social action to alter the social conditions which permit more or less individual freedoms.

One might hypothesise that to the extent to which a society can engender its own critical analyses and to the extent to which its leaders are genuinely responsive to demands for changes however radical, dramatic conflicts can be avoided. The regime or ruling group which backs its claim to eternal domination with force and coercion will be acting as a prompt for a revolutionary analysis. If social change is a constant factor in social life, then attempts to suppress all changes and criticisms will be self-defeating in the long term. The exigencies of power today are no insurance against overthrow tomorrow. If one is searching for a constant social psychological factor in the continual processes of social change, then perhaps one might follow the lead of Maquet (1970). He observes the collapse of the traditional structure of group domination in Ruanda; in spite of the tradition of inequality, the "naturally inferior" Hutu finally rose against their Tutsi masters. The illusion of permanent social stability was destroyed because, to use a universal but non-organismic explanation, "people seem never to resign themselves to social inequality" (Maquet, 1970, p. 215).

10

Concluding Remarks

In the preceding discussions of the various social psychological approaches to the study of intergroup relations, one of the main themes to emerge has been the opposition to individualistic reductionism. The trend towards reductionist thinking in social psychology has been a strong one and has a long history within the discipline. Criticisms of the reductionist approach have been offered for a variety of approaches reducing large-scale social phenomena to matters of individual, or at best interpersonal, psychology. This applies, for instance, to social psychological descriptions of intergroup phenomena based upon infantile and unconscious strivings, basic asocial drives, individual feelings of anger, interpersonal relations and personal motivations. In the majority of these cases it has been suggested that the concentration upon the individual or interpersonal aspects has prevented a wider social analysis; in particular, it has prevented an analysis of the social structures of the groups themselves. In this way the individualistic approach prevents any critical comment on those structures; by considering the social structure as a constant given, there must inevitably be an implicit conservative bias in favour of the *status quo*.

Throughout the criticisms of the various reductionist approaches, the importance of social-cognitive variables was emphasised. Simple psychological paradigms were deemed to be insufficient models of intergroup relations insofar as they ignored, or systematically reduced, social-cognitive variables. Thus in the discussions of the frustration-aggression hypothesis, or psychoanalytic theories of displacement and projection, and of game theory rationality, one of the main arguments was to direct attention to the importance of irreducible social factors. As a consequence it was argued that, even in restricted and essentially interpersonal experimental situations, a specifically social analysis was required, especially one that took into account the subjects' perceptions of the experimental situation. There is currently within social psychology a move to interpret experimental social psychological findings in terms of the subjects' beliefs and cognitions; adherents of this approach consider that intersubjective meanings should be the subject matter of social psychology, and these meanings should not be reduced to a more "basic" paradigm, i.e. to more "basic" psychoanalytic, or stimulus-response, processes. Examples of this new approach are the symbolic interactionism of Alexander and Weil (1969) and Alexander et al. (1970) or the ethogenic approach of Harré and Secord (1972) and Harré (1974). Consequently a number of the criticisms and reinterpretations of social psychological experimentation, especially with respect to frustration-aggression and gaming-behaviour, can be seen as being in accord with this trend within social psychological theorising.

However, there are important differences between the present approach and the symbolic interactionist, or ethogenic, perspective. Both approaches share the same non-reductionist orientation. Nevertheless it is the present position that an opposition to reductionism does not of itself constitute an adequate enquiry. Thus Sherif's non-reductionist account of intergroup relations was criticised as being limited. His account, based upon "group goals", was held to be insufficient to explain why groups will pursue "irrational" goals and what the social genesis of group goals could be. In this respect, it was argued that his theory paid too little attention to ideological aspects and particularly to the formation of group identity. To remedy this it was suggested that social identity should be examined in its social context and that particular emphasis should be placed upon the power relations within that context. The concept of "false consciousness" in particular should be linked directly to such power relations, and the intergroup nature of ideology emphasised. In this way a wider social analysis is made possible, and such an analysis can act as a critique of existing social forms.

In this, more is being suggested than is contained in the symbolic interactionist or ethogenic approaches. Their concentration is upon intersubjective meanings and the cognitive import of social situations. However, this emphasis upon linguistically and socially significant meanings should not be held to replace a wider social enquiry. In stressing the social basis of language and the meanings of social rituals, one should not forget the wider questions that relate to the ideological functions of language, and the social structures which enable the rituals to take place. Therefore the stress upon the social-cognitive aspects of social identification is not an end in itself—the objective significance of such aspects must then be sought. The fact that social identification is mediated by linguistic processes of categorisation, which seem themselves to have certain social psychological effects, does not of itself constitute a full description of social identity in an inter-group context: there is also the need to investigate the wider ideological issues and their underlying material preconditions. In this sense the present position recommends a social psychological analysis which is more explicitly tied to general social theory, than that which is normally recommended by symbolic interactionists or ethnomethodologists. It is, on the other hand, in agreement with the position of Moscovici (1972) who argues that "the central and exclusive object of social psychology should be the study of all that pertains to *ideology* and to *communication* from the point of view of their structures, their genesis and their function" (p. 55, italics in original). In effect this means looking beyond the interpersonal forms of social interaction in order to seek their societal significance.

The relationship of ideology to underlying material conditions has been underlined, and this relationship has been characterised as a dialectical one. Changes in social identity arise from, and can also be said to mediate, changes in the objective basis of society—the infra-structure and superstructure of a society in this sense are dialectically intertwined. The way that an ideology mirrors underlying material conditions is by no means a simple one, and for this reason the present analysis has stressed the importance of the concept of "false consciousness". In particular false consciousness has been related to an inter-group context, in which a dominant group exerts some degree of control over the ideology of an inferior group, and thereby prevents that group from acting in its own interests. Instead, the falsely conscious group acts in the interests of the existing hegemony. The wide interpretation given to the concept of ideology ensures that there are strong ideological implications in designating the beliefs of any group as "false" or "true" consciousness; similarly, most social scientific investigations contain such ideological implications and it has been argued that the social scientist should not seek to avoid ideological or political presuppositions.

In many respects, the arguments that have been advanced, have followed certain lines of thought derived from the works of Marx. The concepts of ideology and false consciousness clearly owe their origin to Marx; similarly, the choice of the terms "group-in-itself" and "group-for-itself" was deliberately intended to follow Marx's distinction between a "class-in-itself" and a "class-for-itself". However it is also possible to discern a stronger emphasis upon the cognitive elements of ideology in the present work. In a sense this is inevitable in a discussion which is explicitly social psychological. However, it is also possible to argue that developments in technology during the past century have made the issues of true and false consciousness more crucial than hitherto. Improvements in mass communication inevitably entail problems involving the mass manipulation of thought. It is possible nowadays for ideas to gain widespread acceptance in a short period of time, and the means exist for the dissemination of half-truths and lies. More than ever do dominant groups possess the tools for creating and maintaining an ideological dominance—the consciousness of the public can be affected, not only by the incessant promotion of particular ideas and assumptions, but also just as much by the systematic exclusion of other potentially radical notions. These processes can be observed in the so-called "free" democracies as well as in societies with overtly totalitarian regimes.

This development in mass communication means that the cognitive elements of ideology constitute prominent practical issues for those attempting to pierce the veil of "official ideological" standpoints. Problems relating to the ideological aspects of false consciousness have a contemporary significance, especially as subordinate groups attempt to forge their own ideologies, to change themselves from groups-in-themselves to become groups-for-themselves. Over a century ago in *The Eighteenth Brumaire of Louis Bonaparte*, Marx could describe the peasants of France as a distinct class-in-themselves because of their similar modes of economic production. However, this mode of production ensured that the peasants were physically separated one from another, and because of this isolation "the identity of interests begets no community, no national bond and no political organisation among them" (Marx and Engels, *Selected Works*, 1968 edn.). As a consequence the peasants could not be called a class-for-themselves, acting in their own class interests. Today, similarly, physical separation can act as a barrier to the creation of effective group organisation; for instance, unionisation can be more difficult among those trades which are scattered throughout many small places of employment (Chivers, 1973). On the other hand, physical isolation today presents no barrier to ideological influences—television, newspapers, radio etc. can ensure that the isolated social group can share in the "official" ideology of the society. In this sense, the modern equivalent of the French peasant, at least in a developed society, is not merely hampered by the physical difficulties involved in becoming a group-for-itself, but also its problems are increased with respect to overcoming a received false consciousness.

As a result the problem of false consciousness can be seen as a particularly acute one in modern society. One possible way of extending the present theoretical analysis of the concept of false consciousness would be to link it with the concept of alienation. Such a link has been suggested by Adorno (1967) but his conception of false consciousness, unlike the present one, was not directly linked to the intergroup situation. The concept of alienation as outlined by Marx in the *Economic and Philosophic Manuscripts of 1844* is essentially a social and objective concept. Unlike more recent derivations from Marx's notion, alienation specifically refers to more than perceived feelings of frustration or powerlessness (for discussions of the irreducibly social nature of Marx's concept of alienation, see Meszaros, 1970, and Israel, 1971; for a comparison of Marx's objectivist concept of alienation with the subjectivist and individualistic concept that has been used by American sociologists, see Plasek, 1974). Marx discusses the way in which the worker is alienated from his work—the product of the worker's labour is appropriated from him and as a result it confronts him in a hostile manner. Similarly it can be argued that the dominant group may not merely appropriate the products of the inferior group's labour, it also can appropriate its conscious life. It attempts to determine the ideology and social identity of the subordinate group, and therefore the subordinate group's social identity confronts it as something that is not its own. In this sense, false consciousness, derived from intergroup inequality, can be seen as being essentially alienating. The ideology and social identity of the subordinate group will in a sense be the property of the dominant group.

However, in suggesting that a dominant group might be able to own the social identity of a subordinate group, the universality of false consciousness should not be exaggerated. It is one thing to describe possible means by which public opinion can be moulded and manipulated, it is another matter to assert that such means are necessarily successful. To assert this would be to presume that social processes are essentially static and that the dominant group is always the dominant group and the subordinate group is always the subordinate group. The processes of social change ensure that situations of intergroup dominance are by no means stable. In chapter eight, the ethnocentric hypothesis was criticised; in particular it was argued that subordinate group members may have a negative ingroup identification. In terms of the present analysis, such a negative ingroup identification can be described as a form of false consciousness: the subordinate group members are adopting the ideological values of the dominant group, and such values impede the development of the subordinate group into a group-for-itself. If such negative ingroup identification is considered the norm for intergroup situations of dominance, then it is hard to see how any subordinate group would be able to transcend its dominated position by developing its own ideology in opposition to that of the existing ruling group. This is so, especially if it is assumed that its conscious life must be owned by the dominant group. Nevertheless it was suggested that the control of the dominant group over the ideology of the subordinate group may be less than total. The ideology fashioned by the dominant group for the benefit of the subordinate group will fail to reflect entirely the experience of the latter. In this way there may well be a mis-match between the social experience of a group and elements of its professed ideology. This ideological tension may itself reflect the processes by which a group-in-itself becomes a group-for-itself.

It is crucial to look beyond the outward symbols of an ideology to assess its social significance. Marx's assertion that the dominant ideas of every age are the ideas of the ruling class, is both a practical and methodological guide to investigate the underlying material conditions presupposed by the ideology. In this sense Marxist analysis has been sometimes compared to Freudian analysis in that both refuse to accept outward meanings at their face value and seek instead their underlying, and often hidden, determinants. The analogy is far from perfect for a number of reasons—not the least being that the Freudian infrastructure, the id, is timeless and immutable, whereas the Marxist infrastructure, the modes of economic and practical activity, dialectically changes with the ideological superstructure. However, the similarity resides in the fact that both are essentially critical disciplines; the Freudian is basically critical of the individual and his motivations; the consequence is the critical *ad hominem* form of argument, which reappears throughout the writings of psychoanalysts. The Marxist must be critical of the "ruling ideas" and relate such ideas to the interests of the various elements within society; the structure of society must be analysed to reveal the objective significance of the subjectively-held ideologies. Thus the "official" ideologies of any society with a ruling class must contain latent social meanings, which need to be un-covered by critical analysis. This form of social criticism is especially apposite for those societies with antagonistic classes, as defined by objective social structure. However, the critique must extend beyond existing class structures—one might assert that, in order to achieve, and then to preserve, a classless society, the debate about the underlying significance of "official" ideologies must be continued. Otherwise ideological forms take on a coercive function for one particular power élite, and ossify into a dogma which conceals the objective structure of society.

In this way the social functions of ideology must be related to dynamic social changes; social psychological analysis as a result must allow for the flux of history, by which groups change their social relations. Thus Marx wrote that:

> There is a continuous movement of growth of the productive forces, of destruction of social relations, of formation of ideas; nothing is immutable but the abstract movement—*mors immortalis*. (Marx, 1963 edn., p. 109, italics in original.)

Therefore a critical social theory must not be based upon a static model of social processes. So much of contemporary social psychology ignores the possibility of structural changes, and as a result is content to examine social psychological relationships within a given social structure. The conflict-resolution approach cannot deal with conflicts that pose a challenge to the social structure, within which the conflict-resolver himself has to operate. In a similar way, the frustration-aggression theorist seems to be forced by his methodological presuppositions to condemn as irrational and impulsive any challenge to the existing *status quo*. The social psychological approach, based upon the examination of interpersonal relations of political and diplomatic leaders, seems in itself to preclude a wider and more critical analysis —in particular, such social psychologists do not raise questions about how a handful of world leaders come to be in a position to make life and death decisions for large numbers of mankind. The simple instinct theorist is even more restricted in his outlook—he must interpret all social phenomena in terms of unchanging instincts, and he dismisses *a priori* the possibility of fundamental social change. Thus none of these social psychological approaches can offer an adequate framework, on its own, for studying the processes of social change, especially as they relate to changes in patterns of intergroup relations.

It is, however, important to realise the limited scope of a critical theory merely built upon relating group ideologies to dynamic large-scale social processes. There is one crucial element missing from such a critical account, which would ensure that its criticism could be of a radical nature. This element is a specifically historical analysis which attributes specific forms to the movement of history. Without any concept of historical development or progression, the dynamic processes of history can be seen as being essentially cyclical. It could be assumed that every age will see a ruling class, attempting to impose its ideas on the rest of society. This attempt will, at best, only meet with partial success, and then only for a limited period of time. The classes that are excluded from power will then develop their own ideologies to challenge the ruling classes. They will thus become classes-for-themselves, and given the right historical conditions they will depose the former ruling class. In doing this, they, or at least certain power groups within this ascendant group, will become the new ruling class. In time the whole process will repeat itself, as a new opposition group is formed to challenge the new masters and their new ideologies. The cyclical interpretation of historical processes, thereby, condemns mankind to a perpetual dialectical struggle between revolution and reaction, in which the only constant is the appearance and reappearance of ruling groups. Freedom from domination is seen as an illusory ideal, that can never be realised in practice.

Such a cyclical account of historical forces is contained in Dahrendorf's (1969) essay on social inequality. Dahrendorf emphasises the permanence of social inequality, which he sees as an inevitable concomitant of any social organisation. Social inequality is, according to Dahrendorf, the factor that ensures the never-ending cycle of revolution producing a new *status quo*, which in turn will be overthrown by revolutionary forces. Thus he argues that the unprivileged of every age will strive against the privileged. This is a historical constant, which ensures that "every system of stratification generates protest against its principles and bears the seeds of its own destruction" (Dahrendorf, 1969, p. 42). The victorious underprivileged become the new masters and initiate a new system of inequality. Human history sees the endless repetition of *le roi est mort—vive le roi!*

A similar cyclical interpretation of history can be found in the writings of Mannheim. Like Dahrendorf he stresses the dialectical relation between social order and revolution; in particular Mannheim directly relates revolutionary (or utopian) thought to the existing "official" ideologies of the *status quo*. He considers that every age produces its own visions of a future utopia, and that these visions contain the "unrealised and unfulfilled" needs of the time. Mannheim argues that the dialectical relationship between utopian thought and the prevailing ideologies of the *status quo* is "the explosive material for bursting the limits of the existing order". In this way ideology produces counter-ideology: "the existing order gives birth to utopias which in turn break the bonds of existing order, leaving it free to develop in the direction of the next order of existence" (1972, p. 179).

The cyclical view of history is essentially a pessimistic one: it implies that libertarian movements will only achieve a limited success. The outcome of a revolutionary movement will be the replacement of one set of masters by a new set. A radical transformation of the conditions that produce dominance itself is not considered feasible. As such, this cyclical view is at variance with the Marxist concept of historical progression. Marx did not hold that man was doomed to the endless cycle of replacing old systems of dominance by new systems of dominance. He admitted that in previous eras revolutionary struggle may have been followed by a renewal of repression and domination, but he claimed that the capitalist society gives birth to the class that can achieve a radically different type of social order. Not only does the proletariat overthrow the bourgeois social order, according to Marx, but it also revolutionises the underlying means of production, which have been left unscathed by all previous revolutions. As such the communist revolution "is directed against the preceding *mode* of activity, does away with *labour*, and abolishes the rule of all classes themselves, because it is carried through by the class which no longer counts as a class in society, is not recognised as a class, and is in itself the expression of the dissolution of all classes, nationalities, etc. within the present society" (Marx and Engels, *The German Ideology*, 1970 edn., p. 94). In this way, Marx and Engels envisage that the proletarian revolution will herald a new era of history in which previous group relations will be radically transformed. History is a progression towards the proletarian victory and is therefore to be seen as a positive development.

The practical differences between the cyclical view of history and the Marxist view of historical progression are fundamental and not to be underestimated. It is not the case that the difference resides in historiographical analysis, which is to be tacked on to more "basic" sociological and social psychological theories. If it is assumed that social scientific analysis is in itself an ideological endeavour and that ideology has practical ramifications, then it becomes fairly simple to locate the practical differences between the two theories of history. The cyclical viewpoint is essentially pessimistic, in that it suggests that inequality, domination and struggle are the permanent lot of mankind, and that it is unreasonable to expect a radical transcendance of man's present condition. In practical terms this view breeds a cynicism, which blunts the edge of all ideologies which aim to transform radically present conditions; it assumes that such attempts will only produce a new system of domination, and as a result its cynicism gives rise to a philosophy of non-action and a resigned detachment. The belief in historical progression, on the other hand, involves a positive commitment to a future, which will be radically different from the past. Thus Marx wrote that "communism is the riddle of history solved and it knows itself to be this solution" (*Economic and Philosophic Manuscripts of 1844*, 1973 edn., p. 135) and also that it is "the *real* movement which abolishes the present state of things" (*German Ideology*, 1970 edn., p. 57). As such it constitutes an ideology of action; the overthrow of existing capitalist society and its replacement by an order which will mark the end of domination and exploitation.

It is the failure of countries, which have experienced proletarian revolutions, to bring about immediate solutions to the riddles of history that has encouraged the pessimism of the cyclical viewpoint. Accordingly, it is held by adherents of the cyclical view that the proletariat must inevitably produce its own social élite, and that consequently the proletarian dictatorship will be no different from any other dictatorship. Similarly, the cyclical view will contend that Lenin's conception of the Communist Party as the vanguard of the working-class must inevitably aid this process of élitism: with the success of the revolution the vanguard will become the new élite, and thereby the ideology of the Party will be geared to defending the privileged position of the new élite. In this way the proletariat's party will come to act against the interests of the people and fail to ensure what Marx called "the development of complete individuals" and "the positive transcendence of private property", (*Economic and Philosophic Manuscripts*, 1973, pp. 132–146; *German Ideology*, 1970, pp. 52–57). Certainly schisms within the communist movement have encouraged this form of pessimism; there can hardly be a communist today who holds that the revolutionary ideal has never been betrayed by any of the Parties in positions of power. Thus the revolutionary struggle itself can be no guarantee that in the post-revolutionary period the leaders will not be divorced from the people and that new élites will not arise.

The critical approach lends itself to two views of history. On the one hand the critical analysis of social processes can lead to the resigned pessimism of the cyclical interpretation. On the other hand it can lead to a more optimistic belief in progress. In this guise the critical approach carries with it an injunction to translate analysis into critical practice. This optimism must however face the fact that the classless and egalitarian society is neither the immediate nor it seems the inevitable sequel to a communist revolution. This produces a dilemma which is both theoretical and practical.

Marx could envisage an ideal state of being which would be "the *genuine* resolution of the conflict between man and nature and between man and man" (*Economic and Philosophic Manuscripts of 1844*, 1973 edn., p. 135). This would entail a total transformation of social relations and of individual psychology. The gap between the image of the ideal and present imperfections calls for drastic and fundamental social changes. The dilemma for the critical approach is whether to retain this image of the ideal or to concentrate upon more limited goals of social improvement and opposition to oppression. On a theoretical level the dilemma is whether social analysis (including social psychological analysis) is sufficient or whether it needs to be accompanied by the development of an idealised individual psychology.

References

Abrahamsson, B. (1970). Homans on exchange: hedonism revised. *American Journal of Sociology*, **76**, 273–285.

Abric, J.C. and Kahan, J.P. (1972). The effects of representatives and behaviour in experimental games. *European Journal of Social Psychology*, **2**, 129–144.

Abudu, M.J.G., Rawe, W.J., Burbeck, S.L. and Davison, K.K. (1972). Black ghetto violence: a case study inquiry into the spatial pattern of four Los Angeles riot event-types. *Social Problems*, **19**, 3, 408–427.

Adamek, R.J. and Lewis, J.M. (1973). Social control violence and radicalisation: the Kent State case. *Social Forces*, **51**, 3, 342–347.

Adorno, T.W. (1951). Freudian theory and the pattern of Fascist propaganda. In *Psychoanalysis and the Social Sciences*, Vol. III (Ed. G. Roheim). International Universities Press, New York.

Adorno, T.W. (1967). Sociology and psychology. *New Left Review*, **46**, 67–80.

Adorno, T.W., Frenkel-Brunswik, E., Levinson, D.J. and Sanford, R.N. (1950). *The Authoritarian Personality*, Harper, New York.

Alexander, C.N. and Weil, H.G. (1969). Players, persons and purposes: situational meaning and the prisoner's dilemma game. *Sociometry*, **32**, 121–149.

Alexander, C.N., Zucker, L.G. and Brody, C.L. (1970). Experimental expectations and the autokinetic experiences: consistency theories and judgmental convergence. *Sociometry*, **33**, 108–122.

Alexander, F. (1937). Psychoanalysis and social disorganisation. *American Journal of Sociology*, **42**, 781–813.

Alger, C. (1965). Personal contact in intergovernmental organisations. In *International Behavior* (Ed. H. Kelman). Holt Rinehart and Winston, New York.

Allen, S. (1973). The institutionalisation of racism. *Race*, **15**, 99–106.

Amir, Y. (1969). Contact hypothesis in ethnic relations. *Psychological Bulletin*, **71**, 319–342.

Anderson, W.A., Dynes, R.R. and Quarantelli, E.L. (1974). Urban counterrioters. *Society*, March/April, 50–55.

Apter, D.E. (1964). *Ideology and Discontent*. Collier-Macmillan, London.

Archer, E.J. (1966). The psychological nature of concepts. In *Analyses of Concept Learning* (Ed. H.J. Klausmeier and C.W. Harris). Academic Press, London.

Aronson, E. (1973). *The Social Animal*. W.H. Freeman and Co., San Francisco.

Aubert, V. (1963). Competition and dissensus: Two types of conflict and of conflict resolution. *Journal of Conflict Resolution*, **7**, 26–42.

Bakan, D. (1958). *Sigmund Freud and the Jewish Mystical Tradition*. Van Nostrand, Princeton.

Baker, K. (1974). Experimental analysis of third-party justice behaviour. *Journal of Personality and Social Psychology*, **30**, 307–316.

Bandura, A., Ross, D. and Ross, S.A. (1963). Vicarious reinforcement and imitative learning. *Journal of Abnormal and Social Psychology*, **67**, 601–607.

Bandura, A. and Walters, R.H. (1963). *Social Learning and Personality Development*. Holt, Rinehart and Winston, New York.

Barnet, R. (1969). *The Economy of Death*. Atheneum, New York.

Baron, R.A. (1971). Exposure to an aggressive model and apparent probability of retaliation from the victim as determinants of adult aggressive behaviour. *Journal of Experimental Social Psychology*, **7**, 343–355.

Baron, R.A. (1971a). Reducing the influence of an aggressive model: the restraining effects of discrepant modelling cues. *Journal of Personality and Social Psychology*, **20**, 240–245.

Baron, R.A. (1972). Aggression as a function of ambient temperature and prior anger arousal. *Journal of Personality and Social Psychology*, **21**, 183–189.

Baron, R.A. (1973). Threatened retaliation from the victim as an inhibitor of physical aggression. *Journal of Research in Personality*, **7**, 103–115.

Baron, R.A. (1974). The aggression-inhibiting influence of heightened sexual arousal. *Journal of Personality and Social Psychology*, in press.

Baron, R.A. and Bell, P.A. (1973). Effects of heightened sexual arousal on physical aggression. *Proceedings, 81st Annual Convention, American Psychological Association*.

Barry, H., Child, I.L. and Bacon, M. (1959). Relation of child training to subsistence economy. *American Anthropologist*, **61**, 51–63.

Bastide, R. (1967). Color, racism and Christianity. *Daedalus*, **96**, 312–327.

Baxter, G.W. (1972). Personality and attitudinal characteristics and cooperation in two-person games: a review. In *Cooperation and Competition* (ed. L.S. Wrightsman, J. O'Connor and N.J. Baker). Brooks/Cole Pub., Belmont, Calif.

Baxter, G.W. (1973). Prejudiced liberals? Race and information effects in a two-person game. *Journal of Conflict Resolution*, **17**, 131–161.

Becker, H.S. (1963). *Outsiders: Studies in the Sociology of Deviance*. The Free Press, New York.

Becker, H.S. (1964). *The Other Side: perspectives on deviance*. The Free Press, New York.

Bentley, S. (1972). Identity and community cooperation: a note on terminology. *Race*, **14**, 69–76.

Berger, P.L. and Luckman, T. (1967). *The Social Construction of Reality*. Allen Lane, London.

Berkowitz, L. (1962). *Aggression: a social psychological analysis*. McGraw-Hill, New York.

Berkowitz, L. (1965). Some aspects of observed aggression. *Journal of Personality and Social Psychology*, **2**, 359–369.

Berkowitz, L. (1965a). The concept of aggressive drive: some additional considerations. In *Advances in Experimental Social Psychology*. Vol. II. (Ed. L. Berkowitz). Academic Press, New York and London.

Berkowitz, L. (1966). On not being able to aggress. *British Journal of Social and Clinical Psychology*, **5**, 130–139.

Berkowitz, L. (1969). The frustration-aggression hypothesis revisited. In *Roots of Aggression* (Ed. L. Berkowitz). Atherton Press, New York.

Berkowitz, L. (1970). Aggressive humor as a stimulus to aggressive responses. *Journal of Personality and Social Psychology*, **16**, 710–717.

Berkowitz, L. (1971). The study of urban violence: some implications of laboratory studies of frustration and aggression. In *When Men Revolt and Why* (Ed. J.C. Davies). The Free Press, New York.

Berkowitz, L. (1972). Frustrations, comparisons and other sources of emotional arousal as contributors to social unrest. *Journal of Social Issues*, **28**, 77–91.

Berkowitz, L. (1974). Some determinants of impulsive aggression: role of mediated associations with reinforcements for aggression. *Psychological Review*, **81**, 165–176.

Berkowitz, L. and Alioto, J.T. (1973). The meaning of an observed event as a determinant of its aggressive consequences. *Journal of Personality and Social Psychology*, **28**, 206–217.

Berkowitz, L. and Geen, R.G. (1966). Film violence and the cue properties of available targets. *Journal of Personality and Social Psychology*, **3**, 525–530.

Berkowitz, L. and Geen, R.G. (1967). Stimulus qualities of the target of aggression: a further study. *Journal of Personality and Social Psychology*, **5**, 364–368.

Berkowitz, L. and Green, J.A. (1962). The stimulus qualities of the scapegoat. *Journal of Abnormal and Social Psychology*, **64**, 293–301.

Berkowitz, L. and Holmes, D.S. (1959). The generalisation of hostility to disliked objects. *Journal of Personality*, **27**, 565–577.

Berkowitz, L. and Holmes, D.S. (1960). A further investigation of hostility generalisation to disliked objects. *Journal of Personality*, **28**, 427–442.

Berkowitz, L. and Knurek, D.A. (1969). Label-mediated hostility generalisation. *Journal of Personality and Social Psychology*, **13**, 200–206.

Berkowitz, L. and LePage, A. (1967). Weapons as aggression-eliciting stimuli. *Journal of Personality and Social Psychology*, **7**, 202–207.

Berkowitz, L., Lepinsk, J.P. and Angulo, E.J. (1969). Awareness of own anger level and subsequent aggression. *Journal of Personality and Social Psychology*, **11**, 293–300.

Bettelheim, B. and Janowitz, M. (1950). *Dynamics of Prejudice*. Harper and Bros., New York.

Bettelheim, B. and Janowitz, M. (1964). *Social Change and Prejudice*. Collier-Macmillan, London.

Beynon, H. (1973). *Working for Ford*. Penguin Books, Harmondsworth.

Bickman, L. (1974). The social power of a uniform. *Journal of Applied Social Psychology*, **4**, 47–61.

Billig, M. (1972). Social categorisation and intergroup relations. Unpublished Ph.D. dissertation, University of Bristol.

Billig, M. (1973). Normative communication in a minimal intergroup situation. *European Journal of Social Psychology*, **3**, 339–343.

Billig, M. (1975). Review of Deutsch's *The Resolution of Conflict*. *European Journal of Social Psychology*, **5**, 409–414.

Billig, M. and Tajfel, H. (1973). Social categorisation and similarity in intergroup behaviour. *European Journal of Social Psychology*, **3**, 27–52.

Bird, B. (1957). A consideration of the etiology of prejudice. *Journal of American Psychoanalytic Association*, **5**, 490–513.

Birrell, D. (1972). Relative deprivation as a factor in conflict in Northern Ireland. *Sociological Review*, **20**, 317–343.

Bixenstine, V.E. and Wilson, K.V. (1963). Effects of levels of cooperative choice by the other players in the prisoner's dilemma game: part II. *Journal of Abnormal and Social Psychology*, **67**, 139–147.

Blake, R.R. and Mouton, J. (1962). The intergroup dynamics of win-lose conflict and problem-solving collaboration in union-management relations. In *Intergroup Relations and Leadership* (Ed. M. Sheriff). Wiley, New York.

Blake, R.R., Mouton. J.S. and Sloma, R.L. (1965). The union-management intergroup laboratory: strategy for resolving intergroup conflict. *Journal of Applied Behavioral Science*, 1, 25–57.

Blake, R.R., Shephard, H.A. and Mouton, J.S. (1964). *Managing Intergroup Conflict in Industry.* Gulf Publishing Co., Houston, Texas.

Blascovich, J., Veach, T.L. and Ginsburg, G.P. (1973). Blackjack and the risky-shift. *Sociometry*, 36, 42–55.

Bolt, C. (1971). *Victorian Attitudes to Race.* Routledge and Kegan Paul, London.

Borden, R.J. and Taylor, S.P. (1973). The social instigation and control of physical aggression. *Journal of Applied Social Psychology*, 3, 354–361.

Bourne, L.E. (1966). *Human Conceptual Behaviour.* Allyn and Bacon, Inc., Boston.

Brenner, C. 1971. The psychoanalytic concept of aggression. *International Journal of Psychoanalysis*, 52, 137–143.

Brewster, B. (1969). Fighting to Win. *New Left Review*, 58, 93–96.

Brooks, R. (1969). Domestic violence and America's wars: an historical interpretation. In *Violence in America* (Ed. H.D. Graham and T.R. Gurr). Bantam Books, New York.

Brown, B.R. (1968). The effects of need to maintain face on interpersonal bargaining. *Journal of Experimental Social Psychology*, 4, 107–122.

Brown, B.R. (1973). Reflections on missing the broadside of a barn. *Journal of Applied Behavioral Science*, 9, 450–458.

Brown, N.O. (1968). *Life Against Death.* Sphere Books, London.

Brown, P. (1973). Male supremacy in Freud. In *Radical Psychology* (Ed. P. Brown). Tavistock, London.

Brown, R. (1965). *Social Psychology.* Collier-Macmillan, London.

Burhams, D.T. (1973). Coalition game research: a reexamination. *American Journal of Sociology*, 79, 389–408.

Burnstein, E. and Worchel, P. (1962). Arbitrariness of frustration and its consequences for aggression in a social situation. *Journal of Personality*, 30, 528–541.

Burton, J.W. (1974). A systems approach to international relations. *International Social Science Journal*, 26, 22–33.

Buss, A.H. (1961). *The Psychology of Aggression.* Wiley, New York.

Buss, A.H. (1963). Physical aggression in relation to different frustrations. *Journal of Abnormal and Social Psychology*, 67, 1–7.

Buss, A.H. (1966). Instrumentality of aggression, feedback and frustration as determinants of physical aggression. *Journal of Personality and Social Psychology*, 3, 153–162.

Buss, A.H., Booker, A. and Buss, E. (1972). Firing a weapon and aggression. *Journal of Personality and Social Psychology*, 22, 296–302.

Byrne, D. (1969). Attitudes and attraction. In *Advances in Social Psychology, Volume IV*. (Ed. L. Berkowitz). Academic Press, New York and London.

Byrne, D. (1971). *The Attraction Paradigm.* Academic Press, New York.

Calley, M. (1965). *God's People: West Indian Pentecostal sects in England.* Oxford University Press, London.

Campbell, D.T. (1956). Enhancement of contrast as a composite habit. *Journal of Abnormal and Social Psychology*, 56, 350–355.

Campbell, D.T. (1958). Common fate, similarity, and other indices of the status of aggregates of persons as social entities. *Behavioral Science*, 3, 14–25.

Campbell, D.T. (1965). Variation and selective retention in socio-cultural evolution. In *Social Change in Developing Areas: a reinterpretation of evolutionary theory* (Ed. H.R. Barringer, G.I. Blanksten and R.W. Mack). Shenkman, Cambridge, Mass.

Campbell, D.T. and LeVine, R.A. (1968). Ethnocentrism and intergroup relations. In *Theories of Cognitive Consistency: a source book* (Ed. R.P. Abelson, et al. Rand McNally and Co., Chicago.

Cannavale, F.J., Scarr, H.A. and Pepitone, A. (1970). Deindividuation and the small group: further evidence. *Journal of Personality and Social Psychology*, **16**, 141–147.

Caplan, N. (1970). The new ghetto man: a review of recent empirical studies. *Journal of Social Issues*, **26**, 59–73.

Caplan, N. and Paige, J. (1968). A study of ghetto rioters. *Scientific American*, **219**, 15–21.

Carr, E.H. (1961). *What is History?* Macmillan, London.

Carver, C.S. (1974). Facilitation of physical aggression through objective awareness. *Journal of Experimental Social Psychology*, **10**, 365–370.

Chabat, J-C. (1973). Social ideology and symbol: a semiotic approach. *International Journal of Symbology*, **4**, 39–47.

Chase, L.J. and Mills, N.B. (1973). Status of frustrator as a facilitator of aggression: a brief note. *Journal of Psychology*, **84**, 225–226.

Chase, M. (1971). Categorisation and affective arousal: some behavioral and judgmental consequences. Unpublished doctoral dissertation, Columbia University.

Cheney, J., Harford, T. and Solomon, L. (1972). The effect of communicating threats and promises upon the bargaining process. *Journal of Conflict Resolution*, **16**, 99–107.

Chivers, T.S. (1973) The proletarianisation of a service worker. *Sociological Review*, **21**, 633–650.

Chomsky, N. (1957). *Syntactic Structures*. Mouton, The Hague.

Chomsky, N. (1965). *Aspects of the Theory of Syntax*. Mouton, The Hague.

Chomsky, N. (1969). *American Power and the New Mandarins*. Pantheon, New York.

Chomsky, N. (1973). *The Backroom Boys*. Fontana/Collins, London.

Chomsky, N. (1973a). Reporting Indochina: the news media and the legitimation of lies. *Social Policy*, **4**, 4–20.

Chomsky, N. (1973b). *For Reasons of State*. Fontana, London.

Christie, R. (1954). Authoritarianism re-examined. In *Studies in the Scope and Method of "The Authoritarian Personality"* (Ed. R. Christie and M. Jahoda). Free Press, New York.

Clark, G. and Sohn, L.B. (1960). *World Peace Through World Law*. Harvard University Press, Cambridge, Mass.

Claude, I.L. (1962). *Power and International Relations*. Random House, New York.

Cohen, A.R. (1955). Social norms, arbitrariness of frustration and status of the agent of frustration in the frustration-aggression hypothesis. *Journal of Abnormal and Social Psychology*, **51**, 222–226.

Cohen, R. and Middleton, J. (1970). *From Tribe to Nation in Africa: studies in incorporation processes*. Chandler, Scranton, Pa.

Cohn, N. (1967). *Warrant for Genocide: the myth of the Jewish world conspiracy and the protocols of the Elders of Zion*. Chatto Heinemann, London.

Cohn, N. (1970). *The Pursuit of the Millenium*. Paladin, London.

Coleman, J.S. (1966). Introduction: in defence of games. *American Behavioral Scientist*, 10, 3–4.

Conklin, H.C. (1955). Hanunúoo colour categories. *Southwestern Journal of Anthropology*, 11, 339–344.

Conklin, H.C. (1964). Ethnogenealogical method. In *Exploration in Cultural Anthropology* (Ed. W.H. Goodenough). McGraw Hill, New York.

Connell, R.W. (1972). Political socialisation in the American family: the evidence re-examined. *Public Opinion Quarterly*, 36, 323–333.

Connell, R.W. and Goot, M. (1972–3). Social science and ideology in American "political socialisation" research. *Berkeley Journal of Sociology*, 17, 165–194.

Coser, L. (1956). *The Functions of Social Conflict*. Free Press, Glencoe, Ill.

Cowen, E., Landes, J. and Schaet, D.E. (1959). The effects of mild frustration on the expression of attitudes. *Journal of Abnormal and Social Psychology*, 58, 33–38.

Crawford, T.J., and Nadditch, M. (1970). Relative deprivation, powerlessness and militancy: the psychology of social protest. *Psychiatry*, 33, 208–223.

Crow, W.J. (1966). Simulation: the construction and use of functioning models in international relations. In *The Psychology of Egon Brunswik* (Ed. K.R. Hammond). Holt Rinehart and Winston, New York.

Dahrendorf, R. (1969). On the origin of inequality among men. In *Social Inequality* (Ed. A. Beteille). Penguin Books, Harmondsworth.

Davies, J.C. (1962). Toward a theory of revolution. *American Sociological Review*, 27, 5–19.

Davis, J.A. (1959). A formal interpretation of the theory of relative deprivation. *Sociometry*, 22, 280–296.

Davis, N.J. (1972). Labeling theory in deviance research: a critique and reconsideration. *Sociological Quarterly*, 13, 447–474.

Davis, R.H. (1966). The international influence process: how relevant is the contribution of psychologists? *American Psychologist*, 21, 236–243.

Dawes, R.M. (1973). The commons dilemma game: an N-person mixed-motive game with a dominating strategy for defection. *Oregon Research Institute Bulletin*, 13, No. 2.

Dawes, R.M., Delay, J. and Chaplin, W. (1974). The decision to pollute. *Environmental and Planning A*, 6, 3–10.

Deese, J. (1967). Meaning and change of meaning. *American Psychologist*, 22, 641–651.

Deese, J. (1969). Behavior and fact. *American Psychologist*, 24, 515–522.

DeLamater, J. (1974). A definition of "group". *Small Group Behavior*, 5, 30–44.

Deutsch, M. (1962a). Psychological alternatives to war. *Journal of Social Issues*, 18, 97–119.

Deutsch, M. (1962b). A psychological basis for peace. In *Preventing World War III* (Ed. Q. Wright, W.M. Evan and M. Deutsch). Simon and Schuster, New York.

Deutsch, M. (1962c). Cooperation and trust: some theoretical notes. *Nebraska Symposium on Motivation*, 10, 275–319.

Deutsch, M. (1969a). Socially relevant science: reflections on some studies of interpersonal conflict. *American Psychologist*, 24, 1076–1092.

Deutsch, M. (1969b). Conflict and its resolution. In *Conflict Resolution: contributions of the behavioral sciences* (Ed. C.G. Smith). University of Notre Dame Press, London.

Deutsch, M. (1969c). Conflicts productive and destructive. *Journal of Social Issues*, **15**, 7–41.

Deutsch, M. (1973). *The Resolution of Conflict: constructive and destructive processes*. Yale University Press, New Haven and London.

Deutsch, M. and Krauss, R.M. (1960). The effect of threat upon interpersonal bargaining. *Journal of Abnormal and Social Psychology*, **61**, 181–189.

Deutsch, M. and Krauss, R.M. (1962). Studies of interpersonal bargaining. *Journal of Conflict Resolution*, **6**, 52–76.

Deutsch, M., Thomas, J.R.H. and Garner, K. (1971). Social discrimination on the basis of category membership. Unpublished ms. Columbia University.

Dicks, H.V. (1950). Personality traits and national socialist ideology. *Human Relations*, **3**, 111–154.

Dicks, H.V. (1966). Intra-personal conflict and the authoritarian character. In *Conflict in Society* (Ed. A. de Reuk and J. Knight). Churchill Ltd., London.

Dicks, H.V. (1972). *Licensed Mass Murder: a socio-psychological study of some SS killers*. Chatto Heinemann, London.

Dion, K.L. (1973). Cohesiveness as a determinant of ingroup-outgroup bias. *Journal of Personality and Social Psychology*, **28**, 163–171.

Dion, K.L. (1973a). Dogmatism and intergroup bias. *Representative Research in Social Psychology*, **4**, 1–10.

Divale, W.T. (1974). Migration, external warfare and matrilocal residue. *Behavior Science Research*, **9**, 75–133.

Doise, W. (1969). Intergroup relations and polarisation of individual and collective judgments. *Journal of Personality and Social Psychology*, **12**, 136–143.

Doise, W., Csepely, G., Dann, H.D., Gouge, C., Larsen, K. and Ostell A. (1972). An experimental investigation into the formation of intergroup representations. *European Journal of Social Psychology*, **2**, 202–204.

Doise, W. and Sinclair, A. (1973). The categorisation process in intergroup relations. *European Journal of Social Psychology*, **3**, 145–153.

Dolbear, F.T. and Lave, L.B. (1967). Inconsistent behaviour in lottery choice experiments. *Behavioral Science*, **12**, 14–23.

Dollard, J. (1937). *Caste and Class in a Southern Town*. Yale University Press, New Haven.

Dollard, J., Doob, L.W., Miller, N.E., Mowrer, O.H. and Sears, R.R. (1939). *Frustration and Aggression*. Yale University Press, New Haven.

Donnerstein, E., Donnerstein, M., Simon, S. and Ditrichs, R. (1972). Variables in interracial aggression: anonymity, expected retaliation and a riot. *Journal of Personality and Social Psychology*, **22**, 236–245.

Doob, A.N. and Gross, A.E. (1968). Status of frustrator as an inhibitor of horn-honking responses. *Journal of Social Psychology*, **76**, 213–218.

Doob, A.N. and Kirshenbaum, H.M. (1973). The effects on arousal of frustration and aggressive films. *Journal of Experimental Social Psychology*, **9**, 57–64.

Doob, A.N., and Wood, L.E. (1972). Catharsis and aggression: effects of annoyance and retaliation on aggressive behaviour. *Journal of Personality and Social Psychology*, **22**, 156–162.

Doob, L.W., Foltz, W.J. and Stevens, R.B. (1969). The Fermeda workshop: a different approach to border conflicts in Eastern Africa. *Journal of Psychology*, **73**, 249–266.

Drabman, R.S. and Thomas, M.H. (1974). Does media violence increase children's toleration of real life aggression? *Developmental Psychology*, **10**, 418–421.

Drabman, R.S. and Thomas, M.H. (1974a). Exposure to filmed violence and children's toleration of real life aggression. Paper presented at Conference of American Psychological Association, New Orleans.

Druckman, D. (1971). Understanding the operation of complex social systems: some uses of the simulation design. *Simulation and Games*, **2**, 173–195.

Druckman, D. and Zechmeister, K. (1970). Conflict of interest and value dissensus. *Human Relations*, **23**, 431–438.

Druckman, D. and Zechmeister, K. (1973). Conflict of interest and value dissensus: propositions in the sociology of conflict. *Human Relations*, **26**, 449–466.

Dummett, A. (1973). *A Portrait of English Racism*. Penguin Books, Harmondsworth.

Durkin, J.E. (1972). Moment-of-truth encounters in the prisoner's dilemma. In *Cooperation and Conflict* (Ed. L.S. Wrightsman, J. O'Connor and N. Baker). Brooks/Cole Publishing Co., Belmont, Calif.

Eckhardt, W. and Newcombe, A.G. (1969). Militarism, personality and other social attitudes. *Journal of Conflict Resolution*, **13**, 210–219.

Eckhardt, W. and Newcombe, A.G. (1972). Comments on Ray's "Militarism, authoritarianism, neuroticism and anti-social behavior". *Journal of Conflict Resolution*, **16**, 353–355.

Eide, A. (1974). A value-based approach: methods and problems in peace research. *International Social Science Journal*, **26**, 119–133.

Eiser, J.R. (1971). Categorisation, cognitive consistency and the concept of dimensional salience. *European Journal of Social Psychology*, **1**, 435–454.

Eiser, J.R. and Stroebe, W. (1972). *Categorisation and social judgment*. Academic Press, London.

Eissler, K.R. (1971). Death drive, ambivalence and narcissism. *Psychoanalytic Study of the Child*, **26**, 25–78.

Ellis, D.P., Weinir, P. and Miller, L. (1971). Does the trigger pull the finger? An experimental investigation of weapons as aggression-eliciting stimuli. *Sociometry*, **34**, 453–465.

Elms, A.C. (1970). Those little old ladies in tennis shoes are no nuttier than anyone else, it turns out. *Psychology Today*, (Feb.), 27–59.

Ember, C.R. (1974). An evaluation of alternative theories of matrilocal versus patrilocal residue. *Behavior Science Research*, **9**, 135–149.

Ember, M. (1974). Warfare, sex ratio and polygyny. *Ethnology*, **13**, 197–206.

Ember, M. and Ember, C.R. (1971). The conditions favoring matrilocal versus patrilocal residence. *American Anthropologist*, **73**, 571–594.

Engels, F. (1968). The origin of the family, private property and the state. In *Marx and Engels, Selected Works*. Lawrence and Wishart, Ltd., London.

Epstein, S. and Taylor, S.P. (1967). Instigation to aggression as a function of degree of defeat and perceived aggressive intent of the opponent. *Journal of Personality*, **35**, 265–289.

Erikson, E.H. (1945). Childhood and tradition in two American Indian tribes. *Psychoanalytic Study of the Child*, **1**, 319–350.

Erikson, E.H. (1946). Ego development and historical change. *Psychoanalytic Study of the Child*, **2**, 359 396.

Erikson, B., Holmes, J.G., Frey, R., Walker, L. and Thibaut, J. (1974). Functions of a third party in the resolution of conflict: the role of a judge in pretrial conferences. *Journal of Personality and Social Psychology*, **30**, 293–306.

Evans, G.W. and Crumbaugh, C.M. (1966). Effects of prisoner's dilemma format on cooperative behavior. *Journal of Personality and Social Psychology*, **3**, 486–488.

Eysenck, H.J. (1956). The psychology of politics and the personality similarities between fascists and communists. *Psychological Bulletin*, **53**, 431–438.

Fanon, F. (1967). *The Wretched of the Earth*. Penguin Books, Harmondsworth.

Fanon, F. (1968). *Black Skin, White Masks*. MacGibbon and Kee Ltd., London.

Feierabend, I.K. and Feierabend, R.L. (1966). Aggressive behaviour within politics, 1948–1962: a cross-national survey. *Journal of Conflict Resolution*, **10**, 249–271.

Feierabend, I.K. and Feierabend, R.L. (1966). Aggressive behavior within political violence: cross-national patterns. In *Violence in America* (Ed. H.D. Graham and T.R. Gurr). Bantam Books, New York.

Feierabend, I.K., Feierabend, R.L. and Nesvold, B.A. (1973). The comparative study of revolution and violence. *Comparative Politics*, **5**, 393–424.

Fellman, J. (1973). Language and national identity: the case of the Middle East. *Anthropological Linguistics*, **15**, 244–249.

Fenigstein, A. and Buss, A.H. (1974). Association and affect as determinants of displaced aggression. *Journal of Research in Personality*, **7**, 306–313.

Ferguson, C.K. and Kelley, H.H. (1964). Significant factors in the overevaluation of own group's products. *Journal of Abnormal and Social Psychology*, **69**, 223–228.

Festinger, L. (1954). A theory of social comparison processes. *Human relations*, **7**, 117–140.

Festinger, L. (1957). *A Theory of Cognitive Dissonance*. Row Peterson, New York.

Festinger, L. (1964). *Conflict, Decision and Dissonance*. University Press, Stanford.

Festinger, L., Pepitone, A. and Newcomb, T. (1952). Some consequences of deindividuation in a group. *Journal of Abnormal and Social Psychology*, **47**, 382–389.

Festinger, L., Riecken, H.W. and Schachter, S. (1956). *When Prophecy Fails*. University of Minn. Press, Minneapolis.

Fink, H.C. (1971) Fictitious groups and the generality of prejudice: an artifact of scales without neutral categories. *Psychological Reports*, **29**, 359–365.

Fisher, R. (1964). Fractionating conflict. *Daedalus*, **93**, 920–941.

Fisher, R. (1969). *International Conflict for Beginners*. Harper and Row, New York.

Fishman, J.A., Ferguson, C.A. and Gupta, J.D. (1968). *Language Problems in Developing Nations*. John Wiley and Sons, New York.

Fogelson, R.M. (1970). Violence and grievances: reflections on the 1960's riots. *Journal of Social Issues*, **26**, 141–163.

Foot, P. (1965). *Immigration and Race in British Politics*. Penguin Books, Harmondsworth.

Fortune, R.F. (1939). Arapesh warfare. *American Anthropologist*, **41**, 22–41.

Forward, J.R. and Williams, J.R. (1970). Internal-external control and black militancy. *Journal of Social Issues*, **26**, 75–92.

Frank, J.D. (1967). *Sanity and Survival: psychological aspects of war and peace*. Barrie and Rockliff, London.

Fraser, C., Gouge, C. and Billig, M. (1971). Risky shifts, cautious shifts and group polarisation. *European Journal of Social Psychology*, **1**, 7–30.

Frenkel-Brunswik, E. (1954). Further explorations by a contributor to the 'Authoritarian personality'. In *Studies in the Scope and Method of 'The Authoritarian Personality'* (Ed. R. Christie and M. Jahoda). Free Press, New York.

Freud, A. (1972). Comments on aggression. *International Journal of Psychoanalysis*, **53**, 163–171.

Freud, S. (1953-1964). *Standard Edition of the Complete Psychological Works* (Ed. J. Strachey). Hogarth Press, London.

Freud, S. (1905). Three essays on the theory of sexuality. *Stand. Ed.* Vol. VII.

Freud, S. (1910). The antithetical meaning of primary words. *Stand. Ed.* Vol. XI.

Freud, S. (1913). Totem and taboo. *Stand. Ed.* Vol. XIII.

Freud, S. (1914). Letter to Frederick Van Eeden. *Stand. Ed.* Vol. XIV.

Freud, S. (1915). Thoughts for the times on war and death. *Stand. Ed.* Vol. XIV.

Freud, S. (1917). Mourning and melancholia. *Stand. Ed.* Vol. XIV.

Freud, S. (1918). The taboo of virginity. *Stand. Ed.* Vol. XI.

Freud, S. (1920). Beyond the pleasure principle. *Stand. Ed.* Vol. XVIII.

Freud, S. (1921). Group psychology and the analysis of the ego. *Stand. Ed.* Vol. XVIII.

Freud, S. (1923). The ego and the id. *Stand. Ed.* Vol. XIX.

Freud, S. (1925). Some psychological consequences of the anatomical distinction between the two sexes. *Stand. Ed.* Vol. XIX.

Freud, S. (1925). An autobiographical study. *Stand. Ed.* Vol. XX.

Freud, S. (1926). Address to the society of B'nai B'rith *Stand. Ed.* Vol. XX.

Freud, S. (1927). The future of an illusion. *Stand. Ed.* Vol. XXI.

Freud, S. (1930). Civilisation and its discontents. *Stand. Ed.* Vol. XXI.

Freud, S. (1933). New introductory lectures on psycho-analysis. *Stand. Ed.* Vol. XXII.

Freud, S. (1933a). Why war? *Stand. Ed.* Vol. XXII.

Freud, S. (1937). Analysis terminable and interminable. *Stand. Ed.* Vol. XXIII.

Freud, S. (1939). Moses and monotheism. *Stand. Ed.* Vol. XXIII.

Friedland, N., Arnold, S.E. and Thibaut, J. (1974). Motivational bases in mixed-motive interactions: the effects of comparison levels. *Journal of Experimental Social Psychology*, **10**, 188–199.

Friedlander, F. (1973). The innocence of research. *Journal of Applied Behavioral Science*, **9**, 459–468.

Friedman, D.J. (1974). Marx's perspective on the objective class structure. *Polity*, **6**, 318–344.

Friedman, N. (1967). *The Social Nature of Psychological Research: the psychological experiment as a social interaction*. Basic Books Inc., New York.

Froman, L.A. and Cohen, M.D. (1969). Threats and bargaining efficiency. *Behavioral Science*, **14**, 147–153.

Fromm, E. (1941). *Escape from Freedom*. Rinehart, New York.

Fromm, E. (1971). *The Crisis of Psycho-analysis: essays on Freud, Marx and social psychology*. Jonathan Cape, London.

Furnivall, J.S. (1956). *Colonial Policy in Practice*. Cambridge University Press, New York.

Gaebelin, J.W. and Hay, W.H. (1974). Third party instigation of aggression as a function of attack and vulnerability. *Journal of Research in Personality*, **7**, 324–333.

Gallo, P.S. (1968). Prisoners of our own dilemma. Paper presented at Western Psychological Association, San Diego, March.

Gallo, P.S. and McClintock, C.G. (1965). Cooperative and competitive behavior in mixed-motive games. *Journal of Conflict Resolution*, **9**, 68–78.

Gardin, H., Kaplan, K.J., Firestone, I.J. and Cowan, F.A. (1973). Proxemic effects of cooperation, attitude, and approach-avoidance in a prisoner's dilemma game. *Journal of Personality and Social Psychology*, **27**, 13–18.

Garnier, M.A. (1973). Power and ideological conformity: a case study. *American Journal of Sociology*, **79**, 343–363.

Geen, R.G. and Berkowitz, L. (1967). Some conditions facilitating the occurrence of aggression after the observation of violence. *Journal of Personality*, **35**, 666–676.

Geen, R.G. and O'Neal, E.C. (1969). Activation of cue-elicited aggression by general arousal. *Journal of Personality and Social Psychology*, **11**, 289–292.

Geen, R.G. and Pigg. R. (1970). Acquisition of an aggressive response and its generalisation to verbal behavior. *Journal of Personality and Social Psychology*, **15**, 165–170.

Geen, R.G. and Pigg, R. (1973). Interpretation of arousal and its effects on motivation. *Journal of Social Psychology*, **90**, 115–123.

Geen, R.G. and Rakosky, J.J. (1973). Interpretations of observed aggression and their effect on GSR. *Journal of Research in Personality*, **6**, 289–292.

Geen, R.G., Stonner, D. and Kelley, D.R. (1974). Aggression, anxiety and cognitive appraisal of aggression-threat stimuli. *Journal of Personality and Social Psychology*, **29**, 196–200.

Geertz, C. (1964). Ideology as a cultural system. In *Ideology and Discontent* (Ed. D.E. Apter). Collier MacMillan, London.

Gentry, W.D. (1970). Effects of frustration, attack and prior aggressive training on overt aggression and vascular processes. *Journal of Personality and Social Psychology*, **16**, 718–725.

Gerard, H.B. and Hoyt, M.F. (1974). The distinctiveness of social categorisation and attitude toward ingroup members. *Journal of Personality and Social Psychology*, **29**, 836–842.

Gerard, R.W. Truth detection. In *Preventing World War III* (Ed. Q. Wright, W.M. Evan and M. Deutsch). Simon and Schuster, New York.

Gergen, K.J. (1967). The significance of skin color in human relations. *Daedalus*, **96**, 390–406.

Geschwender, J.A. (1973). The change in role of violence in the Black revolt. *Sociological Symposium*, **9**, 1–15.

Gilbert, G.M. (1951). Stereotype persistence and change among college students. *Journal of Abnormal and Social Psychology*, **46**, 245–254.

Gillespie, W.H. (1971). Aggression and instinct theory. *International Journal of Psycho-analysis*, **52**, 155–159.

Goddard, D. (1973). Anthropology: the limits of functionalism. In *Ideology in Social Sciences* (Ed. R. Blackburn). Fontana/Collins, London.

Goldstein, J.H. and Arms, R.L. (1971). Effects of observing athletic contests on hostility. *Sociometry*, **34**, 83–90.

Goldstein, J.H., Davis, R. and Herman, D. (1975). The escalation of aggression: experimental studies. *Journal of Personality and Social Psychology*, **31**, 162–170.

Goodman, M.E. (1964) *Race Awareness in Young Children*. Collier Books, New York.

Goranson, R. and King, D. (1971). Rioting and daily temperature: analysis of the U.S. riots in 1967. Unpub. ms.

Gorer, G. (1968). Man has no "killer instinct". In *Man and Aggression* (Ed. M.F.A. Montague). Oxford University Press, New York.

Glover, E. (1946). *War, Sadism and Pacifism*. Paton and Sons, Edinburgh.

Green, J. (1972). *Psychololinguistics: Chomsky and Psychology*. Penguin Books, Harmondsworth.

Greenwell, J. and Dengerink, H.A. (1973). The role of perceived versus actual attack in human physical aggression. *Journal of Personality and Social Psychology*, **26**, 66–71.

Gruder, C.L. (1970). Social power in interpersonal negotiation. In *The Structure of Conflict* (Ed. P. Swingle). Academic Press, London.

Guetzkow, H., Alger, C.F., Brody, R.A., Noel, R.C. and Snyder, R.C. (1963). *Simulation in International Relations.* Prentice-Hall, Englewood Cliffs, N.J.

Gumpert, P., Deutsch, M. and Epstein, Y. (1969). Effect of incentive magnitude on cooperation in the Prisoner's Dilemma game. *Journal of Personality and Social Psychology,* 11, 66–69.

Gurr, T.R. (1969). A comparative study of civil strife. In *Violence in America* (Ed. H.D. Graham and T.R. Gurr). Bantam Books, New York.

Gurr, T.R. (1970). *Why Men Rebel.* Princeton University Press, Princeton.

Gurr, T.R. (1972). The calculus of civil conflict. *Journal of Social Issues,* 28, 27–47.

Gurr, T.R. (1973). The revolution-social-change nexus: some old theories and new hypotheses. *Comparative Politics,* 5, 359–392.

Gurr, T.R. and Duvall, R. (1973). Civil conflict in the 1960's: a reciprocal theoretical system with parameter estimates. *Comparative Political Studies,* 6, 135–169.

Gutiérrez, A. and Hirsch, H. (1973). The militant challenge to the American ethos: 'Chicanos' and 'Mexican Americans'. *Social Science Quarterly,* 830–845.

Guyer, M.J. and Rapoport, A. (1972). 2 × 2 games played once. *Journal of Conflict Resolution,* 16, 409–431.

Hahn, H. (1969). Ghetto sentiments on violence. *Science and Society,* 33, 2, 197–208.

Hall, R.A. (1968). The scapegoat theory of prejudices. Unpub. Master's thesis, Colorada State University.

Hanratty, M.A., O'Neal, E. and Sulzer, J. (1972). Effect of frustration upon imitation of aggression. *Journal of Personality and Social Psychology,* 21, 30–34.

Harford, T. and Solomon, L. (1967). "Reformed sinner" and "lapsed saint" strategies in the Prisoner's Dilemma game. *Journal of Conflict Resolution,* 11, 104–109.

Harré, R. (1974). Blueprint for a new science. In *Reconstructing Social Psychology* (Ed. N. Armistead). Penguin Books, Harmondsworth.

Harré, R. and Secord, P. (1972). *The Explanation of Social Behaviour.* Blackwell, Oxford.

Hartley, E.L. (1946). *Problems in Prejudice.* King's Crown Press, New York.

Hartmann, D.P. (1969). Influence of symbolically modeled instrumental aggression and pain cues on aggressive behavior. *Journal of Personality and Social Psychology,* 11, 280–288.

Hartmann, H. (1951). Some psycho-analytic comments on "Culture and personality". In *Psychoanalysis and Culture* (Ed. G.B. Wilbur and W. Muensterberger). International Univ. Press, New York.

Hartmann, H. (1958). *Ego Psychology and the Problem of Adaptation.* International Univ. Press, New York.

Hartmann, H. (1964). *Essays on Ego Psychology.* Hogarth Press, London.

Hartmann, H., Kris, E. and Loewenstein, R.M. (1949). Notes on the theory of aggression. *Psychoanalytic Study of the Child,* 3, 9–37.

Hartmann, R. and Husband, C. (1974). *Racism and the Mass Media.* Davis-Poynter, London.

Heinila, K. (1966). Notes on the inter-group conflicts in international sport. *International Review of Sport Sociology,* 1, 31–40.

Hendrick, I. (1942). Instinct and ego during infancy. *Psycho-analytic Quarterly,* 11, 33–58.

Hiro, D. (1973). *Black British, White British*. Penguin Books, Harmondsworth.

Hoedemaker, E.D. (1968). Distrust and aggression: an interpersonal-international analogy. *Journal of Conflict Resolution*, **12**, 69–81.

Hodge, R.W. and Treiman, D.J. (1968). Class identification in the United States. *American Journal of Sociology*, **78**, 535–547.

Hokanson, J.E. (1970). Psychophysiological evaluations of the catharsis hypothesis. In *The Dynamics of Aggression* (Ed. E.I. Megargee and J.E. Hokanson). Harper and Row, New York.

Hokanson, J.E. and Burgess, M. (1962). The effects of three types of aggression on vascular processes. *Journal of Abnormal and Social Psychology*, **62**, 446–449.

Hokanson, J.E., Burgess, M. and Cohen, M.F. (1963). Effects of displaced aggression on systolic blood pressure. *Journal of Abnormal and Social Psychology*, **67**, 214–218.

Hokanson, J.E. and Shelter, S. (1961). The effect of overt aggression on physiological arousal. *Journal of Abnormal and Social Psychology*, **63**, 446–448.

Holmes, D.S. (1972). Aggression, displacement and guilt. *Journal of Personality and Social Psychology*, **21**, 296–301.

Holsti, O.R. (1970). Individual differences in "definition of the situation". *Journal of Conflict Resolution*, **14**, 303–310.

Homans, G.C. (1951). *The Human Group*. Routledge and Kegan Paul, London.

Homans, G.C. (1961). *Social Behavior: its elementary forms*. Harcourt, Brace and World, New York.

Horney, K. (1937). *The Neurotic Personality of Our Time*. Kegan Paul, Trench, Trubuer and Co., London.

Horney, K. (1939). *New Ways in Psycho-analysis*. Kegan Paul, Trench, Trubuer and Co., London.

Horowitz, D.L. (1973). Direct, displaced and cumulative ethnic aggression. *Comparative Politics*, **6**, 1–16.

Horowitz, I.L. (1963). *The War Game: studies of the new civilian militarists*. Ballantine, New York.

Horowitz, I.L. (1967). *The Rise and Fall of Project Camelot: studies in the relationship between social sciences and practical politics*. M.I.T. Press, Cambridge, Mass.

Horowitz, I.L. (1970). Deterrence games: from academic casebook to military codebook. In *The Structure of Conflict* (Ed. P. Swingle). Academic Press, London.

Howard, N. (1966). The theory of meta-games. *General Systems*, **11**, 167–186.

Howe, L.P. (1955). Some sociological aspects of identification. In *Psychoanalysis and the Social Sciences*, Vol. IV. (Ed. W. Muensterberger and S. Axelrad). International Univ. Press, New York.

Hsu, F.L.K. (1973). Prejudice and its intellectual effect in American anthropology: an ethnographic report. *American Anthropologist*, **75**, 1–19.

Hull, C.L. (1920). Quantitative aspects of the evolution of concepts. *Psychological Monographs*, **28**. (Whole no. 123).

Imai, S. and Okumura, A. (1973). The effect of group structure upon risk-taking behavior and game-playing strategies in a single-vs-group game. *Japanese Psychological Research*, **15**, 109–119.

Innes, J.M. and Fraser, C. (1971). Experimenter bias and other possible biases in psychological research. *European Journal of Social Psychology*, **1**, 297–301.

Isherwood, C. (1968). *Down There on a Visit*. New English Library Ltd., London.

Israel, J. (1971). *Alienation: from Marx to modern society*. Allyn and Bacon, Boston, Mass.

Jackman, M.R. and Jackman, R.W. (1973). An interpretation of the relation between objecive and subjective social status. *American Sociological Review*, **38**, 569–582.

Jacobson, A.L. (1973). Intrasocietal conflict: a preliminary test of a structural-level theory. *Comparative Political Studies*, **6**, 62–83.

Janis, I.L. and King, B.T. (1954). The influence of role-playing upon opinion-change. *Journal of Abnormal and Social Psychology*, **49**, 211–218.

Janowitz, M. (1969). Patterns of collective racial violence. In *Violence in America* (Ed. H.D. Graham and T.R. Gurr). Bantam Books, New York.

Jaspars, J.M.F., van de Geer, J., Tajfel, H. and Johnson, N.B. (1972). On the development of national attitudes. *European Journal of Social Psychology*, **2**, 347–369.

Jones, G.S. (1972). History: the poverty of empiricism. In *Ideology and Social Science* (Ed. R. Blackburn). Fontana/Collins, London.

Joseph, N. and Alex, N. (1972). The uniform: a sociological perspective. *American Journal of Sociology*, **77**, 719–730.

Kanouse, D.E. and Wiest, W.M. (1967). Some factors affecting choice in the prisoner's dilemma. *Journal of Conflict Resolution*, **11**, 206–213.

Kaplowitz, S.A. (1973). An experimental test of a rationalistic theory of deterrence. *Journal of Conflict Resolution*, **17**, 535–572.

Kardiner, A. (1946). *The Individual and His Society*. Columbia University Press, New York.

Karlins, M., Coffman, T.L. and Walters, G. (1969). On the fading of social stereotypes: studies in three generations of college students. *Journal of Personality and Social Psychology*, **13**, 1–16.

Katz, D. (1965). Nationalism and strategies of international conflict resolution. In *International Behavior: a social psychological analysis* (Ed. H.C. Kelman). Holt Rinehart and Winston, New York.

Katz, D. and Braly, K.W. (1933). Racial prejudice and racial stereotypes. *Journal of Abnormal and Social Psychology*, **30**, 175–193.

Katz, I., Glass, D.C. and Cohen, S. (1973). Ambivalence, guilt and the scapegoating of minority group victims. *Journal of Experimental Social Psychology*, **9**, 423–436.

Kelley, H.H. (1965). Experimental studies of threat in interpersonal negotiations. *Journal of Conflict Resolution*, **9**, 79–105.

Kelley, H.H. (1967), Attribution theory in social psychology. *Nebraska Symposium on Motivation*, **15**, 192–238.

Kelley, H.H. (1968). Interpersonal accommodation. *American Psychologist*, **23**, 399–410.

Kelley, H.H. and Stahelski, A.J. (1970). Social interaction basis of cooperators' and competitors' beliefs about others. *Journal of Personality and Social Psychology*, **16**, 66–91.

Kelman, H.C. (1968). *A Time to Speak: on human values and social research*. Jossey-Bass, San Francisco.

Kelman, H.C. (1972). The rights of the subject in social research: an analysis in terms of relative power and legitimacy. *American Psychologist*, **27**, 989–1016.

Kelvin, P. (1970). *The Bases of Social Behaviour: an approach in terms of order and values*. Holt, Rinehart and Winston, London.

Kiernan, V.G. (1972). *Lords of Human Kind: European attitudes toward the outside world in the imperial age*. Penguin Books, Harmondsworth.

Kilham, W. and Mann, L. (1974). Level of destructive obedience as a function of transmitter and executant roles in the Milgram obedience paradigm. *Journal of Personality and Social Psychology*, **29**, 696–702.

King, B.T. and Janis, I.L. (1956). Comparison of the effectiveness of improvised versus non-improvised role playing in producing opinion changes. *Human Relations*, **9**, 177–186.

Kirscht, J.P. and Dillehay, R.C. (1967). *Dimension of Authoritarianism*. University of Kentucky Press.

Kissinger, H.A. (1969). *Nuclear Weapons and Foreign Policy*. W.W. Norton and Co., Inc., New York.

Klein, M. (1948). *Contributions to Psycho-analysis, 1921–1945*. Hogarth Press and Institute of Psycho-analysis, London.

Klein, M. (1959). *Our Adult World and its Roots in Infancy*. Tavistock Pamphlet, No. 2, London.

Klineberg, O. (1962). Intergroup relations and international relations. In *Intergroup Relations and Leadership* (Ed. M. Sherif). John Wiley and Sons, Inc., New York.

Knight, G.P. and Mack, D. (1973). Race and behaviour in the prisoner's dilemma game. *Psychological Record*, **23**, 61–64.

Knopf, T.A. (1974). Race, riots and reporting. *Journal of Black Studies*, **4**, 303–327.

Knott, P.D. and Dross, B.A. (1972). Effects of varying intensity of counter-aggression. *Journal of Personality*, **40**, 27–37.

Kochanek, S.A. (1973). Perspectives on the study of revolution and social change. *Comparative Politics*, **5**, 313–319.

Kohler, A.T., Miller, J.C. and Klein, E.B. (1973). Some effects of intergroup experience on study group phenomena. *Human Relations*, **26**, 293–305.

Konecni, V.G. and Doob, A.N. (1972). Catharsis through displacement of aggression. *Journal of Personality and Social Psychology*, **23**, 379–387.

Kornhauser, W. (1960). *The Politics of Mass Society*. Routledge and Kegan Paul, London.

Kovel, J. (1970). *White Racism: a psychohistory*. Allen Lane, London.

Krech, D., Crutchfield, R.S. and Ballachey, E.L. (1962). *Individual in Society*. McGraw Hill, New York.

Krocber, A.L. (1920), "Totem and taboo": an ethnologic psycho-analysis. *American Anthropologist*, **22**, 48–55.

Kubie, L. (1965). The ontogeny of racial prejudice. *Journal of Nervous and Mental Diseases*, 265–273.

Kuhn, D.Z., Madsen, C.H. and Becker, W.C. (1967). Effects of exposure to an aggressive model and "frustration" on children's aggressive behavior. *Child Development*, **38**, 739–746.

Kuhn, T.S. (1962). *The Structure of Scientific Revolutions*. Univ. of Chicago Press, Chicago.

Kuhn, T.S. (1970). Reflections on my critics. In *Criticism and the Growth of Knowledge* (Ed. I. Lakatos and A. Musgrove). Univ. Press, Cambridge.

La Barre, W. (1971). Material for a history of crisis cults: a bibliographic essay. *Current Anthropology*. **1**, 3–44.

Ladner, R. (1973). Strategic interaction and conflict: negotiating expectations in accounting for actions. *Journal of Conflict Resolution*, **17**, 175–184.

Lambert, W.E. and Klineberg, O. (1967). *Children's Views of Foreign Peoples: a cross-national study*. Appleton-Century-Crofts, New York.

Lamm, H. (1973). Intragroup effects on intergroup negotiation. *European Journal of Social Psychology*, **3**, 179–192.

Lamm, H. and Kogan, N. (1970). Risk taking in the context of intergroup nego-
tiation. *Journal of Experimental Social Psychology*, **6**, 351–363.
Lange, A. (1971). Frustration-aggression. A reconsideration. *European Journal
of Social Psychology*, **1**, 59–84.
Lange, A. and Van de Nes, A. (1973). Frustration and instrumentality of aggres-
sion. *European Journal of Social Psychology*, **3**, 159–177.
Lantz, D. and Stefflre, V. (1964). Language and cognition revisited. *Journal of
Abnormal and Social Psychology*, **69**, 472–481.
La Torre, R. (1973). Sexual stimulation and displaced aggression. *Psychological
Reports*, **33**, 123–125.
Lawrence, D. (1974). *Black Migrants: White Natives: a study of race relations in
Nottingham*. Cambridge University Press, London.
Leach, E. (1966). Anthropological aspects of language: animal categories and
verbal abuse. In *New Directions in the Study of Language* (Ed. E.H. Lenneberg).
M.I.T. Press, Cambridge, Mass.
Le Bon, G. (1897). *The Crowd: a study of the popular mind*. T. Fisher Unwin,
London.
Lemaine, G. (1966). Inégalité, comparison, et incomparabilité: esquisse d'une
théorie de l'originalité sociale. *Bulletin de Psychologie*, **20**, 1–9.
Lemert, E.M. (1967). *Human Deviance, Social Problems and Social Control*
Prentice Hall, Englewood Cliffs, N.J.
LeVine, R.A. (1965). Socialisation, social structure and intersocietal images. In
International Behavior: a social psychological analysis (Ed. H.C. Kelman). Holt,
Rinehart and Winston, New York.
LeVine, R.A. and Campbell, D.T. (1972). *Ethnocentrism: theories of conflict,
ethnic attitudes and group behavior*. John Wiley and Sons, Inc., New York.
Lévi-Strauss, C. (1966). *The Savage Mind*. Weidenfeld and Nicolson, London.
Lévi-Strauss, C. (1969). *Totemism*. Penguin Books, Harmondsworth.
Lewicki, R.J. and Alderfer, C.P. (1973). The tensions between research and inter-
vention in intergroup conflict. *Journal of Applied Behavioral Science*, **9**, 424–449.
Lewin, K. (1948). *Resolving Social Conflicts*. Harper and Bros., New York.
Lewis, D. (1973). Anthropology and colonialism. *Current Anthropology*, **14**, 581–
591.
Leyens, J.P. and Picus, S. (1973). Identification with a winner of a fight and name
mediation: their differential effects upon subsequent aggressive behaviour.
British Journal of Social and Clinical Psychology, **12**, 374–377.
Liberman, A.M., Harris, K.S., Hoffman, H.S. and Griffiths, B.C. (1957). The
discrimination of speech sounds within and across phoneme boundaries. *Journal
of Experimental Psychology*, **54**, 358–368.
Lichtheim, G. (1974). *Imperialism*. Penguin Books, Harmondsworth.
Lieberson, S. and Silverman, A.R. (1965). The precipitants and underlying con-
ditions of race riots. *American Sociological Review*, **30**, 887–898.
Lindzey, G. (1950). An experimental examination of the scapegoat theory of
prejudice. *Journal of Abnormal and Social Psychology*, **45**, 296–309.
Lipset, S.M. (1960). *Political Man: the social bases of politics*. Doubleday, Garden
City.
Litwak, E., Hooyman, N. and Warren, D. (1973). Ideological complexity and
middle-American rationality. *Public Opinion Quarterly*, **37**, 317–332.
Locke, J. (1960). *An Essay Concerning Human Understanding*. Collins, the
Fontana Library, London.
Loew, C.A. (1967). Acquisition of a hostile attitude and its relationship to
aggressive behavior. *Journal of Personality and Social Psychology*, **5**, 335–341.

Loewenstein, R.M. (1947). The historical and cultural roots of anti-Semitism. In *Psychoanalysis and the Social Sciences*, Vol. I. (Ed. G. Roheim). International University Press, New York.

Lorenz, K. (1967). *On Aggression*. Bantam Books, New York.

Lorenz, K. (1974). *Civilized Man's Eight Deadly Sins*. Methuen and Co., London.

Lovaas, O.I. (1961). Effects of exposure to symbolic aggression on aggressive behavior. *Child Development*, **32**, 37–44.

Lowenthal, L. and Guterman, N. (1972). *Prophets of Deceit*. Pacific Books, California.

Lowry, R.P. and Rankin, R.P. (1972). *Sociology*. Scribner, New York.

Luce, R.D. and Raiffa, H. (1957). *Games and Decisions*. John Wiley and Sons, New York.

Lumsden, M. (1973). The Cyprus conflict as a prisoner's dilemma game. *Journal of Conflict Resolution*, **17**, 7–32.

Lupsha, P.A. (1971). Explanation of political violence: some psychological theories versus indignation. *Politics and Society*, **2**, 89–104.

Lussier, A. (1972). Panel on aggression. *International Journal of Psycho-analysis*, **53**, 13–21.

Mack, D. (1972). Personality, payoff information and behavior in a two-person bargaining game. *Acta Psychologica*, **36**, 125–144.

Mack, D., Auburn, P.N. and Knight, G.P. (1971). Sex role identification and behavior in a reiterated prisoner's dilemma game. *Psychonomic Science*, **24**, 280–281.

Mack, D. and Knight, G.P. (1974). Identification of other player's characteristics in the reiterated prisoner's dilemma. *Psychological Record*, **24**, 93–100.

Mack, R.W. and Snyder, R.C. (1957). The analysis of social conflict: toward an overview and synthesis. *Journal of Conflict Resolution*, **1**, 212–248.

Mandelbaum, S.J. (1968). Consistency, creativity and modernization. In *Theories of Cognitive Consistency: a source book* (Ed. R.P. Abelson *et al.*). Rand McNally and Co., Chicago.

Mann, L. (1972). Cross national aspects of riot behaviour. Paper delivered at Conference of International Association for Cross Cultural Psychology, Hong Kong.

Mannheim, K. (1972). *Ideology and Utopia*. Routledge and Kegan Paul, London.

Manning, S.A. and Taylor, D.A. (1975). The effects of viewed violence and aggression: stimulation and catharsis. *Journal of Personality and Social Psychology*, **31**, 180–188.

Maquet, J.J. (1961). *The Premise of Inequality in Ruanda: a study of political relations in a central African community*. Oxford University Press, London.

Maquet, J.J. (1970). Societal and cultural incorporation in Ruanda. In *From Tribe to Nation in Africa: studies in incorporation processes* (Ed. R. Cohen and J. Middleton). Chandler, Scranton, Pa.

Marcuse, H. (1968). *One Dimensional Man*. Sphere Books, London.

Marcuse, H. (1969). *Eros and Civilization*. Sphere Books, London.

Marcuse, H. (1971). *Soviet Marxism: a critical analysis*. Penguin Books, Harmondsworth.

Marcuse, H. (1972). *An Essay on Liberation*. Penguin Books, Harmondsworth.

Marlowe, D., Gergen, K.J. and Doob, A.N. (1966). Opponent's personality, expectations of social interaction and interpersonal bargaining. *Journal of Personality and Social Psychology*, **3**, 206–213.

Marwell, G., Ratcliffe, K. and Schmitt, D.R. (1969). Minimizing differences in a maximizing difference game. *Journal of Personality and Social Psychology*, **12**, 158–163.

Marx, G.T. (1967). *Protest and Prejudice: a study of belief in the black community.* Harper and Row, New York.

Marx, G.T. (1970). Civil disorder and the agents of social control. *Journal of Social Issues*, **26**, 19–57.

Marx, G.T. (1974). Thoughts on a neglected category of social movement participant: the agent provocateur and the informant. *American Journal of Sociology*, **80**, 402–442.

Marx, K. (1963). *Selected Writings in Sociology and Social Philosophy* (Ed. T.B. Bottomore and M. Rubel). Penguin Books, Harmondsworth.

Marx, K. (1973). *Economic and Philosophic Manuscripts of 1844* (Ed. D.J. Struik). Lawrence and Wishart, Ltd., London.

Marx, K. (1973). *Grundrisse: foundations of the critique of political economy.* Penguin Books, Harmondsworth.

Marx, K. and Engels, F. (1968) *Selected Works.* Lawrence and Wishart, Ltd., London.

Marx, K. and Engels, F. (1970). *The German Ideology* (Ed. C.J. Arthur). Lawrence and Wishart, Ltd., London.

Mazur, A. (1968). A nonrational approach to theories of conflict and coalition. *Journal of Conflict Resolution*, **12**, 196–205.

McCann, E. (1974). *War and an Irish Town.* Penguin Books, Harmondsworth.

McClendon, M.J. (1974). Interracial contact and the reduction of prejudice. *Sociological Focus*, **7**, 47–65.

McClintock, C.G., Harrison, A.A. Strand, S. and Gallo, P. (1963). Internationalism-isolationism, strategy of the other player and two-person game behavior. *Journal of Abnormal and Social Psychology*, **67**, 631–636.

McClintock, C.G. and McNeel, S.P. (1966). Reward level and game playing behavior. *Journal of Conflict Resolution*, **10**, 98–102.

McClintock, C.G. and McNeel, S.P. (1967). Prior dyadic experience and monetary reward as determinants of cooperative and competitive game behavior. *Journal of Personality and Social Psychology*, **5**, 282–294.

McClintock, C.G. and Nuttin, J.M. (1969). Development of competitive game behavior in children across two cultures. *Journal of Experimental Social Psychology*, **5**, 203–218.

McClintock, C.G., Nuttin, J.M. and McNeel, S.P. (1970). Sociometric choice, visual presence and game playing behavior. *Behavioral Science*, **15**, 124–131.

McCord, W., McCord, J. and Howard, A. (1961). Familial correlates of aggression in nondelinquent male children. *Journal of Abnormal and Social Psychology*, **62**, 79–93.

McGuire, W.J. (1960a). Cognitive consistency and attitude change. *Journal of Abnormal and Social Psychology*, **60**, 345–353.

McGuire, W.J. (1960b). A syllogistic analysis of cognitive relationships. In *Attitude Organization and Change* (Ed. M.J. Rosenberg and C.I. Hovland). Yale University Press, New Haven, Conn.

Mead, M. (1935). *Sex and Temperament.* Morrow, New York.

Meeker, R.J. and Shure, J.H. (1969). Pacifist bargaining tactics: some "outsider" influences. *Journal of Conflict Resolution*, **13**, 487–493.

Melman, S. (1970). *Pentagon Capitalism.* McGraw Hill, New York.

Menninger, K. (1942). *Love Against Hate.* Harcourt, Brace and Company, New York

Menninger, K. (1959). *A Psychiatrist's World: selected papers.* Viking Press, New York.

Messé, L.A., Dawson, J.E. and Lane, I.M. (1973). Equity as a mediator of the effect of reward level on behavior in the prisoner's dilemma game. *Journal of Personality and Social Psychology,* **26**, 60–65.

Messick, D.M. (1967). Interdependent decision strategies in zero-sum games: a computer controlled study. *Behavioral Science,* **12**, 35–48.

Messick, D.M. and McClintock, C.G. (1968). Motivational bases of choice in experimental games. *Journal of Experimental Social Psychology,* **4**, 1–25.

Meszaros, I. (1970). *Marx's Concept of Alienation,* Merlin Press, London.   –

Meyer, T.P. (1972). Effects of viewing justified and unjustified real film violence on aggressive behavior. *Journal of Personality and Social Psychology,* **23**, 21–29.

Meyer, T.P. (1972a) The effects of sexually arousing and violent films on aggressive behavior. *Journal of Sex Research,* **8**, 324–333.

Michelini, R.L. (1971). Effects of prior interaction, contact, strategy and expectation of meeting on game behavior and sentiment. *Journal of Conflict Resolution,* **15**, 97–103.

Middleton, J. and Tait, D. (1958). *Tribes Without Rulers: studies in African segmentary systems.* Kegan Paul, London.

Milgram, S. (1963). Behavioral study of obedience. *Journal of Abnormal and Social Psychology,* **67**, 371–378.

Milgram, S. (1965). Some conditions of obedience and disobedience to authority. *Human Relations,* **18**, 57–76.

Milgram, S. (1974). *Obedience to Authority.* Tavistock Publ., Ltd., London.

Miliband, R. (1973). *The State in Capitalist Society.* Quartet Books, London.

Miller, N.E. (1941). The frustration-aggression hypothesis. *Psychological Review,* **48**, 337–442.

Miller, N.E. (1948). Theory and experiment relating psychoanalytic displacement to stimulus-response generalisation. *Journal of Abnormal and Social Psychology,* **43**, 155–178.

Miller, N.E. and Bugelski, R. (1948). Minor studies in aggression: the influence of frustrations imposed by the in-group on attitudes toward out-groups. *Journal of Psychology,* **25**, 437–442.

Millett, K. (1970). *Sexual Politics.* Doubleday, New York.

Mills, C.W. (1963). *Power, Politics and People.* Ballantine Books, New York.

Mills, C.W. (1963a). *The Marxists.* Penguin Books, Harmondsworth.

Milner, D. (1971). Prejudice and the immigrant child. *New Society,* **18**, 469, 566–569.

Milner, D. (1973). Racial identification and preference in "black" British children. *European Journal of Social Psychology,* **3**, 281–295.

Mintz, A. (1951). Nonadaptive group behavior. *Journal of Abnormal and Social Psychology,* **46**, 150–159.

Mitscherlich, A. (1971). Psychoanalysis and the aggression of large groups. *International Journal of Psycho-analysis,* **52**, 161–167.

Mixon, D. (1972). Instead of deception. *Journal of Theory of Social Behavior,* **2**, 145–177.

Moerman, M. (1965). Ethnic identification in a complex civilisation: who are the Lue? *American Anthropologist,* **67**, 1215–1230.

Moerman, M. (1968). Being Lue: use and abuses of ethnic identification. In *Essays on the Problem of Tribe* (Ed. J. Held). Uiversity of Washington, Seattle.

Moinat, S.M., Raine, W.J., Burbeck, S.L. and Davison, K.K. (1972). Black ghetto residents as rioters. *Journal of Social Issues*, **28**, 45–62.

Money-Kyrle, R.E. (1950). Varieties of group formation. In *Psychoanalysis and the Social Sciences*, Vol. II. (Ed. G. Roheim). International University Press, New York.

Money-Kyrle, R.E. (1951). *Psycho-analysis and Politics*. Duckworth, London.

Money-Kyrle, R.E. (1961). *Man's Picture of His World*. Duckworth, London.

Moore, M.F. and Mack, D. (1972). Dominance-ascendence and behaviour in the reiterated prisoner's dilemma game. *Acta Psychologica*, **36**, 480–491.

Morgan, W.R. and Clark, T.N. (1973). The causes of racial disorder: a grievance-level explanation. *American Sociological Review*, **38**, 611–624.

Morland, J.K. (1966). A comparison of race awareness in Northern and Southern children. *American Journal of Orthopsychiatry*, **36**, 22–31.

Morris, R.T. and Jeffries, V. (1970). Class conflict: forget it! *Sociology and Social Research*, **54**, 306–320.

Moscovici, S. (1972). Society and theory in social psychology. In *The Context of Social Psychology: a critical assessment* (Ed. J. Israel and H. Tajfel). Academic Press, London.

Moscovici, S. and Zavalloni, M. (1969). The group as a polariser of attitudes. *Journal of Personality and Social Psychology*, **12**, 125–135.

Muench, G.A. (1960). A clinical psychologist's treatment of labor-management conflicts. *Personnel Psychology*, **12**, 165–172.

Murdock, G. and Golding, P. (1973). For a political economy of mass communications. *Socialist Register*, Merlin Press, London.

Murdock, P. and Rosen, D. (1970). Norm formation in an interdependent dyad. *Sociometry*, **33**, 264–275.

Murphy, R.F. (1957). Intergroup hostility and social cohesion. *American Anthropologist*, **59**, 1018–1035.

Murphy, R.F. (1959). Social structure and sex antagonism. *Southwestern Journal of Anthropology*, **15**, 89–98.

Murphy, R.F. and Kasdan, L. (1959). The structure of parallel cousin marriage. *American Anthropologist*, **61**, 17–29.

Nardin, T. (1971). *Violence and the State: a critique of empirical political theory*. Sage Professional Papers, Beverly Hills.

Nemeth, C. (1970). Bargaining and reciprocity. *Psychological Bulletin*, **74**, 297–308.

Nicolaus, M. (1969). The unknown Marx. In *New Left Reader* (Ed. C. Oglesby). Grove Press, New York.

Nobles, W.W. (1973). Psychological research and the Black self-concept: a critical review. *Journal of Social Issues*, **29**, 11–31.

Noel, J. (1971). White anti-black prejudice in the United States. *International Journal of Group Tensions*, **1**, 59–77.

Nydegger, R.V. (1974). Information processing complexity and gaming behavior: the prisoner's dilemma. *Behavioral Science*, **19**, 204–210.

O'Connor, J., Baker, N. and Wrightsman, L.S. (1972). The nature of rationality in mixed-motive games. In *Cooperation and Conflict* (Ed. L.S. Wrightsman, J. O'Connor and N. Baker). Brooks/Cole Publ. Co., Belmont, Calif.

Ofshe, R. and Ofshe, S.L. (1970). Choice behaviour in coalition games. *Behavioral Science*, **15**, 337–449.

O'Leary, M.R. and Dengerink, H.A. (1973). Aggression as a function of the intensity and pattern of attack. *Journal of Research in Personality*, **7**, 61–70.

Oliva, P. (1971). *Sparta and Her Social Problems*. Adolf M. Hakkert, Amsterdam.

Orne, M.T. (1962). On the social psychology of the psychological experiment: with particular reference to demand characteristics and their implications. *American Psychologist*, **17**, 776–783.

Orum, A.M. (1974). On participation in political protest movements. *Journal of Applied Behavioral Science*, **10**, 181–207.

Orwell, G. (1961). *1984*. New American Library, New York.

Osgood, P. and Tannenbaum, P.H. (1955). The principle of congruity in the prediction of attitude change. *Psychological Review*, **62**, 42–55.

Oskamp, S. (1970). Effects of programmed initial strategies in a prisoner's dilemma game. *Psychonomic Science*, **19**, 195–196.

Oskamp, S. (1971). Effects of programmed strategies on cooperation in the prisoner's dilemma and other mixed-motive games. *Journal of Conflict Resolution*, **15**, 225–259.

Oskamp, S. (1974). Comparison of sequential and simultaneous responding, matrix and strategy variables in a prisoner's dilemma game. *Journal of Conflict Resolution*, **18**, 107–116.

Oskamp, S. and Kleinke, C. (1970). Amount of reward in a variable in the prisoner's dilemma game. *Journal of Personality and Social Psychology*, **16**, 133–140.

Ossowski, S. (1963). *Class Structure in the Social Consciousness*. Routledge and Kegan Paul, London.

Otterbein, K.F. (1968). Internal war: a cross-cultural study. *American Anthropologist*, **70**, 277–289.

Otterbein, K.F. and Otterbein, C.S. (1965). An eye for an eye, a tooth for a tooth: a cross-cultural study of feuding. *American Anthropologist*, **67**, 1470–1482.

Page, M. and Scheidt, R. (1971). The elusive weapons effect: demand awareness, evaluation and slightly sophisticated subjects. *Journal of Personality and Social Psychology*, **20**, 304–318.

Paige, J.M. (1970). Changing patterns of anti-White attitudes amongst Blacks. *Journal of Social Issues*, **26**, 69–88.

Paige, J.M. (1971). Political orientation and riot participation. *American Sociological Review*, **36**, 810–820.

Pastore, N. (1952). The role arbitrariness in the frustration-aggression hypothesis. *Journal of Abnormal and Social Psychology*, **47**, 728–731.

Parsons, A. (1961). A schizophrenic episode in a Neapolitan slum. *Psychiatry*, **24**, 109–121.

Parsons, T. (1952). The superego and the theory of social systems. *Psychiatry*, **15**, 15–25.

Parsons, T. (1954). The father symbol: an appraisal in the light of psychoanalytic and sociological theory. In *Symbols and Values* (Ed. L. Bryson, L. Finkelstein, R. MacIver and R. McKeon). Harper and Row, New York.

Parsons, T. (1958). Social structure and the development of personality. *Psychiatry*, **21**, 321–340.

Patchen, M. (1965). Decision theory in the study of national action: problems and a proposal. *Journal of Conflict Resolution*, **9**, 164–176.

Peabody, D. (1968). Group judgements in the Philippines: evaluative and descriptive aspects. *Journal of Personality and Social Psychology*, **10**, 290–300.

Pepitone, A. and Kleiner, R. (1957). The effect of threat and frustration on group cohesiveness. *Journal of Abnormal and Social Psychology*, **54**, 192–199.

Pettigrew, T.F. (1967). Social evaluation theory: convergences and applications. *Nebraska Symposium on Motivation*, **15**, 241–311.
Pilisuk, M. and Hayden, T. (1973). Is there a military-industrial complex that prevents peace? In *Peace and War* (Ed. C.R. Beitz and T. Herman). W.H. Freeman and Co., San Francisco.
Pilisuk, M., Kiritz, S. and Clampitt, S. (1971). Undoing deadlocks of distrust: hip Berkeley students and the ROTC. *Journal of Conflict Resolution*, **15**, 81–95.
Pilisuk, M., Potter, P., Rapoport, A. and Winter, J.A. (1965). War hawks and peace doves: alternative resolutions of experimental conflicts. *Journal of Conflict Resolution*, **9**, 491–508.
Pilisuk, M. and Rapoport, A. (1964). Stepwise disarmament and sudden destruction in a two-person game: a research tool. *Journal of Conflict Resolution*, **8**, 36–49.
Plasek, W. (1974). Marxist and American sociological conceptions of alienation: implications for social problems theory. *Social Problems*, **21**, 316–328.
Plon, M. (1969–1970). A propos d'une controverse sur les effets d'une menace en situation de négociation. *Bulletin de Psychologie*, **281**, 268–282.
Plon, M. (1972). Sur quelques aspects de la rencontre entre la psychologie sociale et la théorie des jeux. *La Pensée*, **161**, 53–80.
Plon, M. (1973). Sur le sens de la notion de conflict et de son approche en psychologie sociale. Unpub. ms., Ecole des Hautes Etudes, Paris.
Pokrovsky, G.I. (1962). Improving the world: the basis for peaceful coexistence. In *Preventing World War III*. (Ed. Q. Wright, W.M. Evan and M. Deutsch). Simon and Schuster, New York.
Political and Economic Planning. (1967). *Racial Discrimination*, PEP, London.
Pollis, A. (1973). Intergroup conflict and British colonial policy: the case of Cyprus. *Comparative Politics*, **5**, 575–599.
Porter, D.J. (1973, Dec.). How scholars lie: the cultivated misunderstanding of Hanoi's leadership. *Worldview*, 22–27.
Proshansky, H.M. (1966). The development of inter-group attitudes. In *Review of Child Development Research*, Vol. II. (Ed. L.W. Hoffman and M.L. Hoffman). Russell Sage Foundation, New York.
Pruitt, D.G. (1967). Reward structure and cooperation: the decomposed prisoner's dilemma game. *Journal of Personality and Social Psychology*, **7**, 21–27.
Pushkin, I. and Veness, T. (1973). The development of racial awareness and prejudice in children. In *Psychology and Race* (Ed. P. Watson). Penguin Books, Harmondsworth.
Rabbie, J.M., Benoist, F., Oosterbaan, H. and Visser, L. (1974). Differential power and effects of expected competitive and cooperative intergroup interaction on intragroup and outgroup attitudes. *Journal of Personality and Social Psychology*, **30**, 46–56.
Rabbie, J.M. and Horwitz, M. (1969). Arousal of ingroup-outgroup bias by a chance win or loss. *Journal of Personality and Social Psychology*, **13**, 269–277.
Rabbie, J.M. and Wilkens, G. (1971). Intergroup competition and its effect on intragroup and intergroup relationships. *European Journal of Social Psychology*, **1**, 215–234.
Rainwater, L. (1966). Crucible of identity: the Negro lower-class family. *Daedalus*, **95**, 172–216.
Rapoport, A. (1960). *Fights, Games and Debates*. University of Michigan Press, Ann Arbor.
Rapoport, A. (1964). *Strategy and Conscience*. Harper and Row, New York.

Rapoport, A. (1965). Game theory and human conflict. In *The Nature of Human Conflict* (Ed. E.B. McNeil). Prentice Hall, Englewood Cliffs.

Rapoport, A. (1968). Prospects for experimental games. *Journal of Conflict Resolution*, **12**, 461–470.

Rapoport, A. (1970). Conflict resolution in the light of game theory and beyond. In *The Structure of Conflict* (Ed. P. Swingle). Academic Press, London.

Rapoport, A. (1970a). Can peace research be applied? *Journal of Conflict Resolution*, **14**, 277–286.

Rapoport, A. (1972). Gaming: editorial comments. *Journal of Conflict Resolution*, **16**, 95–96.

Rapoport, A. (1974). *Conflict in Man-Made Environment*. Penguin Books, Harmondsworth.

Rapoport, A. and Chammah, A.M. (1965). *Prisoner's Dilemma: a study in conflict and cooperation*. The University of Michigan Press, Ann Arbor.

Rapoport, A. and Guyer, M.J. (1966). A taxonomy of 2×2 games. *General Systems*, **11**, 203–214.

Ray, J.J. (1972a). Militarism, authoritarianism, neuroticism and anti-social behavior. *Journal of Conflict Resolution*, **16**, 319–340.

Ray, J.J. (1972b). Militarism and psychopathology: a reply to Eckhardt and Newcombe. *Journal of Conflict Resolution*, **16**, 357–361.

Reardon, B. and Mendlovitz, S.H. (1973). World law and models of world order. In *Peace and War* (Ed. C.R. Beitz and T. Herman). Freeman and Co., San Francisco.

Reich, W. (1946). *Mass Psychology of Fascism*. Orgone Institute Press, New York.

Rex, J. (1969). Race as a social category. *Journal of Biosocial Science*, Suppl. No. 1, 145–152.

Rex, J. (1972). Nature versus nurture: the signification of the revived debate. In *Race, Culture and Intelligence* (Ed. K. Richardson and D. Spears). Penguin Books, Harmondsworth.

Rex, J. and Moore, R. (1963). *Race, Community and Conflict: a study of Sparkbrook*. Oxford University Press for the IRR.

Rieff, P. (1955). Psychology and politics. *World Politics*, **7**, 293–305.

Rigby, T.H. (1973). The first proletarian government. *British Journal of Political Science*, **4**, 37–51.

Ring, K. (1967). Experimental social psychology: some sober questions about frivolous values. *Journal of Experimental Social Psychology*, **3**, 113–123.

Roazen, P. (1970). *Freud: political and social thought*. Vintage Books, New York.

Roberts, R.C. (1969). On the origins and resolution of English working-class protest. In *Violence in America* (Ed. T.R. Gurr and H.D. Graham). Bantam Books, New York.

Robinson, J.A. and Snyder, R.C. (1965). Decision-making in international politics. In *International Behavior: a social psychological analysis* (Ed. H.C. Kelman). Holt, Rinehart and Winston, New York.

Robinson, P.A. (1972). *The Sexual Radicals: Reich, Roheim and Marcuse*. Paladin, London.

Roheim, G. (1925). *Australian Totemism*. Kegan Paul, London.

Roheim, G. (1930). *Animism, Magic and the Divine King*, Kegan Paul, Trench and Trubuer, London.

Roheim, G. (1934). Evolution of culture. *International Journal of Psychoanalysis*, **4**, 387–418.

Roheim, G. (1941). The psychoanalytic interpretation of culture. *International Journal of Psychoanalysis*, **22**, 147–169.

Roheim, G. (1941a). Play analysis with Normanby Island children. *American Journal of Orthopsychiatry*, **11**, 524.

Roheim, G. (1943). The origin and function of culture. *Nervous and Mental Diseases Monograph*, No. 69.

Roheim, G. (1943a). Children's games and rhymes in Duan. *American Anthropologist*, **45**, 99–119.

Roheim, G. (1945). War, crime and the covenant. *Journal of Clinical Psychopathology*. Monograph Series, No. 1.

Roheim, G. (1949). Technique of dream analysis and field work in anthropology. *Psychoanalytic Quarterly*, **18**, 4.

Roheim, G. (1950). *Psychoanalysis and Anthropology: culture, personality and the unconscious*. International University Press, New York.

Rokeach, M. (1960). *The Open and Closed Mind*. Basic Books, New York.

Rose, E.J.B. (1969). *Colour and Citizenship*. Oxford University Press for the IRR.

Rose, S., Hambley, J. and Haywood, J. (1973). Science, racism and ideology. *Socialist Register*. Merlin Press, London.

Rosenbaum, H.J. and Sederberg, P.C. (1974). Vigilantism: an analysis of establishment violence. *Comparative Politics*, **6**, 541–570.

Rosenberg, M.J. (1960). An analysis of affective-cognitive consistency. In *Attitude Organization and Change* (Ed. M.J. Rosenberg and C.I. Hovland). Yale University Press, New Haven.

Rosenthal, R. (1966). *Experimenter Effects in Behavioral Research*. Appleton-Century-Crofts, New York.

Rothaus, P. and Worchel, P. (1960). The inhibition of aggression under non-arbitrary frustration. *Journal of Personality*, **28**, 108–117.

Rotter, J.B. (1966). Generalised expectancies for internal versus external control of reinforcement. *Psychological Monographs*, **80**, 1–28.

Rudé, G. (1964). *The Crowd in History, 1730–1848*. Wiley, New York.

Rudé, G. (1974). *Paris and London in the 18th Century*. Fontana, London.

Rule, J. and Tilly, C. (1972). 1830 and the unnatural history of revolution. *Journal of Social Issues*, **28**, 49–76.

Rummel, R.J. (1963). Dimensions of conflict behavior within and between nations. *General Systems Yearbook*, **8**, 1–50.

Runciman, W.G. (1966). *Relative Deprivation and Social Justice*. Routledge and Kegan Paul, London.

Sahlins, M. (1960). The origin of society. *Scientific American*, **203**, 76–87.

Sallach, D.L. (1974). Class domination and ideological hegemony. *Sociological Quarterly*, **15**, 38–50.

Samuel, W. (1973). On clarifying some interpretations of social comparison theory. *Journal of Experimental Social Psychology*, **9**, 450–465.

Sanford, N. (1973). The roots of prejudice: emotional dynamics. In *Psychology and Race* (Ed. P. Watson). Penguin Books, Harmondsworth.

Sathyamurthy, T.V. (1973). Social anthropology in the political study of new nation-states. *Current Anthropology*, **14**, 557–565.

Sawyer, J. and Guetzkow, H. (1965). Bargaining and negotiation in international relations. In *International Behavior: a social-psychological analysis* (Ed. H.C. Kelman). Holt, Rinehart and Winston, New York.

Schachter, S. (1959). *The Psychology of Affiliation*. Stanford University Press, Stanford, Calif.

Schachter, S. (1964). The interaction of cognitive and physiological determinants of emotional state. In *Advances in Experimental Social Psychology*, Vol. 1. (Ed. L. Berkowitz). Academic Press, New York.

Scheier, M.F., Fenigstein, A. and Buss, A.H. (1974). Self-awareness and physical aggression. *Journal of Experimental Social Psychology*, 10, 264–273.

Schelling, T.C. (1960). *The Strategy of Conflict*. Harvard University Press, Cambridge, Mass.

Schelling, T.C. (1966). *Arms and Influence*. Yale University Press, New Haven, Conn.

Schervish, P.G. (1973). The labelling perspective: its bias and potential in the study of political deviance. *American Sociologist*, 8, 47–57.

Schuck, J. and Pisor, K. (1974). Evaluating an aggression experiment by the use of simulating subjects. *Journal of Personality and Social Psychology*, 29, 181–186.

Scolnick, J.M. (1974). An appraisal of studies of the linkage between domestic and international conflict. *Comparative Political Studies*, 6, 485–509.

Secord, P.F. (1959). Stereotyping and favorableness in the perception of Negro faces. *Journal of Abnormal and Social Psychology*, 59, 309–315.

Secord, P.F. and Backman, C.W. (1964). *Social Psychology*. McGraw Hill, Tokio.

Secord, P.F., Bevan, W. and Katz, B. (1956). The Negro stereotype and perceptual accentuation. *Journal of Abnormal and Social Psychology*, 53, 78–83.

Sedgwick, P. (1966). Natural science and human theory: a critique of Herbert Marcuse. *Socialist Register*, Merlin Press, London.

Segall, M.H., Campbell, D.T. and Herskovits, M.J. (1963). Cultural differences in the perception of geometric illusions. *Science*, 139, 769–771.

Sermat, V. (1967). The effect of initial cooperative or competitive treatment upon a subject's response to conditional cooperation. *Behavioral Science*, 12, 301–313.

Sermat, V. (1970). Is game behavior related to behavior in other interpersonal situations? *Journal of Personality and Social Psychology*, 16, 92–109.

Shallice, T. (1973). The Ulster depth interrogation techniques and their relation to sensory deprivation research. *Cognition*, 1, 385–405.

Sherif, M. (1936). *The Psychology of Social Norms*. Harper, New York.

Sherif, M. (1966). *Group Conflict and Co-operation: their social psychology*. Routledge and Kegan Paul, London.

Sherif, M. and Harvey, O.J. (1952). A study in ego functioning: elimination of stable anchorages in individual and group situations. *Sociometry*, 15, 272–305.

Sherif, M., Harvey, O.J., White, B.J., Hood, W.R. and Sherif, C. (1961) *Intergroup Conflict and Cooperation. The Robber's Cave experiment*. University of Oklahoma, Norman, Oklahoma.

Sherif M. and Hovland, C.I. (1961). *Social Judgment: assimilation and contrast effects in communication and attitude change*. Yale University Press, New Haven, Conn.

Sherif, M. and Sherif, C.W. (1953). *Groups in Harmony and Tension*. Harper, New York.

Shils, E. (1968). Ideology: the concept and function of ideology. In *International Encyclopedia of the Social Sciences*. Macmillan and Free Press, New York.

Shomer, R.W., Davis, A.H. and Kelley, H.H. (1966). Threats and the development of coordination. Further studies of the Deutsch and Krauss trucking game. *Journal of Personality and Social Psychology*, 4, 119–126.

Shortell, J., Epstein, S. and Taylor, S.P. (1970). Instigation to aggression as a function of degree of defeat and the capacity for massive retaliation. *Journal of Personality*, 38, 313–328.

Shubik. M. (1964). *Game Theory and Related Approaches to Social Behavior.* Wiley, New York.

Shubik, M. (1970). Game theory, behaviour and the paradox of the prisoner's dilemma: three solutions. *Journal of Conflict Resolution,* **14,** 181–193.

Shubik, M. (1971). The dollar auction game: a paradox in noncooperative behavior and escalation. *Journal of Conflict Resolution,* **15,** 109–112.

Shuntich, R.J. and Taylor, S.P. (1972). The effects of alcohol on human physical aggression. *Journal of Research in Personality,* **6,** 34–38.

Singer, J.D. (1963). Inter-nation influence: a formal model. *American Political Science Review,* **57,** 420–430.

Sinha, A.K.P. and Upadyaya, O.P. (1960). Change and persistence in the stereotypes of university students toward different ethnic groups during the Sino-Indian border dispute. *Journal of Social Psychology,* **52,** 31–39.

Siverson, R.M. (1973). Role and perception in international crisis: the case of Israeli and Egyptian decision makers in national capitals and the United Nations. *Internatioal Organization,* **27,** 329–345.

Slusher, E.A., Roering, R.J. and Rose, G.L. (1974). The effects of commitment to future interaction in single plays of three games. *Behavioral Science,* **19,** 119–132.

Smelser, N.J. (1963). *Theory of Collective Behavior.* The Free Press, New York.

Smelser, N.J. (1972). Some additional thoughts on collective behaviour. *Sociological Inquiry,* **62,** 91–101.

Spilerman, S. (1971). The causes of racial disturbances: test of an explanation. *American Sociological Review,* **36,** 427–442.

Stabler, J.R. and Goldberg, F.J. (1973). The black and white symbolic matrix. *International Journal of Symbology,* **4,** 27–35.

Stabler, J.R. and Johnson, E.E. (1972). The meaning of black and white to children. *International Journal of Symbology,* **3,** 11–21.

Stagner, R. and Congdon, C.S. (1955). Another failure to demonstrate displacement of aggression. *Journal of Abnormal and Social Psychology,* **51,** 695–696.

Staples, R. (1973). Race and ideology: an essay in Black sociology. *Journal of Black Studies,* **3,** 395–421.

Steiner, I.D. (1974). What ever happened to the group in social psychology? *Journal of Experimental Social Psychology,* **10,** 94–108.

Stephens, J. (1973). The Kuhnian paradigm and political enquiry: an appraisal. *American Journal of Political Science,* **17,** 467–488.

Sterba, R. (1947). Some psychological factors in Negro race hatred and in anti-Negro riots. In *Psychoanalysis and the Social Sciences* (Ed. G. Roheim). International Universities Press, New York.

Stevenson, P. (1973). The military-industrial complex: an examination of the nature of corporate capitalism in America. *Journal of Political and Military Sociology,* **1,** 247–259.

Stillwell, R. and Spencer, C. (1973). Children's early preferences for other nations and subsequent acquisition of knowledge about those nations. *European Journal of Social Psychology,* **3,** 345–349.

Storr, A. (1964) Possible substitutes for war. In *The Natural History of Aggression* (Ed. J.D. Carthy and F.J. Ebling). Academic Press, London.

Storr, A. (1968). *Human Aggression.* Penguin Books, Harmondsworth.

Storr, A. (1972). *Human Destructiveness.* Chatto Heinemann, London.

Sullivan, H.S. (1936–7). A note on the implications of psychiatry, the study of interpersonal relations, for investigations in the social sciences. *American Journal of Sociology,* **42,** 848–861.

Sullivan, H.S. (1938–9). A note on formulating the relationship of the individual and the group. *American Journal of Sociology*, **44**, 932–937.

Sullivan, H.S. (1950). Tensions interpersonal and international: a psychiatrist's view. In *Tensions that Cause Wars* (Ed. H. Cantril). University of Illinois Press, Urbana, Ill.

Sumner, W.G. (1906). *Folkways*. Ginn, Boston.

Swingle, P. and Gillies, J. (1968). Effects of emotional relationships between protagonists in prisoner's dilemma. *Journal of Personality and Social Psychology*, **8**, 160–165.

Taft, P. and Ross, P. (1969). American labor violence: its causes, character and outcome. In *Violence in America* (Ed. H.D. Graham and T.R. Gurr). Bantam Books, New York.

Tajfel, H. (1957). Value and the perceptual judgement of magnitude. *Psychological Review*, **64**, 192–204.

Tajfel, H. (1959). Quantitative judgement in social perception. *British Journal of Psychology*, **10**, 16–29.

Tajfel, H. (1969). Social and cultural factors in perception. In *The Handbook of Social Psychology*, 2nd edition. (Ed. G. Lindzey and E. Aronson). Addison-Wesley, Reading, Mass.

Tajfel, H. (1969a). Cognitive aspects of prejudice. *Journal of Social Issues*, **25**, 79–97.

Tajfel, H. (1970). Experiments in intergroup discrimination. *Scientific American*, **223**, 96–102.

Tajfel, H. (1972). Experiments in a vacuum. In *The Context of Social Psychology: a critical assessment* (Ed. J. Israel and H. Tajfel). Academic Press, London.

Tajfel, H. (1972a). La catégorisation sociale. In *Introduction à la Psychologie Sociale*, Vol. I. (Ed. S. Moscovici). Larousse, Paris.

Tajfel, H. and Billig, M. (1974). Familiarity and categorisation in intergroup behaviour. *Journal of Experimental Social Psychology*, **10**, 159–170.

Tajfel, H., Billig, M., Bundy, R. and Flament, C. (1971). Social categorisation and intergroup behaviour. *European Journal of Social Psychology*, **1**, 149–175.

Tajfel, H. and Jahoda, G. (1966). Development in children of concepts and attitudes about their own and other countries. *Proceedings of the 18th International Congress of Psychology*, Moscow Symposium, **36**, 17–33.

Tajfel, H., Nemeth, C., Jahoda, G., Campbell, J.D. and Johnson, N.B. (1970). The development of children's preferences for their own country: a cross-national study. *International Journal of Psychology*, **5**, 245–253.

Tajfel, H., Sheikh, A.A. and Gardner, R.C. (1964). Content of stereotypes and the inference of similarity between members of stereotyped groups. *Acta Psychologica*, **22**, 191–201.

Tajfel, H. and Wilkes, A.L. (1963). Classification and quantitative judgement. *British Journal of Psychology*, **54**, 101–114.

Tajfel, H. and Wilkes, A.L. (1963a). Salience of attributes and commitment to extreme judgements in the perception of people. *British Journal of Social and Clinical Psychology*, **2**, 40–49.

Tanter, R. (1966). Dimensions of conflict behaviour within and between nations, 1958–1960. *Journal of Conflict Resolution*, **10**, 41–64.

Tanter, R. (1969). International war and domestic turmoil: some contemporary evidence. In *Violence in America* (Ed. H.D. Graham and T.R. Gurr). Bantam Books, New York.

Taylor, I. (1971). Soccer consciousness and soccer hooliganism. In *Images of Deviance* (Ed. S. Cohen). Penguin Books, Harmondsworth.

Taylor, S.P. and Epstein, S. (1967). Aggression as a function of the interaction of the sex of the aggressor and the sex of the victim. *Journal of Personality*, 35, 474–486.

Terhune, K.W. (1968). Motives, situation and interpersonal conflict within prisoner's dilemma. *Journal of Personality and Social Psychology*, 8, 3, Part 2 (Monog. Supp.).

Terhune, K.W. (1970). The effects of personality in cooperation and conflict. In *The Structure of Conflict* (Ed. P. Swingle). Academic Press, London.

Thibaut, J.W. (1950). An experimental study of the cohesiveness of under-privileged groups. *Human Relations*, 3, 251–278.

Thibaut, J.W. (1968). The development of contractual norms in bargaining. *Journal of Conflict Resolution*, 12, 102–112.

Thibaut, J.W. and Faucheux, C. (1965). The development of contractual norms in a bargaining situation under two types of stress. *Journal of Experimental Social Psychology*, 1, 89–102.

Thibaut, J.W. and Gruder, C.L. (1969). The formation of contractual agreements between parties of unequal power. *Journal of Personality and Social Psychology*, 11, 59–65.

Thibaut, J.W. and Kelley, H.H. (1959). *The Social Psychology of Groups*. John Wiley and Sons, New York.

Thio, A. (1973). Class bias in the sociology of deviance. *American Sociologist*, 8, 1–12.

Thoden van Velzen, H.U.E. and van Wetering, W. (1960). Residence, power groups and intrasocietal aggression. *International Archives of Ethnography*, 49, 169–200.

Thompson, E.P. (1963). *The Making of the English Working-class*. Victor Gollancz, London.

Thompson, R.J. and Kolstoe, R.H. (1974). Physical aggression as a function of strength of frustration and instrumentality of aggression. *Journal of Research in Personality*, 7, 314–323.

Tilly, C. (1963). The analysis of a counter-revolution. *History and Theory*, 3, 30–58.

Tilly, C. (1969). Collective violence in European perspective. In *Violence in America* (Ed. H.D. Graham and T.R. Gurr). Bantam Books, New York.

Tilly, C. (1973). Does modernisation breed revolution? *Comparative Politics*, 5, 425–447.

Titus, H.E. and Hollander, E.P. (1957). The California F scale in psychological research. (1950–1955). *Psychological Bulletin*, 54, 47–74.

Toch, H. (1966). *The Social Psychology of Social Movements*. Methuen and Co., London.

Tomlinson, T.M. (1970). Ideological foundations for Negro action: a comparative analysis of militant and non-militant views of the Los Angeles riot. *Journal of Social Issues*, 26, 93–119.

Toulmin, S. (1967). Conceptual revolutions in science. *Synthese*, 17, 75–91.

Tropper, R. (1972). The consequences of investment in the process of conflict. *Journal of Conflict Resolution*, 16, 97–98.

Turner, C.W. and Berkowitz, L. (1972). Identification with the film aggressor (covert role taking) and reactions to film violence. *Journal of Personality and Social Psychology*, 21, 256–264.

Turner, J. (1973). Competition and category-conflict: self versus group for social value versus economic gain. Unpub. ms., University of Bristol.

Turner, J. (1975). Social comparison and social identity: some prospects for intergroup behaviour. *European Journal of Social Psychology*, **5**, 5–34.

Van den Berghe, P.L. (1967). *Race and Racism: a comparative perspective*. John Wiley and Sons, New York.

Vanneman, R.D. and Pettigrew, T.F. (1972). Race and relative deprivation in the urban United States. *Race*, **13**, 461–486.

Vaughan, G.M. (1964). The development of ethnic attitudes in New Zealand school children. *Genetic Psychology Monographs*, **70**, 135–175.

Vidmar, N. and McGrath, J.E. (1970). Forces affecting success in negotiating groups. *Behavioral Science*, **15**, 154–163.

Vinacke, W.E. (1969). Variables in experimental games: toward a field theory. *Psychological Bulletin*, **71**, 293–318.

Voissem, N.H. and Sistrunk, F. (1971). Communication schedule and cooperative game behavior. *Journal of Personality and Social Psychology*, **19**, 160–167.

Von Neumann, J. and Morganstern, D. (1947). *The Theory of Games and Economic Behaviour*. Princeton University Press, Princeton, N.J.

Vygotsky, L. (1962). *Thought and Language*. Wiley, New York.

Wagatsuma, H. (1967). The social perception of skin color in Japan. *Daedalus*, **96**, 407–443.

Wallace, A.F.C. and Atkins, J. (1960). The meaning of kinship terms. *American Anthropologist*, **62**, 58–80.

Wallace, D. and Rothaus, P. (1969). Communication, group loyalty and trust in the PD game. *Journal of Conflict Resolution*, **13**, 370–380.

Wallace, M.D. (1973). Alliance polarisation, cross-cutting and international war, 1815–1964. *Journal of Conflict Resolution*, **17**, 575–604.

Wallach, M.A. (1958). On psychological similarity. *Psychological Review*, **65**, 103–116.

Wallis, R. (1974). Ideology, authority and the development of cultic movements. *Social Research*, **41**, 299–327.

Walters, R.H., Thomas, E.L. and Acker, C.W. (1962). Enhancement of punitive behavior by audio-visual displays. *Science*, **136**, 872–873.

Walton, R.E. (1970). A problem-solving workshop on border conflicts in Eastern Africa, *Journal of Applied Behavioral Science*, **6**, 453–490.

Watson, G.L. (1973). Social structure and social movements: the Black Muslims in the U.S.A. and the Ras-Tafarians in Jamaica. *British Journal of Sociology*, **24**, 188–204.

Watson, G.L. (1974). Patterns of Black protest in Jamaica: the case of the Ras-Tafarians. *Journal of Black Studies*, **4**, 329–343.

Weatherley, D. (1961). Anti-Semitism and the expression of fantasy aggression. *Journal of Abnormal and Social Psychology*, **62**, 454–457.

Weller, J.M. and Quarantelli, E.L. (1973). Neglected characteristics of collective behavior. *American Journal of Sociology*, **79**, 665–685.

Westergaard, J.H. (1973). Sociology: the myth of classlessness. In *Ideology in Social Science* (Ed. R. Blackburn). Fontana, London.

Wheeler, L. (1966). Motivation as a determinant of upward comparison. *Journal of Experimental Social Psychology*, Suppl. **1**, 27–31.

Wheeler, L., Shaver, K.G., Jones, R.A., Goethals, G.R., Cooper, J., Robinson, J.E., Gruder, C.L. and Butzine, K.W. (1969). Factors determining choice of a comparison other. *Journal of Experimental Social Psychology*, **5**, 219–232.

Whitworth, R.H. and Lucker, W.G. (1972). Effective manipulation of cooperation with college and culturally disadvantaged populations. In *Cooperation and Competition*. (Ed. L.S. Wrightsman. J. O'Connor and N. Baker). Brooks/Cole Publ. Co., Belmont, Calif.

Wiberg, H. (1972). Rational and non-rational models of man. In *The Context of Social Psychology: a critical assessment* (Ed. J. Israel and H. Tajfel). Academic Press, London.

Wichman, H. (1970). Effects of isolation and communication on cooperation in a two-person game. *Journal of Personality and Social Psychology*, **16**, 114–120.

Wilkins, J.L., Scharff, W.H. and Schlottmann, R.S. (1974). Personality type, reports of violence and aggressive behavior. *Journal of Personality and Social Psychology*, **30**, 243–247.

Williams, J.E. and Stabler, J.R. (1973). If white means good, then black . . . *Psychology Today*, July, 50–54.

Wilson, A. (1970). *War Gaming*. Penguin Books, Harmondsworth.

Wilson, G.D. (1973). *The Psychology of Conservatism*. Academic Press, London.

Wilson, G.D. and Nias, D.K.B. (1973). The need for a new approach to attitude measurement. In *The Psychology of Conservatism* (Ed. G.D. Wilson). Academic Press, London.

Wilson, J. (1973). *Introduction to Social Movements*. Basic Books Inc., New York.

Wilson, W. (1971). Reciprocation and other techniques for inducing cooperation in the prisoner's dilemma game. *Journal of Conflict Resolution*, **15**, 167–195.

Wilson, W., Chun, N. and Kayatani, M. (1965). Projection, attraction and strategy choices in intergroup competition. *Journal of Personality and Social Psychology*, **2**, 432–435.

Wilson, W. and Kayatani, M. (1968). Intergroup attitudes and strategies in games between opponents of the same or a different race. *Journal of Personality and Social Psychology*, **9**, 24–30.

Wilson, W. and Miller, N. (1961). Shifts in evaluation of participants following intergroup competition. *Journal of Abnormal and Social Psychology*, **63**, 428–431.

Wilson, W. and Robinson, C. (1968). Selective intergroup bias in both authoritarians and non-authoritarians after playing a modified prisoner's dilemma game. *Perceptual and Motor Skills*, **27**, 1051–1058.

Wilson, W. and Wong, J. (1968). Intergroup attitudes towards cooperative vs. competitive opponents in a modified prisoner's dilemma game. *Perceptual and Motor Skills*, **27**, 1059–1066.

Wilson, W.J. (1973). *Power, Racism and Privilege*. Macmillan Co., New York.

Winnicott, D. (1950). Some thoughts on the meaning of the word "democracy". *Human Relations*, **3**, 175–186.

Wirsing, R. (1973). Political power and information: a cross-cultural study. *American Anthropologist*, **75**, 153–170.

Wittgenstein, L. (1953). *Philosophical Investigations*. Blackwell, Oxford.

Wolin, S.S. (1973). The politics of the study of revolution. *Comparative Politics*, **5**, 343–358.

Wrightsman, L.S. (1966). The effect of real vs. imaginary rewards. *Journal of Personality and Social Psychology*, **4**, 328–332.

Wrightsman, L.S., Davis, D.W., Lucker, W.G., Bruininks, R.H., Evans, J.R., Wilde, R.E., Paulson, D.G. and Clark, G.M. (1972). Effects of other person's strategy and race upon cooperative behavior in a prisoner's dilemma game. In

Cooperation and Competition (Ed. L.S. Wrightsman, J. O'Connor and N. Baker). Brooks/Cole Publ. Co., Belmont, Calif.

Wrightsman, L.S., Lucker, W.G., Bruininks, R.H. and Anderson, W. (1972). Effects of subject's training and college class and other's strategy upon cooperative behavior in a prisoner's dilemma game. In *Cooperation and Conflict* (Ed. L.S. Wrightsman, J. O'Connor and N. Baker). Brooks/Cole Publ. Co., Belmont, Calif.

Wrightsman, L.S., O'Connor, J. and Baker, N. (1972). *Cooperation and Conflict: reading on mixed-motive games.* Brooks/Cole Publ. Co., Belmont, Calif.

Young, J. (1971). The role of the police as amplifiers of deviancy, negotiators of reality and translators of fantasy: some consequences of our present system of drug control as seen in Notting Hill. In *Images of Deviance* (Ed. S. Cohen). Penguin Books, Harmondsworth.

Young, O.R. (1967). *The Intermediaries: third parties in international crises.* Princeton University Press, Princeton.

Zavalloni, M. (1973). Social identity: perspectives and prospects. *Social Science Information,* **12**, 65–91.

Zavalloni, M. (1973a). Subjective culture, self concept and the social environment. *International Journal of Psychology,* **8**, 183–192.

Zechmeister, K. and Druckman, D. (1973). Determinants of resolving a conflict of interest: a simulation of political decision-making. *Journal of Conflict Resolution,* **17**, 63–88.

Zilboorg, G. (1947). Psychopathology of social prejudice. *Psychoanalytic Quarterly,* **16**, 303–324.

Zillman, D. (1971). Excitation transfer in communication-mediated aggressive behavior. *Journal of Experimental Social Psychology,* **7**, 419–434.

Zimbardo, P. (1969). The human choice: individuation, reason and order vs. deindividuation, impulse and chaos. *Nebraska Symposium on Motivation,* **17**, 237–307.

Zinnes, D.A. (1966). A comparison of hostile behavior of decision-makers in simulate and historical data. *World Politics,* **18**, 474–502.

Author Index

Subject Index